Martin Bucer's Doctrine
of Justification

Martin Bucer's Doctrine of Justification

Reformation Theology and Early Modern Irenicism

BRIAN LUGIOYO

UNIVERSITY PRESS

2010

OXFORD
UNIVERSITY PRESS

Oxford University Press, Inc., publishes works that further
Oxford University's objective of excellence
in research, scholarship, and education.

Oxford   New York
Auckland   Cape Town   Dar es Salaam   Hong Kong   Karachi
Kuala Lumpur   Madrid   Melbourne   Mexico City   Nairobi
New Delhi   Shanghai   Taipei   Toronto

With offices in
Argentina   Austria   Brazil   Chile   Czech Republic   France   Greece
Guatemala   Hungary   Italy   Japan   Poland   Portugal   Singapore
South Korea   Switzerland   Thailand   Turkey   Ukraine   Vietnam

Copyright © 2010 by Oxford University Press, Inc.

Published by Oxford University Press, Inc.
198 Madison Avenue, New York, New York 10016

www.oup.com

Oxford is a registered trademark of Oxford University Press

Library of Congress Cataloging-in-Publication Data
Lugioyo, Brian, 1976–
Martin Bucer's doctrine of justification : reformation theology and early modern irenicism / Brian
Lugioyo.
p. cm.—(Oxford studies in historical theology)
Includes bibliographical references and index.
ISBN 978-0-19-538736-0
1. Bucer, Martin, 1491–1551. 2. Reformation. 3. Church history—16th century. 4. Justification—
History of doctrines—16th century. I. Title.
BR350.B93L84   2010
234'.709409031—dc22   2009049119

9 8 7 6 5 4 3 2 1
Printed in the United States of America
on acid-free paper

For Nicole

Acknowledgments

The production of this book is a result of innumerable kindnesses. While the inadequacies and shortcomings that remain are my own, I would like to thank those who made this work especially possible. I am thankful, first of all, to Nicholas Thompson, who enthusiastically took me on as one of his doctoral students at the University of Aberdeen. His invaluable aid throughout, as well as his belief in the project and in me, made this book possible. I also am grateful to Anthony N. S. Lane, who in addition to offering several helpful suggestions has allowed me to include, in appendix D, his translation of Article 5. Among the many who have given various kinds of help and inspiration I would like to mention and thank Ray S. Anderson, Nathan P. Feldmeth, John L. Thompson, Donald Wood, Francesca A. Murphy, John Webster, Benjamin Reynolds, Christopher Asprey, Jonathan Norgate, Andrew Stobart, Thomas Holsinger-Friesen, Richard Cornell, Preston Sprinkle, Thomas R. V. Forster, David Nelson and Fr. Bill Anderson. I am indebted to my dear friend Morton A. E. Gauld, whose Latin tutelage made reading Martin Bucer's Latin slightly enjoyable. I must also give my appreciation to the meticulous eyes of the editors at Oxford University press, particularly Susan Ecklund and Jennifer Kowing, who have saved me from committing many blunders.

I am deeply grateful to my mom, dad, *abuelo*, and *abuela* for their lifelong encouragement, and to John and Lidy Baars and Oma for their support during the writing of this project. Thanks, finally and especially, to my wife, Nicole Lugioyo, for her companionship, good humor, and love. This book is dedicated to her.

Contents

Abbreviations

ARC   *Acta Reformationis Catholicae ecclesiam Germaniae concernantia saeculi XVI.* Edited by G. Pfeilschifter. 6 vols. Regensburg: Friedrich Pustet, 1959–1974.

ASD   *Opera Omnia Desiderii Erasmi Roterodami Recognita et Adnotatione Critica Instructa Notisque Illustrata.* 9 vols. Amsterdam: North Holland, 1969–2003.

BCor   *Correspondance de Martin Bucer.* Vols. 1–. Leiden: Brill, 1979–.

BDS   *Martin Bucers Deutsche Schriften.* Vols. 1–. Gütersloh: Gerd Mohn, 1979–.

BEph   *Epistola D. Pauli ad Ephesios . . .* (1527); (*Bibliographie* 25). *Praelectiones Doctiss. in Epistolam D. P. ad Ephesios . . .* (1562); (*Bibliographie* 229).

BGospels   *Enarrationum in Evangelia Matthaei, Marci, & Lucae . . .* (1527); (*Bibliographie* 22). *Enarrationes perpetuae, in Sacra Quatuor Evangelia . . .* (1530); (*Bibliographie* 39). *In Sacra Quatuor Evangelia, Enarrationes perpetuae . . .* (1536); (*Bibliographie* 77).

Bibliographie   *Martin Bucer—Bibliographie.* Compiled by Holger Pils, Stephan Ruderer, and Petra Schaffrodt. Gütersloh: Gütersloher Verlagshaus, 2005.

BOL   *Martini Buceri Opera Latina.* Vols. 1–. Paris, 1955-; Leiden, 1979–.

BPsalms   *Psalmorum libri quinque ad Hebraicam Veritatem Traducti* . . . (1554); (*Bibliographie* 201).

BRom   *Metaphrasis et Enarrationes Perpetuae* . . . *in Epistolam ad Romanos* . . . (1536), (*Bibliographie* 76); (1562), (*Bibliographie* 223).*CO Iohannis Calvini Opera Quae Supersunt Omnia.* 59 vols. Berlin: Schwetschke, 1863–1900.

CP   *Common Places of Martin Bucer.* Trans. and edited by David F. Wright. Appleford: Sutton Courtenay Press, 1972.

CR   *Corpus Reformatorum. Philippi Melanchthonis Opera Quae Supersunt Omnia.* 28 vols. Halle: Schwetschke, 1834–1860.

Enchiridion   *Canones Concilii Provincialis Coloniensis* . . . *quibus adiectum est Enchiridion christianae institutions* . . . Paris: Nicolaus Boucher, 1545.

LCC   *Library of Christian Classics.* 26 vols. Louisville, KY:: Westminster John Knox Press, 1963–2006.

Lenz   *Briefwechsel Landgraf Philipp's des Grossmüthigen von Hessen mit Bucer.* Edited by Max Lenz. 3 vols. Leipzig: Verlag von S. Hirzel, 1880, 1887, 1891. Reprint, Osnabrück: Otto Zeller, 1965.

LW   *Luther's Works.* American Edition. 55 vols. St. Louis and Philadelphia: Concordia and Fortress Press, 1955–1986.

MW   *Melanchthons Werke in Auswahl.* 5 vols. Gütersloh: Gerd Mohn, 1961–1965.

OER   *The Oxford Encyclopedia of the Reformation.* Edited by Hans J. Hillerbrand et al. 4 vols. Oxford: Oxford University Press, 1996.

PL   *Patrologiae cursus completus.* Series Latina. 221 vols. Edited by J. P. Migne. Paris, 1844–1864.

Pollet   *Martin Bucer études sur la correspondance.* Edited by J. V. Pollet. 2 vols. Paris: Presses Universitaires de France, 1958–1962.

Schiess   *Briefwechsel der Brüder Ambrosius und Thomas Blaurer 1509–1548.* Edited by T. Schiess. 3 vols. Freidburg i. Br.: Fehsenfeld, 1908–1912.

ST   Thomas Aquinas, *Summa Theologiae*. Ed. and trans.
Blackfriars. 60 vols. London: Eyre and
Spottiswoode, 1962–1980.

TAE   *Quellen zur Geschichte der Täufer* 7–8, 15–16. (*Täuferakten Elsass* I–IV). Edited by Jean Rott et al. 4 vols.
Gütersloh: Gerd Mohn, 1959–1988.

WA   Martin Luther. *Luthers Werke. Kritische Gesamtausgabe.
Schriften.* 65 vols. Weimar: H. Böhlau, 1883–1993.

WA.Br.   Martin Luther. *Luthers Werke. Kritische Gesamtausgabe.
Briefwechsel.* 18 vols. Weimar: H. Böhlau,
1930–1985.

WA.DB.   Martin Luther. *Luthers Werke. Kritische Gesamtausgabe.
Die deutsche Bibel.* 15 vols. Weimar: H. Böhlau,
1906–1961.

WA.Tr.   Martin Luther. *Luthers Werke. Kritische Gesamtausgabe.
Tischreden.* 6 vols. Weimar: H. Böhlau, 1912–1921.

ZW   *Huldreich Zwinglis Sämtliche Werke.* 15 vols. Leipzig:
Heinsius; Zurich: Verlag Berichtshaus, Theologischer
Verlag, 1905–1966.

Martin Bucer's Doctrine
of Justification

I

Introduction

Martin Bucer, a Consistent Theologian

Characterizations of Martin Bucer's theology have generally been
influenced by his irenicism, an irenicism that, unfortunately, has
been represented as a zeal for unity at the expense of the truth.[1] This
perspective is characterized by Gordon Rupp's cricket analogy stating
that Bucer was "the greatest ecclesiastical spin bowler of the age,
the very model of a modern ecumenical."[2] Yet, such a pragmatic
caricature cannot be wholly substantiated in regard to Bucer's
negotiations over the doctrine of justification with his colleagues that
were loyal to the traditional church.[3] Bucer's doctrine of justification
has its own inner coherence, rooted in his understanding of the truth.

---

1. The most recent scholar to advance this perspective has been Thomas Kaufmann, who
describes Bucer's role in the Supper strife as outrageous and dishonest. Kaufmann, however,
neglects the secondary theological role that the Lord's Supper played for Bucer during these early
years. See Thomas Kaufmann, *Die Abendmahlstheologie der Straßburger Reformatoren bis 1528*
(Tübingen: J. C. B. Mohr, 1992).

2. Gordon Rupp, *Protestant Catholicity: Two Lectures* (London: Epworth Press, 1960), 24.

3. This is a line of thought that follows some of the more recent research in Bucer studies.
See particularly Reinhold Friedrich, *Martin Bucer—"Fanatiker der Einheit"?: Seine Stellungnahme zu
theologischen Fragen seiner Zeit (Abendmahls- und Kirchenverständnis) insbesondere nach seinem
Briefwechsel der Jahre 1524–1541* (Bonn: Verlag für Kultur und Wissenschaft, 2002); Friedrich,
"Martin Bucer—Ökumene im 16. Jahrhundert," in *Martin Bucer and Sixteenth Century Europe: Actes
du colloque de Strasbourg (28–31 août 1991)*, ed. Christian Krieger and Marc Lienhard, vol. 1 (Leiden:
Brill, 1993), 257–268; and Volkmar Ortmann, *Reformation und Einheit der Kirche: Martin Bucers
Einigungsbemühungen bei den Religionsgesprächen in Leipzig, Hagenau, Worms und Regensburg,
1539–1541* (Mainz: Verlag Philipp von Zabern, 2001). Friedrich sees Bucer as worthy of being called
an ecumenic, making concessions at Worms and Regensburg, but unwilling to reach concord at
any price. Friedrich focuses on Bucer's letters to understand how Bucer understood his role in the

Bucer believed that the truth was one.[4] In his theology the Holy Spirit was the guarantor of truth.[5] Bucer believed that by the inspiration of the Spirit the truth, clearly expressed in scripture, could also be found in the church fathers and in a diffused manner through the philosophers (though their thought was always tested against scripture).[6] Likewise, Bucer's thought categorized Christian theological truths (of the disputed doctrines of the day) into a hierarchy, the doctrine of justification being of high importance for the Church. As such, difficulties over other doctrines like the Lord's Supper could be pragmatically defined and resolved so as to preserve the unity that was held in the truth of justification.

Bucer was in agreement with Luther's occasional rhetoric that the teaching of justification was the article upon which "stands all that we teach and practice against the pope, the devil, and the world."[7] For both Luther and Bucer this doctrine was pivotal; it defined the Church as Church. Yet the manner in which Bucer understood justification is noticeably different. Unfortunately, the distinctions between Bucer and Luther, primarily in regard to their understanding of faith, have been the cause of various value judgments by a few confessionally minded scholars that have evaluated Bucer's thought in terms of an orthodox Reformation understanding of justification, for example, Luther's view.[8] Both reformers advocated justification *sola fide*, but they understood faith in different ways. It is important to realize that the evangelical doctrine of justification was not a statically set proposition early in the sixteenth century but a doctrine that was developing and whose boundaries are more allusive than many

---

Protestant Eucharist debate as well as the negotiations with Catholics, but he does not address Bucer's theology. Likewise, Ortmann's work investigates the activity of Bucer during these negotiations, arguing that Bucer's approach to these negotiations was consistent. He presents a thorough historical commentary on these colloquies, and I am indebted to him on many points. However, as he confesses, he does not attempt a thorough theological evaluation of Bucer's theology.

4. See *BRom* (1536), 28; (1562), 27–28. There is no critical edition of Bucer's *Romans Commentary*, but one is forthcoming in the *BOL* series.

5. See Bucer's dialogue with Conrad Treger, where on the question of how he could know that the Bible was the word of truth he replied, "The Spirit, the comforter, who guides us in all truth according to Christ's promise, it is he who tells me this." *BDS* 2, 93, ll. 15–17.

6. *BRom* (1536), 28; (1562), 28. For Bucer's use of the church fathers, see Irena Backus, "Martin Bucer and the Patristic Tradition," in Krieger and Lienhard, *Martin Bucer and Sixteenth Century Europe*, 1:55–69; also for a detailed examination of Bucer's use of the patristic tradition in regard to the Sacrifice of the Mass, see Nicholas Thompson, *Eucharistic Sacrifice and Patristic Tradition in the Theology of Martin Bucer 1534–1546* (Leiden: Brill, 2005).

7. Luther, *Smalcald Articles*, in *Concordia* (Dresden, 1580), 137(r): "Und auff diesem Artickel stehet alles das wir wider den Bapst, Tueffel und Welt, leren und leben." Both Luther and Bucer would have held other doctrines as primary, for example, the doctrine of the Trinity. Within the theological world of the sixteenth century, where the doctrine of the Trinity was generally undisputed, the doctrine of justification became of prime importance.

8. Such judgments can be found in the works of Karl Koch, Ernst-Wilhelm Kohls, and more recently Athena Lexutt.

assume.[9] For the various evangelical reformers, the doctrine of justification *sola fide* acted as a theological compass that radically steered the evangelicals away from a theology that focused on individual merit. From this foundation an evangelical doctrine of sin developed to marginalize the salvific efficacy of good works. At this stage of evangelical development, the articulations of this doctrine, which holds these emphases, will be what I take to be an early evangelical doctrine of justification, especially in light of the fact that the majority of Protestant reformers at this point were willing to accept multiple articulations of this central doctrine, which prioritized faith and marginalized merit. The precise doctrinal exposition of Bucer's thought as well as the thought of Johannes Gropper, a moderate Catholic, will further reveal the nuances of evangelical and Catholic thought at this time.

As Robert Stupperich states, "Bucer's theology was a theology of the Church."[10] His nuanced ecclesiology, a combination of his emphasis of love of neighbor and the Pauline metaphor of Christ's body, emphasized the responsibility and function of every Christian (limbs of Christ's body) toward one another.[11] In a letter to Philip of Hesse, the landgrave, he wrote, "God is a God of community. Thus as our Lord and head, Christ desires to rule and bless us as his limbs in this way: that he would not carry out the work of salvation for us except through all the limbs and the true community of these."[12]

With Christ as the head, Christians become limbs through the forgiveness of sins. Thus the doctrine of justification by faith was crucial for establishing reform and unity in the Church and as a result played a key role in the discussions with Catholics from 1539 to 1541.

My central thesis is that throughout these discussions Bucer's understanding of justification remained consistent with his most thorough formulation of the doctrine found in his *Romans Commentary* (1536). This does not mean that tact

---

9. Alister McGrath points to three distinguishing marks of the Protestant doctrine of justification: (1) justification is a forensic declaration of righteousness that changes status and not nature; (2) the Protestants made a systematic distinction between justification and sanctification; and (3) the formal cause of justification is the alien righteousness of Christ that is imputed to believers. See Alister McGrath, *Iustitia Dei: A History of the Christian Doctrine of Justification*, 3rd ed. (Cambridge: Cambridge University Press, 2005), 212–213. McGrath's claim that these criteria were part of a broad consensus held by Protestant reformers between 1530 and 1730 is highly misleading. McGrath's boundaries are characteristic but not as definitive as he supposes. This is particularly true in light of the way Luther has been recently interpreted by the Finnish school. Concise generalizations over the doctrine of justification at times are helpful, but during this point in history they can be misleading.

10. Robert Stupperich, "Martin Bucer als Theologe und Kirchenmann," *Die Zeichen der Zeit* 5 (1951): 253–258, quote on 254. More recently Gottfried Hammann has also described Bucer's ecclesiology as pivotal to his theology as a whole. See Hammann, *Martin Bucer: Zwischen Volkskirche und Bekenntnisgemeinschaft*, trans. Gerhard Ph. Wolf (Speyer: Verlagsgemeinschaft Evangelischer Presseverlag Pfalz, 1989), 90.

11. Stupperich, "Martin Bucer als Theologe," 255.

12. Letter to the landgrave (5 April 1546), Lenz 2, no. 231, 427; "Gott ist ein Gott der gemeinschaft. So will unser herr und haupt Christus uns als seine glider also regiren und selig machen, das er das werk unsers heils nicht dann durch alle glider und wahre gemeinschaft derselbigen fuere uns ußrichte."

was absent from these discussions; ambiguity is often the result of any irenic endeavor. Nevertheless, when Bucer's doctrine of justification is clearly expounded and seen as part of his program for reform and unity, the resulting formulations with old Christians can be partially seen as missiological—a step toward the recovery of lost sheep under the power of the Antichrist.[13]

Issues in Bucer Research

> Peacemakers are often forgotten, while the strenuous fighting men of their time live in the memory of the generations that follow; and yet, how often the hardest work of the warrior would be without permanent result if it were not for the compromises of the diplomat, grudgingly accepted and soon forgotten?[14]

Martin Bucer's theological contribution on the doctrine of justification has been generally neglected. The reason for this neglect is perhaps evidenced in Thomas M. Lindsay's quotation: the peacemaker defies confessionalization. James M. Kittelson suggested that Bucer's unique theology in general was neglected because between 1549 (when the reformer was exiled from Strasbourg) and 1598, "Strasbourg's Reformation came to be understood in terms of theological doctrines and ecclesiastical practices rather than the heartfelt character of anyone's faith and life."[15] During this period of confessionalization, the irenic impulse in his thought went against a rigid confessional stance, and as a result his theology remained in the shadows of confessionalized Lutheranism and Calvinism.

Knowledge of Bucer's life and teachings steadily arose from obscurity roughly in 1860 with Johann W. Baum's work on the Strasbourg Reformation, which highlighted the early careers of Wolfgang Fabricius Capito and Martin Bucer.[16] This important contribution to Bucer studies resulted in generating further interest in the chief reformer of Strasbourg, yet it was fifty years later, in 1914, when a more focused yet still incomplete biography of the reformer's

---

13. The missiological motif I take up here is in agreement with Scott H. Hendrix's thesis that the unifying project of the reformers was the Christianization of Christendom. See Hendrix, *Recultivating the Vineyard: The Reformation Agendas of Christianization* (Louisville, KY: Westminster John Knox Press, 2004).

14. Thomas M. Lindsay, "Martin Bucer and the Reformation," *Quarterly Review* 220 (1914): 116–133, quote on 116.

15. James M. Kittelson, "Martin Bucer: Forgotten Man in the Late 16th Century?" in Krieger and Lienhard, *Martin Bucer and Sixteenth Century Europe* 2:714.

16. Johann W. Baum, *Capito und Butzer: Strassburgs Reformatoren: Nach ihrem handschriftlichen Briefschatze, ihren gedruckten Schriften und anderen gleichzeitigen Quellen* (Elberfeld: Verlag von R. L. Friderichs, 1860). Baum's work focused only on the early years of the Strasbourg reformation.

life was published.[17] The first thorough biography was Hasting Eells's *Martin Bucer*, published in 1931, which was described by Bard Thompson as "a full and thoroughly documented biography, written by an able Bucer scholar."[18] Only recently has Eells's work been superseded. In 1990, a year before the 500th anniversary of Bucer's birth, Martin Greschat published *Martin Bucer: Ein Reformator und seine Zeit*.[19] Fourteen years later it was translated into English and incorporated the most recent studies on Bucer's life and thought, making it by far the best resource on Bucer's life.[20] These works in combination with hundreds of other monographs, dissertations, and articles have broadened the scope of Bucer research.

In Bucer studies, two predominant trajectories have influenced the way in which Bucer's theology is understood. One regards his theological influence upon the young Calvin; the other trajectory can be broadly described as the attempt to map the influences of his own thought.

Scholars have recognized that Calvin's three years in Strasbourg were influential for the future shape of the Geneva church, and thus Calvin scholars have been keenly interested in what Calvin accomplished in Strasbourg as well as his relationship with Bucer.[21] Max Scheibe was one of the first scholars to identify Bucer's doctrine of predestination as a source of Calvin's doctrine.[22] Scheibe's work in combination with the work of Reinhold Seeberg had an influential role in Bucer studies in that thence Bucer studies became a subcategory

17. Gustav Anrich, *Martin Bucer* (Strasbourg: Karl J. Trübner, 1914). Anrich himself saw that a complete study could only follow more in-depth Bucer research.

18. Hasting Eells, *Martin Bucer* (New Haven, CT: Yale University Press, 1931); Bard Thompson, "Bucer Study since 1918," *Church History* 25 (1956): 64. Stupperich politely disagreed because he thought it too difficult to write such a biography in America due to the lack of critical editions of Bucer's works. See Robert Stupperich, "Stand und Aufgabe der Butzer-Forschung," *Archiv für Reformationsgeschichte* 42 (1951): 250. I believe Eells's work is still a very good resource, primarily based on his thorough examination of Bucer's correspondences. The next twenty years saw the publication of three shorter biographical works, two of which were prompted by the 400th anniversary of Bucer's death: Robert Stupperich, *Martin Bucer: Der Reformator des Elsasses und Einiger des deutschen Protestantismus* (Berlin: Heliand, 1941); Alfred Erichson, *Martin Bucer: Zum 400 jährigen Todestag des elsässischen Reformators* (Strasbourg: Librairie Oberlin 1951); and François Wendel, *Martin Bucer: Esquisse de sa vie et sa pensée publiée à l'occasion du 4e centenaire de sa mort, 28 février 1551* (Strasbourg: Société Pastorale, 1951).

19. Martin Greschat, *Martin Bucer: Ein Reformator und seine Zeit* (Munich: Beck, 1990); French edition: *Martin Bucer (1491–1551): Un réformateur et son temps*, trans. by Matthieu Arnold (Paris: Presses Universitaires de France, 2002); and English edition: *Martin Bucer: A Reformer and His Times*, trans. Stephen E. Buckwalter (Louisville, KY: Westminster John Knox Press, 2004).

20. Though Greschat provides a thorough treatment of Bucer's life, the work has been criticized for its treatment of Bucer's thought. Gerald Hobbs believes it still only scratches the surface. See Hobbs's review in *Church History* 61 (1992): 243–244.

21. Some scholars have even attributed Calvin's conversion in France to Bucer's influence. See, for instance, Eells's essay, "Martin Bucer and the Conversion of John Calvin," *Princeton Theological Review* 22 (1924): 402–419. Eells concludes that the evidence is weak.

22. Max Scheibe, *Calvins Prädestinationslehre: Ein Beitrag zur Würdigung der Eigenart seiner Theologie und Religiosität* (Halle: M. Niemeyer, 1897), esp. 17–19 and 69–71.

of Reformed or Calvin studies.[23] This trajectory, though not as strong as in the past,[24] has most recently been championed by the works of Willem van't Spijker.[25] These works, though valuable to Calvin studies, are of little interest to this book.

More important to this study is the trajectory investigating Bucer's influences, prompted by the fact that Bucer occupied a space "in between." He lived in between Wittenberg and Zurich, and near France and on the edge of Germany. He was neither Lutheran nor Reformed. He saw himself as a follower of Luther and a mentor to Calvin. He was a humanist and theologian, pastor and diplomat, author and disputer. He mediated between Protestants, Anabaptists, and Catholics. He was a reformer in between.

This "betweenness" has led some scholars to map his theological influences, resulting in neat genetic blueprints of Thomism, humanism, Zwinglianism, or Lutheranism. Reinhold Seeberg viewed Bucer's theology as an example of *Vermittlungstheologie* (mediating theology),[26] an amalgamation of Zwinglian and Lutheran thought.[27] Later Otto Ritschl saw Bucer as a combination of Thomism, Erasmianism, and an early 1518 version of Lutheranism.[28]

---

23. Reinhold Seeberg's influence in this approach to Bucer's theology is evidenced in that the short section on Bucer comes under the heading "Die Theologie Calvins in ihrer dogmengeschichtlichen Bedeutung" in *Lehrbuch der Dogmengeschichte*, vol. 2 (Erlangen: A. Deichert'sche Verlagsbuchhandlung Nachf, 1898), 379–383. This work was republished in 1920 with some minor emendations. Here he states that Bucer's thought was "but the stepping-stone to Calvinism." He saw the progression of Bucerian thought to Calvinism as the transfer of a low form of theology to a higher form. Likewise, Gottfried Hammann believes that part of the reason Bucer's theology was overshadowed by Calvin's is that Bucer's theology attempted, sometimes unsuccessfully, to harmonize seeming contradictions; see Hammann, *Martin Bucer: Zwischen Volkskirche*, 334–337.

24. Marijn de Kroon, in his analysis of the two reformer's responses to Jacopo Sadoleto, has ably demonstrated that there is not as much continuity as usually supposed between the two reformers. See de Kroon, *Martin Bucer und Johannes Calvin: Reformatorische Perspektiven Einleitung und Text*, trans. Hartmut Rudolph (Göttingen: Vandenhoeck & Ruprecht, 1991), esp. 119–125.

25. See Willem van't Spijker, "Bucer und Calvin," in Krieger and Lienhard, *Martin Bucer and Sixteenth Century Europe*, 2:461–470; Spijker, "Bucer's Influence on Calvin: Church and Community," in *Martin Bucer: Reforming Church and Community*, ed. David F. Wright (Cambridge: Cambridge University Press, 1994), 32–44; Spijker, "Calvin's Friendship with Bucer: Did It Make Calvin a Calvinist?" in *Calvin Studies Society Papers 1995, 1997: Calvin and Spirituality (1995) & Calvin and His Contemporaries: Colleagues, Friends and Conflicts (1997)*, ed. David Foxgrover (Grand Rapids, MI: CRC Product Services, 1998), 169–186.

26. See Seeberg, *Lehrbuch der Dogmengeschichte*, 2:382. Seeberg seems to be the first to designate Bucer's theology as a *Vermittlungstheologie*. It must be noted that the use of this term as a designator of Bucer's theology is problematic. The term was first used as a designation of a school of thought in the nineteenth century that openly attempted to mediate between biblical faith and the modern scientific spirit and was led by Karl Immanuel Nitzsch (1787–1868), August Detler Christian Twesten (1789–1876), and Isaak August Dorner (1809–1884). Thus it carries with it anachronistic baggage when used as a designator of a sixteenth-century theology. In addition, this designation influenced the manner in which Bucer's thought was understood. Thus the labeling of his theology as a *Vermittlungstheologie* has resulted in much of Bucer scholarship examining Bucer in an almost genetic fashion as one part Erasmian or Zwinglian, and one part Lutheran.

27. Ibid., 380.

28. Otto Ritschl, *Die reformierte Theologie des 16. und 17. Jahrhunderts in ihrer Entstehung und Entwicklung* (Göttingen: Vandenhoeck & Ruprecht, 1926), 3:122–156. Ritschl explains Bucer's ethical interest as founded in

The impetus behind the works of Stupperich, Henri Strohl, and Friedhelm Krüger has been to determine the humanistic blueprint in Bucer's theology.[29] Ernst-Wilhelm Kohls has argued that Bucer's Erasmianism places his theology in opposition to that of Luther.[30] And Hans Emil Weber emphasized the tension between an objective system and subjective appropriation in Bucer's thought, which is partially why he, rather oddly, describes Bucer's thought as "eine christozentrische ethische Geistmystik."[31] All these descriptions of Bucer's influences are extremely helpful, and indeed necessary for understanding Bucer's thought; they have not, however, always allowed Bucer to speak with his own voice, which is something I hope this project will achieve.

The *Vermittlung* approach to understanding his theology has resulted in hasty representations of his doctrine of justification, seen generally as somewhere in between the thought of Erasmus and Luther. This perspective has been deeply influenced by Bucer's early letter to the humanist Beatus Rhenanus, where he writes:

his humanism, paired with an early Lutheran theology. Ritschl, like Seeberg, sees him as a *Vermittlungstheologe*, who is trying to balance Luther and Zwingli on the Eucharist as well as wanting to hold together Melanchthon's idea of election with some sense of free will (124). A more nuanced understanding of these influences has been provided by works of Greschat, particularly his "Die Anfänge der reformatorischen Theologie Martin Bucers," in *Reformation und Humanismus*, ed. Martin Greschat and J. F. G. Goerters (Witten: Luther Verlag, 1969), 124–140; "Der Ansatz der Theologie Martin Bucers," *Theologische Literaturzeitung* 103 (1978): 81–96; and "Martin Bucer als Dominikanermönch," in *Bucer und seine Zeit*, ed. Marijn de Kroon and Friedhelm Krüger (Wiesbaden: Franz Steiner, 1976), 30–53.

29. Robert Stupperich, *Der Humanismus und die Wiedervereinigung* (Leipzig: M. Heinsius Nachfolger, 1936), esp. 22–26. Stupperich states that Bucer learned the true gospel from Erasmus and saw Luther as going only one step further. Henri Strohl, "Deux etudes sur Bucer," *Revue d'Histoire et Philosophie Religieuses* 10 (1930): 571–578; Strohl, "Théologie et humanisme à Strasbourg au moment de la création de la haute-école," *Recherches Théologiques* 17 (1937): 435–456; Strohl, "Un aspect de l'humanisme chrétien de Bucer," *Revue d'Histoire et Philosophie Religieuses* 18 (1939): 432–447; Strohl, "Bucer, interprète de Luther," *Revue d'Histoire et Philosophie Religieuses* 18 (1939): 223–261. Strohl in focusing on Bucer's humanism has also highlighted Bucer's relationship with Jacob Sturm in regard to opening the school, thus emphasizing the combination of Church and education. Like those before him, Strohl also sees Bucer as a precursor of Calvinism. In this line of research Friedhelm Krüger's work is by far the most thorough: *Bucer und Erasmus: Eine Untersuchung zum Einfluss des Erasmus auf die theologie Martin Bucers (bis zum Evangelien-Kommentar von 1530)* (Wiesbaden: Franz Steiner Verlag, 1970); see also Krüger, "Bucer and Erasmus," *Mennonite Quarterly Review* 68 (1994): 11–23.

30. Ernst-Wilhelm Kohls, *Die Schüle bei Martin Bucer in ihrem Verhältnis zu Kirche und Obrigkeit* (Heidelberg: Quelle & Meyer, 1963), esp. 114–118; Kohls, "Martin Bucer als Anhänger Luthers," *Theologische Zeitschrift* 33 (1977): 210–218; and Kohls, "Martin Bucer: Erasmien et Martinien tel que la Montre su Conception du Baptême," in *Strasbourg au cœur religieux de XVI* siècle: hommage à Lucien Febvre: actes du Colloque international de Strasbourg*, ed. Georges Livet and Francis Rapp (Strasbourg: Librairie Istra, 1977), 167–183. Kohl's analysis of Bucer's thought in relation to Erasmus and Luther seems to be preconditioned by his confessional commitment, which seems to have elevated Luther's theology to the status of infallibility; hence anything less is a corruption of the truth. A similar judgment is made by Johannes Müller in his *Martin Bucers Hermeneutik* (Gütersloh: Gütersloher Verlagshaus Gerd Mohn, 1965), esp. 22–40. Here Müller sees Bucer's intellectualizing of faith as a corruption of evangelical truth. A more careful appreciation of Luther's influence on Bucer can be found in Greschat's article "Der Ansatz."

31. Hans Emil Weber, *Reformation, Orthodoxie und Rationalismus*, vol. 1 (Gütersloh: Gütersloher Verlagshaus Gerd Mohn, 1937), 203–217, quote on 203.

I return to the topic of Martin Luther: although our foremost men refuted him with all their strength, he was not moved a finger's breadth from his propositions. His charm in responding was wonderful, his patience in listening was incomparable, in his elucidations you would have recognized the acumen of Paul, not of Scotus; with his answers so brief, so ingenious and drawn out from the stocks of Holy Scripture, he easily persuaded everyone toward admiration of him. On the following day, away from witnesses, I had a familiar and friendly conversation with the man, and also a dinner prepared with the most chosen doctrines rather than with food. He lucidly explained whatever I asked. He agrees with Erasmus in all things, except it seems that he excels in one thing, that what Erasmus merely insinuates he teaches openly and freely.[32]

Bucer's comment that Erasmus and Luther agree has led various scholars to examine Bucer's description of Luther's Heidelberg theses to determine whether or not Bucer had correctly understood Luther.[33] Those who believe that Bucer misunderstood Luther see this as a result of his strong Erasmian influence. Others like Greschat believe that Bucer understood Luther.[34] Hence, on account of Bucer's conversion to the Reformation at Heidelberg, the tendency has been to describe his soteriology as somewhere between that of Erasmus and that of Luther.

The main difference between Bucer and Luther is their understanding of faith. Lang, Koch, and Johannes Müller emphasize Bucer's intellectualizing view of faith, which for them is weaker than Luther's existential view.[35] Yet

---

32. *BCor* 1, 61, ll. 46–56; "Ad Martinum illum Lutherium redeo: ut summa quidem vi nostri primores amolirentur, ne latum unguem tamen ab instituto suis argutiis. Mira in respondeno suavitas, in audiendo incomparabilis longanimitas; in dissolvendo Pauli agnovisse acumen, non Scoti, adeo scitis eque divinarum scripturarum penu depromptis responsis in sui admirationem facile cunctos adduxit. Fuit postridie cum viro familiaris mihi et procul arbitris amica confabulatio, sed et coena non dapibus, sed doctrinis longe paratissima optatissimaque. Quaecunque sciscitarer, luculentissime explicabat. Cum Erasmo illi conveniunt omnia, quin uno hoc praestare videtur, quod quae ille duntaxat insinuat, hic aperte docet et libere."

33. Karl Koch is representative of the view that Bucer misunderstood Luther; see *Studium Pietatis: Martin Bucer als Ethiker* (Neukirchener: Neukirchener Verlag, 1962), 10–15; see also McGrath, *Iustitia Dei*, 251–252. Recently two works have argued that Bucer accurately understood Luther's theology at Heidelberg; see Martin Brecht, "Martin Bucer und die Heidelberger Disputation," in *Calvin: Erbe und Auftrag*, ed. Wilhelm H. Neuser and Willem van't Spijker (Kampen: Kok Pharos, 1991), 214–218; and Thomas Kaufmann, "Bucers Bericht von der Heidelberger Disputation," *Archiv für Reformationsgeschichte* 82 (1991): 147–170.

34. Greschat's thesis that Bucer's Dominicanism and love for all things Erasmus helped shape his thought before meeting Luther is most convincing. Greschat states that Bucer "was thus not *tabula rasa* upon encountering Luther but interpreted the Wittenberg theologian according to his own background and theological agenda" (Greschat, *Martin Bucer*, 28). This does not mean that he misunderstood Luther, just that his theology would appropriate Luther's insights within his own interpretive scheme. Extremely helpful is Greschat's essay "Der Ansatz," 81–96.

35. August Lang, *Der Evangelienkommentar Butzers und die Grundzüge seiner Theologie* (Leipzig: Neudruck der Ausgabe, 1900; reprint,: Aalen: Scientia Verlag, 1972), 107–116; Koch, *Studium Pietatis*, 43–50; and Müller, *Bucers Hermeneutik*, 22–40. See also Krüger, *Bucer und Erasmus*, 157–162.

rather than seeing this difference as a corruption of evangelical doctrine, the difference between Bucer and Luther can be, and I believe ought to be, seen as one of emphasis.

The tendency to categorize Bucer's theology as a combination of two or three influences has meant that the nuances and subtleties of his soteriology have been neglected, resulting in the generalizing description of "double justification."[36] As I will show, such a designation requires much substantial qualification.

The first major work to deal with Bucer's soteriology was Karl Koch's influential monograph, which was dedicated to understanding Bucer's ethical impulse in relation to his theology. In it Koch presents the thesis that Bucer was a man of praxis rather than theology (as if the two where mutually exclusive).[37] I am unconvinced. The first and only work devoted solely to Bucer's doctrine of justification is Horst-Martin Barnikol's 1961 doctoral dissertation.[38] With this work Barnikol provides the starting point for any investigation into Bucer's soteriology. He argues against the theme that Bucer's ethics drove his theology and also that there is in Bucer a reasonable and clear systematic picture to his thought.

Barnikol's work, however, abates the strong rational nature of Bucer's structure of thought[39] and neglects what I see as a foundational concept of Bucer's soteriology, the Socratic dictum that "to know the good is to do the good."[40] This dictum underlies Bucer's doctrine of justification, and as such it helps to explain how his doctrine joins faith and works, while advocating *sola fide*.

Summary

This book argues that Bucer's doctrine of justification is consistent through the period of the religious colloquies of 1539–1541.[41] As a result of this consistent

---

36. Ritschl, *Dogmengeschichte*, 148–152; Stupperich, *Der Humanismus*, 22–26; Weber, *Reformation, Orthodoxie*, 213; Koch, *Studium Pietatis*, 48–50; among others.

37. Koch, *Studium Pietatis*. This work is based on his Mainz dissertation of 1960. Koch sees Bucer as influenced by Thomas Aquinas and Erasmus, and thus at odds with the evangelical theology represented by Luther.

38. Horst-Martin Barnikol, "Bucers Lehre von der Rechtfertigung: Dargestellt an seinem Römerbriefkommentar" (Ph.D. diss., Georg-August-Universität Göttingen, 1961).

39. An area that has been more thoroughly investigated by Müller and Krüger.

40. For the origin of this maxim, see Plato, *Protagoras*, 352b. Aristotle agrees with this position in the *Nicomachean Ethics* 7.iii.

41. Rather than providing a lengthy literature review here, I have chosen to deal with the relevant literature in the body of the book.

theology of justification, Bucer's irenicism was not of an ambiguous or flabby type.

I begin by elucidating Bucer's missiological and unitive strategy centered on the doctrine of justification. I argue that Bucer believed that if agreement was achieved on this doctrine, then other more peripheral matters could be tolerated. In addition, he believed that agreement on justification would result in a slow reformation from within.

In chapter 3 I explain Bucer's doctrine of justification. I limited the scope of this chapter to his *Romans Commentary* of 1536 (considered his most theologically mature work), where he most thoroughly covers the topic. As mentioned earlier, I show how the Socratic dictum is paradigmatic for his soteriology, highlighting the importance of his intellectualizing view of faith and its relation to works.

Because I am concerned with showing the coherence of Bucer's thought, I have dedicated chapter 4 to understanding the moderate Catholic view of justification in Johannes Gropper's *Enchiridion* of 1538. Because Gropper was instrumental in formulating the agreements on justification reached at Worms in 1540–41 and Regensburg in 1541, understanding his view is helpful for seeing Bucer's influence in the article. Here I will show how Gropper's view of incorporation into Christ within the sacramental structures of the Church is important for understanding his soteriology.

After examining the doctrine of justification in the thought of Bucer and Gropper, my final chapter turns to the agreement reached at Regensburg on justification (including the evaluation of formulations on the doctrine of justification from important preceding colloquies and conferences). Throughout this chapter I argue that Bucer believed that the evangelical understanding of justification was present in the formulations from Leipzig (1539), Worms (1540–41), and Regensburg (1541)[42] and that they are compatible with Bucer's earlier view found in the *Romans Commentary*. For Bucer reform could not be achieved at the expense of the truth of justification as he understood it.

In the end the project will show that Bucer had a coherent and unified doctrine of justification, one that I hope contributes to a broader and more complete understanding of Reformation theology. Likewise, I hope that this exposition of an irenic reformer's view of justification may inspire and give strength to modern-day ecumenical discussions surrounding this important doctrine of the Christian faith.

---

42. Thus, I also argue for the evangelical credentials of the Regensburg article on justification. My primary dialogue partner in this chapter is Athena Lexutt, who sees the evangelical stance in this article as compromised. See Lexutt, *Rechtfertigung im Gespräch: Das Rechtfertigungsverständnis in den Religionsgesprächen von Hagenau, Worms und Regensburg 1540/41* (Göttingen: Vandenhoeck & Ruprecht, 1996).

Notes on Usage

A permanent divide was unfathomable to the key ecclesiastical players prior to the Council of Trent, and therefore it is imperative that we constantly remind ourselves that those who we gladly call the Protestant reformers were writing and pushing their programs of reform not as those outside the Catholic Church but from within it as monks, secular priests, professors, and so forth. On that account, as Diarmaid MacCulloch has noted in his masterful work on the Reformation, the labels "Catholic" and "Protestant" as appellations for two rival factions are problematic.[43] No reformer would have wanted to concede that their disputants or collocutors were Catholic, indicating they were not. The term "Protestant" also has its own peculiarities that stem from a minority group of princes and cities that sided with the reform beliefs of a monk from Wittenberg and a Swiss priest against the emperor during the imperial diet at Speyer on 1529. Though the term "Protestant" specifically designates those who signed the *Protestatio* in 1529, it now tends to cast a wider net, including every estate that later took on the reforming programs of Wittenberg and Zurich.

I have chosen to tackle this terminological difficulty by trying to be as faithful as possible to the terms that were used at the time by the significant players. For the Protestant group I will often use the term "evangelical," since they commonly used this term to refer to themselves (though many Catholics would not have wanted to surrender that term).[44] When referring to imperial politics, I will primarily use the term "Protestant" because the evangelical reformers also often designated themselves as the protesting estates.

For the Catholic group there is a tendency to refer to the papal church as Roman Catholic or the Roman Church, but the use of "Rome" or "Roman" as a designator of the traditional church may be more appropriately placed in the nineteenth century than the sixteenth. Aware of the difficulties, for my purposes I will predominantly use the term "Catholic" to designate the church that broadly remained loyal to the pope in Rome, since this is the term the Catholics used of themselves. At times I may refer to this church as traditionalist or to Catholics as old believers (*Altglaubig*), adopting the manner in which some evangelical reformers referred to their Catholic brethren. In addition, this work follows MacCulloch's advice on the capitalization of the Church. As he states, "The body of the faithful, the worldwide organization called the Church,

43. Diarmaid MacCulloch, *Reformation: Europe's House Divided 1490–1700* (London: Allen Lane, 2003), xix–xx.

44. Erasmus and other reforming Catholics at times referred to the evangelical reformers as pseudo-evangelicals.

deserves a capital, although a building called a church does not."[45] These terminological decisions will keep this study both historically appropriate and internally consistent.

Lastly, throughout the book there are many translated excerpts and quotations from primary sources, the majority of which have never been translated into English. Where the translations of these passages are my own I have placed the original Latin or German text in the footnote. Though this may at times make the notes cumbersome many of the primary sources used for this work are without modern critical editions, and thus, these extensive notes provide the reader ready access to the original languages. In addition to the large excerpts within the body of the book, I have attached three important English translations from Martin Bucer's *Romans Commentary* in the appendix. These translations add a valuable perspective for understanding Bucer's view of the doctrine of justification and supplement the portions of the *Romans Commentary* already wonderfully translated by David F. Wright in *Common Places of Martin Bucer*.[46]

---

45. MacCulloch, *Reformation*, xxv–xxvi.

46. Martin Bucer, *Common Places of Martin Bucer*, trans. and edited by David F. Wright (Appleford: Sutton Courtenay Press, 1972). Throughout the work when Wright has provided a translation of a relevant text I have used his translation and noted it in the footnotes with the abbreviation *CP*.

2

Martin Bucer's Irenic Approach to Reform

The Saxon chancellor Gregor Brück, in a letter to the elector John Frederick, stated that Bucer was "among all the theologians now living, truly an excellent man for negotiating in theological affairs after the manner of the world."[1] Yet this skill for negotiating, praised by Brück, was more commonly viewed as an eagerness to compromise in line with how Margaret Blaurer (sister to Ambrosius and Thomas) called Bucer "the *politicus* and *fanaticus* of union."[2] Heinrich Bullinger, during the controversy between the Swiss and the Lutherans, coined the verb *bucerisare* to describe Bucer's method of reconciling divergent views on the Lord's Supper.[3] During the negotiations at Regensburg, Vice Chancellor Burkhart stated that Bucer seemed to be "nearly wavering."[4] Prince Wolfgang of Anhalt described Bucer's speeches as proceeding from the corner of his mouth.[5] Likewise, Georg Spalatin had many suspicions over Bucer's negotiating zeal,[6]

---

1. Letter to John Frederick (23 October 1539), *CR* 3, no. 1864, 795; "Ich muß bekennen, daß Bucerus warlich unter allen Theologen, die jetzund leben, in theologischen Sachen nach der Welt Weise zu handeln, ein vortrefflicher Mensch ist."

2. Quoted in Baum, *Butzer und Capito*, 500; "theuern Politicus und Fanatiker der Eintracht."

3. Letter to Ambrosius Blaurer (10 October 1544), *Schiess* 2, no. 1134, 308.

4. Letter to the elector John Frederick (14 May 1541), *CR* 4, no. 2230, 291; "so ist doch Bucerus fast wankend."

5. Letter to the Elector John Frederick (14 May 1541), *CR* 4, no. 2231, 293; "seine Reden gemeiniglich mit halben Munde gehen."

6. Letter to Justus Jonas (27 July 1541), *CR* 4, no. 2346, 611; "Bucerus suspectissimum se reddidit."

and Luther, after Bucer's efforts at Regensburg, lost all trust in him.[7] Bucer's negotiations with the traditional church lost him the trust of many. This troubled his younger friend Calvin, who from Regensburg stated: "I am grieved that Bucer is incurring hatred from so many people. Because he has the best of intentions, he is more confident than he ought to be."[8] Bucer's confidence, that in his negotiations he was aiming at advancing the gospel, enabled him to endure the ridicule of his colleagues.

It is no surprise that with the rise of the ecumenical movement in the twentieth century, interest in this reformer and his negotiations with Catholics has increased. The connection between the ecumenical movement and Bucer's efforts for concord has led to Bucer's designation as the "ecumenical reformer."[9] Yet, if for no other reason than the danger of anachronism, it seems appropriate to ask if we have accurately appropriated Martin Bucer as an ecumenist. To describe Bucer's discussions with those loyal to the pope as ecumenical or irenic may obscure the truth of his own intentions, not least because Bucer's thought is never easily categorized.

His motivations for engaging in irenic dialogue are multifaceted. Thus scholars have variously accounted for his efforts. Heinrich Bornkamm noted: "One must see Bucer's endeavors for the unity of the Church in connection with his emphasis of mission, which he more earnestly advocated than any other reformer."[10] Friedrich Kantzenbach saw Bucer's unitive work as stemming from his theological understanding of the true Church as the invisible elect joined as members in the body of Christ.[11] Thomas Brady and Thomas

7. *WA.Tr.* 5, no. 5461, 166; "Buccerus. Da leckerlein hat den glauben gar bei mir vorlorn. Ich trau ihm niemer. Er hat mich zu offt betrogen. Er hatt sich auff dem tag ißt zu Regenspurg ubel gehalten; er hat wollen mediator sein zwischen mir und dem babst, hat gesagt: Ei, es ist ein arm ding, das soviel sehlen sollen umbkomen umb eines odr zwen artickel willen!"

8. Letter to William Farel (12 May 1541), *CO* 11, no. 309, 217; "Male autem me habet quod Bucerus invidia se apud multos gravet. Quia sibi est optime conscius, securior est quam utile sit."

9. See Rudolf Stählin, "Martin Butzer und die Einheit der Kirche," *Evangelisch-lutherische Kirchenzeitung* 6 (1952): 55–59; Jean Erbes, "Martin Bucer (1491–1551): Enfant de Sélestat, réformateur de Strasbourg, précurseur de l'Oecumenisme," *Annuaire de la Société des amis de la Bibliothèque de Sélestat* 4 (1954): 131–147; Erbes, "Martin Bucers Concordienbestrebungen und die heutige Lage der Ökumene," *Kirchenblatt für die Reformirte Schweiz* 121 (1965): 196–201; John T. McNeill, *Unitive Protestantism: The Ecumenical Spirit and Its Persistent Expression* (London: Epworth Press, 1964), 144–162; Rupp, *Protestant Catholicity*, 21–24; Rupp, "Martin Bucer: Prophet of a New Reformation," in *Prospect for Theology: Essays in Honour of H. H. Farmer*, ed. F. G. Healey (Digswell Place: James Nisbet, 1966), 183–199; James Atkinson, "Martin Bucer (1491–1551): Ecumenical Pioneer," *Churchman* 79 (1965): 19–28; and David Wright's introductory essay, "Martin Bucer: Ecumenical Theologian," in *CP* 17–71.

10. Heinrich Bornkamm, *Martin Bucers Bedeutung für die europäische Reformationsgeschichte*, Schriften des Vereins für Reformationsgeschichte 169 (Gütersloh: C. Bertelsmann Verlag, 1958), 27n4. Peter Matheson's article, on Bucer's *Concilium Theologicum* (1541), also highlights Bucer's missiological motivation for Protestant and Catholic dialogue: "Martyrdom or Mission? A Protestant Debate," *Archiv für Reformationsgeschichte* 80 (1989): 154–172.

11. Friedrich W. Kantzenbach, *Das Ringen um die Einheit der Kirche im jahrhundert der Reformation: Vertreter, Quellen und motive des 'ökumenischen' Gedankens von Erasmus von Rotterdam bis Georg Calixt* (Stuttgart: Evangelisches

Kaufmann have characterized Bucer's unitive zeal as politically pragmatic.[12] Reinhold Friedrich viewed Bucer's pursuits as a result of his deep concern for love of neighbor.[13] In a nuanced appraisal, Wilhem Neuser describes Bucer's 1540s model for unity as twofold, "a unity in faith and reformation of the Church."[14] To some extent following Bornkamm, Volkmar Ortmann, in his thorough evaluation, views Bucer's irenic strategy as founded on the prospect of conversion rather than Church unity, again highlighting a missionary agenda.[15] Far from being mutually exclusive, these emphases demonstrate the multifaceted motivations of Bucer's irenicism and the difficulty of reducing his efforts for concord to one key theme.

The purpose of the chapter is twofold. First, I wish to offer a broad but coherent account of Bucer's motives for negotiating with his Catholic brothers. The theme that seems to me to connect the varying emphases best is the uncontested belief that Bucer was a reformer and as such saw himself as returning and reeducating the Church in the restored truth of justification by faith.[16] Thus to say that Bucer was irenic or that he was even an ecumenist requires qualification. To demonstrate this I have offered a brief outline of Bucer's work as a preacher, commentator, negotiator, and teacher.

Second, I wish to describe Bucer's irenic strategy. Here I will demonstrate the centrality of the doctrine of justification for Bucer's program for unity and reform. This evangelical doctrine was for him at this time the basis for the Church and therefore the grounds for unitive discussions. Once clarity was granted over this doctrine, external rites and other issues that separated the Church could be handled with tolerance in a spirit of ἐπιείκεια (fairness, equity). For Bucer, as well as for all the reformers, a divided Church was unfathomable.

Verlagswerk, 1957), 119–141, esp. 122–123. He states here that the theological view of the Church as the limbs of Christ's body "drives Bucer's endeavors for a united Christendom." A shorter summary of his understanding of Bucer's irenicism is found in his article "Martin Butzer: Streiter für Einheit der Kirche in der Reformationszeit," in *Ökumenische Profile: Brückenbauer der einen Kirche*, ed. Günter Gloede, vol. 1 (Stuttgart: Evang. Missionsverlag, 1961), 42–50.

    12. Thomas Brady, "Martin Bucer and the Politics of Strasbourg," in Krieger and Lienhard, *Martin Bucer and Sixteenth Century Europe*, 1:129–143; Kaufmann, *Die Abendmahlstheologie*, 265–272; and his essay "Streittheologie und Friedensdiplomatie die Rolle Martin Bucer's im Frühen Abendmahlsstreit," in Krieger and Lienhard, *Martin Bucer and Sixteenth Century Europe*, 1:239–256.

    13. Friedrich, *Martin Bucer*, 195–198; see also his essay "Martin Bucer—Ökumene im 16. Jahrhundert," 257–268.

    14. Wilhelm Neuser, "Bucers Programm einer 'guten, leidlichen reformation'" (1539–1541)," in *Horizons Européens de la Réforme en Alsace*, ed. Marijn de Kroon and Marc Lienhard (Strasbourg: Librairie Istra, 1980), 227–239, quote on 236.

    15. See Ortmann, *Reformation und Einheit*, 281–282.

    16. See his preface to Thomas Cranmer in *BRom* (1536), iii–iv.

Bucer's Path to Strasbourg

Bucer spent nearly fourteen years under the influence of the Dominicans, an order known for its strong emphasis on education and reputation for combating heresy. The Dominicans instructed him in the scriptures, the works of Thomas Aquinas, and the works of Aristotle.[17] When Bucer was transferred to Heidelberg, he taught scripture and elementary philosophy classes; his superiors, influenced by the spirit of Erasmus, also allowed him to lecture to the younger monks on Erasmus's *Praise of Folly* and *Complaint of Peace*.[18] The Dominicans whetted his appetite for knowledge and provided him with the skills of teaching and disputing that would serve him the rest of his career.

Erasmus's ideas and critiques plowed the field of Bucer's mind, and Luther would seed them in 1518. During Luther's Heidelberg disputation, the critiques of the old church's theology in combination with Erasmus's critiques of Church practice began to shape the contours of Bucer's theology, setting him at odds with the Dominican order.[19] In 1521 Bucer sought his freedom from the order.

Jean-Jacques Boissard's etching depicts Bucer grasping the Bible, yet it might have been more appropriate to illustrate the Bible grasping Bucer. Like many of his time, Bucer viewed the scriptures as the primary vehicle of God's truth and fundamental to the reformation of the Church; thus, immediately after having been released from the Dominican order in April 1521, Bucer began preaching the gospel—an office he had come to believe had been suppressed by the Antichrist (i.e. the pope).[20] For about a year Bucer participated in the entourage of knight Franz von Sickingen, where he spent his time proclaiming the gospel as a court chaplain for Count Palatine Frederick and as the pastor of the parish church in Landstuhl. In November 1522 Bucer was in Wissembourg as Heinrich Motherer's

17. See Greschat, "Martin Bucer als Dominikanermönch," 30–53; Greschat, *Martin Bucer*, 13–35; and Lambert Leijssen, "Martin Bucer und Thomas von Aquin," *Ephemerides Theologicae Lovanienses* 55 (1979): 266–296.

18. *BCor* 1, 74, ll. 42–44. In a letter to Beatus Rhenanus (14 September 1518); "quamquam Heidelbergenses meos patres eo perduxerim, ut Moriam primo, dein et Querimoniam pacis praelegerim nostrae iuventuti." Bucer's introduction to humanism most likely stems from his time in the Latin school in Sélestat. See Greschat, *Martin Bucer*, 7–10.

19. Shortly after Luther's Heidelberg disputation of April 1518, Bucer received his *baccalaureus biblicus*. The Heidelberg faculty then gave him a one-year sabbatical to study Lombard's *Sentences* so that he could prepare his lectures for a two-year course. After studying over this period, Bucer returned to present a series of theses for disputation in the summer of 1519, which dealt with loving one's neighbor (over love of self) as an expression of one's love for God. This rejection of self-love in the Thomist tradition resulted in an uproar. In a letter to Rhenanus describing the uproar, Bucer noted "potissimum quod offendebat, erat, quod tuebar charitatem ordinatam esse a proximo." *BCor* 1, 81, ll. 46–47. Greschat has noted that this position seems to be a result of Luther's *Sermo de duplici iustitia*, which was published in March 1519 (*WA* 2, 143–152). See Greschat, "Die Anfänge," 124–140, esp. 137–138. See also Greschat, *Martin Bucer*, 29–30.

20. See his letter to Jean Sapidus (7 July 1522), *BCor* 1, 185–187.

chaplain. Here his zeal for the gospel coupled with his attacks on the old church led to his excommunication and his expulsion from the city, causing him to seek refuge in Strasbourg, where his now elderly parents lived.

By the time Bucer arrived in Strasbourg, he was already firmly convinced that the laity had been systematically deceived. The reckless extravagance and growing greed of the Church seemed to have encumbered the gospel and the truth of salvation to a point of unrecognizability.[21] Instead of proclaiming the truth of salvation, the Church had obscured the scriptures and placed in their stead masses, images, pilgrimages, and a host of other abuses. Under such desperate circumstances, it was the serious task of the reformers to recover the word of God "from those things which are cancerous growths on the papist flock."[22] The campaign to recover the truth of salvation in Strasbourg took shape in a vigorous program of reeducation in the pure Word of God.[23] Thus while in Strasbourg, as Greschat states, "Bucer demanded of the ruling authorities that they permit the free preaching of God's truth, and also do away with false teaching and with forms of worship that contradicted God's commandments."[24] The council gradually complied. Bucer would become Strasbourg's most influential preacher, author, diplomat, and educator.

Bucer's Work in Strasbourg: Sermon, Commentary, Dialogue, and School

Before granting him license to preach in Strasbourg, the council asked Bucer to defend his preaching in Wissembourg, resulting in his *Summary of His Preaching*.[25] In this work he reaffirmed the need for the unencumbered preaching of the Word of God, stating that what is not in keeping with the apostolic writings is of the Antichrist, since the scriptures are from the Spirit of God.[26]

Bucer began preaching the evangelical message that through faith in Christ believers receive eternal life, are given the Spirit, and become children of God, and as a result Christians no longer live for themselves but for their neighbor.[27]

---

21. See Peter Matheson, "Martin Bucer and the Old Church" in Wright, *Martin Bucer: Reforming Church and Community*, 9.

22. Bucer, *De Caena Dominica* . . . (1524), (*Bibliographie* 4), in BOL 1, 57, ll. 9–10: "ab iis quidem qui papistici gregis carcinomata sunt."

23. See Miriam Usher Chrisman, *Strasbourg and the Reform: A Study in the Process of Change* (New Haven, CT: Yale University Press, 1967), 98–117.

24. Greschat, *Martin Bucer*, 79–80.

25. Bucer, *Summary seiner Predig* . . . (1523), (*Bibliographie* 2), in BDS 1, 71–147.

26. BDS 1, 87, ll. 6–8. "Wobey gewisslich und klar verstanden würdt, das der Apostel schrift uß dem geist gottes ist, und alle die mit ir nit stimpt, uß dem geist des Antichrists."

27. BCor 2, 148, ll. 23–37; and 149, ll. 67–70.

He expounded further on this theme in *That No One Should Live for Themselves but for Others*.[28] Christ's summary of the law and the prophets (Matt. 22:37–40) shaped Bucer's understanding of the gospel. From the report of his preaching endeavors in Wissembourg we can get a glimpse of the manner in which he proclaimed this gospel:

> All the law and the prophets are based on two commandments: You shall love God with your entire heart et cetera and you shall love your neighbor as yourself. That which is in accordance with these commandments is godly; that which is not is without any doubt diabolic. Yet what relation does it have to the love of God when they say that Christ Jesus, whom we ought to obey by the commandment of the Father, has not taught us everything that is necessary to save us and to make us acceptable to the Father, and contrary to love of neighbor whereby one ought to help one's brother, they teach us at great expense to build churches, provide foundations for Masses, endow brotherhoods, purchase good works, burn candles, and all sorts of absurdities? Nobody would spend money on these things which are not commanded by God, for himself if he suffered hunger, thirst, frost, or other need. He would look after himself first and practice on himself the compassion which God desires rather than sacrifice (though toward one's neighbor in particular).[29]

The idea that lighting a candle could replace compassion toward one's neighbor necessitated a program of vigorous preaching, preaching of the gospel that frequently led to attacks against the traditional church and certain practices.[30]

Teaching the gospel was at the heart of Strasbourg's reformation. Almost as soon as Bucer arrived in Strasbourg, he was allowed to teach for one hour a day on the Gospel of John. His teaching prowess was noticed and resulted in

---

28. Bucer, *Das ym Selbs niemant, sonder Anderen Leben Soll . . .* (1523), (*Bibliographie* 1), in *BDS* 1, 31–67. English translation: Martin Bucer, *Instruction in Christian Love (1523)*, trans. Paul T. Fuhrmann (Richmond, VA: John Knox Press, 1952).

29. *BDS* 1, 88, ll. 11–23. "Alle gesatz und propheten hangen an den zweyen gebotten: Hab gott lieb von gantzem hertzen etc. und dein nechsten als dich selb; was disem gemäß ist, ist götlich, was nit, ist on allen zweifel teüffelisch. Wie stot aber mit der liebe gottes, sagen Christus Jhesus, dem wir auß gebott des vatters gehorchen sollen, hab uns nit alles zür seligkeit nutz und dem vatter gefellig gelernet, und lernen wider die liebe des nechsten mis so grossem kosten, domit man den brüdern helffen solt, kirchen bauwen meß stifften, brüderschafft uffrichten, ire güte werck kauffen, wachs brennen und was der unsinnigkeit mer ist? Deren ding, dieweil sye von gott nit gebotten, keiner ym selb umbs gelt kauffte, der hunger, durst, frost oder andere not lytte, er würde ym vor helffen und an ym selb barmhertzikeit, die gott will und nis das opfer (aber furnemlich gegen dem nechsten), üben."

30. Chrisman, *Strasbourg and the Reform*, 125; Chrisman indicates that the *Summary* of his early sermons "assumed a bitter and uncompromising attitude toward his opponents and was quick to hold them up to scorn and ridicule."

his appointment as the preacher of Saint Aurelia in the summer of 1524.[31] From this pulpit Bucer helped established the Reformation in Strasbourg.

Gripped by the evangelical message, Bucer was eager to spread the truths of scripture in writing.[32] Between 1525 and 1527 he translated Luther's *Postils* into Latin for the benefit of evangelicals in Italy, France, and the Low Countries.[33] He later consolidated some of his lectures into his own biblical commentaries: on the Synoptic Gospels (1527), Ephesians (1527), the Gospel of John (1528), Zephaniah (1528), Psalms (1529), Romans (1536), and Judges (1544). These works were intended to help preachers and readers come to the true meaning of scripture. In the preface to the *Synoptic Gospels Commentary* he states that "it is necessary that nothing other than the certain words of God be preached in the churches, words on which reason can rely beyond doubt."[34] Bucer's commentaries were written to aid the preacher in preaching the gospel.

Bucer proclaimed the truth from the pulpit as well as defending it in the conference hall. In 1524, when Conrad Treger published one hundred theses defending the primary authority of the Church and councils over scripture, the Strasbourg preachers, and especially Bucer, were quick to defend the authority of the scriptures resolutely.[35] They invited Treger to a public disputation, but he refused; [36] four years later, however, an opportunity to debate him in Bern arose. In Bern, Bucer demonstrated his skill as a public disputer and encouraged the city council to adopt the Reformation.[37]

At Heidelberg, Bucer was taught the art of *disputatio* as a means for championing the truth against error. This training equipped Bucer to champion the truth in the public disputation as well as in public dialogue, and influenced his pedagogical preference for face-to-face discussion rather than for the written polemic, characteristic of the 1530s and 1540s. His unceasing travels across Europe highlight that he was a man who preferred personal interaction rather

---

31. See Greschat, *Martin Bucer*, 54–61.

32. For a good overview of Bucer as a biblical commentator, see David Wright's essay "Martin Bucer," in *Historical Handbook of Major Biblical Interpreters*, ed. Donald K. McKim (Downers Grove, IL: InterVarsity Press, 1998), 157–164.

33. See Greschat, *Martin Bucer*, 83–84; and Greschat, "Martin Bucer and Church Renewal in Europe," *Reformation and Renaissance Review* 5, no. 1 (2003): 95.

34. *BGospels* (1527), 6; "Atqui in Ecclesiis nihil nisi certa Dei verba loqui oportebat, quibus citra ullam dubitationem mens niti queat."

35. See Bucer, *Handel mit Conrat Treger* (1524), (*Bibliographie* 6), in *BDS* 2, 15–173.

36. For this letter from the Strasbourg preachers, see *BCor* 1, 222–224.

37. In regard to Bucer's activities there, see the dedicatory preface to the Bernese ministers in his *John Commentary* in *BOL* 2, 1–15. See also Greschat, *Martin Bucer*, 78–79, who states: "In these debates, Bucer assumed a position entirely in line with what he had proclaimed up to this point: faith is all that counts; the Holy Spirit is of central importance; decisive for church unity is that all agree on the doctrine of justification—everything else can be tolerated, if necessary; there is no fundamental criterion other than the Bible; people become convinced of its truth through the work of the Holy Spirit."

than impersonal polemics. As such he used his personality and skill in negotiations to advance the truth. David Wright notes: "For him the colloquy no
less than the pulpit could be an arena for the extension of the kingdom of
Christ through the word of Christ. In other words he was a great believer in
dialogue."[38]

The opportunities for public disputation increased as more and more Anabaptists arrived in the tolerant city of Strasbourg, requiring Bucer to debate
notable Anabaptists such as Michael Sattler, Hans Denck, and Pilgrim Marpeck.
The influx of separatists caused difficulties for the uniformity of the Strasbourg
reformation, which caused the Strasbourg preachers to plead that the council
aid the preachers in establishing a more disciplined reformation. In response
to these pleadings the council called a synod in June 1533. During the various
sessions, Bucer had the opportunity to question and debate Clemens Ziegler,
Melchior Hoffman, and Caspar Schwenkfeld, and though he was unsuccessful
in converting them to the evangelical cause, Theobald Schwarz in a letter to
Wolfgang Musculus praised his disputatorial skills:

> Furthermore, above all I wish that you could have seen and heard
> what amount of grace the Lord bestowed on Bucer as he responded
> to all the arguments of his opponents; such that many (I know I am
> saying the truth), who previously were never able to endure Bucer's
> name are beginning to admire him sincerely. Likewise some Papists,
> who thus far thought wrongly concerning the gospel, declared
> themselves in agreement and are beginning to abandon their views.
> Glory and praise be to the Lord.[39]

Bucer's greatest success with Anabaptists came in 1538 at Hesse, when Philip
the Landgrave asked for Bucer's aid in negotiating a peace. In Hesse, Bucer
ably convinced the Anabaptist leaders to reintegrate into the local church,
promising that their valid concerns of moral laxity would be addressed with a
stronger plan of church discipline. As a result of these discussions Bucer insti-
tuted an evangelical form of confirmation in Hesse.[40]

38. *CP* 48.

39. *TAE* 2, no. 405, 118, ll. 10–15; "Velim porro ante omnia te vidisse et audivisse, quantam gratiam dominus
dederit Bucero ad omnia inimicorum argumenta respondere, ita us multi (scio me verum dicere), qui nunquam
prius nomen Buceri audire potuerunt, hominem incipiant ex animo colere. Item papistae nonnulli, hactenus de
evangelio pessime sentientes, dicunt sibi satisfactum et incipiunt sua derelinquere. Domino sit laus et gloria!"

40. See Amy Nelson Burnett, *The Yoke of Christ: Martin Bucer and Christian Discipline* (Kirksville, MO:
Sixteenth Century Journal Publishers, 1994), 113–121. On Bucer's form of evangelical confirmation, see Burnett's
articles "Martin Bucer and the Anabaptist Context of Evangelical Confirmation," *Mennonite Quarterly Review* 68
(1994): 95–122; and "Confirmation and Christian Fellowship: Martin Bucer on Commitment to the Church,"
Church History 64 (1995): 202–217.

Bucer believed that in a face-to-face dialogue it would be easier to persuade one's opponents of the truth.[41] That is precisely why Bucer would repeatedly argue for a public dialogue at Regensburg against the suggestions from Wittenberg for a written debate instead;[42] Bucer knew well that written documents were subjected to differing interpretations.[43]

His preference for public dialogue also influenced many of his written works, which adopted the literary genre of a fictional dialogue.[44] In these works, he would exemplify how men of differing opinions could peaceably and gradually arrive at agreement on the truth. This gradual approach was illustrative of his pedagogy for persuading and teaching others the truth of God's Word.

This pedagogy is seen in his *Catechism* as well,[45] intended to teach the truth to children. Michèle Monteil, in comparing Bucer's *Catechism* (1534) to Luther's *Small Catechism* (1529), helps highlight Bucer's approach, showing how Luther preferred to impart knowledge with small summaries, whereas Bucer preferred to impart knowledge by means of a dialogue that only gradually culminated into concrete forms.[46]

In addition to catecheses, the Strasbourg preachers wanted to educate the community in the gospel in schools. In 1528, urged on by Bucer, the city council established a German and Latin school in the old Dominican monastery.[47] In 1534, Bucer, with the aid of Ambrosius Blaurer, founded "a nursery for sacred studies" to train the clergymen of Strasbourg and neighboring cities.[48]

The sermon, commentary, dialogue, and school were all methods that Bucer used to spread and defend the truths of scripture. I have pieced them together to highlight the manner in which he championed the truth. I believe that in so doing one can better understand Bucer's goals during his discussions with Catholics. As Stupperich has asserted, for Bucer unity would result not from compromise but from the clarification of misunderstandings that enable a unity in the truth.[49] His efforts as a preacher, commentator, negotiator, and

---

41. On mediation during the sixteenth century, see Peter Matheson's *Rhetoric of the Reformation* (Edinburgh: T&T Clark, 1998), 215–237.

42. *CR* 3, no. 1918, 926–945.

43. *Lenz* 1, no. 47, 135.

44. Representative of this literary genre are his *Vergleichung D. Luthers unnd seins gegentheyls vom Abentmal Christi* (1528), *Fürbereytung zum Konzil* (1533), *Dialogi oder Gesprech* (1535), *Von Nürnbergischen fridestand* (1539), *Von Kirchengütern* (1540), and *An statui et dignitate* (1540), among others.

45. See *BDS* 6/3 for the 1534, 1537, and 1543 versions.

46. Michèle Monteil, "Le petit catéchisme (1529) de Luther et la brève explication écrite (1534) de Bucer: Deux modèles d'instruction catéchétique," *Études Germaniques* 50 (1995): 447–466.

47. See Kohls, *Die Schüle bei Martin Bucer*; and J. V. Pollet, "Bucer et l'ecole," *Bibliothèque d'Humanisme et Renaissance* 26 (1964): 559–572, esp. 563 and 567.

48. Letter to Ambrosius Blaurer (24 September 1533), *Schiess* 1, no. 363, 424; ". . . plantarium sanctorum studiorum."

49. Stupperich, "Martin Bucer als Theologe," 256.

teacher could be founded on one goal—advancing the truth and thus strengthening the visible reign of Christ. Under this light Bucer is seen as a missionary-minded reformer.

Bucer's Quest for a United Church

On 20 February 1529, the fervent sermons and writings by the Strasbourg reformers eventually caused the Strasbourg Assembly of the Three Hundred to decide to suspend the Mass until it could be proved that it was acceptable to God.[50] A significant victory had been gained in the long battle against the bishop, the canons, and the traditional church of Strasbourg.

In the same year, after the Diet of Speyer, Strasbourg signed the "Protestation," partly because it was no longer able to conform to the Edict of Worms (1521), having installed married preachers and having recently suspended the Mass. With this decision, Strasbourg had taken a stand against not only the emperor but also the traditional church, as a result confirming that the Reformation would continue in their city. Under these circumstances Bucer found himself to a certain degree free from the "menace of his Catholic adversaries."[51]

Having gained this relative freedom from the papists, Bucer sought with greater zeal opportunities to recover Christians who remained under the tyranny of the Antichrist.[52] Hence a moderate missionary tone toward his French brothers emerges during this time in his *Psalms Commentary* (1529),[53] published under the pseudonym Aretius Felinus.[54] Therein, controversial issues with the old church are handled moderately. Gerald Hobbs, in his examination of this commentary, noted that it contained for the first time a moderation that becomes a prominent feature of Bucer's personality and work in the 1530s.[55]

Of course Bucer never stopped attacking the abuses of the old church, nor did he refrain from calling the pope the Antichrist, yet Bucer's view of reform

50. For the development of this decision, see Chrisman, *Strasbourg and the Reform*, 155–176.

51. R. Gerald Hobbs, "An Introduction to the *Psalms Commentary* of Martin Bucer: The Commentary in Its Historical and Exegetical Setting" (Ph.D. diss., Universite de Strasbourg, Faculte de Theologie Protestante, 1971), 80.

52. See Greschat, "Church Renewal," 92–101.

53. For information on the various editions, see Hobbs, "*Psalms Commentary*," 1n6, 2n7.

54. This pseudonym revealed not only Martin's desire to be read by Frenchmen sympathetic to the Reformation but also his desire to be read by those of the old faith who would be averse to reading anything from his pen. See Hobbs, "*Psalms Commentary*," 77–78.

55. Hobbs, "*Psalms Commentary*," 80. See also Friedrich, who sees the *Psalms Commentary* as a work with an irenic purpose, preceding Bucer's more direct irenical work—*Fürbereytung zum Concilio* (1533). Friedrich, *Martin Bucer*, 145n3.

took on a new perspective, especially toward moderately inclined Catholics. He now advocated a more patient and tolerable stance for the future of the Reformation in Catholic territories based on agreement on the chief Christian doctrines, primarily the doctrine of justification.[56]

Justification is the teaching that constitutes the Christian faithful, that is, the elect, and hence in that regard was essential during the sixteenth century in negotiations with Catholic brothers. For Bucer faith is given with and inspired by the Holy Spirit; the Church is the elect community formed by the Spirit within the Church. Through the means of the Church and the agency of the Spirit, God is accustomed to use the preaching of the Word, the right use of the sacraments, as well as Christian discipline to inspire true faith in the elect. By faith Christians are united members of the one body of Christ;[57] on this account justification by faith is a unitive doctrine because it includes the concept of membership. Gottfried Hammann observed that Luther's teaching of salvation acted as a springboard for Bucer to talk about ecclesiology,[58] an ecclesiology based on faith and active in love, which results in the visibility of the Church in its good works.

Faith unites the body of Christ; however, there is still need of structures in the Church (e.g., ministry, "ceremonies," excommunication, and penance), which help encourage faith and growth in holiness. As I will demonstrate below, in many cases the precise form of these structures were for Bucer of secondary importance and could change according to the circumstances of different churches. As long as these structures did not inhibit the gospel, Bucer was willing to allow them, since it was the doctrine of justification that established a common membership, shared by the elect in both the Protestant and Catholic folds.

Bucer understood the Church to be a mixed Church; wheat would always be accompanied by tares, and therefore the visibility of this Church would always be somewhat compromised.[59] In addition, because faith and works were

56. See Neuser, "Bucers Programm," 227–239; and Marijn de Kroon, "Martin Bucer and the Problem of Tolerance," *Sixteenth Century Journal* 19 (1988): 157–168.

57. Peter Stephens states: "For Bucer the saints are thereby depicted as those who have faith in Christ. Thus from the start the church (or the saints) is defined in terms of faith, and in the paragraphs which follow that is related at once to election which precedes it and to love which flows from it, as well as to Christ, in whom one is elected and to whom one is united as a member to the head, and to the Spirit, who leads the heart both to faith in Christ and to love others." See his chapter "The Church in Bucer's Commentaries on the Epistle to the Ephesians," in Wright, *Martin Bucer: Reforming Church and Community,* 48.

58. Hammann, *Martin Bucer: Zwischen Volkskirche,* 36.

59. These sentiments are found in his *Handel mit Treger . . .* (1524), BDS 2, 147, ll. 10–11; the *Tetrapolitan Confession,* BDS 3, 112–114; in his *Fürbereytung zum Concilio . . .* (1533), BDS 5, 290–292; and in his *John Commentary,* BOL 2, 118. Bucer's dual ecclesiology, that is, the multitudinist church (the Christian community identical with the Christian city) and the professing church (the body of Christ identical with the elect), is most thoroughly examined by Gottfried Hammann. Hammann's study provides an important understanding of the manner in

never perfect in this life for the elect, but only after glorification, the Church could never attain visible perfection, only more or less purity. Therefore, after gaining relative autonomy from the pope, the Strasbourg clergy went forward implementing Bucer's strategy to help weaker churches grow in purity, that is, in true evangelical faith.

In his treatise *Preparation for the Council (Fürbereytung zum Concilio)*,[60] printed in September 1533, Bucer stated: "I do hope, however, that there are many dear children of God on both sides, which are improperly named after men and also kept divided [1 Cor. 3]; thus, one should attempt as much as possible to find and use all ways and means in order that all God fearing persons in all camps become united in Christ our Lord."[61]

It was the duty of Christians to love their weaker brethren, who were their neighbors.[62] In his book *On True Pastoral Care (Von der Waren Seelsorge)*, Bucer believed that the lost sheep that have separated must be again integrated into Christ's flock.[63] In various letters to the landgrave, Bucer repeatedly claimed that the Protestant estates had a responsibility toward the many "poor consciences who wished to come to the gospel."[64] This responsibility Bucer deemed at times as allowing for political force; such was the case in 1534 when the landgrave reinstated the Reformation in Württemberg.[65]

For Bucer the expansion and strength of the kingdom of Christ were to a large degree in the hands of the secular authorities. Using Romans 13 as his chief proof text, Bucer argued that ecclesiastical authority could not be distinct from that of the secular rulers.[66] Greschat notes that for Bucer the magistrate assumed the responsibility "not only for the earthly welfare of their subjects, but also for their blessedness, their eternal salvation—although admittedly within defined limits. The political power does not replace the spiritual; on the

---

which Bucer implemented the Reformation in a *corpus mixtum*. Hammann, *Martin Bucer: Zwischen Volkskirche*, passim.

60. Bucer, *Fürbereytung zum Concilio* . . . (1533), (*Bibliographie* 59), in *BDS* 5, 270–362.

61. *BDS* 5, 277, ll. 21–25; "Ich hoffe aber, es seyen zü beden theylen viel lieber kinder Gottes, die mann unbillich den menschen nachnennet und also geteylet haltet, so man mer alle weg und mittel, die ymmer möglich, süchen und an die handt nemen solte, damit die gotsförchtigen zü allen teylrn in Christo, unserem Herren, vereyniget wurden."

62. See Friedrich, *Martin Bucer*, 195.

63. Bucer, *Von der Waren Seelsorge* . . . (1538) (*Bibliographie* 81), in *BDS* 7, 84–245, esp. 155, ll 34–156, l. 4. English translation: Martin Bucer, *Concerning the True Care of Souls*, trans. Peter Beale (East Peoria, IL: Versa Press, 2009).

64. Letter to the landgrave (28 May 1539), *Lenz* 1, no. 24, 72; "armen gewissen auch zu dem h. Evangeli komen möchten." See Neuser, "Bucers Programm," 235.

65. For Bucer's view of "just war," see Koch, *Studium Pietatis*, 162–164.

66. See Marijn de Kroon, *Studien zu Martin Bucers Obrigkeitsverständnis: Evangelisches Ethos und politisches Engagement* (Gütersloh: Gütersloher Verlagshaus Gerd Mohn, 1984), 70–107; and Brady, "Martin Bucer and the Politics of Strasbourg," 133–137.

contrary it assumes it."[67] Hence Bucer was quick to voice his frustration with the princes for their shortsightedness when they accepted the Frankfurt Recess, which forbade new members to the Schmalkaldic League in 1539.[68]

Political and theological motivations cannot be easily separated in the sixteenth century. Thus when the emperor promised a council to settle the religious question in the empire, Bucer was motivated to use this council as a means to edify the Church. From the 1540s, in areas where the "tyranny" of the pope had not been overcome by the protesting princes, Bucer advised those with evangelical leanings who remained in the old church to be patient. In 1541, motivated by 1 Corinthians 9:22, "To the weak I became weak, that I might win the weak; I have become all things to all men, so that I may by all means save some," Bucer privately advised a *quidam vir* who adhered spiritually to the Reformation but who still remained in less than unfavorable circumstances, to piously tolerate the traditions and ceremonies of the old church.[69] He advocated a form of Nicodemitism,[70] that is, the practice whereby the Christian worshiping in the traditional church patiently tolerated the various abuses of that church for the sake of his Christian brother. In this regard Peter Matheson highlights Bucer's emphasis on inner piety, which allowed him to counsel these pious men to separate the wheat from the tares when attending a corrupt worship service, thus subordinating their own interests to the broader missiological interests of the kingdom of Christ.[71]

Throughout his career, Bucer advocated the visible unity of the Church. In his *Ephesians Commentary* he emphasized the unity and oneness that the Church should have in the body of Christ (Eph. 3:6). Christ is the head of his body, and therefore a body without a head is dead.[72] Likewise, in his *John Commentary* he states that the Spirit of the Lord will at length gather the elect into one body.[73] Bucer was convinced that God desired a united body.[74]

---

67. Greschat, "The Relation between Church and Civil Community in Bucer's Reforming Work," in Wright, *Martin Bucer: Reforming Church and Community*, 17.

68. See Bucer's letter to Gereon Sailer (23 October 1539), *Lenz* 1, no. 34, 114.

69. Bucer, *Consilium Theologicum Privatim Conscriptum* (1541), in *BOL* 4, see 586; "Ad hunc vero modum non legimus Dominum ceremonias depravatas ecclesiae penitus abiecisse. Imo, sicut captivitatem antichristi—quae hisce superstitiosis ceremoniis maxime continetur, minatus est, et exigentibus peccatis nostris etiam imposuit—ita pariter promisit ab hac captivitate liberationem, ac ita ceremoniarum omnium et totius administrationis ecclesiasticae repurgationem."

70. See Francis Higman, "Bucer et les Nicodémites," in Krieger and Lienhard, *Martin Bucer and Sixteenth Century Europe*, 2:645–658; and Pierre Fraenkel, "Bucer's Memorandum of 1541 and a 'Lettera Nicodemitica' of Capito's," *Bibliothèque d'Humanisme et Renaissance* 36 (1974): 575–587.

71. See Matheson, "Martydom or Mission," 169; and *BOL* 4, sent. 526, 615.

72. *BEph* (1527), 45.

73. Bucer, *Enarratio in Evangelion Iohannis,* . . . (1528), (*Bibliographie* 32), in *BOL* 2. Cf. *BOL* 2: 366; "Electi enim ex his filii Dei sunt illi dispersi [John 11:51] quos supra oves vocavit, nondum ovili suo adductas [John 10:16]. Hos Spiritus Domini redigit tandem in unum corpus cum sanctis omnibus."

74. *BOL* 2, 71; "voluit arctissimam vitae inter suos societatem esse ut alii aliorum membra, universi ecclesiam velut corpus unum [Rom. 12:5] constituerent."

It was the doctrine of justification, for Bucer, that established that unity; through faith and love, believers were incorporated members of the body of Christ. Therefore, this doctrine was ecclesiologically essential to the reformation of the Church and held a prime place in negotiations with Catholics.

The Chief Doctrine: Justification by Faith

In his *Defense against the Catholic Axiom* (*Defensio contra axioma Catholicum*), Bucer stated: "The chief point [of our debate] concerns justification, that is, the manner in which a man can reach the point at which he is sure about the divine judgment, certain of the goodwill and mercy of God, persuaded that God regards him as one of the just, and a partaker in the blessed life, having been forgiven all things by which he offended him."[75] The primary importance of the doctrine of justification for the evangelical reformation cannot be overstated, such that Bucer believed that "where there is pure teaching on justification and faith in Christ, there will be no peril which may not be easily suppressed."[76]

In the preface to his *Romans Commentary*, Bucer stated that it was his conviction that to "the one who perceives from S. Paul this, the chief matter of our religion, other things will be understandable without great difficulty."[77] Where agreement exists on justification, other differences could be reasonably tolerated. He affirmed this point again in his *Concilium* of 1539, stating: "What can or might in some way co-exist with the article on justification, the protesting estates must leave uncensored or unreproached in these churches, as long as justification and the proper Christian usage of every ceremony is always taught lucidly clearly and completely faithfully."[78]

---

75. Bucer, *Defensio contra axioma Catholicum* . . . (1534) (*Bibliographie* 62); in *BOL* 5, 1–142, quote on 21; "Caput omnium est de iustificatione, hoc est, de ea ratione qua homini possit contingere, ut securus sit iudicii divini, certus benevolentiae et misericordiae Dei, persuasus se haberi Deo inter iustos, et participes vitae beatae, condonatis omnibus quibus ipsum offendit." In this work, which was directed against Robert Ceneau, the bishop of Avranches, Bucer, besides affirming the centrality of the gospel, accepted the authority of the fathers and the observances of the early church in nondoctrinal matters when scripture was ambivalent on these issues.

76. From a letter of Antoine Morelet du Museau to Bucer quoting from the latter's letter to Thomas Blarer and Jean Zwick (16 September 1534), in *Correspondence des réformateurs dans les pays de langue française, ecuellie et publiée*, ed. A. L. Herminjard, vol. 3, 2nd ed. (Paris: H. Georg, Libraire-Editeur, 1878), no. 478, 205; "Ubi de Justificatione pure docebitur et fides in Christum, nihil futurum periculi quod non facile submoveatur."

77. *BRom* (1536), iv(a); "Hoc enim caput religionis nostrae, qui ex D. Paulo rite perceperit, ei reliqua, ut in huius Apostoli scriptis, ita in Scriptura universa haud ita magno negocio intelligi poterunt."

78. Bucer, *Concilium Buceri*, written in the winter of 1539–40, in *BDS* 9/1, 75, ll. 27–31;"Was auch in einigen weg kont ader mocht mit und beÿ dem artickel der justification bestehen, dasselbige musten die protestirenden diesen kirchen vnuorworffen vnd vngetadelt lassenn, So fern das die justification vnd recht Christlicher gebrauch aller Ceremonien jmer hell, klar vnd gantz getrewlich gelert wurden." Earlier on in this short work, he affirms again the centrality of justification in negotiations, calling it the "heubtartigkel." *BDS* 9/1, 75, ll. 10–13. This short work is his advice on how to proceed with a negotiation for unity.

When counseling others on how to deal with differences that did not threaten a sincere and simple faith, he averred: "Our dear brethren, it is entirely sufficient to be one with us on the fundamentals of the faith, namely that we all are nothing and that God desires to save us and make us holy alone through Christ."[79] Bucer did not accommodate on the fundamentals of the Christian faith, justification being the chief fundamental.[80]

The centrality of this doctrine for the Christian Church allowed Bucer flexibility on peripheral matters in negotiations with Catholics. It acted as an anchoring point, which allowed for a circumference of toleration; anything that threatened to move the anchor or fell outside of that circumference would have to be eventually reformed or disregarded.

Unity was thus impossible without some conversion to the truth of this doctrine. Growth in the knowledge of this truth resulted in the correction of behavior.[81] The strong connection between the forgiveness of sins leading to a life of love toward one's neighbor led Bucer to believe that from agreement over this key doctrine a slow and tolerable reformation could begin within Catholic territories.[82] The precise nature of his doctrine of justification, especially the manner in which faith and love are connected, will be thoroughly discussed in the next chapter, which looks exclusively to his *Romans Commentary*, where he believed the doctrine was most fully explicated. Suffice it to say that his doctrine of justification, which incorporates faith in Jesus Christ and love of neighbor, was what constituted a true Christian.[83] These aspects were essential; other external practices could be allowed for with tolerance.[84]

79. Bucer's report on the *Bern Disputation* (Zürich, 1528), (*Bibliographie* 30), in BDS 4, 83, ll. 7–9; "Unsere lieben brüder, genügt wol, wo man in der summ des gloubens mit uns eins ist, namlich das wir alle nichts sind und uns Gott durch Christum allein fromm und sälig machen wil."

80. Though justification was consistently held as the chief teaching of Bucer's reformation, when he spoke of chief points or doctrines, he could include the following: the right use of the sacraments, suitability of clergy, Christian freedom in other customs and ceremonies, and the right use of church property. See *Lenz* 1, no. 24, 73.

81. Hammann, "The Creation of the 'Christlichen Gemeinschaften,'" in Wright, *Martin Bucer: Reforming Church and Community*, 133.

82. See Ortmann, *Reformation und Einheit*, 281–283; Friedrich, *Martin Bucer*, 196; and Bornkamm, *Martin Bucers Bedeutung*, 27. Neuser's distinction between doctrinal consensus and reformation of practices sets up a cleaner separation than Bucer imagined. Such a separation fails to see the significant impact that the gospel, that is, the doctrine of justification, plays in transforming individuals and the church from within. See Neuser, "Bucer's Programm," 235–237.

83. In the preface to the second edition of the *Gospels Commentary*, dedicated to the University of Marburg, Bucer has the marginal the note:, "Quae doctrina satis, ut quis Christianus sit." In this section he describes that it is love from a sincere faith. BGospels (1530), A4a–A4b; quoted in de Kroon, "Problem of Tolerance," 158.

84. See de Kroon, "Problem of Tolerance," 158.

Bucer's View of Tolerance

Having affirmed this mandatory foundation for true Christianity, I now turn to the manner in which Bucer could allow for a relative freedom in external practices. The full title of the *Romans Commentary* is instructive here:

> *Metaphrasis* [a paraphrasing] and continuous *Enarratio* [detailed explanation] of the Epistles of St. Paul the apostle, in which all the arguments and judgments and words of the Apostle are individually examined reverently and more fully, according to the authority of Holy Scripture and the faith of the Catholic Church past and present. Forty-two harmonizations and decisions of seeming contradictions of places in scripture and of the main controversies in religious doctrine today. All things have been accommodated without ill will καὶ ἐπιεικῶς [fairly, reasonably, equitably] and for the general restoration in every way of concord in the Church. Volume I. Containing the *Metaphrasis* and *Enarratio* on the Epistle to the Romans, in which, as the Apostle discussed the principal topics of the whole of theology most accurately and completely, thus in this Volume is explained the greatest part of the whole, not only of Pauline, but also of universal holy Philosophy. By Martin Bucer.[85]

In this work Bucer was convinced that a clear exposition of the scriptures, as well as the church fathers and even some scholastic theologians, would lead the old church to the evangelical truth of the fundamentals of the Christian faith.[86] In addition, here he indicated that he intended to examine Paul's epistles with fairness, referencing the jurisprudential term ἐπιείκεια (fairness, equity). This warrants further explanation.[87]

85. *BRom* (1536), title page; "Metaphrases et Enarrationes perpetuae Epistolarum D. Pauli Apostoli, quibus singularim Apostoli omnia, cum argumenta, tum sententiae et verba, ad autoritatem Divinae scripturae, fidemque Ecclesiae catholicae tam priscae quam praesentis, religiose ac paulo fusius excutiuntur. Dissidentium in speciem locorum Scripturae, et primarum hodie in religionis doctrina controversiarum conciliationes et decisiones XLII. Omnia citra dentem καὶ ἐπιεικῶς et ad communem Ecclesiarum restituendam concordiam modis omnibus accomodata. Tomus Primus continens Metaphrasim et Enarrationem in Epistolam ad Romanos, in qua ut Apostolus praecipuos totius Theologiae locos tractavit quam exactissime et plenissime, ita est hoc Tomo maxima pars totius, non tam Paulinae, quam universae Sacrae Philosophiae explicata. Per Martinum Bucerum."

86. One of his goals in the commentary was to demonstrate to Catholics the consent of the church fathers throughout the ages on justification in his *Romans Commentary*. See his letter to Bullinger (29 January 1535): "Ipse quoque in hac re peccavi in Enarrationibus meis in Evangelistas, sed non tam voluntate quam necessitate; deerat tempus omnia perlustrandi. Scribo nunc, cum ocium est, in epistolas Pauli; his religiosius observo, quod illic non licuit. In hoc sudo, ut ostendam consensum ecclesiae per omnia secula"; quoted in *Pollet* 2:301n4.

87. This Greek Aristotelian jurisprudential term can also be understood by the Latin equivalent *aequitas*. For *aequitas* as a possible Latin equivalent, see de Kroon, *Martin Bucers Obrigkeitsverständnis*, 44n34, 48–49. As *aequitas* it is also used in his *John Commentary*; see BOL 2, 150–151. De Kroon offers a thorough and clear discussion of the origin and use of the term during the sixteenth century in *Martin Bucers Obrigkeitsverständnis*, 37–56, esp. 44–49.

To expound the manner in which Bucer used the term ἐπιείκεια, it is best to first look briefly at how the term συγκατάβασις (divine condescension, accommodation)[88] functioned in Erasmus's plan for unity, titled *On Mending the Unity of the Church*.[89] Such condescension meant, for Erasmus, that "sometimes the pious and simpleminded ought to be tolerated, even if [they are joined] with some error."[90] For in Erasmus's mind was this not what God did for sinful humanity in Christ? In order for the Church to be united, Erasmus believed that one had to allow for differences in externals, since the visible Church was intermixed with the good and the wicked alike.[91]

On that account Christians ought primarily to be focused on mending their own shortcomings rather than judging others. If everyone focused on living a pious life, then there could be accommodation on certain external practices. Hence, Erasmus placed the focal point of Christianity in the good moral life, characterized in his earlier writings as the *philosophia Christi*.[92] This led to the minimizing of theology's importance, since for him God was too mysterious to be grasped completely by mere mortals, making laughable any confidence in theological debates that attempted to explain completely God.[93] Even the doctrine of justification was included as a doctrine upon which there should be some scope for disagreements.[94]

---

88. *ASD* V-3, 304, ll. 617–620; "Accedat illa συγκαταβάσις, ut utraque pars alteri sese nonnihil accommodet, sine qua nulla constat concordia. Sed hactenus obsecundetur, ut ne moveantur τὰ ἀκίνητα, et hactenus feratur hominum infirmitas, ut paulatim invitentur ad perfectiora." On Erasmus's use of συγκαταβάσις, see de Kroon, *Bucers Obrigkeitsverständnis*, 38, 37–56, 70–78.

89. Erasmus of Rotterdam, *Liber de sarcienda Ecclesiae concordia deque sedandis opinionum dissidiis, cum aliis non nullis lectu dignis* (Basil: Froben, 1533). Froben's 1540 edition has the title *De amabili ecclesiae concordia liber*, in *ASD* V-3, 257–313. For the context and history of Erasmus's reply, see Stupperich, "Einleitung," in *ASD* V-3, 247–255; and Jacques V. Pollet, "Origine et structure du *De Sarcienda Ecclesiae Concordia* (1533) d'Erasme," in *Scrinium Erasmianum: Mélanges historiques . . . à l'occasion du cinquième centenaire de la naissance d'Erasme*, ed. Joseph Coppens, vol. 2 (Leiden: Brill, 1969), 183–196. For shorter discussions on this work, see Kantzenbach, *Das Ringen um die Einheit*, 84–92; Cornelis Augustijn, *Erasmus: His Life, Works, and Influence*, trans. J. C. Grayson (Toronto: University of Toronto Press, 1995), 180–182; Krüger, "Bucer and Erasmus," 18–19; and Thompson, *Eucharistic Sacrifice*, 128–131. In regard to Erasmus's general influence on Bucer, see Krüger, *Bucer und Erasmus*.

90. *ASD* V-3, 305, ll. 668–670; "pius ac simplex affectus interdum tolerandus est etiamsi sit cum aliquo conjunctus errore." Bucer earlier had taken a similar stance in regard to error in the Bern Disputation. Cf. *BDS* 4, 83.

91. *ASD* V-3, 270, ll. 400–405; "Nec omnino falsum est, quod dicunt quidam invisibilem esse ecclesiam. Solus enim Deus introspicit corda hominum, ac vere novit qui sint ipsius. Multis tamen argumentis saepe deprehenditur ubi sit Ecclesia Dei, ubi synagoga Satanae. Multorum enim peccata sunt ad judicium. Sed haec ipsa ecclesia visibilis, quae bonis habet admixtos malos, quantum habet alacritatis ac majestatis, quoties ad pietatis cultum convenit." This sentiment is also in Bucer's *Fürbereytung zum Concilio*; cf. *BDS* 5, 290–292.

92. See Augustijn, *Erasmus*, 71–88.

93. *ASD* V-3, 274, l. 543ff. See C. J. de Vogel, "Erasmus and His Attitude toward Church Dogma," in *Scrinium Erasmianum*, ed. J. Coppens, vol. 2 (Leiden: Brill, 1969), 101–132.

94. *ASD* V-3, 304, ll. 626–638.

For many of the reformers this approach was dangerous. Luther believed that "sense of conscience and the truth itself will not tolerate this model of concord."[95] Bucer was more positive. In a letter to Ambrosius Blaurer of 8 January 1534, Bucer praised Erasmus's work: "It seems to us that Erasmus has conceded very much; and I desired it to be well known among the Germans, for whom we can expect certain ruin, if they do not resolve once and for all with seriousness concerning religion."[96]

In response to Erasmus's book and with the purpose of reminding the emperor of his promise to hold a national council in the "Peace" of Nuremburg (1532), Bucer wrote his treatise *Preparation for the Council* (which I have already had various opportunities to mention). It was written in the form of a dialogue between an Erasmian loyalist (Gotpraecht) and a Lutheran (Gothertz). Both parties agreed that with ill will put aside, they could enter into a reasonable dialogue. Bucer believed that through dialogue differences could be gradually resolved if both parties had the same goals and were led by the Holy Spirit.

In contrast to Erasmus's unitive strategy of συγκατάβασις, which was less concerned with theological disputes, Bucer's strategy of ἐπιείκεια was founded on doctrine, specifically the doctrine of justification by faith and love of neighbor, not personal moral effort.

It is in this work, in the fifth chapter, that the term ἐπιείκεια first appears. It arises directly in regard to Gotpraecht's concern for keeping the command of the Sabbath. Gothertz states:

> But now behold how useful and profitable this commandment is and
> how important God held it, that he even prohibited lighting a fire on
> the Sabbath, however, when the disciples of the Lord in their need
> plucked the heads of the grain on the Sabbath, and in doing so gave
> themselves dispensation from it, the Lord defends them among
> others with the fact that the Sabbath was given for man and not man
> for the Sabbath. Take, for example, David who in his need ate of the
> holy bread which under normal circumstances would not have been
> customarily his; he therefore wanted to prove that all ordinances
> ought to serve the good of man and therefore where it goes against
> this good, man always may and ought to do what serves the glory of

---

95. WA 38, 276, ll. 15–16. "sed conscientia et veritas ipsa hanc concordia rationem tolerare non potest."

96. From the Archives Saint-Thomas de Strasbourg 151, 443, no. 110b, quoted in Friedrich, *Martin Bucer*, 147n62; "Visus est nobis Erasmus permulta dedisse; id et ego optabam notum esse Germanis, quibus certum exitium expectamus, si non constituant serio semel de religione." See also Bucer's colleague in Strasbourg, Wolfgang Capito, who translated this book by Erasmus and had the translation printed in Strasbourg. He added a favorable introduction to the work, *Von der kirchen Lieblichen Vereinigung* (On the Lovely Union of the Church). See James M. Kittelson, *Wolfgang Capito: From Humanist to Reformer* (Leiden: Brill, 1975), 207–208.

God, irrespective of how the letter and the divine commandment express themselves. So with all those ordinances concerned with outward rituals, which are bound to a particular time, place, circumstance, and person, which easily change, one can never achieve that which is universally correct and useful, and therefore one has to allow that which the Philosophers call *"to epiices,"* τὸ ἐπιεικές, that is, the appropriate steering and direction of all laws and ordinances toward that which is right and customary for each time and in each circumstance with each person. Those who spoke Latin called this a dispensation.[97]

In regard to the Christian Church, it seems Bucer uses the term ἐπιείκεια out of his concern to justify the various unwritten ordinances of the early church fathers. Though these ordinances may not be suitable today, we should not lightly disregard them, but discern the context of the ordinances before we apply or abolish them. As Nicholas Thompson notes, ἐπιείκεια "stands for Bucer's conviction that every institution should serve the common good (i.e. edification) whatever its 'letter' might appear to demand."[98] Hence, if the Church is focused on the common good, it is able to make decisions over controverted practices equitably (ἐπιείκεια).

Later on in chapter 8 of the *Preparation for a Council,* Gotpraecht asks Gothertz how reconciliation could be possible between two institutions who celebrated two distinct liturgies. The response here is similar to the one Bucer gave in his *Letter in Defense;*[99] the united Church has never been without diversity, even in the earliest centuries.[100] This diversity pertained to peripheral matters, and unity with diversity was possible when differing liturgical traditions were grounded in true faith active in works of love.

97. BDS 5, 321, ll. 12–24; "Nun sihe aber, wie nutzlich und heylsam dis gebot ist und wie theur es Got gehalten hat, das er auch nur ein fheur uff den Sabath anzuzünden verbotten, noch, do die jünger des Herren zu irer notturfft uff den Sabath hatten die eher außgerauffet und in dem mit inen selb dispensieret, vertredigt sie der Herr under anderem auch damit, der Sabath were umb des menschen willen und der mensch nit umbs Sabaths willen. Zoge ein das exempel Davids, der in seiner notdurfft die heyligen brot gessen hat, das im sunst nit gupüret hette, wolte damit bewysen, das alle ordnungen den menschen zu gütem dienen sollen, und derhalb, wo sichs anders zütrage, der mensch allweg das thün möge und solle, das im zun ehren Gottes dienstlich sein wille, unangesehen, wie der büchstab laute auch der göttlichen gebot, dann in allen denen ordnungen, die das eusserlich menschlich thün belangend, welchs an zeyt, stet, maß und person gebunden ist, die sich leichtlich enderen, kan man nimmer das erreychen, das allweg recht und thünlich ist, derhalb müs man allemal dem stat geben, das die Philosophi »to epiices«, τὸ ἐπιεικές heissen, das ist, dem billichen lencken und richten aller gesetzen und ordnugen uff dasjenig, so zu jeder zeyt, an jeder stat, mit jeder person recht und gepürend sein wille, das die Lateinischen »dispensieren« nennen."

98. Thompson, *Eucharistic Sacrifice,* 137.

99. Here in this *Letter in Defense,* Bucer demonstrates his moderation in his concept of *aequitas.* If the early church with fairness could survive diversity in practices, the church of the sixteenth century could as well. See *BOL* 1, 136, l. 22 through 137, l. 3.

100. BDS 5, 355–358. See also Thompson, *Eucharistic Sacrifice,* 138–139.

Now returning to the title of the *Romans Commentary*, we can start to see why Bernard Roussel points out that what Bucer envisioned was "revolutionary."[101] It indicated that his work would be written with ἐπιείκεια, breaking from what might be seen as the polemical tradition of other commentaries. Bucer's desire for fairness in externals was a strategy that he believed could contribute to the edification of the Christian Church, which was menaced by internal divisions. He did not desire to nourish fights of one faction against another;[102] he knew that the truth is difficult to come by through polemics; and it was in the truth that he wanted consensus.

If the fundamentals of the Christian faith could be agreed upon, then the controversies that were plaguing the Church could be accommodated "without ill will καὶ ἐπιεικῶς [fairly, reasonably, equitably] and for the general restoration in every way of concord in the Church."[103]

Bucer's irenicism must be seen as theologically founded on the doctrine of justification. This was the doctrine that constituted the Christian and incorporated him into the Church. As long as that was established in negotiations, then external issues and practices could be resolved with the common good in mind, that is, with ἐπιείκεια.

Summary

I began this chapter with Calvin's assertion that Bucer was confident of his good intentions despite the fact that his efforts were causing him to lose friends. Bucer's conscience was sure because he believed that what he was doing would help advance the reformation of the old church. While an exile in Cambridge reflecting on his efforts for concord, he explained that it was his aim "most fully to consent, first, with the Lord himself and the Holy Spirit, then also with the true and orthodox Church of primitive times, and lastly, with all the sons of God of the present age, regardless of whatever party they may seem to be through human infirmity."[104] He aimed at discerning and spreading the truth.

101. Bernard Roussel, "Martin Bucer lecteur de l'épitre aux romains," 2 vols. (Ph.D. diss., Universite de Strasbourg, Faculte de Theologie Protestante, 1970), 1:30–34.

102. A view he held from early on. See Bucer, *Apologia . . . circa Christi Caenam . . .* (1526), (*Bibliographie* 21); 1b–3a, quoted in *CP* 33; "Right from the time when I first conceived the way of godliness, not from commentaries composed by men but from the Scriptures themselves through the teaching of the Spirit, I purposed at heart both to esteem nothing more highly than love and to keep as far distant as possible from party passions and contentions, especially in matters of religion."

103. *BRom* (1536), title page as quoted above.

104. Letter to Calvin (14 August 1549), *CO* 13, no. 1240, 355; "me quam plenissime consentire, primum cum Domino ipso et spiritu sancto, deinde cum vera et orthodoxa etiam veterum ecclesia, postremo cum filiis Dei praesentibus omnibus, quarumcunque videantur esse adhuc partiam ex humana imbecillitate."

As a champion of the truth, Bucer spread the edifying doctrine of justification by faith from the pulpit, lectern, and conference hall. Through disputa-
tions and dialogues with Catholics or Anabaptists, Bucer believed that he could
gradually convince his brothers of the essential Christian truths. If there was
agreement on the doctrine of justification, which I demonstrated as fundamental to his irenic program, then externals could be accommodated equitably so
long as they served the common good.

On that account, Bucer never saw himself as accommodating on the doctrine of justification. His program for reform and unity was aimed primarily at
inspiring belief in and securing agreement on this doctrine. Likewise, he
believed that once agreement was reached on this evangelical doctrine of true
faith, the internal regeneration of the Church would likewise gradually result in
external reforms.

In this light, his negotiations with Catholics can be seen as the missionary
endeavor to spread the kingdom of Christ. Bucer was dedicated to the gradual
purification of Christ's churches even where gravely deformed in servitude to
Antichrist, because here was thirsty soil for the Word of God. A staunch believer in dialogue, he worked tirelessly, hoping and believing that evangelical
truth would prevail. In regard to the 1540 negotiations he stated that "hope was
small," but "that we can bring down Satan again. Yet good hope exists that we
can still wrest some from his hand and give them to Christ."[105] This meant
educating in and proclamation of the doctrine of justification by faith. It is to
his unique understanding of that doctrine that I now turn.

---

105. Letter to the ministers in Strasbourg (April 1541), CO 11, no. 296, 195; "Ut prorsus Satanam deiicia-
mus spes parva est: ut tamen aliquid ipsi eripiamus et Christo addicamus, bona spes est."

3

Martin Bucer's Doctrine of Justification in His *Romans Commentary* (1536)

For a man's affections and conduct are determined in
their entirety by his mental convictions.[1]

In the previous chapter I highlighted Bucer's irenic strategy for
reform, which centered on his understanding of justification. There I
briefly described his understanding of this doctrine as combining
faith in Jesus Christ and love of neighbor. It is the task of this chapter
to unpack Bucer's doctrine of justification by carefully examining
how he articulated this doctrine in the *Romans Commentary* (1536).[2] I
argue that by focusing on the intellectualizing emphases that govern
much of Bucer's soteriology (particularly the manner in which the
dictum that "to know the good is to do the good" operates as
paradigmatic for his thought), the manner in which Bucer combines
both faith and love in his doctrine of justification will be clear.

This chapter is divided into five major sections. The first offers a
short introduction to Bucer's *Romans Commentary*. The second
section looks at the misinterpretations of Bucer's doctrine of
justification, primarily its interpretation as a "double justification"
theory. The third section demonstrates the manner in which Bucer
understands *iustitia* and introduces the way in which his

---

1. *BRom* (1536), 16; (1562), 16; *CP* 177.
2. Because Bucer's commentary exists only in sixteenth-century editions, and therefore
without a modern edition (though one by the *BOL* committee is forthcoming), I have included
large portions of the text in both the body and the notes of this chapter.

strong rational emphases allow for both an imputed and an imparted aspect to his doctrine of justification. The fourth section, which constitutes most of the chapter, attempts to outline the structure of Bucer's thought by looking at his epistemology, psychology, and anthropology, as well as his views on sin, free choice, and election. The final section deals with Bucer's doctrine of justification; it is divided into subsections on vocation, faith, and works. In the end, with knowledge of the paradigmatic structure of Bucer's thought, one can more clearly understand Bucer's doctrine of justification.

Bucer's *Romans Commentary*

From the pulpit or the lectern the Strasbourg preachers passed on the knowledge of the evangelical message. In 1524, educated laypersons would enter the Dominican monastery to listen to Bucer's lectures on the New Testament, Wolfgang Capito's lectures on the Old Testament, and later on Caspar Hedio's lectures on Church history.[3] In his lectures, Bucer sought to show the true meaning of the scripture's text from its historical context as well as to demonstrate the manner in which the text ought to be handled in preaching.[4] Bucer's students heard him teach on the Pastoral Epistles, Colossians, Ephesians, Timothy, Titus, Hebrews, Thessalonians, James, Matthew, John, Psalms, and Exodus.[5] Though there is no extant record that indicates Bucer ever delivered lectures on the epistle to the Romans, there is reasonable evidence within his commentary that he had at one point lectured on this important epistle.[6] In his lectures, as in his *Romans Commentary*, he sought to instruct pastors and teachers on how to "pass on the philosophy of Christ to the common people."[7] That is to say that his lectures and commentaries were intended to aid the Christianization of Strasbourg and Europe.

It is important to note that the *Romans Commentary* was published after the Wittenberg Concord of 1536, where the Strasbourg theologians and other southern German theologians found agreement with the Wittenberg theologians on the

3. See Müller, *Bucers Hermeneutik*, 10–12; and Eells, *Martin Bucer*, 46–47.

4. In 1531 Bucer wrote a short memorandum entitled "Quomodo S. Literae pro Concionibus Tractandae sint Instructio," which has been published in Latin and in French translation by Pierre Scherding and François Wendel, "Un Traité d'exégèse pratique de Bucer," *Revue d'Histoire et de Philosophie Religieuses* 26 (1946): 32–75. For examinations of Bucer as an exegete, see Bernard Roussel, "Bucer exégète," in Krieger and Lienhard, *Martin Bucer and Sixteenth Century Europe*, 1:39–54; R. Gerald Hobbs, "How Firm a Foundation: Martin Bucer's Historical Exegesis of the Psalms," *Church History* 53 (1984): 477–491; and Wright, "Martin Bucer," in McKim, *Historical Handbook*, 157–164.

5. See Müller, *Bucers Hermeneutik*, 10.

6. See Roussel, "Martin Bucer Lecteur," 1:14–16. Here Roussel observes that the repetitions and breaks in the *Romans Commentary* could point back to a classroom origin.

7. *BRom* (1536), v(r); "eoque minus instructis materiam suppeditare commendandi philosopiam Christi populo."

doctrine of the sacraments; they also subscribed to the Augsburg Confession. From this point on, Bucer's view of the sacraments leaned away from his previously held memorial view, in line with the Swiss reformers. The evidence of this shift is clearly seen in his amendations to the 1536 edition of his *Gospels Commentary*, as well as his views on the doctrine in the *Romans Commentary*. On that account of this shift some may see his *Romans Commentary* as a piece of *Vermittlungstheologie* aimed at intra-Protestant unity and not truly representative of his own thought. I disagree. In Bucer's *Romans Commentary* we find his mature thought, and it is here where he most thoroughly examines the doctrine of justification; hence, the *Romans Commentary* is where one must go to examine his view on the doctrine. From this thorough articulation of the doctrine given in 1536, I will demonstrate how Bucer remained unwavering amid discussions with Catholics on this point.[8]

Within a span of ten years (1532–1542), more than thirty-five commentaries on the epistle to the Romans were published in western Europe (not including the various reprintings and various editions of the more popular commentaries).[9] The impact of Luther's doctrine of justification *sola fide* resulted in a feverish output of texts that fueled heated disputes. For Bucer these disputes over justification revolved primarily around a misunderstanding of the manner in which *opera* were included within the concept of *sola fide*.[10]

The relation between faith and works required careful exegesis, since "the principle religious disagreements in the whole world have arisen and been sustained from the fact that very few indeed have yet paid attention to the status that should be accorded to our works and why it is they have the nature of merits and earn the wages of eternal life."[11]

---

8. Throughout I have tried, where appropriate, to show the parallels of his thought in his earlier works with this work. August Lang believed that Bucer's doctrine of justification had shifted to a more Lutheran point of view from what he had written in the *Gospels Commentary* (*Evangelienkommentar*, 363, 371); however, rather than there being a development solely based on a Lutheran influence, the different ways in which Bucer talks about justification in the *Romans Commentary* can be wholly substantiated on the basis of the Pauline epistle itself—especially since the various theological loci all stem from his exegesis of Paul. That being said, a more substantial work is warranted on Bucer's doctrine of justification in the *Gospels Commentary*.

9. T. H. L. Parker, *Commentaries on Romans, 1532–1542* (Edinburgh: T&T Clark, 1986). For an insightful look at various readings of Romans during the sixteenth century, see Kathy Ehresnsperger and R. Ward Holder, eds., *Reformation Readings of Romans* (New York: T&T Clark, 2008). Of particular interest are the essays "The Law and Its Works in Martin Bucer's 1536 Romans Commentary," by Edwin W. Tait, and "Romans 7 in the Reformation Century," by Mark W. Elliott.

10. In 1542 he remarked again that the whole debate was a result of Catholics' misunderstanding Luther's position so that they believed Luther excluded all good works. See Bucer, *De Vera Ecclesiarum . . . Reconciliatione et Compositione . . .* (Strasbourg, 1542), (*Bibliographie* 124), 12; the first part of this work was published by Walter Friedensburg as "Martin Bucer, Von der Wiedereinigung der Kirchen (1542)," *Archiv für Reformationsgeschichte* 31 (1934): 145–191, see 165–166.

11. *BRom* (1536), 130; (1562), 119; "Haec in hisce tribus huiusmodi locorum conciliationibus, tam fuse libuit disserere, quod praecipua totius orbis circa religionem dissidia, hinc extiterunt et sustentantur, quod perpauci adeo, adhuc satis perspectum habent, quo nam loco nostra opera habenda sint, et unde habeant quod merita sint, et aeternae vitae merces eis rependatur."

The result of his efforts in his *Romans Commentary* generated high praise. Thus Calvin stated:

> Finally, there comes Bucer, who spoke the last word on the subject with the publication of his writings. In addition to his profound learning, abundant knowledge, keenness of intellect, wide reading, and many other varied excellences in which he is surpassed by hardly anyone at present day, this scholar, as we know, is equaled by few and superior to very many. It is to his special credit that no one in our time has been more precise or diligent in interpreting scripture than he.[12]

Bucer's exegesis coupled with his desire to demonstrate the united witness of the church fathers produced an impressive and massive work of early modern biblical scholarship. The breadth of Bucer's reading in the church fathers and the philosophers is one cause of the prolixity of the work, for when he sat down to write, he enthusiastically and without restraint made multiple connections between the ideas of Plato, Aristotle, Cicero, Paul, Augustine, Jerome, Chrysostom, Thomas Aquinas, Melanchthon, and so on.[13]

This exhaustive approach led to the *Romans Commentary*'s run-on style,[14] which is so tedious that even Bucer admitted its faults.[15] Unfortunately, this aspect of his legacy has resulted in many readers finding his theology "often complicated and barely comprehensible."[16] Though at times tedious, the

---

12. In Calvin's dedicatory letter to Simon Grynaeus of Basel prefacing his *Romans Commentary* (18 October 1539), *CO* 10, no. 191, 404; English translation in *LCC* 23, 75; "Tandem Bucerus lucubrationibus suis emissis veluti colophonem imposuit. Siquidem vir ille, ut nosti, praeter reconditam eruditionem copiosamque multarum rerum scientiam, praeter ingenii perspicaciam, multam lectionem aliasque multas ac varias virtutes, quibus a nemine fere hodie vincitur, cum paucis est conferendus, plurimos antecellit, hanc sibi propriam laudem habet quodnullus hac memoria exactiore diligentia in scripturae interpretatione versatus est."

13. Calvin highlights Bucer's prolixity in the same panegyric. *CO* 10, no. 191, 404; English translation in *LCC* 23, 75; "Bucerus et prolixior est quam ut ab hominibus aliis occupationibus districtis raptim legi, et sublimior quam [ut] ab humilibus et non valde attentis intelligi facile queat. Nam ad cuiuscunque argumenti tractationem se contulit, tam multa illi ad manum suggeruntur ab incredibili qua pollet ingenii foecunditate, ut manum a tabula tollere nesciat." His verbosity even led to Luther calling him a chatterbox (*klapper maul*). Luther to Brück (August 1544), in *WA.Br.* 10, no. 4014, 618, ll. 22–25.

14. Such a style was not reserved to his *Romans Commentary* alone. His style is notoriously poor, as my dear friend, the late Morton A. E. Gauld, lecturer of Latin at the University of Aberdeen, never failed to remind me. He was particularly fond of quoting F. L. Cross's description of Bucer, whose "Latin style is notoriously difficult and unattractive." F. L. Cross, ed., *The Oxford Dictionary of the Christian Church*, 3rd ed., ed. E. A. Livingstone (Oxford: Oxford University Press, 1997), 246.

15. *BRom* (1536), v(v).

16. Heinrich Bornkamm, *Das Jahrhundert der Reformation: Gestalten und Kräfte* (Göttingen: Vandenhoeck & Ruprecht, 1961), 107. For Bornkamm, Bucer's thought is complicated because of the mixing together of humanist, Platonist, Reformation, baptist, and Catholic thought.

Romans Commentary contains profound theological insights and is considered by many Bucer scholars to be his most mature thought.[17]

The 500-page commentary comprises three books of *enarrationes* (book I, chapters 1–3; book II, chapters 4–11; and book III, chapters 12–16).[18] For each book Bucer provides his own translation, which he calls a *metaphrasis*, "a rather free conversation."[19] Each book and accompanying *metaphrasis* is then subdivided into the chapters of the epistle. These are then divided into *sectiones*, which are further divided. The first division of a *sectio* is usually Bucer's *expositio*, in which Bucer is concerned with the broad scope and argument of the section that he is interpreting.[20] After the *expositio*, Bucer adds a section called the *interpretatio*, where he proposes "to explain the actual sense of the individual sentences and words of Paul."[21] The purpose of the *interpretatio* consists of literary and linguistic notes on individual points that need clarification; it is here that he also presents various interpretations from the church fathers. Finally, there are the *observations*, where Bucer offers brief essays on key phrases or sentences with the intention of lifting Paul's precepts and teachings from their complicated contexts in order to present them as universal dogmas or theses. In these he seeks to be simple for the less learned.[22]

In addition to these categories and his theological prefaces,[23] he provides within the commentary various *quaestiones* and *conciliationes* (harmonizations) for passages that are more theologically knotty. In a *quaestio* Bucer usually begins by asking a theological question of particular relevance to the text at hand, which

17. See Lang, *Evangelienkommentar*, 371–372; Peter W. Stephens, *The Holy Spirit in the Theology of Martin Bucer* (Cambridge: Cambridge University Press, 1970), 162; and Edwin Tait, who comments that "the Romans commentary represents the pinnacle not only of Bucer's influence and diplomatic activity but arguably of his thought as well." Tait, "The Law and Its Works," 58.

18. His explanations of these categories are found in his dedicatory preface to Thomas Cranmer: *BRom* (1536), iv(v)–v(v). See Roussel, "Martin Bucer Lecteur," 1:16–17; and Parker, *Commentaries on Romans*, 37–40.

19. *BRom* (1536), iv(v); "Metaphrasim Apostoli, hoc est liberiorem, vel certis in locis, conversationem."

20. *BRom* (1536), iv(v); "In Expositione conatus sum perpetua enarratione indicare, quid Apostolus et qua occasione, quoque fini proponat, deinde quibus, quod proposuit, argumentis, qualiterque dispositis et enunciatis, comprobet."

21. *BRom* (1536), v(r); "Interpretationibus proposui germanum sensum explicare singularum sententiarum et verborum Pauli."

22. *BRom* (1536), v(r); "Observationibus sylvulam volui rudioribus proponere."

23. At the beginning of Bucer's commentary on the epistle to the Romans (intended to be the first commentary in the series of all of Paul's epistles), he has twelve prefaces, as follows: (1) on its merits; (2) on the order of the epistles and their dates; (3) on the order of the epistles as they are commonly divided according to their importance and argument; (4) the principle *quaestio* in this epistle, and the general head to which everything must be referred; (5) the argument of the epistle and the explication that the apostle works out in individual chapters; (6) what the church fathers thought on the *quaestio* of the epistle and its case; (7) the sum of the first reason by which he argues the principal *quaestio*; (8) in what signification Saint Paul uses the words "to be justified" and "justification"; (9) what Paul means by the words "faith" and "to believe"; (10) what Paul means by "Law" and "the works of the law"; 11) whether there is in philosophy something that accords with Paul's teaching; and (12) whether St. Paul keeps to the rules of rhetoric.

he then expounds, usually at great length with the help of the church fathers.[24] When Bucer offers a harmonization it is because he has come across a passage of scripture that seems to be in apparent contradiction with another scriptural passage;[25] at these points Bucer's biblicist impulse is revealed. Throughout the commentary he desires to show that what seems to be contradictory at first sight can be overcome if one seeks the illumination of the Spirit.[26]

Of particular interest to this study are four harmonizations in which Bucer illustrates how scripture passages that affirm works as a cause of salvation are compatible with salvation as *sola fide*.[27] In these harmonizations Bucer shows how passages that seem to proclaim differing views of grace, faith, and works are "beautifully harmonious!"[28] He believed that it was only when people interpreted these texts with a lust for victory (φιλονικεία) that they skewed their true meaning. Hence he stated: "I tell you, if we paid attention to these terms [i.e., in the contexts where the writers apply them], we would both see more clearly than in the light of midday how happily these texts agree, and we would employ them always to our certain edification, far from all disagreements and strife."[29]

24. *BRom* (1536), v(v).

25. *BRom* (1536), v(r)–v(v).

26. Bucer's desire to harmonize seemingly conflicting positions is summarized best by Ian Hazlett, who states, "This paradigm determines his thrust towards Christian consensus, harmony, and peace. It also conditions his biblical hermeneutics and understanding of the church fathers: apparent antinomies are resolved if, illuminated by the Spirit, one seeks the 'reality' of one truth underlying the scriptural and patristic diversities. Not seeing beyond dissonance fuels division, sectarianism, obduracy and lack of charity." Ian Hazlett, "Bucer," in *The Cambridge Companion to Reformation Theology*, ed. David Bagchi and David C. Steinmetz (Cambridge: Cambridge University Press, 2004), 106.

27. The first of these harmonizations to explicitly deal with justification is in regard to Rom. 2:5–10, *BRom* (1536), 115–121; (1562), 99–106. The second is in regard to Rom. 2:11–16, *BRom* (1536), 129–130; (1562), 118–119. The third and fourth are in regard to Rom. 4:1–8, *BRom* (1536), 217–219; (1562), 230–233. In addition, his prefaces on justification, faith, and the Law (*BRom* [1536], 11–28; [1562], 11–27) are important for understanding his position. These harmonizations are found in the appendix in English translations.

Bucer also includes a *peroratio*, where he sums up his position on justification by faith against the calumnies made by Jacopo Sadoleto (*BRom* [1536], 370–373; [1562], 424–429). However, since my discussion here is focused, as much as is possible, on describing Bucer's view of justification in regard to his response to the Pauline epistle, and because this book is focused on Bucer's interaction with Johannes Gropper, who was at Regensburg, rather than with Sadoleto, who was not, I have opted not to discuss this *peroratio* here. However, the summary of the doctrine Bucer provides there is in accord with what he has to say elsewhere. What is of chief concern to scholars in the *peroratio* is in regard to Bucer's statement that Sadoleto teaches the same doctrine as the evangelicals. The question then arises as to whether Sadoleto did or did not, and therefore whether Bucer understood him correctly. Bernard Roussel and Parker disagree over this point. Roussel affirms that Bucer did understand Sadoleto, whereas Parker states "that he had not read him very carefully or that he had little theological acumen or that he was sacrificing theological truth to eirenicism." I think that Bucer's agreement is limited to his desire to demonstrate to Sadoleto that evangelicals did not neglect works and thus insofar that works were part of justification, there was general harmony. See Bernard Roussel, "Martin Bucer et Jacques Sadolet: La Concorde possible (automne 1535)?" *Bulletin de la Société de l'Histoire du Protestantisme Français* 122 (1976): 507–524; and Parker, *Commentaries on Romans*, 166–180.

28. *BRom* (1536), 130; (1562), 119; "sic illa Scripturae loca, quae gratiam Dei, quae fidem, quae opera praedicant, evidentia sunt, et pulcherrime consonant."

29. *BRom* (1536), 130; (1562), 119; "haec inquam, si observaremus, et luce meridiana clarius videremus, quam suavissime ista loca conspirent, et cum certa ea semper aedificatione usurparemus, procul ab omnibus dissidiis et pugnis."

Unfortunately, his attempt to harmonize varying scripture passages that teach justification by faith and justification by works has led some, imprecisely, to interpret his doctrine of justification as a double justification theory.

Double Justification?

Bucer's teaching of justification has been generally characterized as the combination of faith and love of neighbor. However, to describe it as double justification is to understand it only in part.[30]

Strictly speaking, a doctrine of double justification is one that states that there are two formal causes in justification, that is, two types of righteousness, imputed and inherent. This was the doctrine presented at the Council of Trent by Girolamo Seripando.[31] In the eighteenth century some theologians used the label double justification to describe a two-stage event, as John Wesley seemed to do in commending the views of his self-appointed successor, John Fletcher. For Fletcher double justification meant that there was a primary justification at conversion that was by faith and a second justification that took place by works that would make one acceptable to God at the end.[32] These uses of the label double justification make its applicability to Bucer's view problematic. Nevertheless, the label's use as usually applied to John Calvin is similar to the way in which the label could be used to describe Bucer's doctrine. Scholars of Calvin have said that he teaches a double justification theory to accommodate the manner in which scripture speaks of God rewarding works as well as attempting his best to keep justification and sanctification together.[33] On this account the variety of meaning that the label double justification can take on makes it a problematic moniker for describing Bucer's doctrine of justification.

30. Marijn de Kroon has pointed out "that it is actually misleading to speak of a double justification in Bucer—a point which has led to misinterpretation." See de Kroon, "Problem of Tolerance," 162. Rather than saying it is a misinterpretation, it may be better to say that it is an incomplete understanding, one that benefits from further investigation. De Kroon is particularly wary of Karl Koch's statement that "good works are for Bucer a watered-down form of a second cause." Though this is partially true, it is imprecise in that Koch does not take into account the structure of thought that allowed him to explain the role of works in salvation as causes. Cf. Koch, *Studium Pietatis*, 46. In addition, difficulty arises when one tries to define the terms "double" and "justification," since the term "justification" alone is difficult to define. See Anthony N. S. Lane, *Justification by Faith in Catholic-Protestant Dialogue: An Evangelical Assessment* (London: T&T Clark, 2002), 129.

31. See McGrath, *Iustitia Dei*, 323–338; and P. Pas, "La doctrine de la double justice au Concile de Trente," *Ephemerides Theologicae Lovanienses* 30 (1954): 5–53.

32. See Henry D. Rack, *The Reasonable Enthusiast: John Wesley and the Rise of Methodism*, 3rd ed. (London: Epworth Press, 2002), 392, 459–460.

33. Calvin explicates this view in the additions he makes to book 3 of his *Institutes* in 1539 (see *Institutes*, III, xvii–xviii). See Cornelis P. Venema, *Accepted and Renewed in Christ: The "Twofold Grace of God" and the Interpretation of Calvin's Theology* (Göttingen: Vandenhoeck & Ruprecht, 2007), 163–170. See also Lane, *Justification by Faith in Catholic-Protestant Dialogue*, 33–38.

At the turn of the twentieth century, Reinhold Seeberg identified Bucer as a representative of a distinct school of thought in southern Germany, which he described as a *Vermittlungstheologie* between Zwinglian spiritualism and Lutheran soteriology.[34] As noted in the introduction, Bucer has been seen as a *Vermittlungstheologe*, which has consequences for the way in which his theology is approached. Writing at about the same time, Augustus Lang, in his examination of Bucer's *Gospels Commentary*, argued that the doctrines of predestination and *Allwirksamkeit* of God functioned as the foundations of Bucer's theology.[35] The term *Allwirksamkeit* is meant to describe the fact that God's action in salvation is supreme; the best English equivalent of the term would be "sovereign action." Hence, *Allwirksamkeit* as a foundational point in Bucer's theology designates a high sovereign view of God for salvation. Lang sees in Bucer's thought a great importance on the kingly office of Christ. Lang shows that for Bucer man is totally devoid of resources for salvation, and thus God must act. This all-powerful sovereign action for salvation is associated with the power of the Spirit in Bucer's theology.[36] Thus this spiritual emphasis leads Lang to describe Bucer's theology as both mystical and spiritual and at the same time devoid of humanist influence.[37] Lang argued that on account of Bucer's emphasis on the Spirit and the kingdom of Christ (both related to *Allwirksamkeit*), Bucer was focused on regeneration and love of neighbor rather than the forgiveness of sins.[38] However, Lang's rejection of any humanistic impulse in Bucer's thought did not allow him to completely grasp Bucer's doctrine of justification. Both these works, the former, which attributed Bucer's theology to a conciliatory character, and the latter, which reduced Bucer's thought to a few elements at the exclusion of others, characterized early twentieth-century views of Martin Bucer's theology as a whole.

In the mid-nineteenth century Matthias Schneckenburger noted that there were strands in Reformed theology in the seventeenth century that he described as doctrines of "double justification."[39] Referencing Schneckenburger, Otto Ritschl identified Bucer as the progenitor of this doctrine of double justification in Protestant theology.[40] He stated that Bucer's theology was a true

---

34. Seeberg, *Lehrbuch der Dogmengeschichte*, 2:256–257.

35. Lang, *Evangelienkommentar*, 104. Lang states: "Butzer religiöse Gedankengange lassen sich um zwei einfache Grundideen gruppieren. . . . Diese beiden Grundgedanken sind: 1. Die Überzeugung von der Allwirksamkeit Gottes; 2. Die Erwählungslehre."

36. See ibid., 121–126.

37. See ibid., 8, 137. Here Lang takes humanism as speculative Neoplatonism. Lang's appraisal of humanism and therefore its influence on Bucer's thought has been amended by Stupperich and others.

38. Ibid., 109–120. Lang did notice that there was a development toward a more forensic understanding in Bucer's later *Romans Commentary*; see 317–322.

39. Matthias Schneckenburger, *Vergleichende Darstellung des lutherischen und reformirten Lehrbegriffs*, vol. 1 (Stuttgart: Verlag der JBM, 1855), 40–41; see also vol. 2, 75–76.

40. Ritschl, *Dogmengeschichte*, 3:122–156, esp. 148

vermittlungstheologischen Gedankenverbindung that was a result of his attempt to harmonize the *iustum pronuntiare* of God and the *iustum efficere* of the Holy Spirit.[41] Agreeing with Lang, Ritschl saw Bucer's understanding of forgiveness of sins as weak.[42] In Ritschl's view this weakness resulted from an Erasmian influence that resulted in an overemphasis on ethics in Bucer's thought; Ritschl states that this ethical impulse "totally predominated his understanding from the outset and thus Bucer was only superficially in a position to do justice to the reformation doctrine of justification."[43] For Ritschl, Bucer's thought could be characterized as double justification because of "idiosyncratic distinctions," that is, he saw in Bucer's doctrine the view that "God's arrangement of salvation materializes in moderate levels, which separated an earlier phase from a later phase of justification."[44] Hence, Bucer misunderstood the Protestant doctrine primarily because he reduced salvation to an analytic judgment based on works.[45]

Ritschl's depiction of Bucer's doctrine as "double justification," however, is incomplete and therefore weak. Because he failed to grasp adequately the manner in which Bucer's theology arranged different doctrines in relation to each other intellectually, he described Bucer's view as a chronological two-stage event. In contrast, Bucer's view of faith and works is more organically connected than Ritschl's analysis of his doctrine as double justification allows. Unfortunately, this misleading label has infected the manner in which Bucer's doctrine has been seen ever since.[46]

41. Ibid., 143.
42. Ibid., 150–151.
43. Ibid., 148.
44. Ibid., 144.
45. Ibid., 3:150.
46. Robert Stupperich confirmed Ritschl's "double justification" view by demonstrating its form in Erasmus, which had a powerful influence on Bucer's thought. Stupperich showed how Erasmus's doctrine of justification was seen as a process of mortification and vivification from which the believer became a new creation. In addition, Stupperich saw a forensic as well as imparted view of justification in humanist thought that was inherited through Thomas Aquinas's understanding of *iustificatio dupliciter dicitur*. See *ST* 1a 2ae q.100 a.12. The emphasis on new creation in addition to a forensic view of justification led to a double justification view that was ultimately focused on moral renewal (Stupperich, *Der Humanismus*, 8–10, esp. 10n4). Stupperich saw this as true not only for Bucer but for an Erasmian school that includes Julius Pflug, Johann Haner, Georg Witzel, and Johannes Gropper. Thus he states: "Da alle Erasmus–Schüler ohne Ausnahme nur zu nahe, daß sie dazu von Erasmus selbst bestimmt sind" (*Der Humanismus*, 10n4). It was along these lines, according to Stupperich, that Bucer developed his doctrine of justification (with its focus on moral regeneration) coupled with his practice of compromising (*Kompromißverfahren*) (*Der Humanismus*, 22–26).

Hans Emil Weber characterized Bucer's theology as *christozentriche ethische Geistesmystik*, which was a way of saying that Bucer emphasized the role of the Spirit in effecting ethical renewal. With this characterization, Weber gave a nuanced view of Bucer's doctrine of justification. He emphasized Bucer's view of progress in works as tied to faith, which was the gift of the Spirit (*Reformation, Orthodoxie*, 1:206–207). This mystical system, Weber believed, allowed Bucer's dual understanding of *iustificare*, containing both the sense of imputation and impartation, to hold true to the Protestant doctrine of *sola fide* (*Reformation, Orthodoxie*, 1:210). However, Weber noted the danger of pietism and perfectionism that resulted from Bucer's attempt to hold together an objective and subjective appropriation of justification (*Reformation, Orthodoxie*, 1:214–215). Weber tries to show the organic nature of

A more recent example of this imprecision can be seen when Alister McGrath states: "Bucer develops a doctrine of double justification: after a 'primary justification,' in which man's sins are forgiven and righteousness imputed to him, there follows a 'secondary justification,' in which man is made righteous."[47] Though he rightly qualifies this statement by saying that it is not a double justification theory *stricto sensu*,[48] he nevertheless describes Bucer's view as tending "to make justification dependent upon the believer's regeneration through the renewing work of the Holy Spirit."[49] If exaggerated, this view leads to a moralistic understanding of justification wherein works, seen as a necessary element in salvation, are separated from faith as well as from the prime cause of God's benevolence, which is adamantly not Bucer's view.

Double justification as a tag is problematic not because it fails to describe Bucer's teaching (it does in part as it does for Calvin) but because it is imprecise. It does not fully or clearly take into account Bucer's thought structure. On the other hand, double justification does at least attempt to describe the relationship between practice and theology, which was of prime importance to Bucer.[50]

Likewise, it is important to note that the tag in modern Catholic theology has sometimes implied two separate justifications, that is, two formal causes, which the Council of Trent perceived and rejected in the teaching of Cardinal Girolamo Seripando.[51] In this regard Bucer consistently holds to one formal cause, which is the goodwill of God. This, however, does not prohibit him from talking about our cooperation in works as a secondary cause that also stems

---

Bucer's thought and succeeds in part, yet he would have been aided by a more thorough examination of Bucer's understanding of intellectual faith and of works as secondary causes, as I will show.

Karl Koch, who focused on the humanist ethical impulse in Bucer's thought, saw Bucer's theology as opposed to Luther's because he believed that for Bucer praxis preceded doctrine. He stated: "The substance of Christian existence, determined by the command of love in combination with the law, shifts from *fides Christi* to *fides viva, syncera, officiosa, vivifica, 'quae per dilectionem operatur,'* thus from the action of God to man who is freed to love, that is, to men's deeds" (*Studium Pietatis,* 77). Koch sees Bucer's view of faith as a "power for moral acttion, which is detached from Christ" (13). Likewise, following Stupperich, he asserts that Bucer teaches double justification, which is more concerned with morality, thoroughly making him a disciple of Erasmus (13). This stems from an exaggeration that in Bucer's thought the gospel is ultimately subordinate to the law, which it is not (67). As I will show for Bucer, both law and gospel can kill without faith, but with true evangelical faith both can reveal the grace and benevolence of God, which for Bucer is demonstrated in the gospel of forgiveness. Overall, it seems that Koch's strong Lutheran sympathies at times seem to inhibit him from presenting a balanced examination of Bucer's thought.

47. McGrath, *Iustitia Dei,* 252. See also Alister E. McGrath, "Humanist Elements in the Early Reformed Doctrine of Justification," *Archiv für Reformationsgeschichte* 73 (1982): 10–14.

48. McGrath, *Iustitia Dei,* 252. It is this "not *stricto sensu*" that I am hoping to clarify by looking at the structure of his thought.

49. Ibid., 255–256.

50. The tag of "double justification" is not wholly without warrant, but it is imprecise. Cf. *BRom* (1536) 116, 218; (1562), 100, 232.

51. See Pas, "La doctrine de la double justice au Concile de Trente," 5–53; and James McCue, "Double Justification at Trent," in *Piety, Politics, and Ethics: Reformation Studies in Honor of George Wolfgang Forell,* ed. Carter Lindberg (Kirksville, MO: Sixteenth Century Journal Publishers, 1984), 39–56.

from God's goodwill.[52] Thus, only to the extent that Bucer's structure of thought allowed some combination of faith and love of neighbor into his understanding of justification can it be described—and then with considerable qualification—as double justification.

What I propose here is to demonstrate how a careful understanding of Bucer's structure of thought helps clarify what has been too easily character- ized as "double justification." In the process, my account can contribute a more precise and balanced understanding of Bucer's doctrine.[53]

Iustitia and Iustificatio

Before considering Bucer's structure of thought, it is worth considering how Bucer understands the concepts of iustitia Dei and iustificatio.[54] Iustitia is both the justice by which God reveals himself to believers and also the justice with which he adorns them.[55] In the first place, iustitia is an attribute of God under- stood as the highest virtue and goodness (summa virtus, summa bonitas).[56] One comes to know that God's righteousness is constituent of his nature because this goodness is manifested in his actions toward humanity; hence the iustitia Dei is revealed to humanity in God's loving actions toward believers:[57]

---

52. *BRom* (1536), 129–130; (1562), 119.

53. The first and only treatise dedicated solely to Bucer's theology of justification is Horst-Martin Barnikol's Ph.D. dissertation from Göttingen, "Bucers Lehre." Barnikol contends against Koch and others that Bucer's theology is the basis for his ethical impulse and that his doctrinal system has its own inner coherence. Neverthe- less, Barnikol tends to keep the framework of two separate justifications when explicating Bucer's teaching, which I believe is rightly averted by noting the importance of the Socratic dictum in Bucer's thought. Hence, still operating under the double justification theme, Barnikol holds that there are two distinct justifications that work independently of one another, the first of forgiveness and the second of works (101). This is incorrect; they do not function independently but are organically related, as I will demonstrate here. Thus, here a contribution to un- derstanding Bucerian thought is made that can help one further understand the manner in which he held faith and works together as an organic unity. Prior to Barnikol's work, Leopold Temmel's also viewed faith and works as separated in Bucer's thought. See Temmel, "Glaube und Gewissheit in der Theologie Martin Bucers, vorneh- mlich nach seinem Römerbriefkommentar" (Ph.D. diss., Erlangung, 1950), 165–167.

54. On Bucer's use of iustitia and iustificari, see Roussel, "Martin Bucer lecteur," 1:189–198; and Barnikol, "Bucers Lehre," 87–90. In the Romans Commentary, Bucer deals with the concept of the iustitia Dei primarily in the interpretatio of Rom. 1:17, BRom (1536), 79–81; (1562), 50–53. On iustificari and iustificatio, see his preface specifically designed for defining these terms; BRom (1536), 11–14; (1562), 11–14; CP 160–167.

55. BRom (1536), 79, 80; (1562), 50, 51; "qua ipse se nobis . . . exhibet," and "qua Deus nos exornat."

56. BRom (1536), 79; (1562), 50; "צדק id est iustitia nomine, Scriptura summam virtutem et bonitatem intelligit, numeraturque fere cum ישועה ope, vel salute, ut intelligas in eo esse dei iustitiam, summam virtutem, summam bonitatem, cum fert opem suis, et servat eos." This understanding of iustitia as the highest virtue comes from Aristotle (Nic. Ethics 5.i.). See Roussel, "Martin Bucer lecteur," 1:190.

57. See BRom (1536), 180; (1562), 186; "Philippus Melanchthon iustitiam Dei hic (sc. Rom. 3:21) pro accep- tatione accipit, qua nos Deus acceptat: id vero cum eo convenit, quod nos per eam intelligimus incomparabilem illam Dei bonitatem in Christo exhibitam, qua et peccata condonat, et iustitiam imputat, et vitam aeternam

Moreover when we look more closely at these [previously mentioned texts] and those remaining, in which the righteousness of God is proclaimed, we generally see the righteousness of God applied to that by which he himself is just—that is, good, and worthy in himself. In other words, he presents himself as a benefactor, and especially in the fact that he bestows the Spirit, who sets us aflame with a zeal for righteousness.[58]

God's *iustitia* is discovered through the revelation of himself to humanity as both the just God and the God who justifies.[59]

The revelation of God's *iustitia* occurs through the bestowal of the Spirit that simultaneously causes a zeal for *iustitia*, also described as a gift of *iustitia*. For Bucer believers change; they become children of God.[60] He states that "by the righteousness of God, I shall gladly understand it as that which God gives to those who believe in him. For since this principal work and gift is the righteousness of God by which he represents himself as just and good, it immediately raises the mind to this."[61] God represents himself as "just and good" in the life and work of Christ, and it is this *iustitia Christi* that a believer's mind is raised to.[62] The *iustitia Dei*, that is, *iustitia Christi*, is revealed to the believer's mind in faith; the believer then by the power of the Spirit contemplates *iustitia* and out of necessity is made zealous for it:

---

largitur, eamque hic adspirando mentem novam, ac pietatis studium, auspicatur." This is repeated from his preface on justification, where he states similarly that "our justification is our free acceptance [*acceptationem*] before God, whereby he pardons our sins, imputes righteousness to us, and bestows on us eternal life; this life is begun here and now and daily increased in us by the Spirit, who is the implanter and cultivator of righteousness and good works." *BRom* (1536), 14; (1562), 14; *CP* 167. Cf. Melanchthon in *CR* 15, 586.

58. *BRom* (1536), 79; (1562), 50: "Porro cum haec, quae modo adduximus, ac reliqua, in quibus iustitia dei praedicatur, propius intuemur, eam videmus iustitiam dei fere dici, qua ipse se nobis iustum, id est, bonum, et se digne, hoc est, benefacientem exhibet, potissimum quidem in eo, quod largitur spiritum, qui nos iustitiae studio incendit."

59. *BRom* (1536), 80; (1562), 51; "Hanc enim omnino dei iustitam hic Apostolus praedicat, qua deus, et iustus, et iustificans agnoscitur."

60. *BRom* (1536), 79; (1562), 50; "Iustitiam vero dei videtur more scripturae, intelligere divinam, et praepollentem eiusmodi iustitiam, ut appareat eam non nisi dei opus et donum esse. Sic filii dei, viri dei, populus dei, civitas dei, arbores dei, montes dei, et caetera huius generis dicuntur." Here Bucer follows the traditional Augustinian understanding, which states that the righteousness of God is that righteousness by which he makes others righteous. See *De Spiritu et Littera*, XI, 18; *PL* 44, 211.

61. *BRom* (1536), 80; (1562) 51; "per iustitiam dei, libenter etiam eam intellexero, quam deus donat in se credentibus. Nam cum haec praecipuum opus ac donum iustitia dei sit qua se iustum bonumque nobis exhibet, illa, in hanc mentem statim subducit."

62. See *BRom* (1536), 12; (1562), 12; *CP* 162, where Bucer comments on this revelation of *iustitia* in regard to Rom. 3:25. There he states that "Christ came to introduce to the world an ἔνδειχιν, that is, a demonstration of divine *iustitia* unmistakable to all." This demontration of *iustitia* in Christ is then immediately correlated to the work of the Spirit who sets believers "aflame with a zeal for righteousness" and "conforms believers to the image of Christ."

Because by faith we embrace this righteousness and benevolence of
God, it shines in us, and thus he imparts himself, so that also we,
too, are driven by some zeal for righteousness. Therefore this
righteousness of God, by which some sort of righteousness also
comes into being in us, is connected with the other, and by that
means under the name, the righteousness of God, they were
proclaimed by the prophets so that both ought to be understood at
the same time.[63]

The *iustitia Dei*, revealed in the mind through faith, causes a correlative *iustitia*
for believers. The righteousness, in which God himself is righteous and shows
himself as righteous, is at the same time the origin of man's own righteousness. Yet humanity's righteousness is derivative and insufficient in itself to
merit salvation.[64]

Hence Bucer's understanding of *iustitia* includes both the aspect of an
attribute of God and at the same time a derivative *iustitia* that is accomplished
in believers: "From all these texts it is evident that God manifests his righteousness in this for the elect, while he also makes them participators of righteousness: and thus his righteousness is rightly called not only that by which he
presents himself just, but also that which he gives to us."[65]

The Spirit, in manifesting God's own *iustitia* to us by faith, compels us to
pursue *iustitia*. Hence the revelation of *iustitia* in the mind of the elect leads to
a life that strives in works pursuant to the *iustitia Dei*. As I will demonstrate, the
Socratic maxim that "to know the good is to do the good"[66] (and therefore to
know true righteousness is to pursue true righteousness) is an underlying paradigm in Bucer's thought.

The Spirit bestowed to believers is understood as the implanter and educator of true *iustitia*.[67] He makes believers zealous for *iustitia* by revealing to them
that they are imputed as just on account that their sins are forgiven, that is, the

---

63. *BRom* (1536), 80; (1562), 51; "Hinc etiam, quod fide illam dei iustitiam et bonitatem amplectimur,
irradiat ea in nos, seque impertit ita nobis, ut nos quoque aliquo iustitiae studio impellamur. Sic ergo illa dei
iustitia, qua se nobis quoque aliquid iustitiae ingeneretur, connexae ita inter se sunt, et eo pacto a prophetis, sub
hoc nomine, Iustitia dei, praedicantur, ut utramque simul intelligere oporteat."

64. *BRom* (1536), 13; (1562), 13; *CP* 164; "It goes without saying that however great a degree of righteousness the
Spirit of Christ might effect in us when we believe, it will none the less never be sufficient to merit our being regarded
as righteous in God's sight, for we remain unprofitable servants even when we have fulfilled all his bidding."

65. *BRom* (1536), 80; (1562), 51; "Ex his omnibus locis istud liquet, deum suam iustitiam in eo electis
exhibere dum et ipsos iustitiae participes facit: ac ita recte eius iustitiam dici, non solum, qua ipse se iustum
praestat, sed etiam quam donat nobis."

66. For this maxim, see Plato, *Protagoras*, 352b. Aristotle agrees with this position in the *Nic. Ethics* 7.iii.
That this is the case for Bucer will be shown throughout.

67. *BRom* (1536), 14; (1562), 14; "quam Spiritu, iustitiae et bonorum operum plantatore et educatore." See
also *BRom* (1536), 49; (1562), 10.

non-imputation of sins, and on account that they are children of God.[68] "For if sin is not imputed to someone, he is happy (*felix*), he is certainly justified, that is, he is numbered by God among those whom God wishes well and whom he has decided to make happy (*felices*)."[69] The Augustinian view of non-imputation of sins is the primary notion that Bucer understands when speaking of imputation.[70] Though elusive, Bucer does hint at a positive imputation of Christ's righteousness similar to the use of Melanchthon and Luther, as I will show.

> Therefore, when Paul asserts that we are justified by faith, the faith whereby we assuredly believe that Christ is our Saviour and our sole peacemaker with the Father, he means that by this faith we are first of all delivered from all doubt that God, on account of the death of Christ undergone on our behalf, forgives us all our sins, absolves us from all guilt, and passes judgment in our favour against Satan and all the ill we may have deserved. Furthermore, God breathes the power of his Spirit into those acquitted and declared righteous before him, to make immediate assault upon their corrupt ambitions and to urge on their suppression and extinction, and on the other hand, to fashion upright attitudes to every aspect of life, to arouse and foster holy desires, conforming us speedily to the likeness of Christ.[71]

This passage is illustrative of the manner in which Bucer defines *iustificatio* as both declarative and effective.[72] The forgiveness of sins is God's undeserved benevolent action toward believers, and once this action is grasped in the mind, by the power of the Spirit, believers become *felices* and are zealous toward *iustitia*.

In this manner *iustificatio* and *iustificari* are defined as incorporating both declarative and effective aspects. Bucer begins his preface on *iustificatio* by showing how the true meaning of *iustificari* ought to be understood within

---

68. Robert Gundry believes that the non-imputation of sins is the only manner in which Paul speaks of a declarative aspect of justification. Robert H. Gundry, "The Nonimputation of Christ's Righteousness," in *Justification: What's at Stake in the Current Debates*, ed. Mark Husbands and Daniel J. Treier (Downers Grove, IL: InterVarsity Press, 2004), 17–45. See Barnikol, "Bucers Lehre," 91–93.

69. *BRom* (1536), 213; (1562), 225; "Nam si cui non imputatur peccatum, felix est, is utique iustificatus, hoc est, a Deo inter eos quibus bene vult, quosque felices reddere decrevit, numeratus est."

70. See *WA* 40/1, 229, ll. 6–30. In Bucer's *Romans Commentary*, the language of imputation is predominantly found in his preface on justification (*BRom* [1536], 14; [1562], 14); in relation to Rom. 3:21 where he takes the *iustitia dei* as *acceptatio* (*BRom* [1536], 180; [1562], 186); and in relation to Rom. 4:5, where the text explicitly demands that he deal with it (*BRom* [1536], 219; [1562], 233).

71. *BRom* (1536), 12; (1562), 12; *CP* 162.

72. Bucer also at times uses the terms *mortificatio* and *vivificatio* to express both of these aspects. The first relates to the forgiveness of sins and the latter to the gift of the Spirit, which propels believers toward a life of righteousness. See *BRom* (1536), 283–285; (1562), 316–318.

Paul's Hebraic background and therefore ought to be understood by the word הִצְדִּיק (hisdîq). Thus, iustificari is: "To have judgment in one's favor, to be declared to be in the right."[73] To justify is to judge positively, and to condemn is to judge negatively. Justification is a positive judgment. He states: "Now Saint Paul, in inquiring into the means of our justification, takes this word in its primary connotation as above, so that it has the same force as God's acquitting us and deciding our case in our favour when our own thoughts and Satan accuse us."[74] For Bucer justification is primarily understood as this acquittal, that is, the forgiveness of sins.

Justification, however, can also for Bucer be described as the believer being pronounced just, a positive imputation of righteousness.[75] This pronouncement is made on account of merits of Christ;[76] at one point he states that "God saves us by his mercy alone and by the contemplation of the merit of Christ, which, when we believe in Christ, is given to us and becomes ours."[77] Likewise, in the preface on justification and similarly repeated in reference to Romans 3:21, Bucer talks about the believer as accepted as righteous; acknowledging Melanchthon, he states that "our justification is our free acceptance [acceptationem] before God, whereby he pardons our sins, imputes righteousness to us, and bestows on us eternal life; this life is begun here and now and daily increased in us by the Spirit, who is the implanter and cultivator of righteousness and good works."[78] It is in this rather undeveloped sense that Bucer holds to a positive imputation of

73. BRom (1536), 11; (1562), 11; CP 160.

74. BRom (1536), 11; (1562), 11; CP 160–161. Melanchthon defines the verb similarly in his Romans Commentary (1532). See MW 5:39–40. Partial English translation of the 1540 edition in Phillip Melanchthon, Commentary on Romans (1540 ed), trans. Fred Kramer (St. Louis, MO: Concordia, 1992), 25; "According to Hebrew usage of the term, to justify is to pronounce or to consider as just. . . . And the word iustitia does not signify the righteousness of the Law, or universal obedience, or our qualities, when it is said, 'By faith there is given us iustitia.' It signifies the imputation of iustitia, or acceptance. And iustus is in this way understood relationally as acceptance to eternal life. But one must know that in the forgiveness of sins there is given at the same time the Holy Spirit, as I have said above, when we raise ourselves up by faith. . . . Thus the gift of the Holy Spirit is connected with justification, which begins not only one virtue,—faith—but also others: fear and love of God, love of the truth, chastity, patience, justice toward the neighbor, as I shall say later about works. But these virtues do not merit forgiveness of sins, nor are they righteousness on account of which a person is accepted though still afflicted with much infirmity."

75. BRom (1536), 10, 12; (1562), 10, 12; "fidem solam illud esse, quo non solum Deus, sed et homines nos iustos pronuncient"; "nos absolvat, iustosque pronunciet, id est, iustificet."

76. BRom (1536), 12; (1562), 12; CP 162. See also BRom (1536), 263; (1562), 289.

77. See BRom (1536), 129; (1562), 118–119; "deum nos servare ex sola sua clementia, et contemplatione meriti Christi, quod cum Christo credimus, nobis donatur, nostrumque fit."

78. BRom (1536), 14; (1562), 14; CP 167. Cf. Melanchthon in CR 15, 586. See also BRom (1536), 180; (1562), 185–186; "iustitia et summa illa bonitas Dei: qua electos non solum peccati apud se absolvit, et pro iustis acceptat; verum etiam verae iustitiae communione exornat. . . . Philippus Melanchthon iustitiam Dei hic (sc. Rom. 3:21) pro acceptatione accipit, qua nos Deus acceptat: id vero cum eo convenit, quod nos per eam intelligimus incomparabilem illam Dei bonitatem in Christo exhibitam, qua et peccata condonat, et iustitiam imputat, et vitam aeternam largitur, eamque hic adspirando mentem novam, ac pietatis studium, auspicatur."

righteousness; however, though this concept is left undeveloped, the language, especially of the giving of Christ's merit to the believer, is compatible with the language of the imputation of the alien righteousness of Christ, which he develops in the 1540s.[79] That being said, the concept of imputation of righteousness is primarily seen as the non-imputation of sins and adoption as children. The declarative aspect of the doctrine of justification for Bucer is understood this way: "God is gracious toward us, forgives the sins which never fail to oppress us, and counts us among his own people."[80]

Bucer often employs *numerari* to designate that justification is to be numbered among God's own;[81] and as God's own, justification is also the revelation of the inheritance of eternal life. Thus it is common for him to describe justification as the forgiveness of sins and the gift of eternal life.[82]

Iustificatio, however, does not only denote this forensic aspect of pronouncing one forgiven and numbering them as heirs of eternal life. For Bucer the verb *iustificari*, following Augustine, also has an effective sense:

> Consequently, since Paul is accustomed to speaking in this way, denoting by the word "justification" first of course the remission of sins, yet at the same time always indicating in addition that imparting of righteousness which God proceeds to work in us by the Spirit, the same Spirit by whom he grants us assurance of the pardon of our sins and of his goodwill towards us, and whom he has established as the seal [σφραγις (sphragis)] of that pardon—because, I say, Paul customarily speaks in these terms, the majority of the holy fathers, bearing in mind no doubt the more visible aspect of justification, have taken δικαιουσθαι [dikaiousthai] to be justified, in the sense of "to be made righteous." So Augustine[83]: "What does 'to be justified' mean but 'to be made righteous?'"[84]

79. A clearer understanding of an imputation of the *iustitia Christi* develops in his *De Vera Reconciliatione*, 122(r); "Hic Paulum per ablutionem, sanctificationem, et iustificationem, non solum remissionem prioris contaminationis, impuritatis et iniustitiae: et imputationem mundiciei, sanctitatis et iustitiae Christi." On the same page he states: "in scribendo et utendo hoc verbo [i.e. *iustificari*], id semper spectarunt, quod iustificatio, quae remissio est peccatorum per Christum, et iustitiae Christi imputatio, nemini sine spiritu, innovatore totius hominis, et iustitiae in homine effectore contingit." I am grateful to David Fink, who pointed this out to me.

80. *BRom* (1536), 11; (1562), 11; *CP* 162; "God is gracious toward us, forgives the sins which never fail to oppress us, and counts us among his own people."

81. *BRom* (1536), 215; (1562), 228; "nos inter suos numerat, et pro iustis habet." See Barnikol, "Bucers Lehre," 93–95.

82. *BRom* (1536), 18; (1562), 18; *CP* 183.

83. Augustine, *De Spiritu et Littera*, XXVI, 45; *PL* 44, 228.

84. *BRom* (1536), 12; (1562), 12; *CP* 163.

To be justified is both to *censeri* and to *reddi iustos*.[85] The effective aspect of our justification is on account of the gift of the Holy Spirit, which empowers the mind to be able to comprehend the *iustitia* revealed in Christ. The Spirit sets believers "aflame with zeal for righteousness" and "conforms believers to the image of Christ."[86]

Justification includes these aspects: the non-imputation of sins, the numbering of the elect as heirs of eternal life, and the gift of the Spirit that effects the *communicatio iustitiae*.[87] From this perspective justification maintains an effective character that renders invalid the old believers' accusation that the formula *sola fide* diminishes works; "by faith true righteousness is effected in us, and this is brought about entirely by faith."[88] This "faith makes us righteous, that is, endowed with every kind of virtue and rich in good works."[89]

Having introduced Bucer's *Romans Commentary* and addressed the misunderstandings of double justification and Bucer's understanding of *iustitia* and *iustificatio*, I will now explain in greater detail the philosophical element underlying the structures of Bucer's thought, which helps illuminate this dual aspect of righteousness.

Bucer's Structure of Thought

As a youth, at the local Latin school, Martin developed a passion for knowledge and learning that subsequently compelled his grandfather, Claus Butzer Sr., to continue his education by intrusting his bibliophile grandson to the reforming Dominicans of Sélestat in 1507. At fifteen years of age Martin received his tonsure and started a three-year course reading Aristotle in the *studium logicale*; these studies developed a philosophical impulse in him that would never leave.[90]

Arguably one of Bucer's greatest contributions to Strasbourg was the founding of the Gymnasium Academicum in 1538. Because the instruction of theology for Bucer was seen as pursuing the knowledge necessary to live a godly life, recourse to the moral philosophers was beneficial to that end; therefore, Bucer ensured that the trivium would be administered with healthy doses

---

85. *BRom* (1536), 5; (1562), 5; "iustificentur, id est, censeantur, reddanturque iustus."
86. See *BRom* (1536), 12; (1562), 12; *CP* 162.
87. See *BRom* (1536), 12; (1562), 12; *CP* 163.
88. *BRom* (1536), 13; (1562), 13; *CP* 166.
89. *BRom* (1536), 13; (1562), 13; *CP* 166.
90. On how Bucer's years as a Dominican affected his career, see Greschat, "Martin Bucer als Dominikanermönch," 30–53.

of Aristotle and Cicero.[91] Bucer believed that "true theology is not theoretical or speculative, but active and practical. The end of it is living, that is, to live a God-like life."[92] For Bucer theology was a transformative enterprise that shaped one's morality.[93] This is especially revealed within his *Romans Commentary*, which he hoped would instruct pastors and teachers on how to cultivate a more Christian society.

Bucer's philosophical investments are highlighted in his preface on philosophy, which was published separately as an offprint in 1536 as *How Sacred Philosophy Has Generally Been Explained* (*Quam universe S. Philosophiae explicata*).[94] In this preface and pamphlet Bucer shows how moral philosophy is closely related to Christian philosophy:

> Now since theology, being the doctrine handed down to us by Holy
> Scripture, is the supreme wisdom by which alone the life of man is
> rightly instituted, one must especially look for the harmony of
> philosophy with theology in the aspect in which it shapes morality.
> For holy doctrine too is properly concerned with morality, that is, the
> art of right and orderly living, and like this portion of philosophy it
> most beautifully and effectively makes use of other arts. And indeed
> since it leads all men to the point where they may benefit whom they
> can according to their ability, it will certainly impel them to pursue as
> well the skills from which the true and thrifty use of things is learned,
> whether they deal with heavenly things or earthly things, and inform
> and instruct the mind or tongue or even the character and all the
> more successfully, the more intimately they involve the Holy Spirit,
> the author of the accomplishments of all those good people who have
> sincerely devoted themselves to the divine teaching.[95]

---

91. Herman J. Selderhuis, "*Vera Theologia Scienta Est*: Bucer and the Training of Ministers," *Reformation and Renaissance Review* 3, no. 1 (2001): 125–139. Cf. *BGospels* (1536), 549; "Vera Theologia scientia est, pie et beate vivendi."

92. *BOL* 2, 433; "Vera theologia non theoretica vel speculativa, sed activa et practica est. Finis siquidem eius agere est, hoc est vitam vivere deiformem." Martin Bucer in his *John Commentary*.

93. *BRom* (1536), 29; (1562), 28; "Nam et sacra doctrina proprie moralis est." This ought not to come as a surprise, since the distinction between theology and ethics stems from the Enlightenment. Cf. Stanley Hauerwas and Samuel Wells, "Why Christian Ethics Was Invented," in *The Blackwell Companion to Christian Ethics*, ed. Stanley Hauerwas and Samuel Wells (Oxford: Blackwell, 2004), 28–38.

94. Martin Bucer, *Quam universe S. Philosophiae explicata* (Strasbourg, 1536). See *BOL* 5, 22n13.

95. *BRom* (1536), 29; (1562), 28; "Iam cum Theologia, nempe doctrina sacris nobis literis tradita, suprema sapientia sit, qua sola vita hominis recte instituitur, concordia Philosophiae cum hac, in ea parte, qua mores format potissimum quaerenda est. Nam et sacra doctrina proprie moralis est, ars nimirum recte et ordine vivendi, utque haec Philosophiae portio usum aliarum artium pulcherrime et efficacissime instituit. Etenim cum huc omnes ducat ut quibus possunt pro viribus prosint, utique ad consectandas quoque artes, ex quibus verus et frugi rerum usus discitur, impellet, sive illae res coelestes, sive terrenas tractent, mentem vel linguam, aut etiam mores informent ac instruant, hocque felicius, quo magis familiarem habent spiritum sanctum, omnium bonorum artium autorem, quicunque divinae se institutioni ex animo tradiderunt."

This theological appropriation of philosophy stands in line with Bucer's background in the Dominican order, whose motto is *Veritas*. Truth is one, and for him, as for Thomas and the theologians associated with the *via antiqua*, there is a first truth, whose discovery is of utter importance for salvation.[96] The search for this truth was intellectual, and understanding it requires coming to terms with Bucer's epistemology and anthropology.

Bucer's Epistemology

Bucer, following Aristotle, believes that knowledge comes from the senses.[97] In the *conciliatio* in regard to Romans 5:3–5 (where he is attempting to understand why the saints are sometimes said to complain about their afflictions and at other times glory in them), Bucer distinguishes between knowledge of the senses and knowledge of reason, the former always preceding the latter.[98] The senses supply "images [*phantasma*] for which the intellectual forms of things are derived,"[99] and the mind makes rational judgments based on the images that reason has gained through the senses.

To further understand the role of the senses in knowledge, it is beneficial to turn to Bucer's discussion on the knowledge of God. In his *expositio* on Romans 1:18–23,[100] Bucer introduces the difference between notions (*notio*) of God and knowledge (*cognitio*) of God, borrowing the distinction from Cicero's *De natura deorum*.[101] The primary purpose of introducing this distinction is to affirm Paul's claim that the gentiles are without excuse for rejecting God, since every human being is given the *notio Dei*.

The *notio Dei* is the notion that God "has power over all things and is the highest good."[102] This notion is given at birth in all people and is a capacity to derive from the created order things about God. Bucer believes that what can be known from birth are the *invisibilia Dei*, which are in a general sense God's power and divinity, and therefore all are without excuse.[103] He calls them invisible because the senses cannot comprehend these things about God on their own; they need this help; they need this gift.

---

96. *BRom* (1536), 28; (1562), 27–28.

97. *BRom* (1536), 240; (1562), 261; "Hominis cognitio a sensibus venit."

98. *BRom* (1536), 241; (1562), 261.

99. *BRom* (1536), 241; (1562), 261; "phantasmata, e quibus formae rerum intellectuales eximuntur."

100. T. H. L. Parker offers a summary of this passage in his *Commentaries on Romans*, 107–111.

101. See Cicero, *De natura deorum*, bk. II.

102. *BRom* (1536), 84; (1562), 57; "Sic certe haec notio Dei, eum in omnia habere potestatem et esse summum bonum."

103. *BRom* (1536), 84; (1562), 57.

This *notio Dei* is established in the order of the world, that is, by means of the *machina mundi*.[104] Bucer distinguishes four separate inborn notions, repeating Cicero's four notions with a biblical twist: (1) foreknowledge of the future, (2) the awareness of temporal benefits, (3) the awe produced in the presence of nature, and (4) the perception of some astronomical order.[105] These four notions are in every human being from birth. However, instead of choosing to love and serve the God to whom these notions point, all choose to love themselves.

In his *conciliatio* on the same passage titled "Harmonization of places in scripture which partly bestow, partly deny knowledge of God to the ungodly," Bucer clarifies this double way of knowing God (*notio* and *cognitio*):

> Therefore there is bound to be a double way to know God, one in a general sense, which one is wont to call it natural because God makes it shine on all mortals who are intact with the faculties of the body and mind. Indeed this is such that it deprives us of any excuse and convinces us of our own wickedness: But it does not have the power to produce true zeal and worship of God.

> But the other knowledge is to such a degree full and solid so that from itself it immediately produces love, and worthy reverence for God. For this reason it is also called eternal life. This is what the Lord promised to his elect through Christ, and makes proper to the partakers of the new covenant: All will know me from the least to the greatest, so that a brother will have no reason to teach his brother [Jeremiah 31:34]. Christ willed to pour this knowledge upon the world just as when the waters of the sea flooded the earth and covered the whole of it. This knowledge of God goes beyond the former natural knowledge to such a degree that those who have been given it are called born again, new creatures, sons of God.[106]

---

104. *BRom* (1536), 85; (1562), 58.

105. *BRom* (1536), 85; (1562), 58. See Cicero, *De natura deorum*, II:13–15.

106. *BRom* (1536), 86; (1562), 60; "Evincitur igitur, duplicem esse notitiam Dei, alteram generalem, quam quia omnibus mortalibus, qui sunt corporis et animi viribus integri, deus irradiat, naturalis dici solet. Haec tanta quidem est, ut omnem nobis excusationem adimat, et nos apud nos ipsos impietatis convincat: at eo usque non valet, ut verum dei studium cultumque parerent. Altera vero plena est adeo, et solida, ut ilico exse gignat amorem, dignamque reverentiam Dei, unde et vita aeterna dicitur. Haec est quam dominus promittit electis suis per Christum, novique foederis particibus propriam facit: Cognoscent me omnes a minimo usque ad maximum, ut non sit causa cur frater fratrem suum doceat. Hanc Christo revelato in orbem inundare voluit ita, ut cum aquae maris effluunt in terram, totamque obtegunt. Ista dei notitia, priorem illam naturalem, tanto excedit interstitio, ut hac donati, dicantur regeniti, nova creatura, filii Dei."

The *cognitio Dei* differs from the *notio Dei* in producing a firmer knowledge of God. To receive this knowledge requires a special inbreathing of the Spirit.

For Bucer "our mind is a particle of the divine breath, ἐντελέχεια,[107] a certain perennial *actus*, dependent on God as the day on the sun, the river on its spring."[108] The knowledge of God is understood using the metaphor of breathing on our minds (and this is true for both the *notio* and *cognitio Dei*). The *notio* or general knowledge of God is sufficient to give people an understanding of original sin,[109] but in order to stop them from sinning there is need of a new breath that is much more powerful than the breath required to grasp the general knowledge of God:

> Therefore knowledge of God and of truth which is common to all is indeed sufficient that we convict ourselves of sin, but that we should avoid it and constantly embrace what is good, is brought about only by the new breath of God and that much more powerfully than that which is common to all. When God breathes this breath more fully and perpetually on his believers, they are never able to devote themselves entirely to sin and to yield with their entire mind to perversity, what Saint John calls sin when he writes that he who is born from God cannot sin, for the reason that the seed of God remains in him. This seed is more fully and certainly the breath of God, which overcomes the desires of the flesh and at last quenches them. This breath is not in fact always thus present to the saints, for sin conquers and the righteous fall seven times in a day, yet it never withdraws from them to the extent that sin conquers and claims them all for itself. When they have sinned in some way, it enters into them again and does not cease to attack the evil lust, which has brought the righteous down, until it has seized and restored the whole heart to God once again. Hence flowed those tears of Peter,

107. Actuality or the actual being of a thing; in Latin *actus*, and opposite to δύναμις, which is potentiality. Aristotle coined the term, calling the soul the ἐντελέχεια of the body. See H. G. Liddell and R. Scott, *A Greek-English Lexicon*, 9th ed. (Oxford: Oxford University Press, 1995).

108. *BRom* (1536), 85; (1562), 59; "Mens siquidem nostra divinae aurae particula est, ἐντελέχεια, perennis quidam actus, ita a Deo pendens, ut dies a sole, rivus a fonte." Parker describes this understanding as "a translation of the Stoic's engraving of the *notio* on man's mind into Aristotelian categories, with the additional idea that therefore there is a relation between the mind and the *notio* and even between the mind and the *cognitio Dei*." Parker, *Commentaries on Romans*, 109–110.

109. According to Bucer, even the philosophers understood something of original depravity. *BRom* (1536), 267; (1562), 294; *CP* 120; "But men advanced beyond the masses in the knowledge of righteousness have adjudged the evil counsels and designs of the mind to be no less sins and no less liable to divine retribution. The Socratics actually went so far as to acknowledge that the wise, that is, the good man ought not to be assailed by even one evil desire. The sounder among them, such as Plato and his true followers, realized that this was the gift of God alone."

hence emerged sincere penance even from David, however late, hence was expressed the confession of the thief, hence arises all true detestation of and amendment for sins in all saints. In fact they had been sealed by this spirit unto the day of the Lord, who, although he sometimes withdraws himself so that they may be admonished of their weakness and perdition, nevertheless never completely leaves them, which is the inevitable fate of the reprobate. For God is accustomed to breathe more powerfully, often even on the reprobate, with his spirit, especially those whom he has determined to use for notable deeds, as when we read about Saul's being impelled by the spirit of God: but he does this only for as long as he has decided to use them for his glory, hence this inbreathing is not everlasting.[110]

It seems—to stretch a metaphor—as if the mind is a balloon into which God is breathing. There is always a little air given by God (the *notio*), but for the elect there is a fuller inbreathing (the *cognitio*), ebbing and flowing, but never leaving completely. God also breathes on the minds of pagans to fulfill his purposes but quickly deflates the balloon when he is finished.

To return to the role of the senses, the *notio* or general knowledge of God, a weak inbreathing of God, is natural and dependent to some extent on the senses, whereas the firmer knowledge of God seems to rely more completely on the Spirit. This distinction allows Bucer to associate knowledge that comes from the senses as being more susceptible to sin. Thus in regard to Romans 7, he states that our sinful tendencies are tied to our knowledge gained from the senses.[111] That being said, the Holy Spirit, as the conveyer of heavenly knowledge, still uses physical means like hearing to bring us to the truth (e.g., Bucer's

---

110. *BRom* (1536), 87; (1562), 61; "Est ergo cognitio Dei, et veritatis, quae communis est omnibus, satis quidem, ut peccati ipsi nos convincamus, at ut illud vitemus, et quod bonum est, constanter amplectamur, id non nisi novo adflatu dei, et eo multo, quam ille qui contingit promiscue omnibus, potentiore efficitur. Quem cum deus credentibus sibi plenius, et perpetuo adflat, numquam possunt hi se peccato penitus addicere, et toto se animo pravitati concedere, id quod D. Ioannes peccare vocat, cum scribit, eum qui natus est ex Deo, non posse peccare, eo quod semen dei maneat apud illum: quod semen, ipse adflatus Dei plenior et certior est, qui carnis cupiditates superat, tandemque extinguit. Hic adflatus non quidem semper sic adest sanctis, et peccatum vincit nam et iustus septies indie cadit, nunquam tamen ita illis se subducit, ut vincat peccatum, sibique illos totos vindicet. Ubi aliquid peccatum ab his est, ingerit rursus se, nec desistit malam cupiditatem, quae iustum prostravit, oppugnare, donec etiam expugnet, totumque cor Deo restituat. Hinc fluebant illi Petri lacrymae, hinc seria et Davidis, quamlibet sera emersit poenitentia, hinc expressa est confessio latronis, hinc omnis peccatorum vera existit in sanctis omnibus detestatio et emendatio. Obsignati siquidem sunt hoc spiritu in diem domini, qui licet subducat se interdum ut suae illi imbecillitatis et perditionis admoneantur, nunquam tamen deserit hos penitus, quod usu venit reprobis. Solet namque deus saepe et reprobos suo spiritu potentius adflare, maxime quibus ad praeclara facinora statuit uti, ut Schaulem actum spiritu dei legimus: sed hoc per id tantum temporis facit, quo illis ad gloriam suam uti decrevit, inde adflatus hic non est perpetuus."

111. *BRom* (1536), 324; (1562), 366; "Duplex autem est homine voluntas, altera qua consentit legi, altera qua facit quod detestatur. Altera sequitur cognitionem haustam a sensibus."

high regard for the preaching office); a person must *hear* the gospel.[112] Knowledge of God comes through the senses; however, that knowledge remains merely historical knowledge until the person is inspired or illuminated. Understanding these two types of knowledge and their dependence on the senses will help us understand Bucer's psychological anthropology and how he understands decision.

Bucer's Theological Anthropology and Psychology

In the *conciliatio* for Romans 5:3–5, Bucer speaks of a "twofold human" (*duplex homo*) in the saints, as well as a twofold will and twofold judgment.[113] These distinctions, which can be characterized as outer and inner humanity, correspond not to body-mind dualism but to a dialectic within the person as renewed by the Spirit and captive to the flesh. Bucer's view that the saint is *duplex homo* is similar to the familiar Lutheran phrase *simul iustus et peccator*.[114]

The idea that the saint is a *duplex homo* functions in two ways, as a dialectic between righteousness and sin and as a constant fluctuation between a partially regenerate judgment and will and a partially unregenerate judgment and will. It functions as a dialectic in that Bucer understands that man is completely innocent on account of the non-imputation of sins, but because the saint remains captive to the flesh and tainted with concupiscence, he is completely a sinner and forever unworthy of that forgiveness. The dialectic aspect of *duplex homo* affirms that humanity is without saving resources, and thus in Lutheran terms he is *simul iustus et peccator*.[115]

In reference to Rom. 5:3–5, Bucer provides the example of visiting a doctor to help illustrate the difference between the sensual and rational appetites in regard to pleasure and pain. When a patient attends a doctor who will need part of the patient's body to be cauterized or even castrated, his sensual appetite and knowledge tell them that this is something to be avoided; however, the patient's rational knowledge and appetite, after contemplating the information received from the senses, determine that there is a benefit to being castrated. Some may disagree here. See *BRom* (1536), 241; (1562), 261–262; "Cum enim medicus ustionis aut sectionis remedium offert quam aegre assentimur, quam gravatim etiam ubi assensi sumus, illa admittimus. Iam solius sensus est dolor qui percipitur, sed usque eo valet illa cognatio, quae est mentis cum corpore, ut quod corpori infert cruciatum, eiusque naturae sentitur adeo dissentaneum, mens difficile queat iudicare expetendum."

112. See Stephens, *Holy Spirit*, 196–212.

113. *BRom* (1536), 241; (1562), 261; "Est sanctis quoque duplex homo, internus et externus. Etsi, inquit Paulus, homo noster ille externus destruitur, internus renovatur in dies. Ut itaque homo duplex, ita est et iudicium duplex, et voluntas duplex. Id quod ipsum dominum nostrum fateri non puduit. Sed non mea, dicebat ad patrem, sed tua voluntas fiat. Eo certe quod aiebat, non quod ego volo, sed quod tu, fiat: voluisse se id quod patrem ostendit: et simul tamen suae voluntatis esse illud agnoscit, Transfer a me calicem istum. Bipartitam igitur, et in speciem secum pugnantem voluntatem dominus a se agnovit."

114. Bucer nowhere uses this phrase; however, his double sense of the self exhibits a similar dialectic to that of *simul iustus et peccator*. See Luther's *Romans Lectures*, WA 56, 269, l. 21through 273, l. 2.

115. For the way in which this phrase acts as a dialectic in Lutheran thought, see Daphne Hampson, *Christian Contradictions: The Structures of Lutheran and Catholic Thought* (Cambridge: Cambridge University Press, 2001), 9–55.

Because Bucer also believes that righteousness has an intrinsic imparted aspect, albeit tainted by the senses, there is in his thought a sense of progress in righteousness, in relation to one's faith. The greater the strength of the Spirit or the stronger the inbreathing that is in the believer, the weaker will be the effects of concupiscence, since the renewed believer has a will and judgment associated with the Spirit that is less dependent on the senses. This fluctuation is similar to the Augustinian view *ex quadam parte iustus, ex quadam parte peccator*.[116]

This dialectic and fluctuation applies only to the believer; the pagan is only single, he has a single will and a single judgment dependent on the senses. He is *solus et totus peccator*. The saint is *duplex homo*, in both a dialectical and fluctuating sense, primarily because for Bucer justification is not understood exclusively in forensic terms. God's forgiveness effects a psychological and anthropological change that cannot be separated from the justification process.

To understand this bipartite aspect of renewed humanity it is best to turn to Bucer's understanding of Romans 7:15.[117] Here Paul states, "I do not understand my own actions. For I do not do what I want, but I do the very thing I hate." It was common for the early church fathers to take this passage to refer to Paul before his Damascus experience, that is, as a non-Christian. The reformers took a different stance.[118]

Melanchthon took this passage as referring to Paul in a regenerate state.[119] Bucer agrees, to an extent. For him Paul is talking about "some sort" of believer, but Paul is not talking about a believer who is fully regenerate with the full power of the Spirit. Here Bucer introduces a three-step gradation of belief. At the lowest end is the unrepentant heathen; next there is an intermediating state, where a person has received knowledge of God through the law but without the stronger illuminating power of the Spirit; and finally there is the believer who has this power of the Spirit fully on him.[120] Here again he references a twofold will.[121]

---

116. Bucer does not use this formulation either, but I introduce it here to help describe his understanding that a person has a partial imparted righteousness. This aspect of the *duplex homo* seems to function like a teeter-totter. See Augustine, *Enarratio in Psalmum CXL*, in *PL* 37, 1825.

117. A helpful exposition of this passage in Bucer can be found in Joel Edward Kok's dissertation, "The Influence of Martin Bucer on John Calvin's Interpretation of Romans: A Comparative Case Study" (Ph.D. diss., Duke University, 1993), 105–109.

118. For a survey of different views on Romans chapter 7 by various reformers, see Elliott, "Romans 7 in the Reformation Century," 171–188.

119. *MW* 5, 223–224; English translation of 1540 ed. in *Commentary on Romans*, 161; "Furthermore, we must refute the false imagination of those who say that Paul is assuming the artificial guise of an ungodly person here. They deny that the struggle which is described here fits the person who is converted and sanctified, as though in the sanctified there were no remnants of sin, or that nature had been wholly renewed and there are no evil impulses."

120. *BRom* (1536), 323–324; (1562), 365–366.

121. *BRom* (1536), 324; (1562), 366.

This relationship between the unregenerate will and the regenerate will is partially understood in relation to the reception of and capacity to contemplate true knowledge. The contemplation of knowledge in the intellect is the foundation for the act of the will. Here we see Thomas Aquinas's intellectual psychology in play; Thomas states that "the act of the will is nothing else than an inclination proceeding from the interior principle of knowledge."[122] Bucer operates with this same intellectual psychology, so for instance when the will is moved by the intellect supplied only with knowledge that depends solely on the senses without the Spirit, the will frequently chooses lesser goods, that is, it chooses sin. This is because knowledge from the senses is easily corruptible, and it allows the stronger sensual appetite for pleasure (in the unregenerate will) a freer rein than if the will were more dependent on the inbreathing knowledge of the Spirit.

For Bucer, King David's senses led him to conclude that it would be pleasant to have sex with Bathsheeba rather than to conclude that to have sex with a married woman is against God's law.[123] Likewise, describing Peter's denial, Bucer believes that if Peter were to have considered the matter thoroughly in the power of the Spirit, he would not have denied Christ for fear of the crowd.[124]

The distinction between the two wills is similar to the Aristotelian understanding that the incontinent person does not have knowledge in the same way as the continent person, the incontinent person's knowledge is like that of a

---

122. *ST* 1a 2ae q.6 a.4. The relationship between the will and the intellect is complex, and Bucer seems to favor the intellect as the mover of the will. However, the attempt to pit one against the other falsely imposes a dichotomy that does not exist in Bucer's mind, as if the will and intellect were completely distinct. I believe that his understanding of the intellect and the will is similar to Aquinas's in the *Summa*. Eleonore Stump's very helpful article on this relationship clarifies that for Thomas "the will is not independent of the intellect. On the contrary, the dynamic interactions of the intellect and the will yield freedom as an emergent property or a system-level feature." Eleonore Stump, "Aquinas's Account of Freedom: Intellect and Will," in *Aquinas's Summa Theologiae: Critical Essays*, ed. Brian Davies (Lanham, MD: Rowman and Littlefield, 2006), 203–222, quote on 203.

123. *BRom* (1536), 326; (1562), 368–369; "De eo vero quod scientes quod bonum est id tamen non facimus, et quod scimus malum, id facimus, Aristoteles scite disserit. 7. Ethicorum ad Nicomachum. Nam interdum habemus quidem recti scientiam, sed non utimur ea: id est, cum agendum est, non iudicamus secundum eam, quo pacto dormientes et ebrii scientiam habent. His similes sunt qui pravis cupiditatibus ita rapiuntur, ut nihil aliud cogitent, quam quo impotens illa perturbatio impellit. Interdum vero consideramus quid illud sit, quod ita fugiendum occurrit, et utimur scientia, verum in universali, non autem in particulari de eo ipso quod nunc ut agendum obiectum est. Ut David indubie dum tentaretur de bathschaba cogitabat: oblectatio quam vetat Deus exitio et fugienda est. Cum autem illa Delectabile persequendum est, simul in mente versaretur, assumptum est ad hanc, cum hac muliere misceri delectabile, et non ad alteram, commisceri cum hac quae uxor aliena est, a Deo vetitum est. Ab hac enim assumptione animus abducebatur cupiditate, ut id solum cogitaret, cum hac muliere misceri oblectabile est: Istuc ergo prosequendum iudicabat, et in adulterium ruit."

124. *BRom* (1536), 325; (1562), 368; "Si iam potuisset Petrus perstare in consideratione, fugiendum esse negationem Christi servatoris, facile assumpsisset, Hic Iesus Christus servator tuus est, indeque firmatis praemissis etiam conclusisset, Ergo Iesus hic meus magister minime negandus est, et sic in confessione eius perstitisset." See also *BRom* (1536), 241; (1562), 261–262.

drunk or sleeping person.[125] What this means is that the incontinent person has a general knowledge that is unable to contemplate the true good or end (in the act of deciding).[126] Peter was like a drunken man when he decided to deny Christ three times; the fear of people did not allow him to contemplate the good of pleasing God, and if he had been endowed with a greater power of the Spirit, he would have kept to his confession.[127] Peter's unregenerate will and judgment, held captive to the senses and the sensual appetite, overwhelmed his regenerate will and judgment because, to pick up the earlier analogy, his balloon was not fully blown up in the Spirit. Having this balloon more fully blown up allows a person to contemplate the true Good better, with more dependence on the Spirit than the senses; thus this person can make better-informed decisions. In this regard we see that, though there is in a believer this twofold aspect, it is one or the other that at times is in stronger control.

As mentioned previously, Bucer's view of knowledge connected to decisions is in line with the Socratic view that nobody acts against what they know to be good, or stated in another way, "to know the good is to do the good" necessarily. And to do good or to sin can be distinguished in Bucer's mind between knowledge that is driven by the senses and contemplative knowledge that takes the truest end into consideration through the agency of the Spirit.

Because decisions take place in the *mens*, sin, free choice, faith, and love are all primarily understood in intellectual ways. Johannes Müller, in his work on Bucer's hermeneutics, speaks of the *Intellectualisierung der Bucerschen Theologie*; Müller explains the intellectualizing theology of Bucer as an emphasis or priority of the mind in Bucer's theological anthropology, such that faith is seen as the result of revealed knowledge and therefore dependent on the mind or reason, hence Bucer's tendency to talk of faith as *persuasio*.[128] Hence, in Bucer's *Gospels Commentary*, he states: "For everything he does is determined by decisions reached in his own mind and thoughts he has found persuasive. The disposition and power of men follows the judgment of the mind."[129] If one has a right conviction, right action will automatically follow;[130] thus knowledge of

---

125. Aristotle, *Nic. Ethics* 7.x.; cf. 7.iii. This sentiment is repeated by Bucer in *BRom* (1536), 326; (1562), 368–369.

126. In his first *conciliatio* in relation to Rom. 1:18–20, Bucer describes the process of making a decision. See *BRom* (1536), 86–87; (1562), 61.

127. *BRom* (1536), 323–324; (1562), 365–366.

128. See Müller, *Bucers Hermeneutik*, 31–40.

129. *BGospels* (1536), 220; "Nam agit omnino quique pro sententia animi sui, et ut est mente persuasus. Animi iudicium, affectus quoque ac vires hominis sequuntur."

130. For him ethics are related to knowledge, in a manner similar to Plato. For Plato knowledge was a virtue, and thus knowledge of the good led to a good life. Without this knowledge a moral life was impossible. See Terence Irwin, *Plato's Ethics* (Oxford: Oxford University Press, 1995). This is why Bucer had such a great affinity for the moral philosophers. See *BRom* (1536), 28–29; (1562), 28.

God is salvific. This emphasis on the intellect in regard to his theology of justification will be explored and illustrated in the following discussion on Bucer's theological anthropology.

BUCER'S THEOLOGICAL ANTHROPOLOGY: SIN. The doctrine of sin and original sin is pivotal for the evangelical doctrine of justification, especially because the doctrine of justification is concerned with responding to a particular problem.[131] Thus it is critical to discuss the nature of that problem in Bucer's thought in order to understand his formulation of the doctrine of justification. Bucer's understanding of sin and the role of the *ratio* therein is fundamental to all his statements on justification and, as noted earlier, is related to a knowledge that is dependent on the senses.

Luther's first eighteen theses at the Heidelberg disputation (1518), where Bucer was first captivated by the great reformer, highlighted humanity's total inability to avoid sinning.[132] This encounter inspired Bucer to incorporate his own radical understanding of sin, without, however, abandoning his Dominican Thomism and Erasmian humanism, which resulted in a unique perspective.[133]

Be that as it may, Bucer's individuality in regard to other reformers on the doctrine of sin is not necessarily a matter of substance but of nuance. For Bucer the reality of sin is a power inhabiting the flesh (for the saint this will always mean *simul peccator*), which is primarily manifested in a depravity of knowledge. The dualities of flesh versus spirit, external versus internal, and sensual knowledge versus true contemplative knowledge lay the foundation for the way in which Bucer understands justification.

In his explication of Romans 5:12–14, Bucer directs his full attention to the doctrine of original sin. In the *interpretatio* he emphasizes the role of the mind and its association with humanity's fallen condition:

> Indeed sin is the pursuit of evil instead of good by mistake, and the neglect of the good instead of evil. What else would you call this than striving toward ruin? Indeed the apostle wanted to express it through ἁμαρτίαν because it is called הטאת in Hebrew. The first thing meant

131. For the Protestant doctrine of salvation, if there is *any real significant* innovation, it is in regard to the radicalization of sin, not grace. One of the main contributions in Protestant theology is discovered in theological anthropology, specifically in the heightened doctrine of sin. This in no way necessitates that man is the starting point for an understanding of the Protestant doctrine of justification, over against grace. It does, however, imply that regardless of the starting point, the reevaluation and emphasis on grace led to a sharpened reformulation of the problem.

132. *WA* I, 350–375.

133. Greschat, "Der Ansatz," 87; "Es war insbesondere die Einsicht in den ebenso radikalen wie unaufhebbaren Charakter der Sündhaftigkeit des Menschen, was Bucer Luther verdankte und wodurch die Soteriologie mit dem Themenkreis Glaube und Rechtfertigung und insofern auch die Christologie in seinem Denken eine neue Dimension gewannen."

by this word is to go wrong, to err, to be mistaken: but it is trans-
posed for the purpose of signifying the depravity of life: because the
crooked mind errs and hallucinates, as Aristotle excellently and truly
affirms in the *Nicomachean Ethics*, book 7.[134] For the beginning of
every evil in life results from a shortcoming of judgment: whereby
the will always pursues what reason judges it should pursue.[135]

Sin has left man unable to choose the true Good. Instead, humanity errs
when making choices, and inevitably chooses evil instead of good.[136] The
mens (*mens*, *ratio*, and *animus* are three common ways in which Bucer
describes the reason)[137] controls decisions. Sin, therefore, is a confusion of
perishable earthly goods over the highest good, ultimately making sin related to ignorance or rather stupidity. This hampered ability to know the true
good in the intellect is a result of original sin, primarily as a consequence of
inherited concupiscence, due in turn to humanity's loss of original
righteousness.[138]

Illuminated knowledge (or the fuller inbreathing of the Spirit) of God is
eternal life,[139] and the corollary, the lack of illuminated knowledge, results in
damnation. The illuminated knowledge of God is progressively revealed to

134. Aristotle, *Nic. Ethics* 7.ii.1.

135. *BRom* (1536), 253; (1562), 276; "Peccatum siquidem est, errore sectari malum pro bono, et bonum
negligere pro malo. Id quid aliud dicas esse quam eniti ad exitium? Apostolus siquidem per ἁμαρτίαν, id
exprimere voluit, quod Ebraice חטאת dicitur. Hoc nomine primum significatur, labi, errare, falli: transfertur vero
ad significandam vitae pravitatem: quia errat et hallucinatur animus pravus, ut Aristoteles scite ac vere affirmat
Eth. Ad Nicomachum 7. Initium namque omnis mali in vita, a depravatione iudicii est: eo quod hoc semper voluntas prosequatur, quod prosequendum iudicarit ratio." See Barnikol, "Bucers Lehre," 20–25; and Müller, who
more than the others emphasizes this intellectual aspect in Bucer; *Bucers Hermeneutik*, 31–35. See also Krüger,
Bucer und Erasmus, 131–137.

136. This primary role of the mind and sin is echoed by Calvin in his *Romans Commentary; CO* 49, 31;
where he says, "Peccatum proprie animi est."

137. See Krüger, *Bucer und Erasmus*, 133.

138. Bucer agrees with the scholastics, who said that original sin is a loss of original righteousness (*carentia
iustitiae originalis*). However, Bucer sees this loss as completely corrupting man and thus qualifies the assertion
that original sin is only privation of original righteousness. *BRom* (1536), 267; (1562) 295; *CP* 123; "The Schoolmen
make the loss of original righteousness, the state in which all our parts were rightly ordered within us, the chief
aspect of this evil of original sin. But surely it is a necessary consequence of this loss that everything in us is now
disordered and distorted and the habit of corrupt desire has possession of man. As a result, subjection to eternal
death is the lot of all whom the Savior's grace does not restore. This grace, imparted in baptism, annuls the
imputation of this evil to us, but nevertheless the 'law of our members,' our corruption which is ever hateful
to God, persists until this perishable nature has put on the imperishable. So long as the Schoolmen accept these
corollaries, I do not see any divergence from the orthodox opinion of the Church." This seems to result in
the same conclusions as those made by Thomas. Thomas understands the privation of original righteousness as
the "formal" element of original sin, but its absence leaves an unbalanced man, and he calls this concupiscence,
which is for him the "material" element of original sin. "So then sin materially is concupiscence, yet formally it
is the lack of original righteousness" (*ST* 1a 2ae q.82 a.3–a.4).

139. *BRom* (1536), 86; (1562), 60; "Nec mirum, cum vita aeterna sit, Deum novisse."

humanity by the Holy Spirit so that, as Müller states, salvation history is the same as revelation history for Bucer.[140]

The emphasis on the role of knowledge or lack thereof when discussing humanity's original depravity does not, however, force Bucer into a platonic anthropological dualism that puts the higher man over the lower man, as if reason was unspoiled and the body was the spoiler. The whole of man is flesh, his reason, emotions, and will.[141] The priority of the "higher" man in regard to the manifestation of original sin does not evacuate or destroy the all-pervasiveness of sin; thus Bucer in his *Ephesians Commentary* states, "Surely idolatry, rivalry and hatred, are works of the chief part of man, but nevertheless they are called works of the flesh by Paul."[142] Further on in that same commentary in relation to Genesis 6:3, Bucer states that "man has begun to be nothing but a beast; the mind and all reason having been turned toward corruption and such obscene things as beasts enjoy doing."[143] The entire person is regarded as *caro*, and the *caro* is corrupt in its entirety, including the *ratio*. Reason is totally blind without the help of God (*ratio hic, naturae lumen, prorsus caeca est*),[144] and it is in the blind *ratio* that the Holy Spirit works. Thus those with only the insufficient-for-salvation natural light (which is still dependent on God) are completely blind, and this insufficient light is given only so that pagans can somehow perceive the right and be without excuse.

In the *Ephesians Commentary*, Bucer states that the flesh, the corrupt nature of man, is the absolute inability to seek anything but the things of the

---

140. Müller, *Bucers Hermeneutik*, 67. See *BRom* (1536), 290; (1562), 322; "Visum siquidem Deo est, filium suum orbi certis gradibus revelare et hoc apertius, quo propius erat, ut in carne nostra toti ipsum orbi manifestarit. Prima itaque illa cum patrum populi sancti, tum religiosorum Ethnicorum baptismata, ablutiones fuerunt peccatorum per Christum cognitum in generali promissione redemptoris generis humani."

141. Müller pits Bucer against Melanchthon's *Loci* (1521), where Melanchthon includes the affections in his definition of sin. Müller asserts that Bucer's rationalizing view of sin disregards or forgets the affections, whereas a true understanding of natural man must see that the affections dominate both reason and will. Thus Müller prefers Melanchthon's description of sin because he locates original sin pervasively throughout reason, will, and especially the affections. Müller, *Bucers Hermeneutik*, 31–35, esp. 34n70. Nevertheless, though the all-pervasive power of sin may not be as strong for Bucer as it is for Luther and Melanchthon, the separation of the intellect from the affections is not wholly warranted. (Krüger sees the separation of the affections from reason as an Erasmian influence [134].) The elevation or priority of the intellect does not in any way create a duality that results in a separation of reason from the will or affections. It is just that for Bucer to err is to sin, and to err is to make a decision based on the knowledge or information you are given by the senses. If this knowledge remains unilluminated, then you cannot know God truly. This priority, however, in no way diminishes the complete depravity of every aspect of man, as Müller and Krüger seem to indicate. Cf. Stephens, *Holy Spirit*, 81.

142. *BEph* (1527), 49; "Certe idolatria, aemulationes et invidia, opera sunt primae in homine portionis, attamen opera carnis a Paulo vocantur."

143. *BEph* (1527), 49; "nihil nisi bestia homo esse, coepit; mente omnique ratione, ad corruptibilia et foeda ista quibus bestiae delectantur, conversa."

144. *BGospels* (1527), bk. 1, 23(r). This priority of the *ratio* is similarly noted in Erasmus; see Krüger, who expounds the interrelation of Bucer's thought on this point with Erasmus; *Bucer und Erasmus*, 136–137.

flesh;[145] in his *John Commentary* he states that the way of the flesh is concupiscence: *caro concupiscit.*[146] Sin is equated with flesh (again what is meant is not some idea of a body but rather the whole unregenerate person as opposed to the spirit, which is the regenerate person). As mentioned previously, the distinction operates as a dialectic; the life of the saint is duplex, both flesh and spirit.

The distinction also operates as a fluctuating continuum. The flesh is closely associated with the senses, and the Spirit is not. As demonstrated earlier, Bucer sees sin as the inability to choose the right, that is, as a result of knowledge dependent on the senses, and this is the state in which humanity finds itself. As such we are children of wrath.

Commenting on Romans 5:18–21, in one of Bucer's *quaestiones*: "What is Original sin, and what is its power?"[147] Bucer describes the all-pervasive character of sin when he says that "original sin is the infection and corruption of the *whole man* which prevents him from recognizing and aspiring after God and his will as the truest good; instead his judgment on anything is warped, he regards and desires nothing in its proper place and rank, but abuses and perverts all things."[148] A bit further on, Bucer's distinction between flesh and spirit comes out again when he says, "If flesh and blood cannot perceive the kingdom of God, if the affection of the flesh is enmity against God, if by nature we are children of wrath, sold under sin, given over to Satan, what is there in man that we can deny has been tainted and ruined from his beginning?"[149] He answers this by saying, "The reality, then, of original sin as we have defined it is plainer than daylight. It is an infection and subversion of man's whole person so radical that we are incapable of comprehending or sincerely desiring what is good, being utterly made over to perversity and hence to eternal death."[150]

Bucer understood the flesh as thoroughly depraved.[151] The remedy, however, is found in the power of the Spirit who bends our minds toward what is right and gives the power to accomplish the good so that it can be said with Paul that it is Christ who lives in me.[152]

---

145. *BEph* (1527), 91; "natura siquidem sibi relicta, non potest nisi sua quaerere." Also *BEph* (1527), 24; "Dicuntur autem ideo caelestia, quod nihil eorum terrenus Adam vel percipit. Dicuntur et spiritualia, quia operatur ea in nobis spiritus Dei, cum nihil tale possit caro et sanguis"

146. *BOL* 2, 320.

147. *BRom* (1536), 267; (1562), 294; "Quid peccatum originale, et quid valeat."

148. *BRom* (1536), 267; (1562), 295; *CP* 122.

149. *BRom* (1536), 267; (1562), 295; *CP* 122.

150. *BRom* (1536), 267; (1562), 295; *CP* 122–123.

151. *BRom* (1536), 322–323; (1562), 364.

152. Gal. 2:20.

The person in an unregenerated state, that is, under original sin, is worthy of God's condemnation. How this is to be understood in regard to God's justice is an unfathomable mystery. Bucer uses the metaphor of a blind man running into things as an example of original sin, highlighting that the commission of sin is not punished but the condition that results in the stumbling is punished:

> If someone punishes a blind man for repeatedly knocking against him, although he cannot help knocking him because of his lack of sight, surely you will say that it is his blindness which is being punished, not the sin of striking the other—which of course he cannot avoid so long as he is blind. Would you punish equally a blind man who does not knock against others and one who does?—for apparently the man who knocks someone because of blindness offends no more than the man who does not, for in his blindness he cannot avoid striking others.[153]

The infant in the state of sin before having performed any actual sin is still punishable because the state of sin within will inevitably lead to a life of wickedness: "For what is the difference between condemning a man after he has committed, in conformity with his inherent corruptness, iniquities and offences to which he was born and which he cannot avoid, and condemning him before he commits them?"[154]

Here one must now distinguish the role of concupiscence (the flesh) in those who have been baptized. Bucer states: "As a result, subjection to eternal death is the lot of all whom the Savior's grace does not restore. This grace, imparted in baptism, annuls the imputation of this evil to us, but nevertheless the 'law of our members,' our corruption which is ever hateful to God, persists until this perishable nature has put on the imperishable."[155]

Those who are baptized have the imputation of original sin annulled, that is, it no longer condemns them. However, concupiscence still remains, and it remains bent toward evil. This evil that inhabits believers will ultimately be eliminated when they receive glorified bodies, and only then will the believer become completely regenerate and no longer double. As I have mentioned, this understanding is similar to the dialectical view that the believer is *simul iustus et peccator*, since for Bucer concupiscence is sin: "So evil desire is also sin, and since a person judges the objects of his desire to be of supreme value and is

---

153. *BRom* (1536), 268; (1562), 297; *CP* 126–127.
154. *BRom* (1536), 268; (1562), 297; *CP* 126.
155. *BRom* (1536), 267; (1562), 295; *CP* 123.

immediately borne unreservedly in their direction, it is even the root of all sin."[156] From this *radix* all actual sins come forth, and thus since concupiscence remains even in the baptized, sin's power remains. In that respect the radicalization of sin in Bucer's thought was far more pervasive than in that of any of his medieval counterparts. In regard to the scholastic distinction between venial and mortal sins Bucer states, in counsel given to the Waldensian pastors (1530), that for the believer all sins are venial except apostasy, and for the unbeliever all sins are mortal.[157]

The Christian does not become free from the flesh (and therefore the indwelling of sin) until glorification; on that account the Spirit is continually curbing the flesh of the baptized. In a section dealing with baptism Bucer states the following:

> Moreover the reason why the baptism now practiced by the Church is not repeated, seems to be that it is a symbol of the fullest revelation of the knowledge of Christ. By virtue of this we now embrace Christ more fully than was granted to the multitude of saints before the advent of the gospel, namely, to such effect that nothing of ourselves is alive in us, but Christ alone and in all things, and we, by participating to the fullest in his death and resurrection, never fall back under the tyranny of sin.[158]

He states further:

> Our baptism has . . . the presentation of the remission of sins and communion with Christ, the one mediator; its distinctiveness is to present so full a participation in Christ that there remains for us only the return of Christ in his glorified flesh to conform our lowly bodies to his glorious body, and our attaining to him with his stature at last full grown in us and his heavenly image perfected.[159]

The association of sinfulness with this flesh allows Bucer to understand our limited righteousness as imperfect righteousness tainted as it is by original sin, because we carry its consequences in the flesh until the very end until Christ overcomes our flesh and gives us heavenly bodies (akin to Augustine's formulation *ex quadam parte iustus, ex quadam parte peccator*). At that point we will cease to be double, but in the meantime we are double, and this is how

---

156. *BRom* (1536), 266; (1562), 294; *CP* 121.

157. Trinity College Dublin MS 259, 104f.; cited in Euan Cameron, *Reformation of the Heretics* (Oxford: Clarendon Press, 1984), 204. Cf. *BRom* (1536), 258; (1562), 283.

158. *BRom* (1536), 290; (1562), 322; *CP* 290.

159. *BRom* (1536), 293; (1562), 326; *CP* 297.

Bucer understands some degree of righteousness to be imparted to believers (as the divine breath) so that we can be said to share in divinity.[160]

This approach illustrates the difference between Bucer and Luther, in that Bucer allows for an imparting of righteousness in the discussion of justification whereas Luther's soteriology cannot bear this. The strong, ever-pervasive power of sin cautioned Luther from talking in anthropological categories of the justified man.[161] Ian Hazlett puts it well when he states:

> If Luther could imagine faith without works, Bucer could not, since, for him, faith and ethical uprightness—not of itself meritorious— were necessarily proximate. The difference can be illustrated respecting the law. If Luther saw it as bringing condemnation and as a bar to true righteousness, Bucer reckoned that that applied only when the law was seen as an external and unwelcome imposition. Genuine faith induces obedience to God's will and receptivity to the Spirit, who enables the law's internal appropriation.[162]

In that Bucer sees the saint as *duplex*, both sinner and just, his thought can be conceived as a dialectic; however, because righteousness is also imparted, the saint has a double will and judgment that are partially sinful and partially righteous, which allows for perfect righteousness to be achieved in glorification. Bucer's thought, in this way, makes use of both a dialectic between sin and righteousness and an intellectual continuum that allows for greater growth in righteousness, that is, a lesser or greater inbreathing of the Spirit.

This greater growth in righteousness is partially on account of the fact that the Spirit enables the law's internal appropriation. For Bucer, the law is inherent in all of creation, that is, it can be detected in nature and the general order of the world, *machina mundi*. Therefore, the law holds a strong position in his theology and subsequently encourages a strong emphasis on practice as theology's main purpose.[163] As a result, love of neighbor is always mentioned when speaking of salvation or justification. This love of neighbor, however, finds its origin in the power of the Spirit enabling a believer to contemplate the knowledge of the supreme Good. The incapacity to contemplate the true good results in a love for the self.

Attempts to seek the good are, in those persons without the Spirit, always bent in error, for theirs is a limited sensual knowledge. That is why original sin

---

160. *BRom* (1536), 322–323; (1562), 364.
161. Greschat, "Der Ansatz," 88.
162. Hazlett, "Bucer," 104.
163. For detailed studies of the law in the theology of Martin Bucer, see Tait, "The Law and Its Works," 57–69. See also his dissertation, "A Method for the Christian Life."

is the aptitude to make wrong decisions constantly, typically described as choosing false goods instead of the true good, that is, God. Inevitably this leads to an egoistic understanding of sin as love of self. Though this may be more clearly articulated in Bucer's earlier works (especially *Das ym selbs*),[164] it is expressed in various forms in the *Romans Commentary*. Regarding Romans 5:18–21, he describes sin as "the scriptural name for our going astray by forsaking the only God, who is man's highest good, in order to pursue unsubstantial and ruinous phantoms of the good."[165]

In the preface on "What the 'Law' and 'works of law' are for Paul," Bucer states:

> The law demands that you commit yourself entirely to God, that you
> love him above all things, and that nothing that displeases him ever
> please you. Yet you are still to some extent without the Spirit of
> Christ, addicted to yourself and a slave to your own desires. It is
> precisely to that extent that you will burn with desire for those things
> from which the law seeks to detach you and with hatred for the God
> who calls you to abandon these things under the threat of eternal
> punishment. This is how we were born and this is the inclination of
> our natural depravity.[166]

Because of the *ratio*'s depravity and its dependence on the senses, it sees things distorted, and results in humanity attaching itself to temporal goods without acknowledging that they ought to be sought from God above all;[167] the effect is love of self and self-preservation.[168]

In defining sin as a love of self, Bucer is in agreement with Erasmus, who in his *Enchiridion* understands Jesus as the supreme model of one who

---

164. Greschat, "Der Ansatz," 83–85. Here Greschat shows how Bucer's emphasis on love toward God and love toward our neighbors was developed. Bucer's understanding of self-love was first developed in contrast to his Dominican training. Thomas held love of self at the center of his theology, but this love of self encompassed love of God and love of neighbor. It was only later that love of self took an emphasis, within later Thomistic scholasticism, which resulted in problems that led Bucer to identify self-love as sin. What Bucer rejected was the monastic striving for one's own personal salvation that was a part of the Dominican order. Monks were concerned for their own salvation and worked meticulously to achieve it, and surely in Bucer's mind, at the expense of their neighbors. This striving for one's own salvation, this self-love, is sin.

165. *BRom* (1536), 267; (1562), 294; *CP* 120.

166. *BRom* (1536), 27; (1562), 26; "quo magis agnoveris legem poscere, ut Deo te totum permittas, unum ames supra omnia, adeo ut tibi iam nihil adlubescat, quod non sit ex illius sententia, hoc ipso si [destitutus] sis spiritu Christi, eoque tibi ipsi adhuc addictus, tuarumque cupiditatum servus, amplius inflammaris, et rerum illarum, quae faciunt ad ingenium tuum, a quibus nimirum lex revocat, cupiditate, et Dei te ab his, sub interminatione sempiterni supplicii revocantis odio. Sic enim nati sumus, ita fert ingenium naturae nostrae depravatum."

167. *BRom* (1536), 30; (1562), 29, quoted above. Here are hints of Augustine's *uti/frui* distinction. Augustine, *De Doctrina Christiana*, I.22.20.

168. *BRom* (1536), 87; (1562), 60–61. Cf. Luther's concept of *homo incurvatus se*. WA 2, 593, ll. 25–28.

did not love himself but rather lived to love God and his neighbors.[169] Similarly, Bucer is in line with Zwingli, who in his *Commentary on True and False Religion* described Adam's quest to be like God as love of self, and therefore the trait that is passed on to all humanity is this aspect of self-love.[170]

THEOLOGICAL ANTHROPOLOGY: FREE CHOICE AND ELECTION.   A weak knowledge of the supreme Good, even in the greatest philosophers, was nevertheless too weak and unable to choose God, for God chooses those to whom he gives his Spirit. On this point Bucer's doctrine of election and the freedom of choice come to bear.[171]

The doctrine of election or predestination is in the background of Bucer's thought.[172] For him the election of the saints from the foundation of the world is accomplished through the merit of Christ.[173] When Bucer approaches a text where there is an "all" in reference to salvation, he interprets it as "all the elect"; thus in his *observatio* on Paul's statement in Romans 11:25–32 that all of Israel will be saved, Bucer interprets "all" to mean all Israel insofar as it is elect.[174]

The warrant for this election is unknowable; it remains in the realm of God's perfect justice.[175] Although God's predestination of the elect remains a

169. Greschat, "Der Ansatz," 86n42.

170. See *ZW* 3, 712, ll. 7–9.

171. For extended discussion on predestination in Bucer's thought, see Lang, *Evangelienkommentar*, 346–358; see Barnikol, "Bucers Lehre," 5–12; Müller, *Bucers Hermenuetik*, 184–199; on free will and its comparison to Erasmus, see Krüger, *Bucer und Erasmus*, 137–152.

172. Stephens, *Holy Spirit*, 23–41. Following Lang, Stephens states, "The doctrine of predestination or election is one that shapes the whole of Bucer's theology. Even where it is not expressed explicitly, its stamp is to be found." In note 2, Stephens goes further to say, "Failure to see the centrality of predestination in Bucer leads to a fundamental misunderstanding of his theology at a number of points." Stephens's assertion is warranted; however, it is a slight exaggeration to claim that predestination is at the center of Bucerian thought. The doctrine of predestination is a buttress for Bucer's thought, consistently in the background but rarely to the fore. The importance of predestination for Bucer stems from the priority of God, i.e., of grace, in the work of justification over against humanity's own efforts through freedom of choice. Thus it may be more suitable to say in a similar manner that grace is at the center of Bucer's thought.

173. Bucer defines προορίζειν in two ways: "first, the election of the saints and their separation from the remaining polluted mass of lost mankind, . . . and secondly, the election of the saints before they were ever born." *BRom* (1536), 358; (1562), 409; *CP* 96. *BRom* (1536), 358; (1562), 409–410; *CP* 96; "Predetermination (προορισμός), then, which we commonly call 'predestination,' is that act of designation on the part of God whereby in his secret counsel he designates and actually selects and separates from the rest of mankind those whom he will draw to his Son, Jesus our Lord, and ingraft them into him (having brought them into this life at his own good time), and whom, when thus drawn and ingrafted, he will regenerate through Christ and will sanctify to fulfill his purposes."

174. *BRom* (1536), 448; (1562), 517.

175. *BRom* (1536), 359; (1562), 410; *CP* 98; "We must accordingly reject the judgment of reason in this area, and confess that the judgments of God are a 'great abyss' and inscrutable, yet righteous. For God is just in all his ways, even when to our reason he seems otherwise."

mystery, Bucer strongly encouraged that this doctrine be preached and taught to all:

> The teaching of Philip Melanchthon answers this very devoutly and faithfully: it is solely in order that you may be more certain of your salvation and may cleave more firmly to the promises of God.[176] The first demand God makes of us is to believe that he is God, that is, the Saviour, so that when we hear him summoning to himself all who are afflicted and distressed we hasten eagerly to him. Now if those whom God calls heed his call, he has assuredly predestined and foreknown[177] them, and will also justify and glorify them. Therefore, the first duty you owe to God is to believe that you have been predestined by him, because unless you believe that, you represent him as making sport of you when he calls you to salvation through the gospel.[178]

Bucer holds this doctrine of election together with a particular understanding of free will or freedom of choice. He can also affirm that the pre-Christian philosophers could be said to possess freedom of choice in a qualified sense—in spite of election. Bucer defines free will as follows:

> Now the freedom of the will is the faculty of acting according to one's own choice and decision without any compulsion. Notice that I say "without compulsion," not "without necessity," for God of necessity wills what is right and cannot will otherwise, and yet has the highest freedom of will. . . . Freedom of will, therefore, and free will (i.e., αὐτεξούσιον) is the capacity for acting according to your own decision, so that you act on your own initiative and are not acted upon contrary to your wish to be acted upon, and this excludes any power which compels or constrains you against your will, but not the God-given invariability and necessity of doing right.[179]

This voluntary aspect is dependent on the intellect. Bucer believes that the doctrine of predestination actually confirms the doctrine of free will because it is only in the elect that the intellect is not hampered so as to constrain the will's ability to choose. Therefore, the will in relation to the intellect always chooses poorly when the intellect is hampered or obstructed.

---

176. CR 21, 451–453; *Loci Communes* (1535).

177. *BRom* (1536), 360; (1562). 412; *CP* 102. Bucer rejects the notion that God's election is based on the foreknowledge of our good works.

178. *BRom* (1536), 359; (1562), 411; *CP* 99.

179. *BRom* (1536), 360; (1562), 413; *CP* 102–103.

Free choice is completely denied if one understands this to mean the ability to pursue the highest good and thereby gain salvation by one's own efforts. This freedom to gain salvation by one's own choice is emphatically denied because an unbeliever is deprived of secure knowledge of the highest good. As a result, Bucer grants freedom of the will only to the elect, who can choose God because the Spirit has revealed to them a stronger revelation of the supreme Good. Predestination establishes the freedom of the will with regard to salvation, since only then are the elect able to know and choose rightly, that is, to choose God.[180] This demonstrates a close correlation between the doctrines of election and justification, which I will touch on later.[181]

Bucer's intellectual psychology, which emphasizes the role of knowledge in salvation, makes allowances for a more nuanced view of free will than does Luther, who in the midst of a highly polemical debate said that if any freedom exists at all, then it is a freedom only to sin.[182] In this debate Luther wanted to affirm that Christ died not only for the "lower" person but also for the "higher" person, who was just as deprived. Bucer's belief that believers will what they deem good (in relation to their knowledge) allows him to speak of free will in a more subtle manner than his Wittenberg colleague. On this account I agree with Müller, who suggests that Bucer's view of free will be understood within an intellectualist anthropology rather than a voluntarist anthropology, since for Müller the problem of freedom of the will in Bucer is more accurately a problem of an *Erkenntnisfreiheit*, that is, freedom of knowledge.[183] The unregenerate are unable to truly know God,[184] because they lack the freedom that only comes with the *cognitio Dei*. Humanity without the knowledge to make proper

---

180. *BRom* (1536), 361; (1562), 413; *CP* 103; "far from destroying the freedom of the will, predestination alone really establishes it. For the Spirit of true freedom who enables you to approve the good for yourself and pursue it of your own choice, on your own initiative, compelled by no one against your will, becomes yours only because God has foreknown and predetermined you to be inspired and directed by this Spirit. It is hardly freedom at all to embrace evil instead of good; it is rather the error and bondage of Satan." See Temmel, "Glaube und Gewissheit," 135–143.

181. See David Fink, "'The Doers of the Law Will Be Justified': The Exegetical Origins of Martin Bucer's *Triplex Iustificatio*," *Journal of Theological Studies* 58 (2007): 485–524.

182. *De servo arbitrio; WA* 18, 634–639, 736–740.

183. Müller, *Bucers Hermeneutik*, 38–40, esp. 38n84. Stephens thinks that Müller's point is exaggerated. Stephens states: "Müller over-emphasises the intellectualism of Bucer, which he seeks to demonstrate by showing that for Bucer faith is *persuasio* rather than *fiducia*, that it is a persuasion of the mind rather than a persuasion of the heart, that it is conceived as knowledge, and that the will and the affections are subordinate to the reason" (*Holy Spirit*, 67). Later on, however, Stephens acknowledges that Bucer's "treatment of free will sometimes lack[s] clarity and betray[s] his not always exact use of terms" (261). Though Bucer is intellectualist (contra Stephens), it is important to note that for Bucer it is not necessary that the intellect and will be understood as divided from each other, but, as inferred earlier, they work together almost as a system, with the intellect playing a necessary role in making decisions.

184. *BRom* (1536), 401; (1562), 462; *CP* 148. Bucer's intellectualism is evident when speaking of free choice, stating: "Let us too, therefore, acknowledge that in the goodness of God man is so constituted that he is endowed with the faculty of reason, and of will consequent upon reason, that is to say, with the faculty of free will; and this is a fact we are all aware of by experience."

decisions granted by the Spirit always chooses false goods rather than the true Good.

THEOLOGICAL ANTHROPOLOGY: THE LAW AND KNOWLEDGE OF SIN.   Knowledge of original sin, that is, the inability to contemplate the supreme Good, cannot be grasped without assistance (the *notio Dei*). This assistance, in addition to the works of creation, comes through the hearing of the law,[185] though this is not the sole function of the law for Bucer. The functions he allots to the law amount to the threefold uses of the general Reformed position.

In relation to Romans 3:20–26 (second *observatio*), Bucer states, "All doctrine is the law of God: for it summons one to righteousness and restrains one from perversity, therefore everywhere it brings sin into the open."[186] This knowledge of our sinfulness humbles us in order to seek forgiveness from God;[187] therefore, the law kindles zeal for greater amendment of life:[188] "Through the law comes knowledge of sin: and when we gather for the purpose of hearing the word of God, when we take the sacred books in our hands, let us reflect that here we ought to especially hear and read, in order to learn how wretched we are and in a dire state in every respect: so that thereby of course we may be rendered truly eager for the grace of Christ."[189] Knowledge is gained by the law.[190]

Elsewhere he states, "From Moses on, this evil began to be censured and acknowledged; likewise the necessity to seek a remedy became urgent for men. But such is the raging strength of this evil that, when provoked and aroused by the law, not only is its venom not restrained, it actually seethes more violently, until it is curbed by the Spirit of Christ."[191] In this respect Bucer remains in line with Luther's primary understanding of the law.[192] That is, it prepares one for the gospel.

---

185. Hence Bucer believes that the philosophers who knew of our inherent corruption received this knowledge from Moses. B*Rom* (1536), 267; (1562), 294; *CP* 120; "However, Plato's recognition that the wise man's mind should be free from even the faintest longing for evil was undoubtedly learnt from our religion." Here Bucer is echoing the likes of Justin Martyr and other early Christian apologists.

186. B*Rom* (1536), 199; (1562), 210; "Omnis doctrina Dei lex est: vocat enim ad recta, et revocat a pravis: ubique ergo peccatum ostendit."

187. B*Rom* (1536), 199; (1562), 210; "eoque ipso oportet hinc ad orandum a Deo veniam, nos humiliari."

188. B*Rom* (1536), 199; (1562), 210; "studium vitae emendatioris accendit."

189. B*Rom* (1536), 199; (1562), 210; "Per legem cognitio peccati: et cum ad audiendum verbum Dei convenimus ubi sacros codices in manus sumimus, cogitemus hic nobis praecipue audiendum atque legendum, unde discamus quam sumus miseri, ac modis omnibus perditi: quo nimirum ad Christi gratiam vere avidi reddamur."

190. See Tait, "The Law and Its Works," 60.

191. B*Rom* (1536), 267; (1562), 294-295; *CP* 121. From the *quaestio* on original sin.

192. See Bernhard Lohse, *Martin Luther's Theology: Its Historical and Systematic Development*, trans. Roy Harrisville (Minneapolis, MN: Fortess Press, 1999), 267-274.

However, Bucer refuses to pit the law against the gospel, for he understands that Paul uses the term "law" in two ways. Paul sometimes refers to the "law" and "works of the law" as the entirety of scripture, which leads to both faith and charity,[193] and in a negative manner, when Paul is speaking about those seeking to be justified by the works of the law, he means the ceremonies of the law.[194] The first use in Paul "supplies the sole knowledge of God, of ourselves, of all that it matters to know which our eternal life is established, that is, steadfast and enduring righteousness, the life of God. Hence it is called by Solomon the fount of life and life itself, and it is declared by Paul to train us for salvation."[195] The law is salvific, "it is given for life."[196]

Although its purpose is to bring life, Bucer also states that the law brings wrath, condemns, and even kills. Except this is the case only for the unbeliever, for "those who lack the faith in Christ, by which the mind can be certain of remission of sins and inflamed with zeal for righteousness, this law can be of so little service that it may even cast them down into death and hell itself. For in the first place it shows us sin; indeed it is given not to the righteous, but to the unrighteous."[197] Yet even this can be known only by the gift of the Spirit, the lesser inbreathing.

In this light Bucer identifies faith as the most important concept when looking at law and gospel. For he states that without faith in Christ even the gospel leads to death;

> For what God commands is one thing and what he promises another thing. Sin is laid bare by his commands, the remedy is offered by his promises; righteousness is demanded by his precepts but offered by

---

193. Both Krüger and Koch see this unwillingness to pit law against gospel as a rejection of the Lutheran law/gospel dichotomy, which elevates the status of law over gospel in Bucer's thought. See Krüger, *Bucer und Erasmus*, 75–76; Koch, *Studium Pietatis*, 66–67. However, as we just mentioned, Bucer can still retain the same sense of the law that leads sinners to their need for Christ, as Luther held. He even states that without Christ one can only expect from the law everlasting destruction. *BRom* (1536), 24; (1562), 24. Contra Koch and Küger, see Edwin Tait, who states, "Bucer did not reject the theological point the Lutherans were making about the relationship between command and promise, but as a matter of philological accuracy he did not think that 'law' should be used primarily to refer to the exclusively condemnatory aspects of divine doctrina." Tait, "The Law and Its Works," 59.

194. From Bucer's preface, "What the Law and Works of the Law Are for Paul," *BRom* (1536), 23; (1562), 23; "Hinc factum, ut Legis nomine, vel potius, operum legis aliquando ceremonias intelligat, nonnunquam quaecunque lex iubet, et maxime pertinentia ad innocentiam."

195. *BRom* (1536), 24; (1562), 23; "Solam nanque eam cognitionem Dei, nostri ipsorum, ac omnium quae nosse refert, suppeditat, qua nobis constat aeterna vita, hoc est solida et perennis iustitia, vita Dei. Hinc fons vitae, et vita ipsa dicitur a Salomone, et Paulo erudire nos ad salutem praedicatur."

196. *BRom* (1536), 25; (1562), 25; "Lex enim Dei, ut fidem cum primis docet, ita per se salvifica est: data enim est ad vitam."

197. *BRom* (1536), 24; (1562), 23; "attamen quibus deest fiducia Christi, qua animus et de remissione peccatorum certus sit, et iustitiae studio incensus, his lex tam nihil commodare potest, aut etiam in mortem, ipsamque gehennam eos praecipitet. Nam primum ostendit nobis peccatum: neque enim iustis, sed iniustis data est."

his promises; consciences are cast down by the one and raised up by the other; but each of them, both law and gospel, if the power of Christ be absent by which is given the power to believe the promises of God, is a letter that kills and a vehicle of condemnation. Therefore the consideration of truth leads us to this conclusion that apart from Christ there is nothing that is not harmful—law, gospel, and whatever else God has given us for our salvation, in good things whether of the mind or of the body; so that on the other hand, if Christ embraces us and imparts his spirit, both law and gospel and all things which nature would otherwise utterly abhor and which Satan devises for our harm certainly work together for salvation, everything in its own place.[198]

For the believer, apart from the civil and condemning uses, there is a third use of the law. The law gives us a moral compass; it trains us in salvation. The Christian is not free from the law; rather:

This is what happens in the case of those who live in the faith of Christ; therefore each is free of the law in proportion to his faith. And now since faith has not advanced in anybody to the point that there does not cling to him still an esteem for other things besides Christ, as a result of which he frequently embraces and pursues things from which faith shrinks or even violently recoils, and shudders at things which faith would judge it necessary to pursue and seek in the first place, there remains in all of us even to the end a generous measure of unrighteousness and hence the law too has in us still both its place and its fruit, as the judge and admonisher of this remaining iniquity of ours: This in fact is still the case even when finally the Spirit of Christ flourishes within us, rightly understanding and applying all things. . . . Therefore one understands that when the Spirit renews us, death and condemnation are stripped away and men are thus endowed with the Spirit and so the law is for them a vehicle of salvation and life and for that reason is by no means abolished, and

198. *BRom* (1536), 28; (1562), 27; "Omnino enim aliud est quod deus iubet, aliud quod pollicetur. Iussis proditur peccatum, promissis offertur remedium: praeceptis iustitia exigitur, pollicitis offertur; his conscientiae deiiciuntur, illis eriguntur. Sed utraque, et lex, et Evangelium, si desit vis Christi, qua datur credere promissis dei, sunt litera occidens, certaque condemnationis administratio. Huc ergo veritatis nos ratio ducit, extra Christum nihil non noxium esse, legem, Evangelium, et quicquid deus ad salutem alioqui nostram nobis donavit, in bonis tam animi quam corporis; ut contra si Christus nos complectatur, et de suo impertiat spiritu, cum lex, tum Evangelium, et omnia quae alio qui natura summe horret, quaeque Satan in nostram molitur pernitiem, certo ad salutem cooperantur, unumquodque suo loco."

has all the more effect in everyone the richer one becomes in the Spirit of Christ.[199]

For him the law signifies salvific teaching in both testaments. That is, the commands and promises contemplated with the fuller inbreathing of the Spirit are a "vehicle of salvation and life." Hence, Bucer believed, as Edwin W. Tait states, that "the Torah deserves all the accolades it receives in the Old Testament, but it cannot justify in and of itself, since it has no power to create the internal dispositions of faith and love in which alone true righteousness consists."[200]

So far I have shown how Bucer in his *Romans Commentary* understood humanity and its plight. Sin is an ever-pervasive power latent in our flesh from birth. This power affects the entire person, both the "higher" and "lower" person. Yet it reveals its power most prominently in its attack on reason. No longer are people able to know the truth, whether it be the law or gospel of God. There is nothing individuals can do to gain this truth; they are completely passive in this respect. The elect depend on the Spirit to breathe on them, enabling them then to know the supreme Good. This knowledge of God, in its purest form, is salvation. From here we will be able to see more precisely how Bucer's view of justification by faith incorporates works of love.

Justification by Faith and Works of Love

It is the gospel message that Christ came to save humanity. Humanity is not required to do anything for its salvation because, "solely for the sake of our Lord Jesus Christ and out of no regard for merit of our own, God forgives us our sins and bestows on us eternal life."[201]

The question of how Christ's perfect work was appropriated to the believer has repeatedly been at the forefront of the Church's theological program.

---

199. *BRom* (1536), 27–28; (1562), 27; "Ita ut fit apud eos, qui in fide vivunt Christi: lege ergo quisque liber est, pro portione fidei. Iam cum haec fides in nemine eo processit, ut non haereat in eo adhuc aestimatio rerum aliarum praeter Christum, ex qua fit, ut saepenum ero amplectatur, et consectetur, a quibus fides abhorret, et contra resiliat, horreatque ab his quae fidei in primis iudicantur expetenda et quaerenda, multa ad finem usque manet in nobis omnibus iniustitiae portio, indeque habet et lex apud nos adhuc suum et locum et fructum, huius nostrae reliquae iniquitatis iudex et admonitrix; id vero tum demum quando viget apud nos spiritus Christi, rite omnia intelligens, et usurpans. . . . Intelligitur ergo legem sicut spiritu renovato re destitutis condemnationis ac mortis, ita hoc spiritu praeditis, salutis et vitae esse administrationem, ac ideo haudquaquam abolitam, sed apud unumquenque eo valere amplius; quo spiritu Christi fuerit ditior."

200. Tait, "The Law and Its Works," 60.

201. *BRom* (1536), 18; (1562), 18; *CP* 183.

How does salvation come to me? Answers to this question abounded in late-medieval Europe. For the predominant school of the fifteenth century and early sixteenth century, the *via moderna*, the answer was found in the Latin phrase *facere quod in se est*. For the evangelicals, this phrase distorted the good news, weakened Christ's complete work, and thus gave humanity partial responsibility for its salvation. The evangelical reformers argued that individuals cannot be a cause of their salvation; they are passive; salvation is given as a gift.

This gift of salvation was given to humanity, according to Bucer, in the following *ordo salutis* (order of salvation). Bucer derived this *ordo salutis* primarily from Romans 8:28–30. In his *quaestio* concerning predestination on this passage of scripture, he states that "the saints may have complete certainty that those whom God has predestined [*praedestinavit*] he will also call [*vocaturum*], justify [*iustificaturum*] and glorify [*glorificaturum*], and those whom he has already called he has also undoubtedly foreknown and predetermined."[202] The order can be characterized as *electio* (or *praedestinatio*)—*vocatio*—*iustificatio*—*glorificatio*.[203]

---

202. *BRom* (1536), 359; (1562), 411; *CP* 100.

203. I say broadly, because various manners of listing the process of salvation in Bucer's corpus have caused debate over what ought to be included in the order and how the order should be understood. I believe that Bucer's *ordo* is best described as follows: election, vocation, justification, and glorification. The recent debate over the *ordo* stems from Peter Stephens's inclusion of sanctification as a separate category within Bucer's order. Stephens himself admits that Bucer inserts *sanctificatio* only once in a short work *Contra Bernard Wacker* (1533), in *TAE* 2, no. 445, 197. See Stephens, *Holy Spirit*, 21. Nevertheless, he holds that the inclusion of *sanctificatio* is warranted because it is implied in both Paul's and Bucer's theology. However, such a move defines *iustificatio* in a way that possibly betrays Bucer's understanding of the term and order. Against Stephens, Alister McGrath, argues that "Bucer does not, as one of his recent interpreters suggests, include sanctification in the *ordo salutis*: what was later termed *sanctificatio* by Calvin is termed 'secondary justification' or *iustificatio pii* by Bucer" (*Iustitia Dei*, 253). Stephens replied to McGrath's critique, stating that McGrath's analysis depends solely on Bucer's later works, and therefore he has neglected Bucer's earlier works, especially the *Ephesians Commentary* (1527) (see Stephens, "Bucer's Commentaries on Ephesians," 48n8). However, even the evidence that Stephens cites for his case, that Bucer uses the term holiness (instead of justification) in his order in both the *Ephesians Commentaries* and the *John Commentary*, does not justify a separation of justification from sanctification. One could argue that, if anything, it confirms the semiotic range that Bucer gives to the concept of justification. Sanctification and justification are understood as organically united. Cf. *BRom* (1536), 355; (1562), 405, *praescitos*—*praedefinitos*—*vocatos*—*iustificatos*—*glorificatos*. Cf. *BGospels* (1536), 771, *ordo salutis*: [*electio* presumed]—*electis annunciatur*—*fidutia et amor nascuntur*; *BEph* (1527), 26, *notandus ordo: electio / praedestinatio*—*vocatio*—*glorificatio*.

The way in which this order should be taken, whether it be chronological or logical, is of second importance. This distinction seems partially unfounded because Bucer himself did not make it. Stephens's logical understanding (against Müller's chronological understanding) seems to stem from his desire to insert *sanctificatio* as a fifth category into the order, separating it logically from *iustificatio*. To do so is an imprecise description of how Bucer understands justification. For Bucer the order of salvation is both chronological (because each point in the order has real implications in and out of time) and logical (because the order proceeds from cause to effects). The two hang together. For Stephens's view, see *Holy Spirit*, 37–38; for Müller's view, see *Bucers Hermeneutik*, 24.

Vocatio

Having already touched upon *electio*, I proceed to *vocatio*. For Bucer *vocatio* is understood logically as two modes: general and particular, or outer and inner.[204]

The outer or general *vocatio* is viewed as the reading or preaching of the gospel, from which arises an encounter with God's revelation and his promise of forgiveness by means of our eyes or ears, that is, the senses.[205] The gospel must be presented externally either "in writing or aurally."[206] This is because knowledge comes from the senses; listening to the gospel grants an attentive listener sensual knowledge of the gospel" "Lest you believe anything about anything, it is necessary that you first hear that which you ought to believe in; faith is received through words. Thus all who call upon God necessarily believe in him, and for those who truly believe it is necessary that they hear the things about God which are fitting to believe."[207]

For salvation to occur, however, this outer or general *vocatio* requires the greater inbreathing of the Spirit, which is understood as the inner or particular *vocatio*.[208] In regard to this particular vocation Bucer states that "the Lord from the beginning adopted these people and he chose them from all the people of the world so that he might impart to them his Spirit, and hence that

204. There are exceptions to this twofold manner when a particular vocation occurs as in the case of Paul's Damascus road experience. God's preferred manner of inspiring faith involves the outer Word in conjunction with the inner. Cf. Stephens, *Holy Spirit*, 43–47. The inner word can be identified as a *vocatio specialis*. *BRom* (1536), 399; (1562), 459; "Sic est ergo ratio Dei, hos ipsi visum est, omnes quidem ad se vocare externo verbo, non autem omnes ad se spiritu suo attrahere." The general or outer *vocatio* can be heard by both the gentile and the elect. However, the particular vocation is primarily understood as *vocatio* proper, given solely to the elect, which explains the text "many are called but few are chosen" (Matt. 21:14). Cf. *duplex vocatio* in *BGospels* (1536), 411.

205. The scriptures are the concrete place where man encounters the revelation of God. *BRom* (1536), 420; (1562) 486, in the *expositio* of Rom. 10:12–17; "Atqui fides requirit praedicationem Evangelii, cui fides adhibenda est, praedicatio missionem praedicatorum."

206. *BRom* (1536), 15; (1562), 15; *CP* 175. Cf. *BGospel* (1536), 220; "Sic ex audito Evangelio fides, id est sacra huiusmodi de Christo persuasio, hoc est, πίστις et אמונה in animo eius provenit."

207. *BRom* (1536), 420; (1562), 486; "Ut enim quidpiam credas de aliquo, necesse est te audire ante, id quod credere de eo debeas, Fides habetur dictis. Ut ergo Deum omnes invocent, necesse est ut omnes ei credant, ut vero credant, necesse est ut id de Deo audiant, quod credere oportet."

208. *BRom* (1536), 410; (1562) 473; "Necesse est igitur, ut a domino [homines] praeveniantur, cum externa praedicatione evangelii, tum interno adflatu spiritus sancti, quo audito Evangelio credant, et credentes iustificentur." Bucer's continual dialogues and debates with Anabaptists, especially Caspar Schwenkfeld and Sebastian Frank, perhaps influenced the close proximity of Word and Spirit in Bucer's thought. See André Séguenny, "Why Bucer Detested the Spiritualists: Some Reflections on Reading Bucer's Dialogues of 1535," *Mennonite Quarterly Review* 68 (1994): 51–58; and R. Emmet McLaughlin, "The Politics of Dissent: Martin Bucer, Caspar Schwenckfeld, and the Schwenkfelders of Strasbourg," *Mennonite Quarterly Review* 68 (1994): 59–78. Bucer's strong insistence when commenting on Rom. 10:17 that faith cannot come without the scriptures administered by men can be seen as deriving from the debate with sectarianism, which elevates the inner word over against the outer word. *BRom* (1536), 422; (1562), 488; "Impossibile igitur est ad fidem pervenire, pervenire ad vitam aeternam, nisi audieris Evangelium, idque administratum per hominem." See Barnikol, "Bucers Lehre," 54–57.

they may live in his glory."[209] The glory for which we are made begins with this chronological-causal understanding of the inspiration of the Spirit:

> Of course, one effect of predestination becomes the cause of another: the inspiration of the Holy Spirit creates soundness of judgment, a sound judgment issues in uprightness of will, an upright will produces holiness of conduct, and holy conduct obtains the reward which the Lord of his boundless goodness bestows on it. But all of these are the result solely of the unmerited kindness of God.[210]

The calling to faith and the gift of faith can be approximately understood under these two modes of *vocatio* in the *ordo salutis*.[211] Admittedly, Stephens highlights the difficulty in separating vocation from justification, yet vocation is always, for Bucer, the first movement toward salvation after election that leads to both justification and glorification.[212] This highlights later the role he gives to justification. Justification is not only about faith but also about love, and hence *vocatio* and justification are associated with faith.[213]

Faith

The medieval scholastics had been toiling over the doctrine of justification and the theology of Paul for decades.[214] In the course of their discussion the schoolmen developed an intricate understanding of faith; they spoke of faith in terms of *fides quae, fides implicita, fides explicita, fides acquisita, fides infusa, fides informis*, and *fides formata charitate*.[215] The evangelical reformers discarded these multifarious

---

209. *BRom* (1536), 186; (1562), 193; "Dominum ab initio populum istum assumpsisse sibi, et ex omnibus populis orbis selegisse in hoc, ut suum eis spiritum impertiret, indeque ipsi in gloriam ipsius viverent."

210. *BRom* (1536), 360; (1562), 412; *CP* 102.

211. In the *Romans Commentary*, Bucer also calls vocation conversion, attraction, or being grafted into Christ. *BRom* (1536), 356; (1562), 407; "D. Augustinus in loco supra adducto ex libro de Corrept. et gratia ait subaudiendum esse: Ad hoc, vocavit, secundum propositum. De vocatione enim hic Apostolus loquitur, quae verbo fit et spiritu Christi adeo efficaci, ut et conversio, attractio, et in Christum insitio sit et vocetur."

212. *BRom* (1536), 400; (1562), 460; "Certum enim est, ut vocationi dei quis pareat, quod est initium totius salutis, id esse donum et opus dei, quod deus aliis largitur, aliis negat. Illis enim suadet ut persuadeat: his non ita: et non possunt non sequi vocantem quibus persuadet, nec sequi quibus non persuadet." At one point in the commentary he associates *poenitentia* (repentance) with *vocatio*. See *BRom* (1536), 446; (1562), 519.

213. Müller, *Bucers Hermeneutik*, 24n38. Here I agree with Müller, who believes that we must not overlook the fact that, for Bucer, *vocatio* is understood as *adoptio in filios*, which is the indication of a knowledge of God closely combined with faith.

214. Heiko A. Oberman, *Forerunners of the Reformation: The Shape of Late Medieval Thought* (Cambridge: James Clarke, 2002), 121–141.

215. *OER* 2:89–93; *fides quae* (the content of faith), *fides qua* (that by which one believes or the subjective act of faith), *fides implicita* (a layperson's faith in everything the Church believes), *fides explicita* (a priest's faith, which understands the meaningfulness of every article of faith), *fides acquisita* (the faith acquired by natural means like listening to a sermon, sometimes said to be equal to historical faith), *fides infusa* (the gift of faith

definitions. For these reformers there was only true faith; any other faith was merely opinion,[216] a human notion and dream.[217] Accordingly, they sought to rescue *fides* from its medieval categories, primarily by delving into the Pauline epistles.

In the beginning of the *Romans Commentary*, Bucer elucidates Paul's understanding of faith in an extensive preface entitled "What Paul Means by the Words '*Fidei*' and '*Credere.*'"[218] Here, Bucer, the accomplished Hebraist,[219] delves into Paul's rabbinic mind in a rigorous attempt to define אמן, πίστις, and *fides.*[220]

Bucer's definition of *fides* there illustrates that for him *fides* is understood as the result of two stages of instruction, which results in trust in God.[221] The first stage takes place in the classroom of God's creation and is the *notio Dei* (the lesser inbreathing). The second stage includes being instructed in the gospel and results in knowledge not only that God exists but also that he is God for us, *pro nobis*. This second stage is a result of the fuller inbreathing of the Spirit, which results in the *cognitio Dei*. Finally, this knowledge of God, which results in assenting to these truths by means of the sure persuasion of the Holy Spirit, leads to complete trust in the promises of God. *Persuasio* leads to *fiducia*.

THE BEGINNING OF FAITH: FIRST LEVEL OF KNOWLEDGE.   Because we are all born into the classroom of God's handiwork, we all possess a general knowledge that God exists. Were it not for the partial inbreathing of the Spirit, we would not even recognize this truth: "For such darkness covered us from our tainted birth that unless fresh light were infused into us from above we could perceive none of the things of God."[222] This is akin to the *notio Dei*, which we have spoken of elsewhere. Apart from creation, in this stage there is also the possibility of gaining further understanding of God by oracles and stories that have been passed on from person to person.

---

supernaturally infused in the soul), *fides informis* (faith unformed by love which can exist with mortal sins), and *fides formata charitate* (faith formed by and active in love).

216. *BRom* (1536), 21–22; (1562), 21; *CP* 192.

217. *WA.DB.* 7, 9.

218. "Quid Paulo Venit Verbis Fidei et Credere," 9th Preface (1536), 14–23; (1562), 14–22.

219. See Gerald R. Hobbs, "Martin Bucer on Psalm 22: A Study in the Application of Rabbinic Exegesis by a Christian Hebraist," in *Histoire de l'exégèse au XVIe siècle: Textes du Colloque International Tenu a Genève en 1976*, ed. Olivier Fatio and Pierre Fraenkel (Geneva: Droz, 1978), 144–163.

220. *BRom* (1536), 21–22; (1562), 21; *CP* 192.

221. Bucer describes a similar threefold movement toward faith in his exposition of the story of the Centurion in his *Gospels Commentary*. First, faith is typically connected to the external preaching of the gospel (akin to the general *vocatio*). Second, the Holy Spirit persuades the hearer that the message is absolutely true (akin to the particular *vocatio*). Finally, this leads to a life that trusts in God. *Persuasio* leads to *fiducia*. The Centurion in the story is depicted as hearing the preached gospel; having heard, his reason gained *fides*, that is, a convincing knowledge of Christ. See *BGospel* (1536), 219–220.

222. *BRom* (1536), 15; (1562), 15; *CP* 174.

In this manner, then, from the contemplation of the wonderful
workmanship of heaven and earth, from the excellent works of
providence which it daily displays, and from the oracles granted to all
peoples and all ages, and thereafter transmitted from mouth to
mouth, from generation to generation, and further by the light
shining from above men first learnt of the being of God, that is, that
he is supreme power and supreme goodness, the supreme power by
which all things both were fashioned and also are preserved, the
Divinity which governs the universe, possessing strength and
goodness to repay every man according to his deeds.[223]

In addition to this understanding of the existence of God, a further understanding can be achieved by means of special revelation.[224] Thus creation, oracles,
and special revelations are the specific classrooms for this first-level knowledge
of God, but it is our heavenly schoolmaster, the Holy Spirit, who is the active
agent teaching us of God's existence (however poor this might be). Without the
Spirit, humanity remains completely ignorant of God.

This first level of knowledge is not faith but the beginning of faith.[225] It is
a preparatory work of the Spirit, which allows the elect to be persuaded of the
gospel at a latter stage (akin to prevenient grace). While describing *fides* and
credere he alludes to this initial faith, stating:

Therefore, "to believe" [*credere*] as not only Paul but the whole of
scripture uses it, if you take it in a general sense, is obviously the
equivalent of "concur with what is said," and "faith" [*fides*], the equivalent
of "the assent we give to what God says." Just as it is essential to have
prior knowledge of God and to regard him as worthy of faith, likewise
unless we accept the testimony he bears of himself to us, we are
incapable of acknowledging him; and only then do we acknowledge
God's own words when he himself shows us, irradiated by his own
light that they are his own. The beginning of faith, then, is to be so
breathed upon by the Spirit of God that we accept all that from the first
he has imparted about himself to our minds, and all that day by day he
instills in them, all too that he declares by the visible testimony of his
wondrous works of the Godhead, which long ago he set forth for men

223. *BRom* (1536), 15; (1562), 15; *CP* 174.
224. *BRom* (1536), 15; (1562), 15; *CP* 174; "To men already imbued with this kind of knowledge and appreciation of God, and further means of revelation he employed, whether the ministry of men or angels, or at other
times a secret prompting, carried his own weight and authority, so as to be received by ready minds, and encountered the response of faith."
225. *BRom* (1536), 15; (1562), 15; *CP* 176.

to behold in the structure of this world, and which daily he performs anew, and finally all that men proclaim to us about him—and accept it all so readily that we do not doubt that he is God, that is, the Supreme Good which has created and preserves and perfects all things.[226]

Consequently, at this preliminary level of instruction we are only able to assent to "God's being and to providence."[227]

Knowledge of God's existence and providence is dependent on God's perceived authority. Hence during this stage we gain the knowledge of his ultimate authority by his Spirit irradiating us: "For when the process of reasoning by which our mind recognizes what is said to be true does not apply and the authority of the speaker alone evokes faith, the will is inevitably inclined toward the speaker and possessed by love and admiration for him."[228]

This preparatory knowledge before true faith illustrates Bucer's anthropological partiality to the mind's role in salvation. Knowledge is necessary to know what to have faith in. This perspective does not, however, necessitate that faith be solely intellectualist; for it is the case that Bucer understands the entire person as being moved in the act of faith, both reason and will, mind and heart.

FAITH: SECOND LEVEL OF KNOWLEDGE.   The second course of instruction builds upon the necessary knowledge of God's existence. Instead of being taught by means of nature or tradition's stories, here we are taught by the gospel. This instruction leads to a greater knowledge not only of God but also of ourselves.

> At this stage it is the gospel we are taught, in which God sets before us what he has bestowed on us, and will henceforth bestow, through our Lord Jesus Christ, for we can attain the knowledge of God only by knowledge of what he is and purposes to be to us. Therefore, through the gospel is presented this promise of his kindness in Christ our Lord, that through him he means to be all things to us, to forgive our sins and make us partakers of eternal life. Assent is given to this promise by those upon whom he breathes by his Spirit; by the Spirit alone can it be acknowledged as the promise of God. This assent is the evangelical faith of which Paul speaks.[229]

This second level of knowledge is granted by a greater illumination of the Holy Spirit. It is here where we learn of God's exhortations to holiness, of the gospel,

---

226. *BRom* (1536), 15–16; (1562), 15; *CP* 175–176.
227. *BRom* (1536), 16; (1562), 15; *CP* 176.
228. *BRom* (1536), 15; (1562), 14; *CP* 173–174.
229. *BRom* (1536), 16; (1562), 15–16; *CP* 176–177.

and, most important, of what God means to be for us (in particular his desire to forgive sins and grant eternal life). When believers assent to this knowledge, it is because all that they have learned has been due to the Spirit's persuasion showing them that these things are certain and true. *Fides* is characterized by *persuasio*.

Bucer defines *fides* primarily as this act of assent, which is better defined by the term *persuasio*. In an exhaustive word study, he states:

> The Hebrew for "faith" and "believe" (אמונה, האמין) are both derived from אמן, which means "sure, settled, firm," so that האמין (to believe) has the force of "to be made firm, to become sure," and אמונה (faith) connotes "assuredness, confirmation." In Exodus 17 it is said of the hands of Moses held up by Aaron and Hur and thereby made steady, "And his hands became אמונה," that is, sureness or firmness, and thus firm and unmoved. Now what word could more fully express the character of faith? For the mind is made completely firm and stable, as it were, by the divine promises, no longer wavering between conflicting conjectures and opinions, and tending in opposite directions. For how can anyone continue to vacillate and waver rather than rest steadfastly and immovably upon the sacred divine promises, once he knows for certain by the influence and illumination of the Spirit of God that they are God's promises and will stand fast when heaven and earth are changed?

> Similarly the Greek term for "faith," πίστις, derived ἀπο τὸ πέπεισμαι, meaning "I am persuaded" [*persuasus sum*], speaks of a persuasion [*persuasionem*] free from uncertainty, a sure confidence in what is said (though as always happens, the Greeks put the word to numerous other uses). Πιστεύω ἀπὸ τôs πίστος, means "I have faith, I am persuaded" [*fidem habeo, persuasum teneo*]. The philosophers confuse πιστίς (faith) with opinion, as Plato does, or make it subsequent to opinion, as Aristotle, but they are speaking of a faith that is of human origin, we of the faith we have in the words of God and under the influence of the Holy Spirit. However, Aristotle also says this, that "being persuaded follows upon faith" (πίστει ἀκολούθει πέπεισθει).

> The Latin term for "faith," *fides*, is also quite appropriate; it is so called because there comes to pass [*fio*] what is said [*dico*]. We are also properly said to "believe" [*credere*] when we apply such faith to another's words or promises that we are free from all doubt.[230] The

---

230. Here Bucer's etymology is contrived. Cf. T. G. Tucker, *Etymological Dictionary of Latin* (Halle: Max Niemeyer, 1931), 96.

Latins accounted credulity [*credulitas*] a fault, but this is a propensity for believing easily in men, who by nature deceive and are deceived. "For every man is vanity and a lie."[231]

Persuasio is Bucer's preferred understanding for πίστις. Bucer's first definition of *fides* in the *Romans Commentary* highlights this case: "Faith is the certain persuasion through the Holy Spirit of God's love and fatherly kindness toward us, in reliance upon our Lord Jesus Christ, who by his death has expiated our sins, and by his life through which he now reigns, makes us partakers of his righteousness."[232] This *certa persuasio* is essential to the definition of faith. For how can faith, a gift from God himself, include any doubt? Such a perfect persuasion through the Holy Spirit must lead to a perfect trust (*fiducia*). The adjective *certa* with *persuasio* clearly demonstrates that faith is this certain conviction.[233]

Bucer's strong correlation of faith with certain persuasion comes out of his zealous pursuit of knowledge and truth. He was driven to put on the black and white habit not by religious anxiety, as it was for Luther, but by truth and the pursuit thereof.[234] The monastery was less a means of ensuring salvation than it was a means for Claus Butzer Sr. to ensure that his grandson received a good education. Ironically, it was this impulse for knowledge, spurred on now by humanist authors, that partially drove him out of the monastery.[235] Thus, if for Luther, faith was entrusting oneself entirely to God as an existential act with the cognitive element of faith attenuated, Bucer came at the question differently.[236] Bucer was "striving after clearer religious knowledge."[237]

---

231. *BRom* (1536), 21–22; (1562), 21; *CP* 192. Similar descriptions are found in his *Ephesians Commentary*. *BEph* (1527), 19. There, Bucer translates πίστις as *persuasio* and sees *fides* as a mistranslation, a μετάληψις (μετάληψις is an alteration in the sense of the word). He states: "Paulo it aque fides propie persuasio est, qua mens de verbis Domini nihil addubitat, persuasa scilicet a Spiritu sancto." See also *BGospels* (1536), 219–220.

232. *BRom* (1536), 6; (1562), 6; *CP* 196n1. See also (1536), 14; (1562) 14; *CP* 172.

233. See Krüger, *Bucer und Erasmus*, 158–159.

234. The certainty of one's salvation was for Luther impossible. Hence, his Reformation discovery was due in part to his lack of certainty, certainty of whether he had genuinely achieved the required minimum of repentance. Faith was for him nothing other than the promise and gift of God, which was completely opposite to any ritual piety. See Heiko A. Oberman, *Luther: Man between God and the Devil*, trans. Eileen Walliser-Schwarzbart (New York: Image Books, 1992), 177.

235. In his *Verantwortung* (1523), (*Bibliographie* 3), in *BDS* I, 160, ll. 3–23. Bucer states that the Dominican monks had forced him to cease his studies and forbidden him to read. See Müller, *Bucers Hermeneutik*, 25–27.

236. For Luther on faith, see Paul Althaus, *The Theology of Martin Luther*, trans. Robert C. Schulz (Philadelphia: Fortress Press, 1966), 43–63.

237. Müller, *Bucers Hermeneutik*, 25. See also Krüger, *Bucer und Erasmus*, 163. This aspect is particularly clear in his citation of Pseudo-Dionysius's *The Divine Names*. Bucer states: "since Dionysius expresses our point quite wonderfully in the sublime, almost inspired characteristic of all his writings, we will quote what his work on *The Divine Names* has to say about faith. 'Faith,' he writes, 'relates to the divine Reason, which is the simple and truly existent truth, and so the solid foundation of believers, establishing both them in the truth and the truth in them with an unwavering permanence. For those who believe and are persuaded possess a simple knowledge of the truth, and this knowledge avails to unite the knower and the objects of knowledge, while ignorance is ever the cause of change and self-discrepancy in the ignorant. Consequently, the man who believes in the truth according to

Understanding Bucer's thought gives us an initial insight into why he understood faith as he did. Faith was a result of instruction, an accumulation of knowledge about God from nature, tradition, miracles, commands, promises, and the gospel illuminated by the Holy Spirit to be true and certain. This certainty, incited by the Spirit, leads to our complete trust in God, the final aspect of a certain persuasion.

TRUST.   The certain *persuasio* of a second-level knowledge results in *fiducia*:

> Those to whom it [evangelical faith] is granted, being now convinced beyond doubt [*pro indubitato habent*] that having clasped them in his ineffable love God will bestow all good things upon them, will be bound to place their whole trust [*fiduciam*] in him, and will love and worship him with all their heart and soul and strength, and as a result only what is approved by God will be pleasing to their mind, and, being on fire with love for their neighbor and an all-consuming zeal for righteousness, they will live only to God, and God will be their whole life.[238]

This trust is the result of the illuminated authority of God's word for believers.[239] Believers trust God, the supreme Good, because he is the highest and most reliable authority.[240]

Again Bucer's intellectualist inclination is founded on the strong conviction that the Spirit's illuminated knowledge of who God is and of who God wants to be toward his elect must result in this perfect trust and love for God.[241] Bucer states: "Similarly, the saints who believe God's promise of remission of

---

the sacred word will never be dislodged from the stable foundation furnished by faith, on which he will surely enjoy the security of immovable and immutable permanence. Indeed, he who is united with the truth knows perfectly that all is well with him, even though the multitude rebuke him for being out of his mind; for it naturally escapes them that he has been rescued from error by the truth through true faith. But he knows well enough for himself that instead of being, as they say, out of his senses, he has been delivered from the unstable and ever-varying twists and turns of protean error through simple, self-consistent, unchanging truth. Hence it is that our chief preceptors in divine wisdom die daily for the truth, thereby bearing witness by both word and deed to that singular knowledge of the truth which Christians profess, testifying that it is more simple and divine than all other forms of knowledge, or rather that it is the only true, the only simple knowledge of God.'" *BRom* (1536), 22; (1562), 22; *CP* 194–195.

238. *BRom* (1536), 16; (1562), 16; *CP* 177.

239. *BRom* (1536), 15; (1562), 15; *CP* 175; "Being quickened by the Spirit of God they at once accepted the authority of the God who offered the gospel, and by giving credence to the gospel they became firmly persuaded of their redemption through Christ as declared by the gospel, and so they believed the gospel, believed in Christ, and obtained salvation."

240. *BRom* (1536), 22; (1562), 22; *CP* 194. Bucer states that we are moved to believe "by his authority alone."

241. *BRom* (1536), 16; (1562), 16; *CP* 178; "Is there anyone who knows beyond doubt that his life and all things lie at someone else's disposal, and that this person grants him a complete pardon when he deserved the ultimate penalty, and singles him out for his love and adopts him as his son and designates him to be his heir, and that there is nothing in the world that can look kindly upon him without the other's behest—is there anyone, tell me, who would not place his whole trust in such a person and honour him above all else?"

sins and eternal life cannot fail to rejoice with confident exultation, and to devote themselves wholeheartedly to God, their supreme benefactor. *For a man's affections and conduct are determined in their entirety by his mental convictions.*"[242] Therefore, this trust in God founded on illuminated knowledge results inevitably in love.

Faith and Love

It is inconceivable that this certain knowledge of a loving God can lead to anything less than love. For how can you know that God loves you, forgives you, and desires only good for you and yet not reciprocate this love? How can one know the good and not choose to do it? For Bucer, faith and works of love are like fire and heat, inseparable.[243]

In this manner, through the knowledge of God's love, love is inspired in the believer. That is, works of love are not divorced from this certain faith.[244] In the preface on faith he objects to the opinion of the schoolmen, who separate faith from love.[245] He states:

> But in one respect they have apparently failed to understand their
> own position; they teach that this assent, though given to the words
> of God out of an ingrafted faith, can exist without the love of God. For
> they make this assent more certain than any acquired knowledge,
> because it rests upon divine truth while knowledge depends on
> human reason, and they also recognize that every person is
> motivated by his will according to the degree to which he becomes
> aware that something is for his good. . . . Now anyone can easily see

---

242. *BRom* (1536), 16; (1562), 16; *CP* 177; emphasis added.

243. *BRom* (1536), 120; (1562), 106.

244. Barnikol and Temmel see faith and works as separate aspects of justification. However, this is because of the failure to understand the strong intellectual framework in Bucer's thought, which demands that true faith results in good works; see Barnikol, "Bucers Lehre," 170; Temmel, "Glaube und Gewissheit," 165–167. See also *BRom* (1536), 16; (1562), 16; *CP* 178, where Bucer criticizes the scholastics for separating faith from love.

245. It seems here that he is going against Thomas, where Thomas can distinguish between formed and unformed faith in *ST* 2a 2ae q.4 a.4. There Thomas states that "the distinction of formed from unformed faith is in respect of something pertaining to the will, that is, charity, and not in respect of something pertaining to the intellect." Here Thomas holds two types of faith (one with love, the other without), yet the latter is not a virtue and therefore not justifying or perfecting faith. Later on in article 7, Thomas asserts that faith is the foremost virtue of the theological virtues, but nonetheless that "to be a foundation a thing requires not only to come first, but also to be connected with the other parts of the building: since the building would not be founded on it unless the other parts adhered to it. Now the connecting bond of the spiritual edifice is charity, according to Col. 3:14: 'Above all . . . things have charity which is the bond of perfection.' Consequently faith without charity cannot be the foundation: and yet it does not follow that charity precedes faith." Therefore, even Thomas held a strong bond between love and faith, as Bucer wishes to maintain.

the serious inconsistency between the claim that faith can exist without love for God, and these other beliefs of theirs. For if a person has been enabled to give credence to the Scriptures and be less in doubt about their message than if he had established its certainty by reasoning, how can he possibly believe with full personal conviction that God is as compassionate and well-disposed towards him as the Scriptures present him to us, and yet fail to love him from the heart and commit himself wholly to him? . . . And will the man who has through faith a certainty greater than that of knowledge, the certainty that in God he lives and moves and has his being, that in his unspeakable goodness and compassion when he deserved eternal death he translated him to share in eternal life by delivering up his own Son to death for his sake—will he then be indifferent towards God?[246]

At the core of this error is the inclusion of uncertainty in one's own salvation. Bucer sees this uncertainty as the result of a mistranslation of Ecclesiastes 9 that resulted in a "gospel" of works righteousness.

The medieval translation of Ecclesiastes 9:1b reads: "Man knows not whether he is worthy of love or of hatred."[247] This Latin translation of the Hebrew, for Bucer, led to misunderstanding.[248] According to Bucer, the Hebrew does not convey the same sense of uncertainty; contrariwise, it grants certainty that all things are in God's hands. Thus, after giving his own translation of the text in question, he concludes, "Whoever reads the whole of this chapter will realize that Solomon means to persuade us to acknowledge that all things are in the hand of God; it is his resolve that in this life so far as our outward lot is concerned, everything happens to good and evil alike, and no definite calculation can be made of all that happens."[249] Consequently, one ought to be content with what happens in one's life, whether it be for good or bad.

This verse was used by theologians of the latter Middle Ages to discourage certainty of forgiveness and thus to encourage a humility that embraced an uncertainty of one's forgiveness of sins. The late-medieval virtuoso Gabriel Biel embodied this interpretation, teaching that one cannot be certain of

---

246. *BRom* (1536), 16; (1562), 16; *CP* 178–179.

247. Eccl. 9:1b; "et tamen nescit homo utrum amore an odio dignus sit."

248. *BRom* (1536), 17; (1562), 17; *CP* 180n41; see also Calvin in *Institutes* III 2. 38, who also discusses this error.

249. *BRom* (1536), 17; (1562), 17; *CP* 180. The verse in Hebrew is terse and ambiguous, yet Bucer's emphasis is echoed by modern exegetes who clarify that the central theme is that death comes to both the righteous and the wicked. Cf. Roland E. Murphy, *Word Biblical Commentary: Ecclesiastes*, vol. 23a (Dallas, TX: Word Books, 1992), 88–94, esp. 94.

possessing grace. For him this very uncertainty is encouraged, in that this "constant oscillation between love and fear is in itself a sign for the *viator* that he is still on the road to the heavenly Jerusalem and that he is sufficiently prepared for the inhabitation of Christ."[250] Out of this theological setting the pastoral theology of the day focused on love and works as granting the populace greater assurance of grace.

But Bucer's exegesis of Ecclesiastes 9 reveals that "there is nothing here to encourage lack of conviction in the saints about God's love towards them."[251] A Christian must hold the contrary. It is from a firm assurance granted by the Holy Spirit that we can cry out to God, "Abba, Father."[252] Hence, if you doubt that God is your Father and your Savior, you cannot love God: "For either you do not acknowledge Christ's redemption at all, or if you do, you will be persuaded to the exclusion of every doubt, that through Christ God is so favorably disposed towards you that you enjoy the position of his son and an heir of eternal life; nor is it for a time only but forever that he has absolved those who are sanctified."[253] This error "is what has caused men to defect from the word of God's promise of grace."[254] The result is that many in the Church have gained a

> vain and ruinous trust in their own righteousness, in others of an
> ineluctable torment of conscience, in many of wholesome despair,
> because no man is able to progress so far in righteousness that, when
> the searchlight of divine judgment shines into his mind, he can avoid
> realizing full well that all he has achieved is far from sufficient to win
> God's reconciliation and his bestowal of eternal life.[255]

This lack of certainty resulted in an overzealous emphasis on love and works, neglecting the truth that salvation is a gift; it cannot be earned. The elect are the elect for salvation by faith.[256] And hence the command to believe in God is fulfilled by God himself, for faith is a gift mysteriously given as a result of the prime cause: God's goodwill.

Love is intimately associated with faith because the certain persuasion in God inevitably results in love. Recruiting Augustine for his cause, he states

250. Quoted in Heiko A. Oberman, *The Harvest of Medieval Theology: Gabriel Biel and Late Medieval Nominalism*, 3rd ed (Grand Rapids, MI: Baker Academic, 2002), 230.
251. *BRom* (1536), 17; (1562), 17; *CP* 181.
252. *BRom* (1536), 17–18; (1562), 17; *CP* 181.
253. *BRom* (1536), 18; (1562), 17; *CP* 182.
254. *BRom* (1536), 18; (1562), 17; *CP* 182.
255. *BRom* (1536), 18; (1562), 17–18; *CP* 182.
256. *BRom* (1536), 359; (1562), 411; *CP* 99.

that "the exclusion of all doubt from this faith was his [Augustine's] regular teaching, especially by means of the arguments that 'faith works through love,' which is a thing faith is unable to do except by relying fully and completely on God's word, and that it is created by that 'teaching of the Father' which all who receive cannot fail to come to Christ, albeit they come perfectly willingly."[257]

Love is the result of faith; lack of love signals a lack of faith. Therefore, Bucer always included love of one's neighbor within his definitions of justification, making his love, as Thomas Torrance remarked, "the most moving and characteristic element in Butzer's theology."[258]

Works

By faith we are saved, and for Bucer this effects a real change in this present life, resulting in true happiness. As experience has taught him, all of humanity desires happiness and preservation of life; humanity was created with these desires. For Bucer happiness (*felicitas*), what the Greeks call εὐθυμία (*euthumia*), can only be realized once we have knowledge that God is favorable to us, and that is why "in all religions means of expiating sins and appeasing the deity have featured first and foremost, for human nature is so constituted that we continually covet our own preservation and prosperity."[259]

This inborn constitution, that is, the pursuit of happiness, produces an uneasy anxiety when a person's sins are not forgiven.[260] The wrath of God toward them obstructs true happiness. Therefore, in a similar manner to that described in Luther's tract *On the Freedom of a Christian* (1520), the believer's anxiety is silenced by the gospel of God's goodwill and mercy, consequently

---

257. *BRom* (1536), 16; (1562), 16; *CP* 178. Augustine's *In Joannis Evangelium Tractatus*, XXIX, 6; *PL* 35, 1631. See also *BRom* (1536), 23; (1562), 22; *CP* 195–196; ". . . let no one be offended at his [Augustine's] describing love of one's neighbor as the definition of faith, a definition in terms of the effect. He meant to reveal faith by reference to that mark through which its integrity is more easily recognizable. Not for a moment did he hold the opinion that our salvation is based upon the merit of this love or any other kind of merit except Christ's alone, as every page of his works bears lucid testimony. But since true faith in Christ never fails to produce this its proper fruit, he considered that what is not so obvious, the essence and character of true faith, should be exhibited, following the apostle's practice, from the more visible reality of love."

258. Thomas F. Torrance, *Kingdom and Church: A Study in the Theology of the Reformation* (1956; reprint, Eugene, OR: Wipf and Stock, 1996), 82.

259. *BRom* (1536), 12; (1562), 12; *CP* 161. For a summary of Aristotle's view of happiness, see W. T. Jones, *A History of Western Philosophy: The Classical Mind*, 2nd ed., vol. 1 (Fort Worth, TX: Harcourt Brace Jovanovich, 1980), 259–287.

260. As noted earlier, for Bucer even the philosophers had an understanding of original sin. See *BRom* (1536), 267; (1562), 294; *CP* 120.

inspiring true happiness resulting in love of one's neighbors.[261] Without this gospel people are ever anxious and seeking various other means toward εὐθυμία. "It is this [εὐθυμία], therefore, that Saint Paul rightly searches out first of all, when ministering appropriate encouragement relevant to our restoration to God and his image in us."[262] Hence, Paul leads us to the Christ who has appeased the Father on our behalf so that, free from anxiety, we can become what we were intended to be.

> Accordingly, Paul quite properly introduces us to Christ the Saviour, and declares that he alone reconciles the Father to us who have always been lost through our sins, whatever degree of righteousness we may appear to have attained, and presents himself as our advocate with the Father, so that the Father lays aside all his displeasure towards us, absolves us, and pronounces us righteous, that is to say, he justifies us. All these things our only Saviour, Jesus Christ, accomplishes for all who trust in him. Moreover, by his Spirit he gives them such assurance of this reconciliation with God and so of justification, that, with every fear of the divine judgment at last outlawed, as they now esteem and revere God as Father, so they flourish in genuine love towards all men, and in every mark of true holiness of life.[263]

Doubt of God's favor is a psychological barrier to good works. When the believer is persuaded of the gospel of God's favor, his present life immediately changes.[264]

It is important to note that Bucer's understanding of salvation is a future reward as well as a new eschatological way of life in the present, resulting in true holiness of life. Salvation is not solely something we wait for; it is a present

---

261. *BRom* (1536), 12; (1562), 12; *CP* 161; "Now our natural constitution is such that we are powerless to serve others and manifest God's likeness—the end for which he created us and to which he summons us by the whole of his law and the teaching of the prophets, seeing that he who loves his neighbour has fulfilled the whole law—unless the spirits have first been raised to a sure hope of happiness and our minds have attained that serenity which the Greeks call εὐθυμία."

262. *BRom* (1536), 12; (1562), 12; *CP* 161.

263. *BRom* (1536), 12; (1562), 12; *CP* 162.

264. See *BRom* (1536), 117; (1562), 102; "Si enim Deum ideo super omnia diligimus, quia summum bonum est, necesse est, ut eum etiam nostrum summum bonum, hoc est, omnia in eo nobis quoque bona agnoscamus. Vitam itaque cum praesentem, et quicquid haec requirit, tum aeternam, ac quicquid ad hanc perducit, in ipso expetamus: deinde cum in deo vivamus, moveamur, simus, adeoque nihil quam dei opus, ab ipso ad suam gloriam conditi simus, utique dei gloriam nemo expetet, qui non simul expetat, ut suo tempore vivat, et iis, quae vita haec requirit, fruatur, donec liberatus corpore mortis huius, aeternum vivat, iam deo plene coniunctus. Haec enim ut ita haberent deus decrevit, ita igitur ut sint, optimum est, eoque a sanctis optandum. Sed quid hac opus philosophia?"

reality that ushers us into the kingdom of Christ.[265] Salvation *sola fide* effects a real change in this present life for Bucer because he is convinced that this Spirit-informed faith necessarily results in good works (akin to the Greek conviction that "to know the good is to do the good"). By faith one is able to contemplate knowledge of the good, resulting in works that please God.

In this way Christians become pleasing people. They live a life that pleases God in the present, and, according to Bucer, a pleasant and comfortable existence is one of salvation's many rewards.[266] Thus, Bucer observes, the saints of the Old Testament constantly pleaded for not only eternal gifts but also for present gifts of wealth and health:[267] "The word of the Lord teaches us on this point sufficiently, and praises in the saints, even as it proposes it to be imitated by us, the fact that they have earnestly prayed to the Lord not only for eternal life, but also present life and whatever is conducive to its being lived pleasantly, and for this reason they have spurred themselves on toward all that is pleasing to God."[268]

Likewise, the Garden of Gethsemane illustrates this pursuit for the preservation of this life.[269] Bucer believed that Jesus Christ knew that this present life was worth living, and that is why he pleaded for his chalice to be removed from him.[270] All, heathen and Christian alike, seek whatever is conducive to living pleasantly. The Christian, however, being free to realize true happiness because of his certain faith in Christ, is able to perform the works that warrant a genuinely pleasant life; the heathen is left doubting in vacant idols and serving himself.

The pleasant life (true happiness) is also understood as being in communion with God. In his "Harmonization of the statements: 'God repays each according to his works' and 'No one will be justified by works,'" dealing with Romans 2:5–10, Bucer describes the happiness of the Old Testament saints in this way: "For their happiness was in a sense their share in divine glory, which they realized from his promises, and God instructed them to seek this with

---

265. This conviction, which Bucer clearly presents later in *De Regno Christi* (1551), is present throughout his career. Wilhelm Pauck states, "It reflects his entire career insofar as in it he sets forth that doctrinal and practical understanding of the Reformation which he had achieved in connection with his work and experience" (*LCC* 19, 157). Cf. Andreas Gäumann, *Reich Christi und Obrigkeit: Eine Studie zum reformatorischen Denken und Handeln Martin Bucers* (Bern: Peter Lang, 2001).

266. Wilhelm Pauck states that the "definition of the Kingdom of Christ may be regarded as a summary of Bucer's theological convictions. It was his basic concern that men should live 'well and happily'" (*LCC* 19, 166).

267. *BRom* (1536), 118; (1562), 103; "Hinc est ut Scriptura ab eo passim Deum praedicat, quod bona malaque huius vitae omnia unus dispensat, quod vitam, prosperam valetudinem, opes, pacem, et optata omnia, observantibus sua praecepta largitur et tuetur: id quod non solum in libris Mose, sed etiam Prophetarum atque Psalmorum denique et novi testamenti, ubique videre est."

268. *BRom* (1536), 117; (1562), 102; "Verbum domini satis hic nos docet, illud in sanctis laudat, et tanquam imitabile nobis proponit, quod illi vitam non modo aeternam, sed praesentem quoque, et quicquid ad eam commode transigendam conduct, enixe a domino orarunt, eaque causa, se ad omnia dei placita exstimularunt."

269. *BRom* (1536), 117–118; (1562), 102.

270. Luke 22:42.

singular zeal: they were unable not to seek it, except in accordance with those promises of God. And in this matter they sought not so much their own concerns but the things of God."[271] The result of faith is this happiness: "For zeal and obedience to God, which is a result of that faith, by which we believe that God wills to behave as a father to us, draws one primarily and with a special power to the things that please God."[272] To share in divine glory is to live zealously pursuing the pleasure of God. We were created with this in mind; its fulfillment is our felicity. The script was written in such a way that good works are fundamental to our happiness, and ultimately to our salvation.[273]

The importance of knowing what our true happiness is, is demonstrated at every opportunity in scripture, which teaches good works with our happiness in mind:

> When scripture is especially concerned to commend good works to us, and so invites us to perform them, it is easily seen how helpful it is that scripture states and expounds only that good works contribute to our felicity. For it is by the will of God that good works have this advantage, that an abundant reward is paid for them, that God judges us in accordance with them and declares us heirs of eternal life; more than that he now fully reveals this eternal life, that is, he justifies us finally and completely: Why then would scripture not express, proclaim, and inculcate this, and all the more so when it has begun to arouse and kindle in us the zeal for good works?[274]

Scripture clearly shows that this present life is to be lived in pursuit of good works; it is how life is intended to be lived.

Scripture also reveals everywhere that there are rewards for good works. It is, according to Bucer, like a mother encouraging her young son to memorize the Lord's Prayer. As a reward, she will give him a handsome bonnet (*elegans pileum*).[275]

271. *BRom* (1536), 118; (1562), 102; "Nam ipsorum felicitas quaedam erat divinae gloriae portio, id quod ex ipsius promissis cognoscebant, hancque ut singulari studio quaerant, praeceperat eis Deus, non potuerunt igitur eam non expetere, sed iuxta illa Dei promissa. Inque eo non tam sua, quam quae Dei sunt, expetierunt."

272. *BRom* (1536), 118; (1562), 102; "Studium enim et observantia dei, quae ex fide illa est, qua credimus deum nobis velle se praestare patrem, in primis et praecipua vi ad placita dei pertrahit."

273. Cf. *Das ym Selb* (1523) (*Bibliographie* I); *BDS* I, 50, I. 32 through 51, I. 7.

274. *BRom* (1536), 130; (1562), 119; "Facile quoque illud videtur, quando Scriptura id nobiscum praecipue agit, ut bona opera nobis commendat, ac ita ad ea invitet, quam nihil ab re faciat, quod id solum memorat et exponit, quod ad felicitatem nostram bona opera conferunt. Habent namque hoc ex voluntate Dei, ut merces eis copiosa rependatur, ut secundum ea ipse nos iudicet, et haeredes vitae aeternae pronunciet, imo iam eam plene exhibeat, hoc est, ultimo et consummate iustificet: cur id igitur Scriptura non exprimeret, praedicaret, inculcaret, ibi dumtaxat, ubi studium horum excitare, inflammareque in nobis instituit?"

275. *BRom* (1536), 116; (1562) 100.

The boy memorizes the prayer and the mother gives the bonnet as agreed. In this case who would deny that the reason why the boy was given a bonnet was that he memorized the prayer? For the mother would not have otherwise given the bonnet. However no one will say that this work, that the boy memorized the prayer, was worth this in itself, but it was because the mother, loving the boy so, wanted it thus.[276]

The handsome bonnet is an inappropriate gift for such a task.[277] However, a benevolent parent gives good rewards for following commands. Thus, the child merits this wonderful bonnet only on account of his mother's goodwill.

Rewards are tied closely to the idea that God desires to be benevolent toward his children who follow his commands. Bucer states:

There is in the fact that scripture proposes a reward for good works, both of this present age and of the future, this advantage, that when any desire for good things comes upon us, either present or future, there immediately comes to one's aid [the thought], "your God alone bestows these things, and has promised them, to those who tread the path of his commandments." This thought, contemplated with faith, immediately sets the mind on fire for the commands of God.[278]

Bonnets aside, scripture presents eternal life as a reward for good works, but according to Bucer, only in a secondary manner.[279] To help illustrate the point, Bucer, knowledgeable of the life of knights and horses, employs a metaphor from a medieval tournament to illustrate how and why good works merit such rewards:[280]

Just as if a king were to designate for himself some nobles for which he were to appoint certain tournaments with most generous prizes: in that situation none receives the prize except the one who contends

---

276. *BRom* (1536), 116; (1562) 100; "Puer precationem ediscit, mater, ut pacta est, pileum rependit. Hic quis non dicat causam, ut donaretur pileo puer, fuisse, quod edidicit precationem? Neque enim pileum alias mater donasset. Nemo autem dicet istud operis, quod precationem puer edidicit, exse hoc valuisse, sed quia ita voluerit amans adeo pueri mater."

277. See also his similar anaology between a father and his son in *BGospels* (1527), bk.1, 135(r).

278. *BRom* (1536), 118; (1562), 102–103; "Praeterea inest in eo, quod Scriptura bonis operibus mercedem, cum huius saeculi, tum futuri proponit, hoc utilitatis, ut cum subit nos cupiditas bonorum quorumlibet, sive praesentium, sive futurorum, statim succurrat, Deus tuus haec solus largitur, et est ea pollicitus iis, qui terunt semitas mandatorum suorum. Id fide perpensum, statim accendit animum ad iussa Dei."

279. *BRom* (1536), 116; (1562), 100; "Omnino igitur probe facta, causae sunt, ut Deus nobis benefaciat, sed non primae, nec per se, verum secundaria, et id etiam non nisi ex ultronea benevolentia."

280. Bucer most likely was introduced to equestrianship during his time in Ebernburg castle under the protection of the knight Franz von Sickingen. See Greschat, *Martin Bucer*, 130.

legitimately and each is repaid in accordance with how he behaved in the tournament and on these terms the legitimate effort expended in the contest is in its own way the reason for the prize. But that effort alone does not deserve a prize of itself nor of its own merit: for many others undergo much more effort and indeed danger in fighting on the prince's behalf; as is also the case when one is fighting earnestly in battle where no prize is awarded, still less such a prestigious and generous prize as is awarded to the participants in the tournament. The fact therefore is that in this situation for the nature of the contest there is awarded a generous prize by the prince who established that order of nobility by his own decision and appointed to it those whom he pleased and who has then announced such prizes as he willed for the contestants.[281]

God is the generous prince who decreed that such worthless deeds merit such extravagant prizes. Hence, here we can see that Bucer's understanding of justification is framed within a *pactum* structure, albeit one that God himself fulfills.[282]

As Stupperich notes, one can see that the scholastic teaching of *meritum de congruo* and *meritum de condigno* did in all probability have an influence on Bucer's understanding of works.[283] For Bucer, because God has decided to grant rewards for good works, there is a sense in which works are seen in a congruous manner. The works of a believer are accepted by God as worthy of merit not because they are so in themselves but because, first, God has decreed them to be such and, second, they are his very works in the believer.

---

281. *BRom* (1536), 119; (1562), 104; "Ita ut si rex ordinem aliquem sibi designet nobilium, cui certa constituat certamina, et vincentibus amplissima praemia: Ibi praemia quidem illa nemo accipit, nisi qui legitime certaverit, rependitur cuique iuxta quod se habuerit in certamine, eoque pacto labor ille certaminis legitimus, suo modo causa est praemii. At id non ex se, non suo merito: nam plerique alii multo plus laboris ac periculi certando pro principe subeunt, etiam ubi serio pugnatur, quibus tamen nihil praemii rependitur, nedum tam insigne, et liberale, ut istis ludentibus. Est ergo quod hic pro ratione certaminis redditur, nihilominus liberale donum principis, qui suo arbitratu ordinem istum nobilium instituit, inque eum, quos ipsi visum est, adlegit, qui denique, quae ipse voluit, certantibus praemia edixit."

282. *BRom* (1536), 116; (1562), 100; "Verum istuc [the merit of works] pacto accipiendum est, ut simul agnoscamus et confiteamur ea, istuc nempe causas beneficiorum Dei, et merita esse et dici, nullo suo merito, sed mera et gratuita Dei in nos benevolentia." See also *BRom* (1536) 116; (1562), 100; "Quantumvis enim pie sancteque vivamus, et omnia recte faciamus, adhuc inutiles servi sumus, nec possunt ulla nostra merita sic esse, ut Deum, vel ad minimum omnium beneficiorum, quae praestat nobis, obligare ullo pacto, ullave etiam summae liberalitatis lege, possimus. Sunt enim quaecunque recte facimus, per omnia ipsius opera, tota et totaliter, ut qui operetur in nobis, et velle, et efficere quod decet, qui finxerit nos ex nihilo. Dona eius sunt, quaecunque in nobis mala non sunt."

283. Robert Stupperich, "Schriftverständnis und Kirchlenhre bei Butzer und Gropper," *Jahrbuch des Vereins für Westfälische Kirchengeschichte* 44 (1951): 113. See also Barnikol, who also makes this connection in "Bucers Lehre," 112–113.

What impels Bucer toward such a view is his desire to preserve God's goodwill as the primary cause of one's salvation in light of passages of scripture that promote works, such as Psalm 61: "Steadfast love belongs to you, O Lord. For you repay to all according to their work." How can one hold this true when Paul states that we are saved by faith, not by works (Eph. 2:9)? Because Bucer holds that scripture cannot contradict itself, there ought to be a way to explain how we can be said to be justified both on account of what we do and not on account of what we do.

In a *conciliatio* on Romans 2:11–16, dealing with this issue, Bucer begins to explain the apparent difficulty by stating that:

> God saves us by his mercy alone and by the contemplation of the
> merit of Christ, which, when we believe in Christ, is bestowed on us
> and becomes ours. For those very deeds done rightly in accordance
> with which God justifies us, that is, assigns to us eternal life, are the
> works of Christ in us, bestowed on us with Christ out of the pure and
> free goodwill of God. As a result the goodness of God is in itself the
> prime and the whole cause of our salvation, as is expressed by the
> phrases "by grace alone" and "by faith alone." By this faith of course,
> we embrace and receive this grace, namely that we are justified and
> not as a result of works.[284]

By faith alone means that in faith Christians contemplate Christ, and because faith comes with the bestowal of the Spirit of Christ, they become possessed by him so that believers now live in him and he in them. In this sense of mutual inhabitation, Christians are allowed to cooperate with God in salvation, since these works are not their own but the work of Christ in them. This agency is expressed in Bucer primarily in terms of the bestowal of the Holy Spirit,[285] being clothed in Christ,[286] participation in Christ,[287] being in communion with Christ,

---

284. *BRom* (1536), 129; (1562), 118–119; "Deum nos servare ex sola sua clementia, et contemplatione meriti Christi, quod cum Christo credimus, nobis donatur, nostrumque fit. Nam illa ipsa recte facta, iuxta quae nos Deus iustificat, hoc est, nobis vitam aeternam adiudicat, Christi in nobis opera sunt, cum illo donata, ex mere Dei et gratuita benevolentia, ut Dei bonitas semper prima, per se, et tota causa sit salutis nostrae, id quod istae locutiones exprimunt, Sola gratia, solaque fide, qua scilicet gratiam hanc amplectimur, et recipimus, nos iustificari, et non ex operibus."

285. *BRom* (1536), 12; (1562), 12; *CP* 162.

286. *BRom* (1536), 290; (1562), 322; *CP* 290; "Now, the death of our sins and the life of God are so perfectly presented that we are said to be buried into death of Christ, incorporated into Christ, clothed with Christ. Therefore, as we can expect no more perfect presentation of Christ, given symbolically for the apprehension of faith, so also it is most inappropriate to repeat our baptism."

287. *BRom* (1536), 296; (1562), 330; *CP* 305.

and so forth.[288] If a believer "does any good, it results from the fact that he is a creation of God, created for good works, works which God himself prepares, makes and performs, so that he rewards in us gifts which are already his."[289] Hence, Bucer follows Augustine's view that "when God crowns our merits, he crowns nothing but his own gifts."[290] Merit is not the result of works but the result of the believer cooperating with the Spirit who works within the believer:

> Nevertheless, when God wants us to cooperate with him by good
> works for our salvation, or rather, even to "work it out"
> (κατεργάζεσθαι) [Phil. 2:10] and has thus determined to repay us
> according to our deeds, there is brought about also in its own way our
> justification; that is, eternal life is assigned to us as a result of works.
> But this is the case only when through our election and the purpose
> of God formed before the ages, there is already assigned to us before
> the foundation of the world this life of God as a result of the grace of
> God and the merit of Christ [Ephesians 1 and 3]. This life moreover is
> assigned to us through faith, that is, after we believe in Christ and
> have in some way become already possessed of him. This of course
> comes about at that blessed beginning of faith which belongs to the
> sons of God through the Spirit, who is the pledge of this inheritance.
> For good works are the fruit of this faith and of the Spirit.[291]

Works are in a sense a cooperating cause, which Bucer speaks about as a secondary cause elsewhere.

288. *BRom* (1536), 292; (1562), 324; *CP* 294; "Moreover, since the faith whereby we embrace these promises of salvation cannot exist apart from the Spirit of Christ and some degree of communion in the nature of Christ, that is to say, in the life of God and in true virtue, the Lord, the one mediator between God and men who is always in the midst of his people and always at work by his Spirit in the holy ministrations of his word and symbols, has likewise always bestowed through the sacraments together with the imparting of the Father's favour his Spirit, but according to a set measure which has varied in accordance with the age."

289. *BRom* (1536), 120; (1562), 105; "Si quid benefacit, id inde est, quod figmentum Dei est, ad bona opera conditus, et ea, quae Deus ipse praeparat, facit, et perficit, ut sua iam in nobis dona remuneret."

290. Augustine, *Epistola CXCIV*, 19; *PL* 33, 880; "cum Deus coronat merita nostra, nihil aliud coronat quam munera sua."

291. *BRom* (1536), 129–130; (1562), 119; "Nihilominus tamen, cum Deus velit nos sibi bonis operibus ad nostram salutem cooperati, imo etiam eam perficere, κατεργάζεσθαι, Philipp. 2. ac ita statuerit nobis secundum nostra facta rependere, fit etiam suo modo iustificatio nostri, hoc est, adiudicatur nobis vita aeterna, ex operibus, sed tum, quando iam haec nobis vita Dei, ex gratia Dei, et Christo merito ante conditum mundum adiudicata est per electionem nostri, et propositum Dei ante saecula factum. Ephe. 1. & 3. adiudicata item per fidem, hoc est postquam credentes Christo, eius iam compotes aliquo modo facti sumus, felici scilicet illo fidei initio, quod est per spiritum filiorum Dei, qui arrabo est huius haereditatis. Sunt enim bona opera, huius fidei et spiritus fructus."

In his *conciliatio* in regard to Romans 2:11–16, Bucer explains the nature of election, faith, and works as *triplex iustificatio*, that is, God assigns eternal life to Christians in three ways:[292]

> The first is that by which he destines us to eternal life and it exists
> solely by his goodness and regard for the merit of Christ. . . . The second
> way is that by which he already reveals eternal life in some way and
> grants that one enjoy it, by the gift of his Spirit, in which we cry "Abba
> Father." This justification exists in addition by reason of our faith, but
> that too is something which God out of his free goodness gives, and
> brings about by his Spirit in us. The third way is when he now reveals
> actually and fully the eternal life or even blessings which we enjoy, no
> longer only by faith and hope. Our deeds contribute to this justification,
> but they too are the gifts and works of the free goodness of God.[293]

The first *iustificatio* is equated with election and acts as the foundation for the following two *iustificationes*, that is, faith and works.[294] As he states thereafter, "The sole goodness of God and merit of Christ is the prime and in itself entire cause."[295] God's divine benevolence is the primary and sole cause of salvation; his election enables the elect to do good works, which then function only as secondary causes.

Later on, in reference to Romans 4:1–8, Bucer speaks of a *prima iustificatio*, that is, "absolution from all impiety,"[296] and a *secundaria iustificatio*,[297] "which is a

---

292. *BRom* (1536), 130; (1562), 119; "Triplex itaque est nostri iustificatio, hoc est, trifariam nobis Deus vitam aeternam adiudicat." For an extended hermeneutical treatment on Bucer's concept of *triplex iustificatio*, see David C. Fink's article "'The Doers of the Law Will Be Justified.'"

293. *BRom* (1536), 130; (1562), 119; "Prima est, qua vitam aeternam nobis destinat, ea constat utique sola ipsius bonitate, et respectu meriti Christi. . . . Altera, qua vitam aeternam iam aliquo modo exhibet, et frui ea donat, donato suo Spiritu, in quo clamamus Abba pater. Haec iustificatio constat praeterea etiam fide nostra, sed quam ipsam quoque nobis Deus ex sua gratuita bonitate donat, et suo in nobis spiritu efficit. Tertia, cum iam re ipsa, et plene vitam aeternam, vel etiam bona, quibus in hac vita fruimur, exhibet, non iam fide tantum et spe. Ad hanc iustificationem concurrunt facta, sed ea ipsa quoque gratuitae bonitatis Dei dona et opera sunt." In *De Vera Reconciliatione* [172(v)–173(r)], Bucer talks of a threefold justification as well; however, there, the first justification is understood as the forgiveness of sins, the grace of God, and communion with the Father and Son; the second justification corresponds to the new life of the believer lived with love and virtues; and the third is the justification by which good works are confirmed and rewarded.

294. On this point Fink believes that the Scotist-Occamist aspect of *acceptio divina* is influencing Bucer's thought, in that there is such a close association between election or predestination and justification. He states, "Whatever Bucer's relationship to the Thomistic theology of his former Dominican order may have been, there can be little doubt that for him, 'the heart of our salvation, that is, our justification,' derives from an act of will on the part of God. . . . Justification is thus primarily God's act of acceptance" ("'The Doers of the Law Will Be Justified,'" 508–509).

295. *BRom* (1536), 130; (1562), 119; "prima et per se totaque causa est, sola Dei bonitas, et Christi meritum . . ."

296. *BRom* (1536), 218; (1562), 232; "prima iustificatione, hoc est, ab omni impietate absolutione . . ."

297. Bucer's use of *secundaria* hints not to a following (*secunda*) but to an inferior or second-rate justification that highlights the superiority of the first. In the *Expositio* that precedes this discussion, he correlates this secondary justification to James, stating: "Illud Iacobi dictum est de secundaria iustificatione, quae consequitur opera, non de primaria et substantiali, de qua hic Paulus." *BRom* (1536), 213; (1562), 224.

result of works."[298] This latter *iustificatio* is in reference to various places in scripture where God states that he will not justify the wicked (Exod. 23:7). Again Bucer
makes the distinction between the prime cause, God's goodwill, and all other secondary causes, which is similar to Aquinas's distinction between a prime cause
and a middle cause that is enveloped within the prime cause.[299] God's goodwill
as the prime cause of salvation does not exclude our cooperation in works as
secondary middle causes,[300] only because good works are contingent on God's
goodwill, the prime cause, demonstrating here Bucer's teaching of *Allwirksamkeit*. The allowance for cooperation in one's salvation in this secondary sense
does not weaken the prime cause.

That good works act as secondary causes of salvation is clearly demonstrated by Bucer when he interprets a passage that seems to inherently contradict salvation by works, for example, the case of the thief on the cross.[301] Because
in Bucer's thought works are subordinately necessary for salvation, the thief
could enter heaven only if he had done good works inspired by the Spirit, which
would then be rewarded. The careless observer may surmise that the thief did
not have time to accomplish a good work, for he died there on a cross, unable
to do anything but have faith and die, but this is to understand good works in a
rather limited way.[302] Bucer states:

> For suppose that somebody lived in the most ungodly manner through-
> out his entire life. The Lord however converts him at the end of his life
> just as he did with the thief who was crucified with our Savior. Now as
> soon as he has embraced the goodness of God by faith, his mind truly
> burns for the glory of God. If he can do nothing else, he confesses his
> sins to the glory of God, and urges others to repent. Even if he cannot
> do it by prayer, he does it by groans and sighs. In this he now has good
> works according to which he may be justified, that is, for which he may
> be judged to deserve admission to the inheritance of eternal life.[303]

298. *BRom* (1536), 218; (1562), 232; "secundaria, quae iusta opera fit."

299. *ST* Ia q.19 a.7; "voluntas Dei, cum sit causa prima, non excludit causas medias."

300. See also *BRom* (1532), 401; (1562), 461; *CP* 146; "But a first cause does not preclude the functioning
of second causes. God does indeed act in us in everything, and acts upon us too according to his good pleasure,
but he does so in such a way that he causes us to act, so that by his action we come to understand an issue, exer-
cise choice, accept or reject, and set our physical powers in motion."

301. Luke 23:43.

302. Faith is the chief good work. See *BRom* (1536), 215–216; (1562), 229; "Credere sane opus est, et
omnium bonorum operum caput, quare Dei opus, hoc est."

303. *BRom* (1536), 119; (1562), 105; "Nam fac esse, vixerit aliquis impientissime per omnem vitam, Dominus vero in extremo eum ad se convertat, ita ut fecit latroni, qui fuit crucifixus cum servatore, iam simul atque is
fide dei bonitatem amplexus est, mens eius vere ardet in gloriam dei si nihil aliud potest, confitetur tamen in
gloriam Dei sua peccata, hortatur alios ad poenitentiam, etiam si oratione nequeat, facit id gemitibus et suspiriis.
Sic iam habet bona opera, secundum quae iustificetur, hoc est, pro quibus iudicetur, esse ad haereditatem
admittendus vitae aeternae."

Good works are essential for the reward of salvation.

It ought to also be mentioned that good works are not only a secondary cause of salvation but also signs of that very salvation, since good works are usually visible. On this account Bucer states that men can judge believers as just on account of the fact that they recognize the *iutitia* of the believer.[304] This is not understood as a justification by men; rather, when believers are inspired by faith toward *iustitia*, these works of *iustitia* are seen by those around who can judge those works as righteous.[305] They give evidence of one's election.[306] Justification is a visibly realized doctrine founded on the dictum that "to know the good is to do the good"; to have true faith is to love your neighbor; to contemplate the *iustitia Dei* is to necessarily pursue *iustitia*.

Justification is *sola fide*. The gift of faith, understood as a deeper inbreathing enabling one to contemplate true *iustitia*, leads a man or woman to pursue this *iustitia* in works. These works are a product of the gift of faith, which leads Bucer to maintain that believers are saved by works produced automatically from true faith. In this light he defends the Augustinian definition of justification by faith that works through love, stating: "But let no one be offended at his [Augustine's] describing love of one's neighbour as the definition of faith, a definition in term of the effect."[307]

God chooses to forgive those whom he chooses. As evidence of this election he bestows upon them faith, or the fuller breath of the Holy Spirit. This gift of faith that comes with the bestowal of the Spirit reveals *iustitia* resulting in a derivative *iustitia*. Thus it is in this manner that Bucer holds together an imputed and imparted aspect in his doctrine of justification.

Summary

For since it is God who gives and inspires all understanding, knowledge, manner, and skill, one cannot doubt that he passes on the doctrine of eternal life in this order, manner, and vividness, so that the human mind is nowhere able to lose, much less to censure, this doctrine, when that light, by which God is accustomed to pour over

304. See Barnikol, "Bucers Lehre," 123–126.

305. *BRom* (1536), 10; (1562), 10; "Non quod nostri iustitificatio hominum quoque iudicio nitatur, verum quod quos Deus iustos habet, id est, quibus peccata remittit, hos simul suo spiritu ita adflet, ut soli ex animo iustitiae studeant, et quamvis in multis continuo et ipsi delinquant, soli tamen quicquid in orbe est iustitiae, obtineant, et hominum iudicio adeo se iustos adprobent, ut cum rem habent cum incredulis, iudicium sibi fieri orent pro sua innocentia et iustitia."

306. See *BRom* (1536), 360; (1562), 412; *CP* 101.

307. *BRom* (1536), 22; (1562), 22; *CP* 196.

us, is rightly enjoyed, with everything else he has been pleased to bestow upon the whole nature of man. As I have said, human nature cannot perceive in full the truth while it is still destitute of the light of faith, unless it is born again.[308]

Bucer's teaching of justification by faith cannot be accurately described as "double justification." Bucer did not conceive of separate judgments, one synthetic and then one analytic based on works, which the tag double justification can tend to insinuate.

Bucer conceives of salvation as founded on God's goodwill; God chooses those whom he chooses to save. Those whom he saves are completely void of any salvific resources, and by the gift of his grace he calls them to be his elect. They are called and instructed in the gospel of Christ's perfect merit, so that now having been taught such wonderful and powerful things, and knowing God's kind disposition toward them by the greater inbreathing of the Spirit, the elect are moved toward deeds of love—deeds of love that in a secondary manner can be said to save, because these works are not the believer's own and these works in themselves are worth nothing. It is just that God accepts them as worthy deeds. God maintains this wonderfully complex circle: he chooses, calls, justifies, and finally glorifies his chosen ones.

Important for understanding his doctrine has been the understanding that Bucer conceives of the saint as being *duplex*. The dialectic of spirit and flesh acts in a similar manner to Luther's *simul iustus et peccator*—the saint is always a sinner because he will always be afflicted by the flesh until he is glorified and given a new heavenly body, but he is also just because God has forgiven him his sins on account of Jesus Christ. In addition, as noted earlier, there is a strong imparted aspect to justification that results in a double will and judgment that can fluctuate according to the power of the Spirit. I have used the analogy of a balloon and the breath of the Spirit to show the way in which Bucer understands Christians to live in this present life fluctuating between knowing true righteousness and being held captive to concupiscence.

The Spirit is seen primarily as the believer's educator in faith. In justification the Spirit as persuader or instructor affects the mind in this manner. Highlighting the dictum that "to know the good is to do the good," I have shown how Bucer connects faith to works, true *iustitia* and partial imparted *iustitia*. To know

308. *BRom* (1536), iv(v)–v(r); "Etenim cum Deus sit, qui omnem intellectum, scientiam, viam et artem, donat et inspirat, dubitari non potest eum doctrinam vitae aeternae eo tradere ordine, via et evidentia, ut in illa nihil uspiam mens humana, lumine illo recte usa, quo perfundere Deus solet, quibuscunque naturam hominis integram largiri dignatur, desyderare, nedum repraehendere possit; utcunque illa ad plenam, ut dixi, veritatem nisi renata, percipere non possit, dum destituitur adhuc luce fidei."

true *iustitia* is to also pursue and be zealous for *iustitia*. Hence Bucer's doctrine of justification *sola fide* wholistically includes works of love in this manner.

Likewise, for him the knowledge of one's non-imputation of sins and one's adoption as a child of God precedes the impartative aspect of righteousness. This knowledge acts as a stimulus. The declarative aspect results in the necessary effective aspect of his understanding of justification. Nevertheless, the priority is on the imputed righteousness. In this way God's declaration is always effective; as McCormack states, "God's verdict creates the reality it declares."[309]

In expounding Bucer's nuanced doctrine of justification, we can see that justification is composed of a synthetic judgment in election based in the mysterious goodwill of God. To the elect this is the evangelical message. For Bucer this is the doctrine he believed he could gradually come to an agreement on with his Catholic brothers. His Catholic brothers' grievance that the evangelicals denied works of love were untrue, and that is what Bucer passionately would try to explain in the dialogues of the 1530s and 1540s. Bucer held that true faith is not dead; it necessarily results in good works.

The dualities of faith and works and imputation and impartation, in Bucer's doctrine, are combined with a coherent integrity that is consistent with the teaching of *sola fide*. As I will demonstrate, Bucer's doctrinal stance was unwavering during his negotiations with Catholics. He was consistent. To demonstrate this consistency, I will in the next chapter explain the manner in which Johannes Gropper understood the doctrine of justification. By doing this I will demonstrate the various similarities and differences that these two men had on the teaching of justification. For Bucer it was the doctrine of justification, the evangelical truth, that established the church, a point I made in the previous chapter. For Gropper the opposite is the case. That is, for Bucer soteriology precedes ecclesiology; for Gropper ecclesiology precedes soteriology. Likewise, for Bucer imputation causes impartation based on the Socratic dictum, whereas for Gropper impartation precedes the imputation of righteousness. Both men believed that it was a gracious and merciful God in whom trust must be placed for salvation; likewise, both believed that justification was a declarative and transformative event. By understanding better these similarities and differences, one will be better equipped to examine the irenic negotiations from 1539 to 1541. It is to Gropper's doctrine that I now turn.

---

309. Bruce L. McCormack, "What's at Stake in the Current Debates over Justification?" in *Justification: What's at Stake in the Current Debates*, ed. Mark Husbands and Daniel J. Treier (Downers Grove, IL: InterVarsity Press, 2004), 107.

4

Johannes Gropper's Doctrine of Justification in the *Enchiridion* (1538)

To the extent that we are grafted into Christ, on that account we are righteous.[1]

The view of justification developed in Johannes Gropper's *Enchiridion christianae institutionis* (1538)[2] attracted Martin Bucer's admiration and encouraged him to see Gropper as a collaborator in Catholic reform.[3] So impressed was Bucer that he presented Gropper with a copy of his *Romans Commentary* at the Colloquy of Hagenau in 1539.

At Hagenau, while meeting at the lodging of the archbishop of Cologne, they discussed how unity might be achieved. Reflecting on this later, Gropper described their discussions, stating: "As far as time allowed I could sense then that Bucer was not very far from my position,

---

1. *Enchiridion*, 142(v) (marg. note); "Eoipso et ob id iusti sumus, quia Christo insiti" (in reference to John 15).

2. Gropper's *Enchiridion christianae institutionis* was first published in 1538 as an appendix to the *Canones* of the provincial synod in 1536: *Canones Concilii Provincialis Coloniensis . . . quibus adiectum est Enchiridion christianae institutiones* (Cologne: Nicolas Wolrab, 1538). The final version of the *Canones* is also in *ARC* 2, 192–305. I am using the octavo edition of the *Enchiridion* (Paris: Nicolaus Boucher, 1545).

3. At Hagenau, Bucer and Gropper had discussed the issue of justification and other problems. See Cornelis Augustijn, "L'espirit d'Erasme au Colloque de Worms (1540)," in *Colloquia Erasmiana Turonensia*, ed. Jean-Claude Margolin (Toronto: University of Toronto Press 1969), 383–384; and Walter Lipgens, *Kardinal Johannes Gropper, 1503–1559 und die Anfänge der katholischen Reform in Deutschland* (Münster: Aschendorff, 1951), 227. For Bucer's view on these initial discussions, see Bucer's *Von den einigen rechten wegen . . .* (Strasbourg, 1545), (*Bibliographie* 145), in *BDS* 11/2, 297–303. For Gropper's view, see *An die Roemsche Keyserliche Maiestat . . . Warhafftige Antwort und gegenberichtung . . .* (Cologne: Iaspar Gennepaeus, 1545), 36b–38a.

though he finished everything with the words: God only wills that a person might undertake such a Christian dialogue in the fear of God, whereby one member kindly listens and instructs the other, in order to help each other return to Christian unity."[4] During this meeting they discussed the main issues in the *Enchiridion* and began a theological courtship that eventually led to the attempted and perhaps premature wedlock of their views in the Worms/Regensburg Book of 1540–1541. For these reasons an exposition of Gropper's teaching on justification is required.

In this chapter I will explain the key features of Gropper's view of justification as expressed in the *Enchiridion* to help distinguish Gropper's thought from Bucer's. Specifically, I will show how Gropper's paradigm of *incorporatio* into the body of Christ (or the vine) governs the way in which he understands the teaching of justification, especially the aspect of impartative righteousness.[5] I will demonstrate how this paradigm emphasizes the transformational-sacramental structures of the traditional church, that is, through the sacraments the members of the body are strengthened, or rather the branch grows in righteousness. The task here is to articulate accurately and concisely how Gropper's doctrine of justification functions within this paradigm of *incorporatio*.[6]

From the start it will be apparent that there are similarities with Bucer's view. This is particularly due to the fact that Gropper was influenced by humanist as well as evangelical thought, particularly Melanchthon's *Loci Communes* (1535), from which he often quotes.[7] Both Bucer and Gropper describe an imputative and impartative aspect in their doctrine, though these are understood in different ways. I will demonstrate that their differences are mainly due to their differing theological priorities. That is, for Bucer the doctrine of justification by faith establishes the Church—it is the chief doctrine among others—while for Gropper the

---

4. Gropper, *Warhafftige Antwort*, 37a; quoted in Lipgens, *Kardinal Johannes Gropper*, 122; "So weit ich damals spüren konnte, war Bucer nicht in vielem wider meine Meinung, sondern endigte alles mit den Worten: Wollte nur Gott, daß man durch ein solches christliches Gespräch, wobei der eine Teil den andern gütig anhört und belehrt, in Gottesfurcht es unternähme, einander wieder zur christlichen Einigkeit zu verhelfen."

5. The paradigm of incorporation is the manner in which Gropper understands what it means to be a Christian. It is based on the impartation of grace in baptism that makes the believer a member of Christ's body. For him the concept of incorporation is another way of describing that impartation.

6. Due to the insightful work of Reinhard Braunisch, Gropper has attracted more attention, especially in ecumenical circles. My indebtedness to Braunisch's work is evident throughout. Braunisch, *Die Theologie der Rechtfertigung im "Enchiridion" (1538) des Johannes Gropper: Sein Kritischer Dialog mit Philipp Melanchthon* (Münster: Aschendorff, 1974).

7. See Reinhard Braunisch, "Johannes Gropper zwischen Humanismus und Reformation: Zur Bestimmung seines geistigen Standorts bis 1543," *Romische Quartalschrift* 69 (1974): 192–209; see also Stupperich, *Der Humanismus*, 15–18. For Gropper's interaction with Melanchthon's *Loci*, see Braunisch, *Die Theologie der Rechtfertigung*, passim.

Church is the locus of justification within the sacramental cycle of baptism, confirmation, Eucharist, and penance; hence soteriology is theologically second to ecclesiology.[8]

Before describing Gropper's doctrine, I will first briefly present an overview of the historical context that gave birth to the *Enchiridion*. Then I will discuss some of the problematic interpretations of Gropper's view in the *Enchiridion*. After identifying some pitfalls, I will give a careful account of Gropper's teaching of justification on the basis of the concept of *incorporatio* into the body of Christ by looking at the sacraments of baptism, confirmation, and the Eucharist, and specifically the sacrament of penance. Within the subsection on penance I will also look at Gropper's understanding of faith, grace, *iustitia*, and the causes of justification. In the end this chapter will provide a means to analyze Bucer's role in the formulation of article 5 of the Worms Book.

Gropper's *Enchiridion*

In 1527, when he was just twenty-four years old, Johannes Gropper's legal and administrative competence was quickly recognized:[9] he became the Keeper of the Great Seal to Hermann von Wied, archbishop of Cologne.[10] Three years later he would accompany the archbishop's entourage to the Diet of Augsburg. Commenting twenty-six years later on this experience, he stated: "In my youth I surrendered my attention to the wisdom of law. From 1530 I began reading first the Bible and then the Holy Fathers concerning the religious questions which were disputed at the Diet

8. Here the argument is similar to that of Hampson in *Christian Contradictions*. There she illustrates the incompatibility of the doctrine of justification in Catholic and Lutheran theology on account of differing structures of thought. She describes Lutheran thought as a dialectic, using the formula *simul iustus et peccator*, and Catholic thought as a transformational *via*. In a similar manner here, I show that Bucer and Gropper construe the doctrine of justification differently, and that Hampson's categories of dialectic and *via* are partially appropriate; however, it is more important to understand that these structures of thought are underpinned by specific priorities. For the Catholics, ecclesiology was their theological priority from which questions of soteriology were answered; for the evangelicals, however, soteriology defined ecclesiology.

9. Much of the following background information can be found in Braunisch, *Die Theologie der Rechtfertigung*, 27–60; Lipgens, *Kardinal Johannes Gropper*, 51–66; Johannes Meier, "Das 'Enchiridion christianae institutionis' (1538) von Johannes Gropper Geschichte seiner Entstehung: Verbreitung und Nachwirkung," *Zeitschrift für Kirchengeschichte* 86 (1975): 289–328; Thompson, *Eucharistic Sacrifice*, 154–157; and Mechtild Köhn, *Martin Bucers Entwurf einer Reformation des Erzstiftes Köln: Untersuchung der Enststehungsgeschichte und der Theologie des "Einfältigen Bedenckens" von 1543* (Wittenberg: Luther Verlag, 1966), 19–33. Gropper graduated from the arts faculty at the University of Cologne on 17 June 1516. Here the *via antiqua* of Thomas Aquinas was thriving and affected the arts faculty. See Lipgens, *Kardinal Johannes Gropper*, 15–23.

10. Reinhard Braunisch, "Johannes Gropper (1503–1559)," in *Katholische Theologen der Reformationszeit*, ed. Erwin Iserloh, vol. 1 (Münster: Aschendorff, 1984), 118.

of Augsburg, however privately without a tutor."[11] Stimulated by the arguments over doctrines, Gropper dedicated himself to the study of theology. His theological studies included various humanist and evangelical writings, from which he was seemingly encouraged toward a moderate position on Church reform.[12]

The 1534–1535 Münster uprising took place a few miles north of the Cologne territory, which forced Archbishop von Wied to take the threat of popular discontent seriously. To stem the tide he decided to institute moderate reforms in his diocese, borrowing from Duke John III's reforms in the duchy of Julich-Cleves. Duke John had issued in 1532/33 a humanistic church order called the *Declaratio* in order to protect the unity of the Church in the face of a growing Protestant reformation, which was spreading in the duchy of Julich-Cleves.[13] The *Declaratio* was a moderate Erasmian example of reform, but influenced as well by the Wittenberg theologians.[14]

With the *Declaratio* as a model, Archbishop von Wied commissioned Gropper to draft an agenda for a provincial synod (to take place in 1536), which outlined various measures for the reform of the Cologne diocese.[15] One of the outcomes of this request was Gropper's *Enchiridion christianae institutionis*, which was appended to the synod's proceedings.

The *Enchiridion* was a pastorally oriented manual for reform. The *Canones* described the *Enchiridion* as follows:

> *A summary of the Christian doctrine brought together in the Enchiridion*:
> Since evangelical and apostolic doctrine tells us (and here the decrees
> of the fathers and councils as well as the Pragmatic Sanction of the
> Diet of Augsburg agree) that preaching and reading in the church of
> God should come only from canonical scripture and the divine
> oracles in accordance with the ecclesiastical interpretation of the holy

11. Letter to Kaspar Hoyer (Jan. 1556), printed in W. E. Schwartz, "Römische Beitrage zu Johannes Groppers Leben und Wirken," *Historisches Jahrbuch* 7 (1886): 417; quoted in Braunisch, *Die Theologie der Rechtfertigung*, 34; "Juventutem iuris prudentiae mancipavi; biblia primum et sanctos patres ab anno trigesimo, quo in comitiis Augustensibus, quibus tum intereram, de religione agebatur, legere coepi, sed privatim sine magistro." Though he was a self-taught theologian, Albert Pighius praised Gropper's theological talent to the papal legate Marcello Cervino (later Pope Marcellus II) in a letter from 1541; "Gropper ist zwar von Beruf Jurist, aber durch Eifer und glückliche Neigung Theologe. Die Theologie hat er keiner Schule gelernt, sondern durch seine Veranlagung und seine Talente. Wenn ich zwischen einem Schultheologen und einem solchen zu wählen hätte, würde ich diesen vorziehen"; quoted in Stupperich, "Schriftverständnis und Kirchenlehre," 115.

12. For his theological influences, see Braunisch, *Die Theologie der Rechtfertigung*, 40–41; Braunisch, "Johannes Gropper zwischen Humanismus und Reformation," 199–200; and Lipgens, *Kardinal Johannes Gropper*, 42–46.

13. See Köhn, *Martin Bucers Entwurf*, 19–23. For the text of the *Declaratio*, see Aemilius L. Richter, *Die evangelischen Kirchenordnungen des sechzehnten Jahrhunderts: Ukunden und Regesten zur Geschichte des Rechts und der Verfassung der evangelischen Kirche in Deutschland*, vol. 1 (Weimar: Landes-Industriecomptoir, 1846), 212ff.

14. See Köhn, *Martin Bucers Entwurf*, 20n12.

15. For a historical background on the Cologne synod, see Braunisch, *Die Theologie der Rechtfertigung*, 27–60; Lipgens, *Kardinal Johannes Gropper*, 51–66; and Köhn, *Martin Bucers Entwurf*, 24–33.

fathers and doctors, it does not seem inappropriate to have a summary of the Bible drawn up for parish priests lest they run aground at some point because they do not know the chief points of scripture.[16]

In that sense the *Enchiridion* was seen as a preaching guide, organized much like a catechism. It is structured as follows: *De Symbolo Apostolorum* (2r–33r), *De Sacramentis Novi Testamenti* (33r–195v), *De Ratione ac Modo orandi Deum* (196r–234r), *De Natura, Distinctione, ui, ac usu legis, cum subiuncta explicatione decalogi* (234v–310r), and also included *Formula ad Quam Visitatio intra Dioecesim Coloniensem Exigetur* (310v–322v).[17]

The *Enchiridion* was extremely popular across Europe, resulting in forty reprintings within twenty-eight years (1541–1568).[18] Unfortunately or ironically, the *Canons'* reforms were never fully implemented in Cologne.[19] The *Enchiridion*'s main influence was within French and Italian reform-minded circles.[20] In addition, the popularity of the work gave it the impetus to reach beyond the Continent. For example, the *Enchiridion* became the basis of Archbishop John Hamilton's catechism in Scotland.[21] Its influence was also recognized at the Council of Trent.[22]

Though the *Enchiridion* was popular among many of the reform-minded, the moderate tone of Gropper's work brought it into disrepute. To post-Tridentine Catholics, it was seen as an attempt to incorporate evangelical (i.e., heretical) teachings into the Catholic faith. Roberto Bellarmino, for example, espoused this view. His criticism of the *Enchiridion* in *Disputationes . . . de controversiis christianae fidei . . .* [23] paved the way to its being placed on the *Index librorum prohibitorum* in 1596.[24] Evangelical opinions of the *Enchiridion* were mixed. Luther and Melanchthon were aggravated by it, feeling that it masked

---

16. *Canones* 6.20, 27(v); "Summa doctrinae christianae in Enchiridion contrahenda: Porro cum secundum evangelicam atque apostolicam doctrinam (quibus decreta patrum ac conciliorum, denique pragmatica sanctio Augustana merito accedant) ecclesia Dei sola canonica scriptura ac divina eloquia secundum ecclesiasticam interpretationem sanctorum patrum ac doctorum et recitari et praedicari debeat, non abs re videbitur parochis summam bibliorum paucissimis praescribere, ne alicubi, dum scripturae metas nesciunt impingant."

17. The section on the sacraments constitutes 50 percent of the entire *Enchiridion*.

18. Meier, "'Enchiridion Christianae Institutionis,'" 315–328.

19. Evidenced by the archbishop's later attempt at reform in 1542.

20. Meier, "'Enchiridion Christianae Institutionis,'" 302–306.

21. Alec Ryrie, "Reform without Frontiers in the Last Years of Catholic Scotland," *English Historical Review* 119 (2004): 43–44; James K. Cameron, "Cologne Reformation and the Church of Scotland," *Journal of Ecclesiastical History* 30 (1979): 39–40.

22. Meier, "'Enchiridion Christianae Institutionis,'" 306–309.

23. Roberto Bellarmino, *Disputationes Roberti Bellarmini Politiani . . . de controversiis christianae fidei, adversus huius temporis haereticos opus* (Ingolstat, 1581–1593). I made use of the 1601 Ingolstat edition, 4:1028, 1096–1097; see note 29 below.

24. Meier, "Enchiridion Christianae Institutionis," 310–314.

various papist errors.[25] Martin Bucer, as noted earlier, was much more positive. In the *Enchiridion* he saw a possible dialogue partner for moderate reform. We will see why.

"Double Justification"?

Gropper begins the subsection *De Iustificatione Hominis* by stating:

> And although, as we hope, we have taught above from the deepest foundations, by what order one attains justification, how it is accomplished in us through God, how it is received through faith (though not without hope and charity), and on whom it is bestowed: nevertheless, because this matter is disputed at this time with more zeal for quarrels than for godliness, we therefore strive to the best of our ability to rescue the truth itself by plumbing more deeply the most clear fountains of Holy Scripture and to render more clearly the opinion of the church. We consider, however, that the opinion of the church in this great matter is solely that which the authority of the apostolic scriptures defend, to which the fathers subscribe, which the universal church of whatever time has approved, and which all the godly not only assert, but also feel in their minds, and experience to be the truth itself.[26]

Gropper's desire to clarify the doctrine of justification from the deep fountains of Holy Scripture unfortunately would be proved by history to be anything but clear. His position that "Iustificatio duo proprie complectitur,"[27] combining forgiveness of sins and regeneration under the one heading of justification, similar to Bucer, has led to confusion over the relationship

---

25. Martin Luther, Justus Jonas, Bugenhagen, and Melanchthon to the Nürnberg Pastors (12 Feb. 1540), in *WA.Br.* 9, no 3444, 52, ll. 49–51; see also *WA.Br.* 8, no. 3287, 349, ll. 6–14. See Braunisch, "Johannes Gropper zwischen Humanismus und Reformation," 202.

26. *Enchiridion*, 132(r); "Et quamquam supra ex penitissimis, ut speramus, fundamentis docuerimus, quo ordine ad iustificationem perveniatur, quomodo per Deum in nobis fiat, quo pacto per fidem (non tamen sine spe et charitate) accipiatur, et cui tribuenda sit: nihilominus, quia haec materia hac tempestate maiori contentionis quam pietatis studio controvertitur, idcirco annitemur ipsissimam veritatem ex limpidissimis scripturae fontibus altius eruere, et ecclesiae sententiam, quod in nobis est, illustriorem reddere. Arbitramur autem ecclesiae sententiam in hac tanta re eam solam esse cui apostolicarum scripturarum patrocinatur authoritas, cui patres subscribunt, quam universa ecclesia cuiuslibet temporis comprobat, et quam omnes pii non tantum asserunt, sed et mente sentiunt, ac experiuntur ipsam veritatem esse."

27. Gropper, *Enchiridion*, 132a.

between *iustitia* and *iustificatio* in the *Enchiridion*. This confusion is primarily due to the failure to recognize Gropper's framework of sacramental incorporation.[28]

Cardinal Bellarmine criticized the work in his *De controversiis* because he believed it taught a "double justification" theory.[29] This criticism was partially due to his attempt to discredit Gropper as a participant at the negotiations at Regensburg, as well as his association of the *Enchiridion*'s view of justification with the view Gropper would later hold in his *Antididagma* (1544), where a double formal cause in justification (i.e., a proper "double justification" theory) is explicitly expressed.[30] The view that the *Enchiridion* advocated a "double justification" theory was advanced again in the twentieth century by Robert Stupperich in his study on the Diet of Regensburg.[31] Such analyses tend to be imprecise. The *Enchiridion* does not teach a "double justification" theory in a strict sense of justification holding to two formal causes, but a nuanced account of *duplex iustitia*, which in no way necessitates a double formal cause in justification.

As McGrath has shown, Gropper's understanding of *duplex iustitia*, which stems from the medieval distinction between *iustitia infusa* and *iustitia acquisita*, differs from a pure "double justification" view.[32] For Thomas Aquinas *iustitia infusa* (an infused habit of grace from God) was the formal cause of justification, whereas *iustitia acquisita*, caused by man's actions, remained insufficient for justification. Thomas states:

28. Braunisch was perhaps the first to demonstrate the importance of sacramental incorporation for Gropper's theology, specifically in the sacrament of the Eucharist. See Braunsich, *Die Theologie der Rechtfertigung*, 263–285, 407–408.

29. Bellarmino, *Disputationes Roberti Bellarmini*, 4:1028; "Bucerus in libro Concordiae, ut fortasse Catholicos aliquos seduceret, ut fecit, duplicem iustitiam excogitavit, a qua formaliter iustificaremur; unam imperfectam, quae in virtutibus in nobis inhaerentibus sita sit, alteram perfectam, quae est ipsa Christi iustitia nobis imputata. Quoniam enim iustitia nostra nunquam talis esse potest, ut iudicium Dei sustineat, ut ipse dicit, ideo necessarium esse imputationem iustitia Christi, ut illa induti, et quodammodo tecti coram Deo compareamus, et iusti pronunciemur. . . . In eandem sententiam sive potius errorem indicit Albertus Pighius in Contr. II et auctores Antididagmatis Coloniensis." See also pp. 1096–1097; "Altera sententia est auctoris Enchiridii Coloniensis in tractatu de Iustificatione, qui ex tribus illis haereticorum erroribus solum tertium non recipit. Vult enim necessarium esse ad iustificationem, ut certo credat unusquisque sibi remissa esse peccata; sed tamen negat, hominem sola fide iustificari: 'Fatemur,' inquit, 'verum esse ad iustificationem hominis omnino requiri, ut homo certo credat, non tantum generaliter, quod propter Christum vere poenitentibus remittantur peccata, sed et quod ipsimet homini credenti remissa sint propter Christum per fidem.' Haec ille. Sed liber is in multis aliis censura Ecclesiastica dignus esse videtur. Certe in modo loquendi doctrinam Melanchthonis et Buceri valde redolet."

30. See Gropper, *Antididagma seu christianae et catholicae religionis . . .* (Louvain: Servatius Zassenus, 1544), 21(v).

31. Stupperich, *Der Humanismus*, 15–18. Cf. McGrath, *Iustitia Dei*, 312–314; and Braunisch, *Die Theologie der Rechtfertigung*, 419–426.

32. See McGrath, *Iustitia Dei*, 312–314. See also Edward Yarnold's article, which discusses various understandings of *duplex iustitia*: "*Duplex Iustitia*: The Sixteenth Century and the Twentieth," in *Christian Authority: Essays in Honour of Henry Chadwick*, ed. G. R. Evans (Oxford: Clarendon Press, 1988), 204–223.

If, however, we take justification in the strict sense, justice may be predicated either of a habitual disposition or of individual acts; and accordingly justification may be taken in two ways. First, according as a man becomes just through acquiring the disposition of justice; second, according as he performs acts of justice and here justification is simply the carrying out of justice. Now justice, like the other virtues, may be acquired or infused, as we have seen. The acquired virtue is caused by man's acts, the infused comes from God himself through grace. The latter is true justice, of which we here speak, and on its account one is said to be just before God, according to Romans [4:2].[33]

Thomas held that justification is due to the *iustitia infusa* and not the acquired virtue. Gropper's position in the *Enchiridion* is similar in that it indicates one sole formal cause of justification that is founded on the *iustitia infusa*, the infusion of God's love into a Christian's heart.[34] There are not two formal causes but two types of righteousness, which do not necessarily result in two formal causes as Stupperich seems to suggest.[35]

Stupperich conflates *iustitia inhaerens* (another term used for *iustitia infusa*) with *iustitia acquisita* when he describes the distinction between *iustitia imputata* and *iustitia inhaerens* as a "double justification" theory.[36] This, however, neglects the incorporational aspect, on which Gropper bases his undeveloped view of *iustitia imputata*.

This aspect of *iustitia imputata* may be better understood by borrowing Luther's early analogy in his *Romans Lectures* of a sick man who has been promised a full recovery by a doctor. The sick man does what the doctor prescribes, trusting in the eventual fulfillment of the doctor's promise, that is, wellness.[37] Luther places an emphasis on trusting the doctor's diagnosis or decree. For Gropper, there is a similar proleptic quality to his understanding of the doctor's diagnosis. However, and this is an important distinction, Gropper's view sees the patient placing his trust in this diagnosis by trusting the medicine prescribed. The emphasis is placed on the medicines that the doctor has decreed as salvific (a kind of seven-step program). In Gropper's view the medicine is being incorporated into the body of Christ, which is decreed as salvific.

---

33. *ST* ia 2ae q.100 a.12.

34. *Enchiridion*, 142(r)–145(r).

35. Stupperich, *Der Humanismus*, 15–18, 10n4. Stupperich's characterization of Gropper's view is in part because he places Gropper within a broader Erasmian school, which he sees as holding a double justification theory: "Da alle Erasmus–Schüler ohne Ausnahme nur zu nahe, daß sie dazu von Erasmus selbst bestimmt sind."

36. Ibid., 10n4, 15–18. Cf. Braunisch, *Der Theologie der Rechtfertigung*, 419–425; and McGrath, *Iustitia Dei*, 312–314.

37. *WA* 56, 272, l. 3 through 273, l. 2.

It is through baptism that a person is incorporated into Christ, that is, imparted righteousness. This incorporation carries with it certain benefits, the first of which is that a believer can trust that, however weak his righteousness might be, Christ's righteousness supplements it. Thus, Gropper views one's incorporated membership into the body of Christ (the infusion of *iustitia* or *charitas*), which results in *iustitia acquisitia*, as the basis for the eschatological declaration of *iustitia*. That is, the recovery of the patient is dependent on the incorporation into Christ, which has with it the promise of final wellness, because what belongs to the head of the body, belongs to its members as well. Stupperich misunderstood the declarative aspect by neglecting the incorporational aspect of Gropper's teaching and conflating the impartative aspect, which is understood by incorporation, with *iustitia acquisitia*.

The rest of the chapter will demonstrate clearly how Gropper's understanding of justification ought to be considered within the transformational-sacramental paradigm of incorporation into Christ. In so doing I have relied heavily on the work of Reinhard Braunisch,[38] as well as Hubert Filser's more recent work on Gropper's ecclesiology and doctrine of the sacraments.[39] By elucidating the ecclesiological structure of his thought, it is possible to more clearly recognize differences between Bucer and Gropper.

Gropper's Doctrine of Justification

Gropper's view of justification is found within his elucidations on the sacraments because, for Gropper, God has decreed to bestow his grace by means of the sacraments, seen as divine accommodations to human nature:

> God could indeed give to us his grace without any visible form;
> however, seeing that we are carnal and very slow to grasp spiritual
> things, because the strength of the body's mind has greatly been
> spoiled and it is weakened in operation and divided from faith, hope,
> and love immediately ruining [it], therefore the weakness of our flesh
> has been repaired, encouraged, educated, nourished, and strength-
> ened under the visible form.[40]

38. See Braunisch's *Die Theologie der Rechtfertigung*. This is the only monograph dedicated to Gropper's teaching of justification.

39. Hubert Filser, *Ekklesiologie und Sakramentenlehre des Kardinals Johannes Gropper: Eine Glaubenslehre zwischen Irenik und Kontroverstheologie im Zeitalter der Reformation* (Münster: Lit Verlag, 1995).

40. *Enchiridion*, 34(r); "Potuit quidem ille sine omni visibili forma gratiam suam nobis dare, sed quoniam carnales sumus, et ad spiritualia capessenda admodum tardi, quia animi robur corporis vitiati mole ac operatione debilitetur ac distrahatur, a fide, spe, et charitate subinde concidens, idcirco fragilitas carnis sub forma visibili reparanda, incitanda, erudienda, fovenda et confortanda erat."

This does not mean that the sacraments are causes of grace in and of themselves, but rather God has chosen to tie to these visible signs the effectiveness of grace, which Gropper sees as the work of the Holy Spirit.[41]

In this manner he follows Peter Lombard's view of the sacraments as "visible signs of the invisible grace of God, which God certainly works in not unworthy recipients, through the sacraments when they are administered openly in the church, which externally bear the likeness of this same grace."[42] As one meditates on the visible sign (the visible word of grace), invisible grace is given to the believer.[43] The efficacy of grace in the sacraments is also described as medicine that is distributed to the sick.[44] Likewise, Gropper sees Christ as the original sacrament.[45] Through his death and resurrection, salvation is attained for humanity. And this accomplishment is passed on in the sacraments, where Christ imparts his grace to believers.[46]

At this point one immediately begins to notice the different ways in which Gropper and Bucer understand *gratia*. Gropper speaks of *gratia* in traditional terms as an imparted gift, which is manifest in various types of *gratia* (i.e., *praeveniens* or *operans, iustificans, subsequens* or *cooperans*).[47] For Bucer, as well as the reformers, *gratia* (the Latin translation for χάρις and חן) was understood as "favor" and "benevolence."[48] The reformers held that grace meant that God was for his elect, whereas Gropper believed God's grace to be an effective force or substance

41. See Braunisch, *Die Theologie der Rechtfertigung*, 286–290.

42. *Enchiridion*, 141(v); "ut signa sint visibilia gratiae Dei, quam Deus per ea quum in ecclesia publice administrantur, in non indigne recipientibus certo operatur, eiusdem gratiae similitudinem extrinsecus gerentia." See *Sentences*, bk 4, dist. 1, in *PL* 192, 1089.

43. *Enchiridion*, 34(v); "Sunt ergo sacramenta novi testamenti principaliter instituta, ut sint certa et efficacia signa, voluntatis et gratiae Dei in sensum externum incurrentia, admonentia et erudientia nos, ut quod foris in specie visibili geri cernimus, intus per Dei in Evangelio propositae." See also *Enchiridion*, 34(v); "Ita per sacramenta tanquam quaedam indicia seu testimonia Dei (quibus testatur se nobis placatum propter Christum filium suum) spiritus sanctus efficaciter operatur salutem et confert gratiam." Gropper takes up from Eck and Aquinas the notion of a threefold sign: *signa rememorativa passionis Christi, signa demonstrativa praesentis gratiae*, and *signa prognostica futurae gloria*. See Filser, *Ekklesiologie und Sakramentenlehre*, 173–174. In regard to the sacraments as the visible word, see *Enchiridion*, 34(v); "In sacramento ergo non tantum elementum seu exteriorem speciem respicimus sed magis verbum."

44. *Enchiridion*, 35(v); "Quanquam vero haec legis novae sacramenta praesentissima remedia sint, quibus Samaritanus ille bonus vulnerato appropinquans, et originalis et actualis peccati vulneribus medetur."

45. See Braunisch, *Der Theologie der Rechtfertigung*, 267.

46. *Enchiridion*, 76(v); "Et quoniam tota virtus passionis Christi, quod ad nos attinet, in applicatione sita est, ut scilicet eam gratiam (quam nobis in ara crucis moriendo promeruit Christus) participemus, dignatus est ipsa quaedam post se sacramenta relinquere, quae suo verbo et promissione firmavit, ut sciremus per eorum legitimum usum, fructum suae passionis, nobis efficaciter et certo communicari."

47. The differentiation of types of grace is borrowed from Augustine and Aquinas and was widely disregarded by the reformers, including Bucer. See Augustine, *De gratia et libero arbitrio*, xvii, 33, in *PL* 44, 901; *ST* 1a 2ae q.111 a.1–5; see Braunisch, *Die Theologie der Rechtfertigung*, 207–238.

48. *BRom* (1536), 53; (1562), 16–17; "Quod Scriptores Novi Testamenti χάρις, hoc scriptura חן vocat. Id nominis sic fere usurpatur, ut apud Latinos gratia, qua praediti dicuntur ii, qui hominibus grati sunt et amabiles, quosque gratiosos vocamus. Ut enim Latini dicunt, hic valet apud principem, aut populum gratia, ita Scriptura dicit: הדא מצא חן בעיני השר אן העם, Iste invenit gratiam in oculis principis vel populi. Hinc quibus Deus se singulariter bene voluisse testatus est, hos commemorat Scriptura invenisse gratiam in oculis Dei, ut Noah, Abraham,

in the elect that also placed them in him. The sacramental system incorporates the believer as a limb into the body of Christ or grafts the believer, as a branch, into the vine.[49] This sacramental incorporation is the governing premise for his discussion of justification, which begins in the sacrament of baptism.

Baptism

In baptism the infant dies with Christ and is raised with Christ.[50] In so doing he becomes a member of Christ's body. In this sacrament all guilt is removed on account of this membership;[51] however, concupiscence is not removed but remains in the baptized as a disposition to sin, though no longer imputed as sin.[52] Gropper states:

> Since in baptism not only all original sin but also all actual sin is forgiven, and the Holy Spirit, who regenerates us into a new creation, is given, who diminishes the tinder of concupiscence (that is, the disorder of appetite and weakness of corrupted nature, which remains after baptism), so that it cannot harm us unless we again assent to sin: it follows that if we had immediately to depart from this world after receiving baptism, baptism alone would suffice, and regeneration would in itself save those who would soon be received into the peace of the blessed world. For he who after baptism meets death spotless with acquired innocence is fortified by death, because he is not able to sin after death.[53]

Mosen, Davidem et alios. Cumque Dominus effecisset, ut Ioseph apud principem custodiae gratia valeret, id memorat Scriptura hisce verbis, הסהד ויתן תן בעיני שר בית, id est, et dedit gratiam eius in oculis principis domus custodiae. Eadem loquendi forma refert Dominum dedisse gratiam populo Israel, in oculis Aegyptiorum, ut quae peteret, Aegyptii ei commodarent. Ita liquet per ח in scripturis, significari favorem et benevolentiam. Cum itaque Deus nullo nostro merito, sed ultronea sua erga nos dignatione et benevolentia nos servat, Paulus gratia Dei servari nos praedicat, et passim pro gratuita Dei benevolentia et misericordia, nomine χάριτος utitur."

49. *Enchiridion*, 142(v) (marg. note); "Eoipso et ob id iusti sumus, quia Christo insiti." See Braunsich, *Die Theologie der Rechtfertigung*, 263–298, 406–408.

50. On baptism, see *Enchiridion*, 36(r)–41(v); see also Filser, *Ekklesiologie und Sakramentenlehre*, 191–213. In his discussion of baptism here, he takes up the theme of mortification and vivification from Romans 6 (*Enchiridion*, 37(r)).

51. *Enchiridion*, 40(v); "in baptismo omnis peccati reatus tollitur, chirographum damnationis nostrae deletur." See also *Antididagma*, 18(r); "Principio de iustifcatione qua increduli, impii, et qui hactenus inimici Dei fuerunt, in summa quotquot a matris utero in peccato originali nati sunt, primum et recenter in homines pios et Dei amicos, per sacrum baptisma regenerantur."

52. *Enchiridion*, 41(r); "Sed manet concupiscentia, quae licet a Paulo interdum peccatum dicatur, veluti quum ait: Si autem quod nolo, illud facio, iam non ego operor illud, sed quod habitat in me peccatum. Tamen post baptismum fomes non imputatur in peccatum, nisi ei mens seu voluntas assentiatur."

53. *Enchiridion*, 42(v); "Quum in baptismo non solum omne peccatum tam originale quam actuale remittatur, sed et spiritus sanctus in novam nos regenerans creaturam, detur, qui et concupiscentiae fomitem (id est,

Here it is important to note that baptism imparts grace and causes regeneration in the infant. It is the washing of regeneration (Titus 3:5);[54] the old man is expunged and the new man is raised. Through baptism this regeneration constitutes membership into the body of Christ; believers are now God's children, the fruits of which are the forgiveness of sins and resurrection from the dead.[55] Incorporation into Christ is the basis for the non-imputation of sins or innocence.

It is also important to note that concupiscence is no longer viewed as sin for Gropper; rather, it is after baptism only an *inclinatio*. As Braunisch states, "The impulse to sin [concupiscence] in man is continuously active; however God has justified man in such a way that he not only no longer condemns it, because he graciously decided to do so, but also because this desire is not worthy of condemnation, since God has created a new creature."[56] Here the evangelical emphasis of concupiscence as sin, that is, something still worthy of condemnation, is absent from Gropper's understanding.[57]

For Gropper baptism in the true Church creates Christians, that is, outside the Church there is no salvation.[58] With a prevenient gift of grace, children who were held captive by the devil now become children of grace.[59] In baptism a person puts on Christ, becoming a member of Christ's body; he is incorporated.

Confirmation

In the next section Gropper talks about the sacrament of confirmation.[60] Because most believers are not so fortunate as to die immediately after baptism, they live

---

appetitus inordinationem et naturae corruptae imbecillitatem, quae in nobis post baptismum reliqua est) sic attenuat, ut ea nobis, nisi rursus peccato assentiamus, nocere non possit: consequens est, ut si continuo ex hoc seculo post receptum baptismum nobis migrandum foret, solus ipse baptismus sufficeret, et regeneratio per se salvaret, mox in pace beati seculi recipiendos. Qui enim post baptismum cum acquisita innocentia immaculatus pervenit ad mortem, ipse morte confirmatur, quod non possit peccare post mortem."

54. Filser, *Ekklesiologie und Sacramentenlehre*, 194–195.

55. *Enchiridion*, 37(r); "Natura nascimur filij irae, sed baptismus regenerat nos filios gratiae, Natura nascimur ex sanguinibus, ex voluntate carnis, ex voluntate viri, hoc est, in peccatis, sed ex baptismo renascimur filij Dei: nimirum Christo filio dei per baptismum inserti, sicut Paulus ait: Quicunque in Christo baptizati estis, Christum induistis [Gal 3:27]." See Filser, *Ekklesiologie und Sacramentenlehre*, 198.

56. Braunisch, *Die Theologie der Rechtfertigung*, 132.

57. Cf. section 3.4.2.1.2.

58. *Enchiridion*, 2(v); "Ecclesia catholica per lavacrum regenerationis nos efficit Christianos." See also *Enchiridion*, 29(v)–30(r); "In ecclesia, inquam, non haereticorum sed sancta, catholica et apostolica, in spiritu Christi congregata, est remissio peccatorum per baptismum, et post baptismum per poenitentiam et claves ecclesiae datas."

59. *Enchiridion*, 30(r); "Innovat siquidem hominem per baptismum qui fecit illum, praevenit gratia etiam ipsam infantiam, ut sint liberi, per Christum liberati, qui in Adam a diabolo tenebantur ante captivi."

60. *Enchiridion*, 42(r)–49(r). See Filser, *Ekklesiologie und Sakramentenlehre*, 213–231.

their lives in a constant battle against concupiscence (seen by Gropper as a defect of both the will and the intellect).[61] Thankfully, God has provided the sacrament of confirmation as a way in which believers can be strengthened against the tactics of Satan, the world, and the flesh:[62] "In baptism we are regenerated into life, after baptism we are strengthened for battle. In baptism we are cleansed, after baptism we are strengthened: in baptism we are received and sealed into the army of Christ, in confirmation we are set aside for the battles and struggles of this world and we are equipped with the proper armor for the fight."[63] In the sacrament of confirmation the believer is strengthened in wisdom, understanding, counsel, strength, knowledge, piety, and the fear of the Lord.[64] These are the weapons given for the battle. By the sacrament of confirmation the baptized are endowed with a strengthening of grace.[65]

The Eucharist

The concept of incorporation is prominent within Gropper's discussion of the sacrament of the Eucharist.[66] By participating in the Eucharist, believers grow in righteousness because they are united with the Spirit, and in the meal they are incorporated into the body of Christ. Gropper states:

This sacrament is also called by the Greeks *synaxis*, that is, a conciliation or communion, because by this mystery it is signified and confirmed a very close union of the mystical body with the head,

61. *Enchiridion*, 3(v); "At posteaquam protoplastes legem dei neglexit, et Satanae legibus optemperare maluit, protinus intellectum, hoc est mentem et rationem, qua iudicaret, quid eligendum, omnis error invasit. Itidem voluntatem, qua expeteret, quod demonstraret ratio, carnalis concupiscentia graviter vitiavit. . . . Utraque ergo parte vitiata, duplici remedio opus erat, fide, quae purificaret cor, hoc est mentem et rationem, ceu fontem animi, et charitate, quae submoveret pravas cupiditates, ut ad ea tantum feramur, quae praescripsit Deus."

62. *Enchiridion*, 43(v); "Hoc ergo in sacramento confirmationis agitur, ut spiritum sanctum, quem in baptismo ad purificationem et emundationem accepimus, ad robur quoque et augmentum virtutis capiamus, quo adversus peccatorum, mundi, et diaboli insultus confirmemur, et facti intrepidi, nullis perturbationibus frangi, nullis tribulationibus succumbre, nullis denique terroribus ac cruciatibus a Christo separari valeamus."

63. *Enchiridion*, 42(v); "Itaque in baptismo regeneramur ad vitam, post baptismum confirmamur ad pugnam. In baptismo abluimur, post baptismum roboramur: in baptismo in milites Christi recipimur ac signamur, in confirmatione ad agones et praelia mundi huius reservandi, armis competentibus instruimur pugnaturi."

64. *Enchiridion*, 45(r); "Immitte in eum spiritum sanctum tuum septiformis gratiae tuae, paracletum, de coelis, spiritum sapientiae et intellectus, spiritum consilii et fortitudinis, spiritum scientiae et pietatis, et imple eum spiritu timoris tui, et signa eum signaculo sanctae crucis, propitiatus, et spiritum sanctum non amittat in vitam aeternam."

65. *Enchiridion*, 42(v); "Ergo spiritus Sanctus, qui super aquas baptismi salutifero descendit illapsu, in fonte pulchritudinem tribuit ad innocentiam: in confirmatione augmentum praestat ad gratiam, quia in hoc mundo tota aetate victuris, inter invisibiles hostes et pericula gradiendum est: quamobrem alia atque alia specie subinde visus est."

66. *Enchiridion*, 49(r)–81(r). See Filser, *Ekklesiologie und Sakramentenlehre*, 232–300; and Thompson, *Eucharistic Sacrifice*, 154–166.

that is, of Christ and the Church, and of all the true professing members of Christ, who truly profess the name of Christ among themselves, a term which has been taken from the words of St. Paul.[67]

Again he says:

Moreover the principal end of the institution of this sacrament is, that it be a witness and a pledge of remission of sins and of future glory gained for us through Christ. For when Christ shares his body with us, and he attaches us as his members to himself, he testifies that his benefits apply to us. For he says: "He who eats my flesh, and drinks my blood, he remains in me and I in him." (John 6[56])[68]

Again he says:

David, foreseeing this restoration [to eternal life], sang: how glorious is my cup of satisfaction. Then since the church is the mystical body of Christ and Christ wanted to commit to us its unity, by the receiving of this sacrament, the matter of bread and wine was very appropriately chosen. For just as one loaf is made from many grains, and wine flows from many grapes, and one body is composed of many members, so the church is a combination of many faithful people bound together by love. Christ in fact consecrated the mystery of our peace and unity on his table. Moreover it was necessary that scripture be thus fulfilled, and that the shadow be dispelled by the supervening light, and the truth correspond to the figure.[69]

By participating in the body and blood of Christ in the Eucharist, believers become more like Christ, that is, more righteous.

67. *Enchiridion*, 50(r); "Dicitur quoque hoc sacramentum a Graecis synaxis, id est conciliatio seu communio, quod hoc mysterio significetur et confirmetur arctissima coniunctio mystici corporis cum capite, hoc est, Christi et ecclesiae, et omnium Christi membrorum, Christi nomen vere profitentium inter se, quae appellatio ex divi Pauli verbis desumpta est, dicentis (1 Cor. 10)."

68. *Enchiridion*, 57(r)–(v); "Praeterea principalis finis institutionis huius sacramenti est, ut sit testimonium et quasi pignus remissionis peccatorum et futurae gloriae nobis per Christum promeritae. Quum enim Christus nobis corpus suum impertit, et nos sibi tanquam membra adiungit, testatur ad nos suum beneficium pertinere. Sic enim ait: Qui manducat carnam meam, et bibit sanguinem meum, in me manet et ego in eo."

69. *Enchiridion*, 52(v)–53(r); "Quam refectionem praevidens David, cecinit: Calix meus inebrians, quam praeclarus est. Deinde quum ecclesia Christi corpus mysticum sit, et illius unitatem, perceptione huius sacramenti Christi nobis commendare voluerit, panis et vini materia conguentissime delecta est. Quoniam sicut ex multis granis conficitur unus panis, et ex pluribus acinis vinum confluit, et unum corpus ex multis membris conponitur, sic ecclesia ex multis fidelibus charitate copulante connectitur. Mysterium siquidem pacis et unitatis nostrae, Christus in sua mensa consecravit. Praetera sic oportebat adimpleri scripturam, et umbram per supervenientem lucem evacuari, et veritatem figurae respondere."

The sacraments are means of progressing in grace and righteousness, so that in baptism believers are initiated into Christ, in confirmation strengthened in Christ, and in the Eucharist partake of Christ. All demonstrate and illuminate and cause the believer's incorporation into the body of Christ. Thus he is able to say that through baptism, confirmation, and the Eucharist Christians are baked into the bread of Christ.[70] In this context of incorporation into the body of Christ, God is the great baker, milling, mixing, and baking the church into Christ's body.

Penance

Half of Gropper's discussion on the seven sacraments of the New Testament deals with the sacrament of penance.[71] It is in this section that Gropper offers his focused discussion on the doctrine of justification because the doctrine, for him, is concerned with adult faith effective in love.[72] True penance is "nothing other than the conversion of men to God."[73]

Gropper proceeds to analyze the sacrament by means of various subdivisions: *De Poenitentia* (which deals with *Contritio*) (81v–102v), *De Confessione* (102v–126v), *De Satisfactione* (126v–132r), *De Iustificatione Hominis* (132r–147v), *De Poenitentia Exteriori* (147v–150v), and *De Poenitentiae Sacramento* (151r–157r). Within these divisions Gropper distinguishes between *poenitentia interior* and *poenitentia exterior*. The first four sections generally deal with the interior form of penance. *Poenitentia interior* is the necessary prerequisite for the *poenitentia exterior*, realized in absolution.[74] Thus, properly speaking, for Gropper, the sacrament of penance is related to the exterior

---

70. *Enchiridion*, 77(v); "Et quo magis huius sacramenti virtus illustretur, ad caeterorum etiam sacramentorum efficaciam conferenda est. Sub baptismum quum exorcizamur, quasi molimur: quando baptizamur, quasi conspergimur: quando spiritus sanctificationem accipimus (quod in confirmatione fit) quasi coquimur: at in hoc sacramento Christi panis efficimur." This image comes from Augustine's *Sermo CCXXIX(a) "De sacramentis fidelium, feria II Paschae,"* in *PL* 38, 1103.

71. *Enchiridion*, 81(v)–157(r). See Braunisch, *Die Theologie der Rechtfertigung*, 183–298; and Filser, *Ekklesiologie und Sakramentenlehre*, 300–341.

72. *Enchiridion*, 143(v) [i.e., 145(v)]; "Nam cum de fide iustificante loquimur maxime in adulto, non accipimus fidem, quatenus habitus quispiam est, sed magis quatenus in actu consistit."

73. *Enchiridion*, 82(r); "Ordiemur ergo a verae poenitentiae descriptione, quae sane nihil aliud est, quam conversio hominis ad Deum, quae tum fit ac peragitur, quum peccata quae vel in nobis experimur, vel commisimus, propter Deum, ex animo non sine gravi animi dolore odimus cum voto ac proposito deinceps non peccandi, sed vitam in melius commutandi."

74. *Enchiridion*, 82(r); "veteres verae poenitentiae tres partes numerarunt, Contritionem, Confessionem, et Satisfactionem. Rursus veram poenitentiam duabus speciebus contineri constat, Interiori et exteriori. Exterior iterum in publicam et privatam scinditur. . . . Hae tamen omnes exteriroris poenitentiae species ut fructuosae sint, interiorem poenitentiam praesupponunt."

form.[75] However, here I will focus on the interior aspect of penance, since it is in these first sections where Gropper elucidates his understanding of faith, grace, and *iustitia*.

THE PROGRESSION OF FAITH.   In the first subsection, dealing primarily with contrition, Gropper explains what he means by faith. For him it is both a revelatory and a transforming act, that is, true faith involves both the intellect and the will. Faith is intellectual in that it is sometimes understood as learning doctrines and punishments, which inspire fear associated with the second use of the law. Likewise, faith affects the will in that it is seen as an infused gift of God that transforms and empowers the will. The manner in which faith affects the intellect and the will is seen in terms of progression. Faith progresses from a general type to a special type, which he clearly describes using the Augustinian distinctions *credere Deum, credere Deo*, and *credere in Deum*.[76]

Both *credere Deum* and *credere Deo* are understood as intellectual faiths: that is, they are tied to learning doctrines, specifically gaining knowledge that God exists, as well as learning about God's promises and his punishments. *Credere Deum* is the first step in faith and is purely a historical faith. It basically believes that there is a God. *Credere Deo*, a second step in faith, is used to describe faith that believes in the promises and truths of scripture, as well as knowing that God is angry with sin and that God punishes wickedness.[77] Both of these two initial faiths are of the general type, which is able to believe the facts of the gospel just as the demons do (James 2:19).[78]

Within the context of penance, these two preliminary faiths (*credere Deum* and *credere Deo*) are associated with the beginning of justification and penance.

75. *Enchiridion*, 82(r); "Intetum costat, illius exterioris poenitentiae, quae proprie sacramentum est . . . vim propemodum totam in absolutione consistere." Gropper leaves his discussion of absolution, exterior penance, at the end of his discussion starting on 147(v) [i.e., 149(v)].

76. *Enchiridion*, 85(r); "nempe duplicem aut triplicem etiam esse fidei seu credendi rationem." On this Augustinian trifold distinction (*Sermo de symbolo* in *PL* 40, chap. 1, 1190–1191), see Th. Camelot, "Credere Deo, Deum, in Deum: Pour l'histoire d'une formule traditionnelle," *Revue des Sciences Philosophiques et Théologiques* 30 (1941–1942): 149–155. See also Braunisch, *Der Theologie der Rechtfertigung*, 196–202. Though Bucer too has a progression in faith, which I described in the previous chapter, he does not agree with the use of these three terms (*credere Deum, credere Deo*, and *credere in Deum*) because the dative and accusative tenses with or without the preposition "in" cannot be distinguished in the scriptures in the same manner that Augustine and the scholastics imply. See *BRom* (1536), 21–22; (1562), 21–22; *CP* 193–194.

77. *Enchiridion*, 85(r); "Aliter, qua Deo credimus, quae persuasio et constans opinio est, qua fidem et promissionibus et comminationibus divinis adhibemus, quam habent iniusti cum iustis communem. Nam . . . revelatur ira Dei super omnem impietatem et iniustitiam hominum eorum qui veritatem Dei in iniustitia detinent: id est, ira Dei revelatur hominibus etiam iniustis, qui veritatem et iustitiam Dei (qua sciunt Deum esse, Deum peccatis irasci, Deum scelera punire) in iniustitia detinent et contemnunt."

78. *Enchiridion*, 85(r); "Siquidem una est, qua Deum esse, ac caetera quae scriptura commemorat, non aliter quam historica quadam fide recitata, vera credimus. Unde et historica fides appellatur quam nobiscum daemones communem habent." See also *Enchiridion*, 144(r).

They spring up from the threats of the law, arousing a fear of God's punishment (*timor servilis*).[79] Here the law serves a double function: first to reveal to
the sinner his own sinfulness and then to also make the sinner aware of God's
righteousness.[80] Prior to this knowledge from the law, similar to Bucer, the
sinner remains ignorant. This ignorance is overcome by the gift of the Spirit
through a progression of grace and faith.[81]

The previous types of faith are generally seen as intellectual, whereas
justifying faith is seen as healing and strengthening the will.[82] Gropper
views the weaker intellectual faiths as providing the basis needed for man to
assent to God, and can be called infused or habitual faith (*fides infusa, habitualis*), whereas true faith, which is effective in love, can be called acquired or
actual faith (*fides acquisita, actualis*).[83] It ought to be clearly noted that true
faith is not separate from the two preceding faiths but envelops them. In this
sense contrition "begins and is conceived in most by a historical faith and a
timor servilis (attrition), but it is not perfected unless by a sincere faith and
timor filialis."[84] True contrition is based on love of God rather than a fear of
punishment. In this way true contrition and true faith are seen as effective
in love:[85]

> Love cannot be absent from a vigorous and sincere faith (that is, on
> account of the third manner of believing [*credere in Deum*], to which
> justification is bestowed). For you believe in vain that God exists and is
> one, unless you believe in such a way that God exists so that you render
> all things received to him and you fasten all your hope for salvation in

79. *Enchiridion*, 87(r)–88(r).

80. See Braunisch, *Die Theologie der Rechtfertigung*, 188.

81. *Enchiridion*, 202(r); "In donis spiritus et virtutibus Christianis gradus sunt quidam. Peccator quum in
altissimus ignorantiae tenebris versatur, secundum carnem vivens, sequens carnales concupiscentias, peccat,
sed propemodum ignorans. Deinde quum respicit in legem Dei condemnantem peccatum, si nondum adiuvet
spiritus, vult quidem secundum legem vivere, sed victus concupiscentia delinquit, idque sciens, et proinde
gravius. Postquam autem accesserit spiritus, quo donante credimus, nobis ex toto corde conversis ab operibus
mortuis ad Deum per Christum remissum iri peccata, ac donari gratiam adiutricem adimplendi mandatum Dei,
tum demum incipit homo agi spiritu Dei."

82. *Enchiridion*, 85(r); "Nec hoc omittendum est, fidem secundum tertiam vero etiam in voluntate, quod
actio fidei sic acceptae (quod est credere, fidere, et adhaerere Deo) non solo intellectu, quem fides illuminat, sed
et voluntate, quam accedente charitate inflammat, perficiatur." See also *Enchiridion*, 3(r)–(v).

83. *Enchiridion*, 85(r); "Haec fides quatenus homini ad assentiendum his quae credenda sunt, a Deo infun-
ditur, fides infusa dicitur: quatenus vero post iustificationem vel per auditum verbi, vel per visa miracula augescit,
acquisita. Rursus, quatenus se non exerit, habitualis: quatenus vero sese exerit, et exercet, actualis appellatur."

84. *Enchiridion*, 86(r); "Haec [i.e., contritio] incipit quidem et concipitur ut plurimum fide historica et
timore servali, sed non perficitur nisi fide syncera et timore servili."

85. *Enchiridion*, 87(r); "Vides ergo, quemadmodum consideratio iustitiae ac iudicii divini, accedente fide
historica, poenitentiam inchoet, consideratio vero bonitatis divinae ex amoris affectu cum fiducia misericordiae,
poenitentiam formet."

him. However, you do not do this unless you join love to faith and afterward demonstrate good works, so that what you believe you love.[86]

Justifying faith is *efficax per charitatem*.[87]

The two weaker faiths cannot bring about justification until there is true justifying faith (associated with *timor filialis, gratia iustificans*).[88] Justifying faith or *timor filialis* is described as trust (*fiducia*) in God by which a believer depends on the mercy and grace of God, that is, the formal cause of justification.[89] Gropper states:

> Actual trust, which now inspires a contrite and humble heart to believe God, seeks mercy and at last contemplates the author and perfector of faith, Jesus; it believes that sins are forgiven to him through Jesus and at the same time receives the Holy Spirit who renews the heart, and imbues the heart with the affection of love; I say this trust (which is the work that God particularly requires in us) obtains and receives justification.[90]

Because true faith is seen as the work that God requires, the *condicio sine qua non*, Gropper can describe it in combination with repentance as a work of congruous merit, inspired by the Holy Spirit.[91] Faith is the means by which God has decreed to justify his people; it is the instrumental cause.[92]

86. *Enchiridion*, 86(r); "Sed fidei integrae ac syncerae (nimirum secundum tertiam credendi rationem acceptae, cui iustificatio tribuitur) non potest abesse charitas. Frustra enim credis, esse Deum, et esse Deum unum, nisi sic credas Deum esse, ut illi omnia accepta referas, omnemque tuae salutis spem in illum defigas. At id non facies, nisi fidei adiungas charitatem, ac postea piis operibus testeris, et quod credas et quod ames."

87. *Enchiridion*, 144(r).

88. *Enchiridion*, 144(v); "Unde Paulus monet, ut accedamus cum vero corde in plenitudine fidei aspersi corda a conscientia mala, ut manifestum sit eos homines, qui vitiosis indulgent cupiditatibus hanc fidem habere vel retinere non posse, licet fidem habeant, quae ipsis vel cum daemonibus vel cum impiis communis est, quae omnem poenitentiam praecedit, sed non iustificat."

89. *Enchiridion*, 85(r); "Tertia fidei ratio est, qua in Deum credimus, solis piis peculiaris, quae certissima quaedam fiducia est qua toto nos Deo submittimus, totique a gratia et misericordia Dei pendemus. Haec et spem complectitur et charitatem individuam comitem habet. Est enim . . . fides, qua amando in Deum itur, nimirum quam Paulus describens ait, fides quem per charitatem operatur." See Braunisch, *Die Theologie der Rechtfertigung*, 312–317. Martin Greschat takes Gropper's understanding of faith as trust to be his major step toward an evangelical understanding of justification (*Martin Bucer*, 177).

90. *Enchiridion*, 143(r) [i.e., 145(r)]; "ipsa actualis fiducia, qua cor contritum et humliliatum iam Deo fidere incipit, misericordiam quaerit, ac tandem aspiciens in authorem fidei et consummatorem Iesum, sibi per eundem peccata remitti credit, ac simul spiritum sanctum cor innovantem ac affectu charitatis imbuentem accipit, ea inquam fiducia (quae opus est quod in nobis Deus praecipue requirit) iustificationem, impetrat et accipit."

91. *Enchiridion*, 144(v). See Braunisch, *Die Theologie der Rechtfertigung*, 232–238.

92. *Enchiridion*, 93(v). See Braunisch, *Die Theologie der Rechtfertigung*, 232–238.

Justifying faith, as the instrumental cause of salvation, however, does not exclude hope and love.[93] Faith, hope, and love are bound together. On this account Gropper sees himself as going against the *plures haeretici* (the reformers) who separate faith and therefore justification from love[94]—a point Bucer later tried to show Gropper was not the case.[95] Suffice it to say that for Gropper true faith is understood in actual rather than habitual or infused terms; justifying faith is known in works.

THE PROGRESSION OF GRACE.   Just as there is a progression in faith, there is a progression in grace. For Gropper grace can be either general or special, the former being the grace that is common to all, that is, the grace of creation.

The *gratia creatoris* is given to humanity on account of its being created in the image of God; specifically, it is understood as the gift of rationality.[96] After the Fall the image of God became so weak that it lost both *iustitia* and the *gratia* of God.[97] Yet on account of *gratia creatoris*, rationality remained, albeit in a darkened form as a *lumen mentis* (also called the *lumen naturae*).[98] This feeble light allowed the Old Testament Israelites to understand the Mosaic Law, and after the time of Christ, it allows people to understand the Gospel Law, in a manner akin to the first levels of faith. Fathoming these laws, however, does not mean the ability to fulfill them. To keep the law and to love God necessitates that the Law of the Spirit enters into a person's heart.[99]

This darkened *lumen* corresponds to the weakening of the *liberum arbitrium*. Before the Fall, Adam and Eve had complete freedom—they were free from

93. *Enchiridion*, 144(r); "Spes proprie futurorum est, fides praesentium. Spes se accepturam confidit, fides vero arripit et accipit. Charitas operosa est, sed non prius operatur, nisi fide pacem erga Deum te assequutum apprehenderis. Ergo cum fidem in Christum, proximum instrumentum iustificationis appellamus, charitatem et spem a iustificatione non excludimus: sed propriam esse fidei rationem, iustificationis donum ac pollicitationem spiritus accipere, cum divo Paulo et Ambrosio ac caeteris catholicis patribus docemus."

94. *Enchiridion*, 139(v); "Sed hic diligenter animadvertendum est, longe alius esse dicere, omni homini quicunque credit sibi remissa esse peccata per Christum, illi statim peccata remitti, quam si dicas: Nemini remitti peccata, nisi remissionem se credat assequutum per Christum, nam hoc verum est, illud falsum. Plures enim ex haereticis invenias qui sic credunt, et tamen remissionem peccatorum non assequuntur quod extra ecclesiam sint et spiritu charitatis vacent. Utrunque ergo requiritur ad iustificationem, nempe ut et credas tibi remissa esse peccata per Christum, et ut te spiritu charitatis renovatum mente, et iam ad opus bonum affectum esse per fidem intelligas."

95. *BDS* 11/2, 298, ll. 10–16.

96. *Enchiridion*, 5(v); "Fecit et hominem ad imaginem et similitudinem suam, in mente homini indita, ibi enim est imago Dei. Ideo mens ipsa non potest comprehendi, ne a seipsa quidem, quia est imago Dei."

97. See *Enchiridion*, 89(r)–90(v).

98. *Enchiridion*, 238(r); "Lumen illud naturae menti primi hominis infusum etsi peccato succedente non penitus extinctum, mirum tamen in modum obtenebratum fuit. Remansit adhuc effigies quaedam et imago divinae sapientiae, quam ipse animis nostris impressit ac insculpsit, sed tenuis, qua tamen nullum est in rerum natura certius Dei vestigium." See *Enchiridion*, 236(v)–237(r).

99. *Enchiridion*, 143(r)–145(v) [i.e., 145(r)–147(v)].

compulsion and able to choose God. After the Fall, the ability to choose God was lost, and the ability to choose without compulsion was weakened. Therefore, in order to choose God, there needed to be given special grace that could restore the *liberum arbitrium*. In other words, fallen humanity cannot choose to love God; it must always wait passively for God's healing grace.[100]

Special grace is properly Christian grace received on account of the mercy of God and administered by the Spirit. It is this special grace that heals and justifies a person's deprived nature.[101] It is also this grace that is further broken down into various types of grace beginning with *gratia preveniens*.[102]

Prevenient grace, also known as *gratia operans*, "is that which precedes and prepares the will—not that the will is created, for even before this grace the will existed—but now the will becomes good, and is freed from its prior state of being enslaved to sin."[103] Prevenient grace prepares the will by means of the intellect, that is, Gropper describes it in intellectual terms as a knowledge that allows the person to acknowledge his own sins. This grace in and of itself is similar to *timor servilis*, which is insufficient for justification. For this there is need of *gratia iustificans*.[104] Justifying grace added to prevenient grace heals the will.[105] It is understood in a parallel sense to the idea of faith, so that if prevenient grace is seen as the weaker form of faith, akin to *timor servilis*, then justifying grace is seen as the gift of true faith, *credere in Deum*, akin to *fides actualis* or *timor filialis*, as described earlier.

Though the distinction can be described in this way, at times Gropper blurs the line between prevenient and justifying grace in regard to the manner in which they affect the will.[106] Both prevenient and justifying grace are seen to

100. *Enchiridion*, 88(v); "Sed interim impii, impoenitentes et praefracti, qui excusationem in peccatis quaerunt, peccatum peccato cumulantes, suae damnationis causam blasphema voce in deum transferunt, causantes (idque ex Paulinis verbis perperam detortis) quod resipiscere ab iniquitate non sit, neque volentis neque currentis hominis, sed solius Dei miserentis. Atque hinc inferre moliuntur, omnem hominis curam in hac re plane supervacaneam esse, asserere non verentes arbitrii libertatem in homine ad bonum prorsus nihil valere. Quae sententia plane impia hac deploratissima tempestate innumerabilem Christiani gregis turbam misere deceptam, in aeternae damnationis barathrum praecipitavit."

101. *Enchiridion*, 91(r); "Gratia vero specialiter accepta, quam doctrina Christiana et demonstrat et praedicat esse propriam Christianorum, non est natura, sed est occulta misericordia Dei, qua per subministrationem spiritus, sanatur ac salvatur natura qua praedestinati vocamur, iustificamur, sanamur et glorificamur."

102. Here Gropper follows Peter Lombard. See Lombard, *Sentences*, bk. 4, dist. 25–26; *PL* 192, 709–714.

103. *Enchiridion*, 91(r)–(v); "Operans ergo gratia est quae praevenit ac praeparat voluntatem, non ut fiat voluntas, quia et ante hanc gratiam voluntas erat, sed ut voluntas bona fiat, et quae prius erat serva peccati, liberetur."

104. *Enchiridion*, 92(v); "Gratia ergo praeveniens, qua Deus hominem incitat ut iustificetur, gratia quidem Dei est eximia, sed non sufficit, nisi accedat gratia iustificans, quae voluntatem sanat, et sola facit ut recte vivatur."

105. *Enchiridion*, 92(v)–94(r).

106. See Braunisch, *Die Theologie der Rechtfertigung*, 219–221.

work with man in a cooperative way, so that Gropper can describe actual faith as *believing* that one's sins are forgiven and at the same time *accepting* the renewing Holy Spirit and the infusion of the affect of love.[107] The gift of grace is free; however, it is also something to be accepted by an assent of the will.[108] The response to the grace of God, however, is the result of God's work in us, enabling us to accept the forgiveness of sins.[109] Elsewhere he states: "We do not deny that an assent of our will is necessary for justification just as Augustine said: 'God who created you without you, does not justify you without you.'"[110] He qualifies this by stating: "We assert that our will is not able to justify itself any more than a blind, ugly, or bent man is by nature able to make himself sighted, beautiful, or straight: so that those who dare to say that the will of man justifies itself are not only ungodly, but clearly mad."[111] True faith is seen as involving the will's response. The will, having been prepared by God, now trusts, assents, and believes.

Because concupiscence is not eliminated by prevenient and justifying grace until the believer is finally glorified,[112] there is need of a third grace, which helps the believer grow in righteousness and charity. *Gratia cooperans* is the grace given to persevere in good works of love.

---

107. *Enchiridion*, 143(r) [i.e., 145(r)].

108. *Enchiridion*, 91(v); "Gratia praeveniens plurimos habet gradus, et ut summatim dicamus, duplex est. Una, qua Deus praevenit peccatorem ut resurgat. Altera, qua peccator praevenienti Deo assentiens iam resurgit. Utraque voluntatem nostram praevenit Deus, sed priorem subministrando solus operatur, in altera voluntas nostra Deum praevenientem subsequens ei per velle seu assensum, remissionem peccatorum accipiendo cooperatur." *Enchiridion*, 94(r); "Hanc autem gratiam iustificantem voluntas nostra (ut supra diximus) comitatur, ac veluti pedissequa subsequitur, non quidem tempore, sed causa tantum et natura. Voluntas enim in iustificatione nostra, gratiae quodammodo cooperatur, sic ut iustificatio nostra sine voluntate et consensu accipiens non perficiatur." See also *Enchiridion*, 144(v).

109. *Enchiridion*, 94(v); "Itaque velle poenitere, velle resipiscere, velle accipere remissionem peccatorum, non est sola voluntate, sed illud nobiscum operatur dominus, dum immutando malevolam voluntatem, eam facit benevolam, et suae voluntati consentientem. Unde voluntatem quidem nostram Deus immutat, et sic operatur in nobis velle, sed tamen quia voluntas invita mutari nequit, Deo cooperatur dum ei consentit."

110. *Enchiridion*, 143(v); "Itidem non inficiamur assensu voluntatis nostrae ad iustificatione opus esse, quemadmodum Augustinus dixit: Deum qui creavit te sine te, non iustificare te sine te." Augustine on Philippians 3, in Lombard, *Collectanea*; PL 192, 243.

111. *Enchiridion*, 143(v); "Sed asserimus, voluntatem nostram non magis seipsam iustificare posse, quam hominem natura caecum, deformem aut incurvum, seipsum facere posse videntem, formosum aut rectum: ut non solum impii, sed plane insani sint, qui dicere ausint: Voluntatem hominis seipsam iustificare."

112. *Enchiridion*, 96(v)–97(r); "In Christo manentes per Christum (qui solus legem implevit) legem imputative implemus, si tamen nullum consensum praebeamus, nec secundum carnis desideria ambulemus, ut ex religua infirmitate, innitentibus nobis super Christum, nihil damnationis sit timendum, quod Christus vim et tyrannidem peccati eneruauerit, ut amodo in nobis mortem operari non possit, nisi rursus a Christo declinantes, per consensum in illud ruamus: In summa statuendum est, nos per gratiam Salvatoris in hac quidem vita proficere, deficiente scilicet sensim cupiditate, et crescente charitate, per subministrationem spiritus sancti: sed perfici demum in illa vita futura, quum cupiditas tota extinguetur, et chartias complebitur."

> Subsequent or cooperating grace accompanies our will, because after
> our will has been healed through justifying grace it now has a
> measure of freedom to fight against its infirmity and to function well,
> not on account of a fear of punishment, but rather with a love for
> God and righteousness, since now it is aided by the Holy Spirit,
> which God imparts to us in justification and which he pours into our
> hearts through the gift of charity.[113]

This is a strengthening grace.[114] It helps the will follow the commands of the
law in good works (similar to a third use of the law). The will freed, with this
helping grace, ought to pursue perfection.[115]

In this general threefold manner (*preveniens, iustificans, cooperans*) a Christian progresses in grace: the believers are prepared, healed, and strengthened
until they are perfected in the end. The branch is grafted into the vine, is
watered by grace, which then produces the fruits of faith and love. True contrition is the combination of *credere Deum* and *credere Deo* with *credere in Deum*;
timor servilis with *timor filialis; gratia praeveniens* with *gratia iustificans*.

IUSTITIA.   In the section titled *De iustificatione hominis*, Gropper deals with
iustitia and the causal framework of justification. He begins by stating, "Justification properly consists in two parts, namely the remission of sins, and the
renewal and purification of the interior mind."[116] He then supplements this
with a third part, which consists in the gift of eternal life (*nempe donationem
vitae aeternae*),[117] leaving one's justification incomplete until its eschatological
fulfillment. These three all happen or take place under the principle of incorporation, that is, membership into Christ's body.[118]

> For after God receives us as children and coheirs of Christ through his
> justifying grace, and does so through faith, it comes to pass that our
> subsequent works performed in faith and *timor filialis*, although not
> entirely perfect and complete, please God as the works of his children,

---

113. *Enchiridion*, 97(r); "Dicitur autem haec gratia subsequens seu cooperans comitari voluntatem nostram,
quod voluntas nostra sanata per gratiam iustificantem, iam nacta sit aliquam libertatem repugnandi infirmitati
suae et bene operandi, non quidem iam timore poenae, sed amore Dei et iustitia quum iam adiuvetur a spiritu
Sancto, quem in iustificatione Deus nobis impertit et per eundem charitatem in cordibus nostris diffundit."

114. *Enchiridion*, 97(r)–98(r).

115. See Braunisch, *Die Theologie der Rechtfertigung*, 398–401.

116. *Enchiridion*, 132(r); "Iustificatio duo proprie complectitur, nempe remissionem peccatorum, et interioris mentis renovationem seu repurgationem."

117. *Enchiridion*, 132(r).

118. Braunisch describes Gropper's idea of *incorporatio* as "der tragende, alle übrigen Aspekte des Verdienstes
verbindende und an die essentielle Erneuerung anknüpfende Faktor." *Die Theologie der Rechtfertigung*, 407–408.

of those reconciled to him, for our persons are now pleasing to him through Christ from whose perfection we supplement our imperfection, since we are members of his body, of his flesh and his bone, all receiving from his fullness and making his righteousness our own.[119]

Within this framework of incorporation, we see that there is an outgrowth of good works that Gropper seems to intimate will be imputed as righteous. That is, by incorporation, which occurs in baptism with the first impartation of grace, believers then perform weak works that are then declared righteous based on the fact that those performing them are members of Christ's body. Their merits alone are always insufficient and therefore they must rely only on the perfect merit of Christ, which supplements their weak merit, a merit that is in process.[120] Justification is predominantly seen as beginning with the believer's weak righteousness, which Gropper insinuates will be imputed as righteous based on the fact that this weak righteousness stems from their incorporation into Christ. For Gropper justification is not purely a forensic occurrence.

When he discusses the definition of the verb *iustificare*, he wishes to distinguish his definition from that in Melanchthon's *Loci* (1535), where Melanchthon states: "Justification means the remission of sins and reconciliation, or the acceptance of a person unto eternal life. To the Hebrews *iustificare* is a forensic term, as if I were to say that the Roman people 'justified' Scipio after he was accused by the tribunes, that is, they absolved him or pronounced him to be just."[121]

Gropper responds by stating that "to be justified in Paul signifies more than to be pronounced just."[122] Quoting Augustine, Gropper defines the verb *iustificare* as "to be rendered just; or to be clothed or adorned with righteousness."[123] Here he shows the importance of the believer being made righteous.

119. *Enchirdion*, 96(v); "Postquam enim deus per gratiam iustificantem nos recipit in filios et cohaeredes Christi, idque per fidem, fit ut postea opera nostra tanquam filiorum et reconciliatorum, in fide et timore filiali facta, licet non admodum perfecta, et absoluta, deo placeant, quia iam placent personae per Christum, ex cuius perfectione nostram imperfectionem supplemus, sumus enim membra corporis eius ex carne et ossibus eius, De plenitudine eius omnes accipientes et iustitiam eius nostram facientes."

120. Braunisch, *Die Theologie der Rechtfertigung*, 366–367; "Christus ergänzt aus seinem Verdienst, was menschlicher Bemühung and Vollkommenheit abgeht, so daß der renovatus das Gesetz 'imputative' erfüllt und vor Gottes Endgericht schließlich bestehen kann. Die iustitia imputata, genauer: das meritum imputatum Christi gehört also nur der 'zweiten' Rechtfertigung zu, insofern Rechtfertigung trotz der prinzipiellen Ereignishaftigkeit von Versöhnung und Wiedergeburt immer zukunftsbezogen bleibt und der Vollendung harrt; die Wandlung zu einem neuen Menschen hatte statt und ist doch in processu."

121. Melanchthon, *Loci Communes* (1535), CR 2, 421; "Iustificatio significat remissionem peccatorum et reconciliationem seu acceptationem personae ad vitam aeternam, Nam Hebraeis iustificare est forense verbum; ut si dicam, populus Romanus iustificavit Scipionem accusatum a tribunis, id est, absolvit seu iustum pronuntiavit."

122. *Enchiridion*, 132(v) (marg. note); "Iustificari plus apud Paulum significat, quam iustum pronuntiari."

123. *Enchiridion*, 132(v); "Quid enim est aliud, iustificari, quam iustus effici; seu iustitia indui ac adornari et quid iustificati aliud, quam iusti facti?" (This sentiment is found in Augustine's *Sermo CCXCII*, in *PL* 38, chap. 6, 1324.)

However, it is critical to understand that this definition does not exclude the idea of imputed righteousness because for Gropper the imputation of righteousness is understood as the believer's adornment by the benefits of the head. This manner of viewing an imputative righteousness, itself left undeveloped, reveals that Gropper prior to his discussions with Martin Bucer was willing to use these terms minimally to demonstrate some aspect of divine declaration in the doctrine of justification.

Forgiveness of sins and renewal are bound together. Imputation and impartation are both parts of the one justification. Therefore, he objects to the emphasis on imputation at the expense of renewal when speaking of the doctrine of justification; for when one stresses imputation, he distorts the Pauline understanding of justification by imposing on it the inappropriate analogy of a legal process.[124] For this reason Gropper challenges the idea that the courtroom of humanity is in any way similar to the courtroom of God, and he claims that the comparison between God's justification of a sinner and Scipio's trial is completely invalid. For in the case of Scipio, he was accused wrongly and therefore pronounced innocent of the charges. But Christians will never be innocent before God's court because the charges against them are always true:

> But God in remitting sins deals far differently with us: for he does
> not declare us innocent, nor, when the law accuses us, does he charge
> it with calumny, nor does he approve of our actions, but he deals with
> us in an altogether different manner. For in the first place he convicts
> us of sin through the law: then when we have been convicted, he
> urges us toward the confession of sin: then when we have confessed,
> he declares us sinners, and as such he condemns us, but afterward,
> when we have been convicted, have confessed, and been condemned,
> he restores us with free mercy when we appeal and have recourse
> through faith to the mercy which Christ has exhibited. And therefore
> the reconciled sinner is more to be compared with one who has
> suffered a sentence and then been restored, than to one who has
> been absolved in a court: because the absolution by which a sinner is
> absolved of his sins, is in no way similar to a forensic absolution.
> Justification, therefore, is our sentence, which not only consists of
> the forgiving or remission of sins, but also embraces righteousness,
> by which, when sins have been remitted, God in addition changes the
> wicked into good, that is, from ungodly to godly, and from those

---

124. See Braunisch, *Die Theologie der Rechtfertigung*, 360–362.

willing evil to those willing good, and this through the gift of the Holy Spirit, which transforms, renews, and reforms our mind and will.[125]

Man is not justified on account of a forensic declaration because when God forgives a man (as Gropper states earlier), he embraces him in righteousness and changes him through grace.

Gropper describes justification as the remission of sins and the renewal of the mind. His primary emphasis is that justification takes place on account of an imparted righteousness, which makes the believer righteous and is understood by incorporational language. When a believer becomes a member of his body, he possesses a certain measure of righteousness demonstrated in good works. However, this measure is unable to merit salvation on its own; thus to merit salvation the believer's righteousness must be supplemented by the imputation of Christ's righteousness. The efficacy of a believer's righteousness always depends on the righteousness of Christ, not of man: "Those remaining in Christ fulfill the law through Christ (who alone fulfilled the law)."[126] Therefore, one's merits are meritorious only when they are in Christ, and one's righteousness is true righteousness only when it is associated with Christ's. In this way the works after justification done with *gratia cooperans* are understood as *meritum de condigno*, only on account of the supplementing righteousness of Christ that is imputed through a believer's incorporation into Christ.[127] For Gropper the primary understanding of imputation is in regard to works righteousness,[128] so that a believer's weak merit is what is imputed, not the believer himself.

Christ is the church's head. And because he is the head and the church his body, believers can count the imputation of Christ's perfect merit as attained, though their imparted righteousness is incomplete, producing weak merits.

---

125. *Enchiridion*, 132(v)–133(r); "At Deus remittens peccata, longe secus nobiscum agit: non enim pronuntiat nos innocentes, nec ipsam legem accusantem nos, calumniae arguit, nec acta nostra approbat, sed omnia contraria agit. In primis enim per legem nos de peccato convincit: convictos, ad peccati confessionem adigit: confessos, peccatores pronuntiat, et ut tales damnat; quamvis postea convictos, confessos, ac damnatos ad misericordiam suam in Christo exhibitam per fidem provocantes ac recurrentes, contra sententiam quam passi sumus, gratuita clementia restituat, ut peccator reconciliatus, magis fit conferendus ad sententiam passum et restitutum, quam ad absolutum in foro: quod absolutio qua peccator a delictis absolvitur, nihil simile habeat cum absolutione forensi. Iustificatio itaque nostra sententia, non in sola condonatione seu remissione peccatorum consistit, sed et iustitiam complectitur, qua Deus remissis peccatis, insuper etiam ex malis bonos, hoc est, ex impiis pios, et ex male volentibus bene volentes facit, idque per donationem spiritus sancti, mentem et voluntatem nostram transmutantis, renovantis, ac reformantes."

126. *Enchiridion*, 96(v); "In Christo manentes per Christum (qui solus legem implevit) legem imputative implemus."

127. See Braunisch, *Die Theologie der Rechtfertigung*, 407.

128. See ibid., 429.

When a believer struggles in his weak imparted righteousness with *gratia coop-erans*, he can be comforted in the thought and fact that Christ's righteousness supplements his deficient righteousness, because as a believer he is a member of Christ's body. In these moments of weakness Gropper counsels the believer to hope in this promise. He says, "Then above all, I ought to remember the word of promise, in which, O Lord, you have given me hope; then, O Christ, I must look to the words you spoke to the woman who was an adulteress, though not yet condemned: 'Neither do I condemn you' . . . O voice of mercy, O the hearing of these joyful words of salvation!"[129]

The weakness of our imparted righteousness or incorporation, for Grop-per, can be increased and therefore is future-oriented. The Eucharist is a pledge of future glory, when one day believers will be the true body of Christ. In the meantime, the believer is a pilgrim gaining greater and greater strength in his incorporation. The believer in this world increases his righteousness through good works and participation in the sacraments. However, these works outside of Christ will never allow us to stand worthily before God. We are always com-pletely reliant on the bestowal of Christ's perfect merit, so that within this scheme the believer progresses in righteousness by grace that will find its ful-fillment in the future, and only then will our justification be completed. He states: "In summary it is established that we indeed make progress in this life through the grace of our Savior, gradually deserting cupidity, and growing in charity, through the aid of the Holy Spirit: but it is perfected finally in that future life, when cupidity will be wholly extinguished and charity will be made complete."[130] In the present, believers are encouraged to work out their salva-tion, knowing that in the end it will be granted on account of Christ's perfect merit. One's works performed through grace are "imputed to justice" (*ad iusti-tiam imputari*)[131] because they please God through Christ.

Gropper understands both the imputation of righteousness and the weak righteousness of works as stemming from one's incorporation into the body

---

129. *Enchiridion*, 140(r)–(v); "Cum ergo suggerit mihi infirmitas mea, quinam sciam me in numero filiorum esse: tunc maxime memorem esse me oportet verbi promissionis, in quo mihi domine spem dedisti: tunc mihi in verba tua Christe respiciendum est, quibus mulieri adulterae, necdum damnatae, dixisti: Nec ego te condemnabo mulier: vade, et iam amplius noli peccare. O vocem misericordiae, o auditum laetitiae salutaris."

130. *Enchiridion*, 96(v)–97(r); "In Christo manentes per Christum (qui solus legem implevit) legem impu-tative implemus, si tamen nullum consensum praebeamus, nec secundum carnis desideria ambulemus, ut ex religua infirmitate, innitentibus nobis super Christum, nihil damnationis sit timendum, quod Christus vim et tyrannidem peccati eneruauerit, ut amodo in nobis mortem operari non possit, nisi rursus a Christo declinantes, per consensum in illud ruamus: In summa statuendum est, nos per gratiam Salvatoris in hac quidem vita profi-cere, deficiente scilicet sensim cupiditate, et crescente charitate, per subministrationem spiritus sancti: sed per-fici demum in illa vita futura, quum cupiditas tota extinguetur, et chartias complebitur."

131. *Enchiridion*, 146(r) [i.e., 148(r)].

of Christ (i.e., the impartation of righteousness). Therefore, one's righteousness is perfect only when it is in Christ. One's works are condign merits only when they are in Christ. A person is therefore justified only when he is in Christ.

THE CAUSES OF JUSTIFICATION.   Gropper has a nuanced view of *duplex iustitia*: the weaker *iustitia* of the believer and the perfect *iustitia* of Christ. But this is not a "double justification" theory strictly speaking. Both Bucer and Gropper hold to one single formal cause, which Gropper describes as the mercy and grace of God, by which God turns our minds to himself.[132] Gropper's discussion of the causes of justification states that the efficient cause is God, the final cause is the humanity of Christ, the formal cause is the grace and mercy of God understood in association with the outpouring of charity in our hearts, and the instrumental cause is faith.[133]

With regard to the efficient cause of justification, Gropper states: "The efficient cause of our justification is God alone, not us ourselves. For it is God alone who justifies, who alone remits sins."[134] God is the agent of justification.[135]

Gropper describes the final cause of justification as the humanity of Christ. He states: "Moreover the final cause, that is, the cause to which God has regard in remitting sins and because of which, and on account of whose worth and merit, properly so-called, he remits our sins, is Christ, not in so far as he is God, for in that respect he effects justification with the Father and the Holy Spirit, but in so far as he is man, that is, in so far as he is made an eternally efficacious victim for sin."[136] It is only because the Son came in human form that he was able to merit forgiveness of sins for believers. Here the purpose of justification is described using strong incorporation language. For it is the purpose or end

---

132. *Enchirdion*, 143(r); "Iam si et formalem causam iustificationis quis requirat, respondebit Apostolus hanc iure dici misericordiam Dei et gratiam, qua anima ad se convertit Deus." Cf. *BRom* (1536), 126–127; (1562), 114–115. Rather than using the termonology of formal, efficient, and instrumental, Bucer here uses the language of first, second, and in this case third cause. Bucer describes God's goodwill as the first cause, the merit of Christ as the second cause (though he believes this really to be an extension of the first cause), and the saints and their good deeds (since they are joined to Christ the head) as a third cause, which is akin to an instrumental cause, for God has ordained to use the saints and their good deeds as instruments in salvation.

133. *Enchiridion*, 142(r)–145(r).

134. *Enchiridion*, 142(r)–(v); "Causa enim efficiens iustificationis nostrae, solus Deus est, non nosipsi. Solus enim Deus est, qui iustificat, qui solus peccata remittit."

135. Comparable to Bucer's view of *Allwirksamkeit*, God is the effector of justification and therefore the efficient cause.

136. *Enchiridion*, 142(v); "Porro causa finalis, hoc est, ea causa quam Deus in remissione peccatorum respicit, et propter quam, et ob cuius dignitatem et meritum proprie dictum, ipse nobis remittit peccata, Christus est, non quatenus Deus, nam eatenus cum patre et spiritu sancto efficit iustificationem, sed quatenus homo, nimirum quatenus factus est hostia pro peccato in sempiternum potens."

of justification that Christians are reconciled in Christ.[137] On this point he relies on both John 15:4 ("I am the vine, you are the branches; he who remains in me, and I in him, he will bear many fruit, because without me you are able to do nothing, because on account of this you are righteous, because you are engrafted in me")[138] and Isaiah 53:6, 11. He states: "Even Isaiah most clearly conveys the final cause of justification in Christ: He states that 'we all like sheep have gone astray, each of us has turned to his own way; and the Lord has laid on him the iniquity of us all;' and after a few words: 'If he laid down his soul for sin, he will see many offspring and longevity, he my servant will justify many in his wisdom, and he will bear their iniquities.'"[139] In this manner being in Christ results in our forgiveness of sins, which is the end or purpose of our justification.[140]

The formal cause deals with the aspect of trans*form*ation. As Edward Yarnold notes, "The formal cause is always intrinsic to the subject—e.g. the formal cause of the whiteness of a wall is the whiteness itself."[141] In regard to justification it can be described as that which God will look upon on the last day and accept.

Gropper states that the formal cause is "the mercy and grace of God, by which God turns back our mind to himself."[142] Justification is being "saved by grace through faith, and this is not from you yourselves: for it is a gift of God, it is not from works, lest anyone should boast" (Eph. 2:8–9).[143] Thus, here Gropper indicates that God will look not to a believer's righteousness but to his mercy to declare him righteous. The believers' righteousness is completely dependent upon God.

However, he proceeds to expand the definition to include the concept of the theological virtues, though not in the same way that *recentiores theologi* blindly state that the formal cause is "*charitas Dei*, which is poured into our hearts by the Holy Spirit" (Rom. 5:5).[144] For Gropper, "Charity is not the formal cause in

137. *Enchiridion*, 142(v); "Rom. 3 [24–25]. Iustificamur gratis gratia ipsius per redemptionem que est in Christo Iesu, quem proposuit Deus propitiatorem."

138. *Enchiridion*, 142(v); "Et quid aliud est, quod Christus apud Ioan. Ait, Ego sum vitis, vos palmites, qui manet in me, et ego in eo, hic fert fructum multum, quia sine me nihil potestis facere, quia propter hoc iusti estis, quia mihi estis insiti."

139. *Enchiridion*, 142(v); "Et clarissime Esaias causam finalem iustificationis in Christum transfert: Omnes, inquit, nos quasi oves erravimus, unusquisque in viam suam declinavit, et posuit Dominus in eo iniquitates omnium nostrum, et post paucas: Si posuerit pro peccato animam suam, videbit semen longaevum, in scientia sua iustificabit ipse servus meus multos, et iniquitates eorum ipse portabit." Isa. 53:6, 10–11.

140. See also Gropper's *Antididagma*, 21(v); "Caeterum, causa finalis iustificationis nostrae nemini est ignota, quum ad hoc potissimum a Deo iustificemur, ut simus in laudem gloriae ipsius, Eph. 1. et obtineamus in Christo salutem animarum nostrarum et vita aeternam. I.Petri.1.&3."

141. Yarnold, "*Duplex Iustitia*," 208n13.

142. *Enchiridion*, 143(r); "Iam si et formalem causam iustificationis quis requirat, respondebit Apostolus hanc iure dici misericordiam Dei et gratiam, qua animam ad se convertit Deus."

143. *Enchiridion*, 143(r); "Item, gratia salvati estis per fidem, et hoc non ex vobis: Dei enim donum est, non ex operibus, ne quis glorietur."

144. *Enchiridion*, 143(r); "Unde consequitur, recentiores theologos temere affirmasse, charitatem Dei, quae per spiritum sanctum in cordibus nostris diffunditur, in iustificatione ratione causae formalis obtinere."

so far as it is from us, but in so far as it is from God."[145] In addition he states referencing 1 John 4:7–13 that "because God is love, in which he abides, he abides in God and God in him. In fact in this we are aware, because we abide in him and he in us, because he gave to us his Holy Spirit, evidently with the pouring of love into our hearts."[146] Therefore, he qualifies the formal cause as "the love of God in so far as it is a gift of God and proceeds from God."[147] He explains that this must be the case because the love in the believer remains imperfect with infirmities of the flesh.[148] Therefore, the infusion of love as a gift from the mercy of God can be seen as the formal cause and that upon which God will look when he pronounces us just.[149]

The last cause of justification that Gropper then touches on is the instrumental cause. Here it is true justifying faith in Christ, which I have described previously.[150]

To summarize the causal structure of justification: God is the efficient cause, the humanity of Christ that reconciles believers to God is the final cause, the mercy and grace of God resulting in the inpouring of his love is the formal cause, and justifying faith is the instrumental cause. There is no cause of justification that stems from believers themselves. A believer's righteousness is always imperfect, unable to merit salvation, and therefore dependent on the righteousness of Christ for salvation. Justification is a free gift.[151]

Summary

Gropper understands justification under the paradigm of incorporation into the body of Christ or being engrafted into the true vine, which is another way of understanding the impartation of righteousness. Consequently, a believer

---

145. *Enchiridion*, 143(r) (marg. note); "Charitas non quatenus ex nobis, sed quatenus ex Deo causa formalis iustificationis."

146. *Enchiridion*, 143(r); "quia Deus charitas est, in qua qui manet, in Deo manet et Deo in eo. Quin in hoc cognoscimus, quoniam in eo manemus, et ipse in nobis, nimirum diffundente charitatem in corda nostra."

147. *Enchiridion*, 143(r); "Dicimus autem diserte charitatem Dei, hoc est, quatenus Dei donum est, et a Deo proficiscitur, causae formalis rationem in iustificatione obtinere, ut meritum nostrae voluntatis, quae haec charitas per fidem accipitur, a ratione causae excludamus."

148. *Enchiridion*, 143(r); "adhuc admodum imperfectus sit, resistente nimirum, quandiu in hoc corporis tabernaculo sumus, infirmitate carnis."

149. Cf. Council of Trent, session 6, chap. 7.

150. *Enchiridion*, 144(r); "Verum causa . . . instrumentalis iustificationis proxima, fides in Christum est, qua credimus, per redemptionem quae est in Christo Iesu, nobis remitti peccata." Bucer in his posthumous *Ephesians Commentary* speaks of faith as the *media causa*. See B*Eph* (1562), 27a.

151. *Enchiridion*, 143(r) [i.e., 145(r)]; "sed ut sciamus, quod gratis iustificemur, hoc est, quod nullis operum praecedentibus meritis iustificatio debeatur: alioqui gratia iam non esset gratia, quae ideo datur, non quia opera bona fecimus, sed ut ea facere valeamus, id est, non quia legem implevimus, sed ut legem implere possimus."

can be described as a detached branch that gets engrafted into the vine, which gradually fuses with the trunk of the vine. This branch (which is partially of the vine but not completely) grows and transforms into the true vine as it is nourished by the sacraments. As it becomes a healthier branch, the quality of its fruit also becomes better. However, this fruit is not as perfectly delicious as the fruit that comes from the true vine itself. Nevertheless, because the weak branch is engrafted in the true vine, its fruit is imputed as perfectly delicious. This engrafting takes place solely by the mercy and grace of God. To pick up Luther's analogy of the sick man that we began with, for Gropper the medicine of the sacraments facilitates the growth in righteousness that allows for the diagnosis/declaration of true righteousness within the framework of incorporation.

Both Gropper and Bucer described justification as having declarative and effective aspects; both understood that justification not only declared someone just but also made them such. They, however, understood these aspects differently.

By highlighting the ecclesiological paradigm of incorporation into the body of Christ, I have demonstrated how the sacraments, which aid one's progression through grace, are emphasized in Gropper's understanding. The impartation of righteousness is the basis for both good works and the imputation of righteousness that these works receive. Hence, merit plays a greater role in Gropper's system than in Bucer's. For Bucer works are necessary on account of God's *pactum*; they have *meritum de congruo*. For Gropper works are necessary for justification because they are what merit salvation and are declared righteous on account of their stemming from the incorporation in Christ, thus giving them *meritum de condigno*. Nevertheless, both affirm that no work of man apart from grace or the Spirit is able to merit anything at all. For Gropper the imputative aspect, though weak, in his thought is understood as a supplementation of one's weak righteousness by Christ's perfect righteousness; this supplementation occurs on the basis that a believer is incorporated into Christ, that is, the imputation of righteousness is dependent on the impartation of righteousness.

For Bucer the emphasis is reversed. The imputation of righteousness, established in election, is revealed to the believer intellectually with the gift of faith through the power of the Spirit. This faith gains knowledge of the non-imputation of sins and of one's adoption as a child of God and therefore the mercy of God, which is also understood as his *iustitia*. Through faith the Spirit reveals this *iustitia* to the believer, which then, on the basis of the dictum that "to know the good is to do the good," accomplishes a derivative *iustitia* in the believer. Rather than a supplementation, Bucer understands imputation as a stimulus. With knowledge of true *iustitia*, the believer pursues that *iustitia* through loving his or her neighbor. But this derivative *iustitia* and good works stem from the imputative aspect of his doctrine.

In addition, for Bucer the imputative aspect of his doctrine is highlighted in his dialectical understanding of the *duplex homo*, which understands concupiscence in the saints to remain as sin (akin to a *simul iustus et peccator*), which Gropper's more progressive sacramental paradigm cannot bear. In other words, Bucer speaks of sin, Gropper of sins. For Gropper there is a sense of fluctuation between being in a state of sin and a state of justice that therefore requires the sacrament of penance. For Bucer the Christian is always righteous, however fluctuating between more or less righteousness. For Gropper the righteousness that a believer has is weak because it is always struggling against concupiscence. For Bucer the Spirit breathes into the balloon of the mind, allowing for an ebbing and flowing of faith. The greater the knowledge dependent on the Spirit and less on the senses, the greater progression in righteousness is achieved.

The main difference, then, between them stems from their distinctive theological priorities, resulting in varying descriptions of the imputative and impartative aspects of their doctrines. Nevertheless, their views are not incompatible on the basis that both desire to highlight how justification is based on the mercy of God and not on one's insufficient righteousness. Their differences are in regard to their emphases.

Having established a clear understanding of the manner in which these two men understood the doctrine of justification, I now turn to the manner in which this doctrine was agreed upon during the Worms and Regensburg colloquies.

5

Martin Bucer's Doctrine of Justification in Sixteenth-Century Dialogue (1539–1541)

Unity of the church stands not in the same ceremonies,
but in the same doctrine, faith, and right use of the sacrament.[1]

Having carefully examined Bucer's doctrine of justification as well as the moderate Catholic view represented in Gropper's *Enchiridion*, I now turn to Bucer's negotiations over justification. By examining the various texts and discussions that took place at these negotiations, I will demonstrate how Martin Bucer remained consistent to his 1536 exposition of the doctrine.

From 1536 onward, Bucer's reconciliatory work was industrious, most notably and perhaps most successfully resulting in the Wittenberg Concord and the reassimilation of Anabaptists in Hesse.[2] However, I will examine what could have been his greatest reconciliatory success, a religious settlement reuniting Germany. The colloquy of Regensburg and the preceding colloquies offered him the unprecedented opportunity to help facilitate a religious peace between the German Roman Church estates and the German protesting

---

1. Bucer, *Von der Waren Seelsorge* . . . (1538) (*Bibliographie* 81), in *BDS* 7, 95, ll. 6–10 (marg. note).
2. At Wittenberg, Bucer negotiated a reconciliation formula on the Lord's Supper, which had divided the Swiss and south German Protestants from the evangelicals allied to Wittenberg. At Hesse, Bucer "vigorously emphasized that not a pious life but the merits of Christ and love constitute the foundation of the church." Greschat, *Martin Bucer*, 155.

evangelical estates. Bucer was optimistic; he sincerely believed in the possibility of this reunion. In 1539 he wrote: "I certainly believe that we can come to an agreement on those things which are truly fundamental to the Christian faith, and leave the rest unresolved in Christian freedom, if we only focus on God with all our hearts."[3] With agreement on justification by faith and the right use of the sacraments, other obstacles could be resolved under the guidance of ἐπιέικια. That is, for Bucer, justification was the basis for recognizing others as Christians, the right use of the sacraments was the basis for recognizing other groups of Christians as churches, and in regard to ceremonies there was flexibility.

The question I will be exploring is whether or not Bucer's understanding of justification is compatible with the various articles on justification during this period. Stated negatively, I will be exploring whether or not Bucer's theology of justification during these discussions was an irenicon.[4] Thus, having analyzed both Bucer's and Gropper's doctrines of justification, I will now examine whether Luther was right to say of article 5 that "therein they are right and we also are right."[5]

3. Bucer, *Nürnbergischer fridestand* (1539), (*Bibliographie* 91), in *BDS* 7, 439, ll. 33–36; "Wolan, ich gibe zü, das man in rechten haupstucken christlicher gemeynschafft sich ja wol könde vergleichen und durch Christliche freihey das andere in Christlicher eynigkeyt gleich onverglichen lassen, Wa man alleyn von hertzen uff Gott sehen wolte."

4. To accomplish this task I have made use of the following works: Max Lenz, *Briefwechsel Landgraf Philipps des Grossmüthigen von Hessen mit Bucer*, 3 vols. (Stuttgart: Verlag von S. Hirzel, 1880–1891), esp. 3:1–148; Ludwig Cardauns, *Zur Geschichte der kirchlichen Unions-und Reformbestrebungen von 1538 bis 1542* (Rome: Loescher, 1910); Hasting Eells, "The Origin of the Regensburg Book," *Princeton Theological Review* 26 (1928): 355–372; Robert Stupperich, "Der Ursprung des'Regensburger Buches' von 1541 und seine Rechtfertigungslehre," *Archiv für Reformationsgeschichte* 36 (1939): 88–116; Reinhard Braunisch, "Die 'Artikell' der 'Warhafftigen Antwort' (1545) des Johannes Gropper: Zur Verfasserfrage des Worms-Regensburger Buches (1540/41)," in *Von Konstanz nach Trient: Beiträge zur Geschichte der Kirche von den Reformkonzilien bis zum Tridentum*, ed. Remigius Bäumer (Munich: Verlag Ferdinand Schöningh, 1972), 519–545; and most recently Volkmar Ortmann's *Reformation und Einheit*, which is by far the most thorough account of the colloquies thus given. These works have explored the genesis of the various articles. For this book, however, the question of origins, especially of the Worms Book, is ancillary, used to support my main argument that Bucer's theology of justification is in keeping with these consensus documents regardless of their genesis.

Among the many studies on the colloquies, Athina Lexutt's monograph *Rechtfertigung im Gespräch*, dealing exclusively with the doctrine of justification during this period, is relevant to this work. Lexutt's position, however, is based on a criterion of true Reformation doctrine that is rather more rigid than what was actually the case in the period under discussion. Likewise, Lexutt argues that Bucer's theology of justification was unclear and unable to accept the doctrine of justification *sola fide*. However, as I have demonstrated, this is not the case. Nevertheless, her thorough analysis is important for discussions of justification during this period. Her position is very similar to the position held by Wilhelm Neuser in "Calvins Urteil über den Rechtfertigungsartikel des Regensburger Buches," in *Reformation und Humanismus*, ed. Martin Greschat (Witten: Luther Verlag, 1969), 176–194. Anthony Lane has argued in a similar manner against both Neuser and Lexutt in his article "Calvin and Article 5 of the Regensburg Colloquy," in *Calvinus praeceptor Ecclesiae: Papers of the International Congress on Calvin Research*, ed. Herman J. Selderhuis (Geneva: Droz, 2004), 233–263. This work, rather than looking at Calvin's understanding, will be looking at Bucer's during these discussions.

5. Luther and Bugenhagen to John Frederick (10–11 May 1541), *WA.Br.* 9, no. 3616, 407, ll. 15–16; "Darin sie recht und wir auch recht haben."

There is no doubt that Bucer's drive for religious unity was determined by an intermixture of theological and political motives, as partially demonstrated in chapter 2. However, the two motives need not be mutually exclusive, since Bucer's political action was underpinned by his concern for strengthening Christendom, that is, it was theologically motivated.[6] My intention here is to show how Bucer was theologically consistent during his negotiations over justification from 1539 to 1541.[7] These negotiations will be evaluated on the basis of their coherence or lack thereof with what Bucer stated in his *Romans Commentary* and Gropper in his *Enchiridion*.

This chapter will look first at the Leipzig article on justification, then at Bucer's campaign for a national council after the Truce of Frankfurt, then at the preparatory Protestant discussions and treatises on justification, the Worms Book article 5, Gropper's redraft of this article, and finally at the final form of the article agreed to at Regensburg. The analysis of these documents and negotiations will demonstrate that Bucer's doctrine of justification from 1536 is compatible with those views expressed during this period and, moreover, that Bucer's doctrine of justification was not an irenicon. Though flexible both as a pastor and as an ecclesiastical diplomat, Bucer remained consistent as a theologian on this central doctrine.

The Leipzig Conference (1539)

Protestant territories in the 1530s experienced relative peace due in part to the Peace of Nuremberg (1532). This imperial edict suspended all legal suits in regard to religion, including those suits on ecclesiastical property. As a result, it enabled the Protestant estates to strengthen and organize, ensuring the heritage of the Protestant Reformation in Germany.

However, during the latter 1530s the estates remaining loyal to the pope felt threatened by the growing Schmalkaldic League. Their anxiety led to two

---

6. This can be stated to be the case because both the politics of the state and the church remained subservient to the kingdom of God. For him the establishment of this kingdom on earth was a primary factor in his pursuit of political and theological unity. For the political contexts of the colloquies and an analysis of Bucer's part therein, see Cornelis Augustijn, "Strasbourg, Bucer et la politique des Colloques," in *Strasbourg au cœur religieux de XVI* siècle: hommage à Lucien Febvre: actes du Colloque international de Strasbourg (25–29 mai 1975)*, ed. Georges Livet and Francis Rapp (Strasbourg: Librairie Istra, 1977), 197–206. See also de Kroon, *Bucers Obrigkeitsverständnis*; and Georg Kuhaupt, *Veröffentliche Kirchenpolitik: Kirche im publizistischen Streit zur Zeit der Religionsgespräche (1538–1541)* (Göttingen: Vanderhoeck & Ruprecht, 1998).

7. Hence we echo Cornelis Augustijn's opinion that "stressing Bucer's diplomatic abilities has to be given up in favour of an effort to understand the connection between his activities and his theology." See Cornelis Augustijn, "Bucer's Ecclesiology in the Colloquies with the Catholics, 1540–1541," in Wright, *Martin Bucer: Reforming Church and Community*, 107–108.

developments that would disrupt the relative peace. The first was the action of the Imperial Chamber Court placing the ban on the city of Minden, in Westphalia, which had adopted the evangelical reformation in 1530. The second was the formation of the Nuremberg League on 10 June 1538. These two events placed Germany on the brink of civil war.

In addition, property disputes aggravated the struggle between evangelical and Roman Church territories. Hence on the deathbed of Duke George of Saxony, his chancellor, George von Carlowitz, sought to protect the ducal territories from an inevitable evangelical takeover by the duke's brother Henry, which would be aided by John Frederick, elector of Saxony.[8] The negotiations stemmed from Carlowitz's desire to create a buffer against an imminent evangelical reformation. Under these circumstances Carlowitz invited the landgrave from Hesse and the Saxon elector to discuss the possibility of a moderate reform in the ducal territories that would preserve the status quo.[9] These meetings recommended themselves to Bucer as part of his broad missionary strategy for Europe.[10]

Bucer had just finished negotiating a peace with Anabaptists in Hesse for the landgrave when the landgrave called on him again. Bucer would lead the negotiations on behalf of Hesse with Philip's chancellor, Johannes Feige. On New Year's Eve of 1538, Bucer arrived in the city of Leipzig disguised as a merchant, blending into the crowd that was arriving for the annual trade fair.[11] The duke, though deathly ill, was still an opponent of the Reformation, and therefore Carlowitz initiated this conference without the duke's approval and asked that the representatives keep these negotiations a secret.[12] The following day Melanchthon and Chancellor Gregor Brück arrived from Electoral Saxony. There to meet them and to negotiate for Ducal Saxony were Carlowitz and the mayor of Leipzig, Ludwig Fachs, who was later replaced by George Witzel as the

---

8. See Greschat, *Martin Bucer*, 168–169; Ortmann, *Reformation und Einheit*, 52. Cf. Eells, *Martin Bucer*, 244.

9. See Günther Wartenberg, "Der Leipziger Religionsgespräche von 1534 und 1539: Ihre Bedeutung für die sächsisch-albertinische Innenpolitik und für das Wirken Georgs von Karlowitz," in *Religionsgespräche der Reformationszeit*, ed. Gerhard Müller (Gütersloh: Gerd Mohn, 1980), 39–40.

10. On the Leipzig Conference, see Ortmann, *Reformation und Einheit*, 49–77; Thomas Fuchs, *Konfession und Gespräch: Typologie und Funktion der religionsgespräche in der Reformationszeit* (Weimar: Böhlau Verlag, 1995), 388–409; Wartenberg, "Der Leipziger Religionsgespräche," 35–41; Pierre Fraenkel, *Einigungsbestrebungen in der Reformationszeit: Zwei Wege—Zwei Motive* (Wiesbaden: Franz Steiner, 1965), 6–36; Cornelis Augustijn, *De Godsdienstgesprekken tussen Rooms-Katholieken en Protestanten van 1538 tot 1541* (Haarlem: F. Bohn, 1967), 16–24; and Stupperich, *Der Humanismus*, 40–49. See Bucer's report to the landgrave (2 January 1539) in Lenz 1, no. 23, 63–68.

11. Georg Witzel, *Warer Bericht von den Acten der Leipsischen und Speirischen Collocution zwischen Mar. Bucern und Georg. Wilcelien* (Cologne: Johann Quentel Erben, 1562), in ARC 6, 18, ll. 5–7 ("*kauffmans gestalt*").

12. See Ortmann, *Reformation und Einheit*, 51–53, and citations to letters and other primary sources there.

leading theological representative. Witzel was the duke's consultant in religious affairs as well as a Lutheran apostate.[13]

They met in the Paulinum (the Dominican monastery) and later continued their discussions in Fach's private residence. On 2 January the negotiations commenced with discussions on what the basis for negotiations would be, that is, what document would help facilitate the discussion. Carlowitz in his opening speech proposed a reform based on early church practices using Gregory the Great's reign as the cutoff point (*Richtscheit*).[14] On that account he proposed a text that had been written by Witzel in 1538, which proposed a moderate reform of the ducal territory based on the early church.[15] This text and approach, however, troubled the evangelical reformers, for there were, in their opinion, already many errors that had crept in during the sixth century, for example, purgatory among others. Only after Carlowitz then suggested the time of Augustine as the *Richtscheit* did the evangelical collocutors, still weary of accepting everything from this period, agree to enter discussion on the basis of this time period, albeit with the qualification that only the chief articles from this period would be seen as normative.

On the following day they discussed faith and works, and it was at this point that Carlowitz called on Witzel to aid in the negotiations. Witzel was convinced that the true church was the Church that remained loyal to the pope, yet he was just as tireless as Bucer in seeking reform. For Melanchthon, negotiations would be difficult with the Lutheran apostate, and thus at the request of his elector he withdrew from the negotiations, which left Bucer as the lead evangelical theological negotiator.[16]

As noted previously, Bucer, in addition to scripture, observed that a thorough exposition of the early church fathers could lead the old church to the

13. For a good introduction to Witzel's unitive program, see Irena Backus, "The Early Church as a Model of Religious Unity in the Sixteenth Century: Georg Cassander and Georg Witzel," in *Conciliation and Confession: The Struggle for Unity in the Age of Reform, 1415–1648*, ed. Howard P. Louthan and Randall C. Zachman (Notre Dame, IN: University of Notre Dame Press, 2004), 106–133, esp. 120ff. See also Barbara Henze, *Aus Liebe zur Kirche Reform: Die Bemühungen Georg Witzels (1501–1573) um die Kircheneinheit* (Münster: Aschendorff, 1995); and Kantzenbach, *Das Ringen um die Einheit*, 176–202.

14. For the use of the apostolic church as a *Richtscheit* at Leipzig, see Magnus Ditsche, "Das 'Richtscheit der Apostolischen Kirche' biem Leipziger Religionsgespräch von 1539," in *Reformata Reformanda*, ed. Erwin Iserloh and Konrad Repgen, vol. 1 (Münster: Aschendorff, 1965), 466–475.

15. Witzel, *Typus ecclesiae prioris: Anzeigung, wie die heilige Kyrche Gottes, inwendig siben und mehr hundert jaren, nach unsers Herrn Auffart, gestalt gewesen sey* (Mainz: Behem, 1541).

16. Some of Melanchthon's displeasure with the path of negotiations was also due to the fact that major theological issues would be left for a later date, allowing these negotiations to be concerned primarily with practical issues. See Greschat, *Martin Bucer*, 169–170. In addition, the elector's relationship with Henry, the duke's brother, played a pivatol role in his pulling Melanchthon from these negotiations. See Günther Wartenberg, "Der Leipziger Religionsgespräche von 1534 und 1539: Ihre Bedeutung für die sächsisch-albertinische Innenpolitik und für das Wirken Georgs von Karlowitz," in *Religionsgespräche der Reformationszeit*, ed. Gerhard Müller (Gütersloh: Gerd Mohn, 1980), 35–41.

evangelical truth of the fundamentals of the Christian faith. The omission of the consensus of the fathers was what he observed as the flaw in his *Gospels Commentary*, which he sought to correct in his *Romans Commentary*.[17] And for Bucer, unlike Melanchthon, Witzel's apostasy from the Lutheran camp had little relevance for the negotiations.

This meeting produced a blueprint for reform in sixteen articles primarily oriented toward practical reforms.[18] Reflecting back on the conference, Witzel stated that the agreement reached in 1539 was primarily penned by Bucer.[19] Bucer also admitted his leading role in drafting these articles.[20]

Bucer's doctrine of justification was at the forefront of the conference. He was convinced that doctrinal unity in the area of justification would again guarantee that there would be a true reformation of the Church. A territory could not be correct in doctrine without also becoming a good tree.

As indicated in chapter 2, Bucer believed that agreement on justification allowed for flexibility in regard to Church structure and ritual. Nevertheless, he did expect that these aspects of Church life would be reformed in a manner consistent with an agreement on justification by faith. That the first article of the sixteen articles deals with the issue of justification therefore is significant; it is upon this article that the subsequent articles are founded.[21]

The Leipzig Articles on Justification

The first three Leipzig articles deal with soteriology specifically: the first deals with the manner in which one is saved from damnation, the second with free choice and good works, and the third with repentance. These three soteriological articles set the tone for the remaining thirteen articles, which are more

---

17. Bucer's letter to Bullinger; *Pollet* 2:301n4.

18. The articles were originally composed in German and can be found in *BDS* 9/1, 13–51; they were subsequently translated into Latin by Michael Helding and can be found in *ARC* 6, 1–20. The Latin text gives the following headings: (1) Quomodo homo ex originali damnatione ad dei gratiam, iustitiam et aeternam salutam redeat, (2) De libero arbitrio hominis et possibilitate bene operandi, (3) De poenitentia eorum, qui baptizati et ecclesiae iam insiti sunt, (4) De sacramento baptismatis, (5) De sacramento corporis et sanguinis Christi, (6) De confirmatione, (7) De ordinatione ministrorum ecclesiae, (8) De electione [clericorum], (9) De extrema unctione, (10) De ieiunio, (11) De delectu ciborum, (12) De monachatu, (13) De veneratione santorum, qui ex hac vita excesserunt, (14) De feriis, (15) De memoria mortuorum, and (16) De officio magistratus.

19. Witzel affirmed that Bucer had written the majority of the articles in his short appendix to the articles, *Warer Bericht von den Acten der Leipischen und Speirischen Collocution . . .* (1562), *ARC* 6, 18, ll. 38 through 19, l. 3.

20. Earlier in 1545 Bucer affirmed that he had been the primary author of the articles in *Ein Christlich ongefärhlich bedencken . . .* (1545), *(Bibliographie* 143). See Ortmann for citations from this work *(Reformation und Einheit*, 68–69).

21. Lexutt, *Rechtfertigung im Gespräch*, 76; "Die Anordnung der Themen ist sicher nicht zufällig. Da das Kapitel zum Topos der Rechtfertigung gleich den Auftakt bildet, ist davon auszugehen, daß hier tatsächlich der eigentlich neuralgische Punkt der Kontroverse gesehen wurde."

ecclesiologically oriented. On this account they are compatible with the Protestant paradigm that prioritizes soteriology over ecclesiology. Hence I will show here how Bucer's understanding of the doctrine of justification is consistent with the Leipzig articles.

The first article is titled "How man damned from birth might come to the grace of God, righteousness, and blessedness."[22] This article begins by stating that humanity is completely vitiated by original sin. A man does not have the natural resources from which he can save himself; he is condemned to eternal damnation and the wrath of God.[23] From the outset it is established that the doctrine of justification is *durch glauben ohne alles wercken.*[24]

The article continues by pairing justification (*gerecht machen*) with adoption (*kinde gottes machen*) and the inheritance of eternal life (*erb der ewigen seligkeit gemacht*). It is telling that in this article the term "justification" does not appear, perhaps highlighting the problem of the word itself. By omitting the problematic term, the authors take a strategy that attempts to downplay the controversy over this doctrine. On the other hand, the term's exclusion is not problematic for Bucer, since he is used to understanding the doctrine using various terms and metaphors, for example, "righteousness," "forgiveness," "adoption," and the gift of eternal life.[25] The article articulates the doctrine of justification in a manner consistent with Bucer's previous understanding by using the biblical concepts of adoption, restoration, forgiveness of sins, and judgement, among others. It states:

> However when the Lord, moved by his pure mercy, sends and gives
> his holy word to man,[26] for him to believe in it truly, so that he knows
> and feels his sin and damnation through the law, and henceforth
> rightly repents and suffers in his heart, and knows and believes from

22. *BDS* 9/1, 23, ll. 16–17; "Wie der Mensch von dem angebornen verderben zur gnaden gottes, fromkheit und seligkeit komme." *ARC* 6, 2; "Quomodo homo ex originali damnatione ad dei gratiam, iustitiam et aeternam salutem redeat." Lexutt notes that the use of *redeat* instead of the passive *reducitur* indicates that the authors view humanity as cooperators in justification. Lexutt's point is well noted; however, the rest of the article makes it clear that nothing can be read into the fact that *redeat/komme* is active. As I will show, the article clearly points out that humanity is without the resources for salvation and that any works that are accomplished in believers are in fact the works of God. It is also curious that Lexutt has chosen to ignore the original German version and works exclusively with the early undated translation from the Catholic Helding. See Lexutt, *Rechtfertigung im Gespräch*, 76–79.

23. *BDS* 9/1, 23, ll. 18–20; "Der Mensch ist durch die erbsunde also verdebt, das er auß seinem naturlichen vermogen nichts gut furnemen mag uund muß sein und aller Creaturen halben ewiglich under dem zorn gottes und verdammet sein." See *ARC* 6, 2, ll. 23–25.

24. *BDS* 9/1, 24, l. 3.

25. See Stephens, *Holy Spirit*, 49n1.

26. The Latin here includes the giving of grace with his word: "verbum suum immittit homini eique donat gratiam." *ARC* 6, 2, ll. 26–27.

the gospel that God from his grace and through the merit of his son, our Lord Jesus wills to forgive all his sins and to give him eternal life, thereupon humanity through this faith without any assistance of the works that he has done before grace, is made righteous, a child of God, and an heir of eternal salvation before God.[27]

Justification stems from God's mercy and the merit of Jesus Christ, which results in the sending of his word. This word, understood as law and gospel, is sent to inspire faith in the promise of forgiveness; as law it reveals sin, as gospel it reveals grace. The authors are clear that the justification event is dependent on the grace of God and that the unbeliever is declared righteous not on account of works but through faith, described as the combination of repentance and contrition.[28]

Works of grace prior to faith are explicitly excluded as a primary cause of one's justification. Nevertheless, Bucer, commenting on the article in 1545, stated that he was troubled over the phrase "die er gethan hat vor der gnaden."[29] He stated: "This addition I would have preferred to leave out, so that nobody would become suspicious of us granting the Pelagian error."[30] Bucer was worried that the statement could justify a view that works after justification would be taken as worthy in themselves and that believers would trust in works rather than in the gospel.

27. *BDS* 9/1, 23, ll. 21 through 24, l. 5. "Wan aber der herr, auß seiner lauther Barmhertzigkeit bewegt, dem mentschen sein heyliges wort zusendet und verleÿhet, demselbigen warlich zuglauben, also das er auß dem gesetz seine sunde und verderben erkennet und fulet Und hat derhalben rechte rewe und hertze leidt, Und auß dem Euangelio erkennet und glaubet, Das jme Gott auß seinen gnaden und durch den verdienst seines sons, unsers hern Jesu, alle seine sundt verzeihen unnd das ewig leben schenken will, Alßdan wirt der mentsch durch diesen glauben one alles zuthun seiner wercken, die er gethan hat vor der gnaden, vor gott gerecht, ein kinde gottes und erb der ewigen seligkeit gemacht." *ARC* 6, 2, ll. 26–33; "Quando autem deus mera sua misericordia motus salutare verbum suum immittit homini eique donat gratiam, ut vere credat verbo, sic ut per legem homo peccatum suum et damnationem agnoscat et sentiat et de peccatis suis vera poenitentia et cordis contritione indoleat, per evangelium vero cognoscat et credat deum per gratiam suam et filii sui domini nostri Jesu Christi meritum omnia peccata ipsius dimittere et aeternam donare vita velle, tunc homo per istam fidem sine adiumento suorum operum, quae fecit, per gratiam coram deo iustus, filius dei et heres aeternae salutis constituitur."

28. There is a very strong similarity here to *Confessio Augustana* 12, 3–5.

29. The two versions of Bucer's *Ein Christlich ongefärhlich bedencken* (1545) differ from the other four transcripts used to create the text in the *BDS* volume. The *Österreichisches Staatsarchiv* transcript (thought to be the most reliable) has the phrase "die er gethan hat *von* der gnaden." Bucer has replaced *von* with *vor*, a change that partially demonstrates the wariness which he had over the phrase because with *von* the idea of *gratia preveniens* is included in the discussion of justification. As I have shown, Bucer did not speak of a progression of grace like his Catholic counterparts; rather, he spoke in terms of the Holy Spirit working on persons rather than persons progressing in grace.

30. Bucer, *Ein Christlich ongefärhlich bedencken* . . . (1545), G3; "Disen beisatz hette ich lieber aussen gelassen, damit niemand ein verdacht darauß schoepffete, als ob wir wolten dem Pelagianischen irthumb statt geben"; quoted in Ortmann, *Reformation und Einheit*, 57n63.

He concluded, "The others told me that this did not necessarily follow. . . . This phrase only denied that works before grace were made pure, therefore as such they concede nothing to works after the reception of grace occurs."[31] On that account Bucer could accept its inclusion so long as it did not elevate the status of works in justification.

Of course the authors were insistent in the article that justifying faith is not without works. True faith bears fruit, a position Bucer always advocated, but Bucer never advocated that works were worthy in themselves. For him works could only be said to be meritorious based on their relation to being the very works of God within believers,[32] a stance that the article takes when it quotes Augustine, "God crowns his own works."[33]

Athina Lexutt and Reinhold Friedrich interpret the Leipzig articles as ecclesially centered, seeing in them an overall Catholic tone, compromising the Reformation position on justification.[34] Their evidence for this view is predominantly from the statement in the first article that justification occurs "through the ministry of the church by the preaching of the word and the practice of the sacraments."[35] Lexutt, therefore, concludes that "*iustificatio* does not occur *sola fide*, but *sola ecclesia*."[36] Yet pitting *sola fide* against *ecclesia* seems to me a false dichotomy.

Bucer, in his *Ein Christlich ongefärhlich bedencken*, states that Mark 16:16 ("He who has believed and has been baptized shall be saved; but he who has disbelieved shall be condemned") ought to be read as the background of this phrase on the role of ministry and the sacraments in justification.[37] The statement that justification occurs through the Church is an affirmation that both Luther and Bucer repeatedly make when speaking of justification in relation to the ministry of preaching and especially in the sacrament of baptism.[38] By

---

31. Bucer, *Ein Christlich ongefärhlich bedencken*, G3–G3v; "Die anderen sagten aber, diß volgete auß dem nicht. . . . Solche rede verneinete allein, das den wercken vor der gnaden nit gepüret, gebe darumb sollichs nit den wercken zü, nach empfangener gnaden beschehen"; quoted in Ortmann, *Reformation und Einheit*, 57n63.

32. See section 3.5.4.

33. BDS 9/1, 24, ll. 20–21; ARC 6, 3, ll. 2–5.

34. Lexutt, *Rechtfertigung im Gespräch*, 75–79; Friedrich, *Martin Bucer*, 163–164; see also Cardauns, *Zur Geschichte*, 4–18, esp. 11–13.

35. BDS 9/1, 24, ll 7–8; "durch den dienst der kurchen mit der predig gotlichs worts und der heyligen sacramenten." See ARC 6, 2, ll 34–36.

36. See Lexutt, *Rechtfertigung im Gespräch*, 77; see also Reinhold Friedrich, who sees the statement of justification mediated through the ministries of preaching the word and the sacraments as an unwarrantable concession to the Catholic position (*Martin Bucer*, 164).

37. See BDS 9/1, 24n9.

38. For Luther, faith was given through the Word and the sacraments; hence he can state, "Therefore he who wants to find Christ, must first find the church. . . . The church is not wood and stone but the assembly of the people who believe in Christ. With this church one should be connected and see how the people believe, live and teach. They certainly have Christ in their midst, for outside the church there is no truth, no Christ, no salvation." WA 10, 140, ll. 8–17; LW 52:39–40. Likewise, Bucer saw the church as indispensable for salvation. In his

means of his word and the sacraments, God inspires and strengthens faith through the Holy Spirit. *Ecclesia* is thus not the antithesis of *sola fide*, as Lexutt would like to suggest. This phrase in the article explains the typical manner in which this faith is given and received.

After indicating the ecclesial place of justification, the article goes on to speak of good works, stating that "when such a man now lives in Christ the Lord, Christ also lives in him, thus good works necessarily follow from him, as good fruits grow from a good and fruitful tree."[39] In a Bucerian fashion, the article states, then, that good works result in both temporal and eternal rewards and that they are necessary for eternal life.[40] This is explained as only being so not on account of the worth of the work but on account of the grace and merit of Christ, who works in believers. Thus the works that are rewarded are his very own works, paraphrasing Augustine.[41]

Lexutt finds the necessity of good works alarming in that it does not specify how this necessity exists.[42] She believes that the necessity of works flings open the door to a dubious inclusion of good works in the justification event, such that the article's position on the necessity of good works "assigns *iustitia operum* a place in the event of justification, which does not do justice to the evangelical understanding."[43] Lexutt seems to understand "evangelical" here to mean a later forensic view in Lutheran theology, which thus ignores the variety of expressions on this doctrine within the evangelical camp of reformers during this preconfessionalized period. As I have shown, within the structure of his thought Martin Bucer understood works within an evangelical framework of *sola fide*. Thus because her analysis lacks a complete understanding of Bucer's position, which understands that works necessarily have a place in justification, albeit in a secondary manner, she excludes the possibility that this article could be read in an authentically evangelical fashion.[44]

The article clearly shows that the works of the believer remain imperfect as long as the believer lives in the flesh, which is compatible with the manner in

---

Gospels Commentary, he states that it is through the preaching of the word and the sacraments that Christ "offers and presents remission of sins, communion in himself, and eternal life." *BGospels* (1536), 485. See also *BDS* 5, 164, ll. 33–34; and *BRom* (1536), 420; (1562) 486.

39. *BDS* 9/1, 24, ll 8–11; "Weÿl dann nhun ein solcher mentsch in Christo, dem hern, lebet und Christus in ime, so sollen von notwegen beÿ jme die guten werck volgen wie gute frucht von einem guten gesunthen baume."

40. See *BRom* (1536), 117; (1562), 102–103.

41. *BDS* 9/1, 24, ll. 16–21. The reference to Augustine is found in *Epistola CXCIV*, 19; *PL* 33, 880.

42. Lexutt, *Rechtfertigung im Gespräch*, 78.

43. Ibid.; "Die necessitas der guten Werke weist der iustitia operum eine Stellung im Rechtfertigungsgeschehen zu, die ihr nach evangelischen Verständnis nicht zukommt."

44. Lexutt's understanding of Bucer's doctrine comes from the secondary literature and is especially reliant on Karl Koch's *Studium Pietatis*.

which Bucer understood the believer to be *duplex homo*, that is, a saint who lives both in the flesh and in the spirit.[45] This imperfection of the justified is articulated again in the second article "on the free choice of men and the possibility of doing good works":

> But those who live in Christ through true faith, he illuminates and drives through the Holy Spirit and he works in them to will and to do, so that they are able to judge, choose, will and accomplish what is good and righteous before God; yet while the faithful live here imperfections and all kinds of defects more or less cling to their every work, even after he was endowed freely more or less with the grace of God and the Holy Spirit.[46]

The conception of faith as an illumination enabling the believer to recognize the good is Bucerian. Free choice is reenabled to some extent by the infilling of grace and the Holy Spirit. As in the *Romans Commentary* the articles understand free choice and faith primarily in intellectualistic terms; this is highlighted by the fact that *erkennen* is used in conjunction with *glauben* when speaking of faith.

Thus, can we say that Bucer's understanding of justification is understood, albeit in condensed form, in the Leipzig article? According to Friedrich, this is not possible. He sees Bucer as accommodating to the Roman Church position, rejecting *sola fide* and asserting works righteousness.[47] However, Friedrich misunderstands Bucer's understanding of faith and its connection to love of neighbor. For Bucer the teaching of the *sola fide* formula is upheld in the article by stating that salvation is by the grace of God *durch diesen glauben*.[48]

---

45. See BDS 9/1, 24, l. 22 through 25, l. 4; "Nachdem aber uns die verderbnus unser Natur, so lanng wir hie leben, anhangt, seindt alle unsere gute werck noch mangelhafftigk, darzu ubereylen uns die bose lust, das wirymmer umb verzeyhung der sunden und gnade zubitten haben, und muissen den waren trost und alle sicherheit unsers gewisses bey Christo, dem hern, durch die Barmhertzigkeit gottes in waren und lebendigem glauben suchen." See also 26, ll. 1–4; "Noch will der streit zwischen dem flesch und dem geist bey uns verharrt, so lang wir leben, wirdet keiner nymmer mher so selig oder volkommen, er muß noch als bekennen, das er sunde hat und umb verzeyhung derselbigen teglich betten." See sections 3.4.2. and 3.5.4.

46. BDS 9/1, 25, ll. 16–21; "Die aber in Christo durch waren glauben leben, die erleuchtet und treibet er durch den heyligen geist, wircket in jnen das wollen und thun, das sie urtheilen, welen, wollen und thun mögen, Das vor gott gut und recht ist, Wiewole, so lang sie hie leben, mit unvolkommenheit und allerlei mengel, Welche einem yeden mher oder minder anhangen, Nachdem er mit der gnaden gottes und heyligen geist mher oder minder reychlich begabt ist."

47. Friedrich, *Martin Bucer*, 163.

48. BDS 9/1, 24, l. 1. For Bucer, the *sola fide* formula was being interpreted so that Roman Church believers accused evangelicals of neglecting works. On that account he at times did his best to articulate the truth that this formula represented without the *sola*. The most striking example of this comes in his *Psalms Commentary*, where he states the following: "I hold it enough to use the word of Scripture, and to say that the just person lives by faith, that by faith we are justified and saved, the *sola* having been left off, because it gives such offense; then I will in no way be reluctant to interpret these, and say: by faith the love of God is created in us, which brings forth a zeal for all virtues, and perfects and renders all men blessed. But I should be unwilling at the same time to condemn

In the Leipzig articles we have a plan for moderate reform of church territories loyal to the pope based on the early church, in which the teaching on justification is in line with evangelical thought as articulated by Bucer. Bucer stated: "In this article everything of my faith is set out."[49] In some of the other articles Bucer remained silent and was criticized for various concessions; however, this silence can be seen as a result of his program of ἐπιείκεια based on the evangelical doctrine of justification.

For further support of the article's evangelical credentials, one can turn to Luther himself, who saw the Leipzig article on justification in a positive light. He acknowledged it as a possible foundation for a settlement. Luther wrote: "Because they acknowledge and propagate the chief article of justification, of communion in both forms, of the rejection of the private mass, of the marriage of priests, and of monkery, thus it may be held entirely with us as an agreement."[50]

Hubert Jedin stated that "while it acknowledges the necessity of good works for salvation, [it] does not state the doctrine of man's intrinsic justification with sufficient clearness."[51] He continues to say that "if the scheme had been carried through, it would have led to the Protestantising of the whole of Germany for it suppressed essential elements of the Catholic faith and in the guise of toleration gave free scope to the dynamics of Lutheranism."[52] In that it prioritizes soteriology over ecclesiology, I agree. When one evaluates the articles from Bucer's perspective, one must take into account his program of ἐπιέικια and the priority of justification, which for him is the basis for enabling reform. Once the truth of justification by faith is established in a territory, reformation will occur from within; that is, purer (more evangelical) practice will follow from this goodly doctrine.

---

for this reason the holy fathers who from scripture have borrowed their *sola*. It is surely not the part of Christians to be offended by words, when there is agreement on the sense." *BPsalms* (1554), 31; "Ut igitur ne veris quidem quisquam offendus est, ita satis habebo, vocibus uti Scripturae, et dicere iustum fide vivere, Fide nos iustificari et salvari: omisso quod tantopereoffendit SOLA. Tum et hac ipsa interpretari, ac dicere, Fide gignitur in nobis Dei amor: hic parit studium virtutum omnium, totosque perficit er beati nihil pigebit. At nolium et simul sanctissimus Patres, qui ex Scripturis suum SOLA mutuati sunt, ideo damnari. Verbis certe, dum de sensu constat, offendi, Christianorum non est."

49. Bucer, *Ein Christlich ongefährlich bedencken* ... (1545), (*Bibliographie* 143), Giii; "In disem artikel ist alles gesetzet auch auß meinem glauben . . ."; quoted in Ortmann, *Reformation und Einheit*, 59n69.

50. *WA.Br.* 8, no. 3425, 652; "Weil sie die heübtstuck als von der Iüstification, von beidergestalt, von abthun der winckel messen, von der priester ehe, von der Monchery bekennen und zü lassen, so mags wol ein vergleichung mit uns heissen." On the Wittenberg opinion of the Leipzig articles, see Ortmann, *Reformation und Einheit*, 73–74. It is worth noting that Julius Pflug also saw the articles as acceptable, though written in a Protestant style. See Ortmann, *Reformation und Einheit*, 69–71.

51. Hubert Jedin, *A History of the Council of Trent*, trans. Ernest Graf, vol. 1 (London: Nelson, 1957), 362.

52. Ibid., 363. See also Ortmann, who sees the articles as foundationally Protestant (*Reformation und Einheit*, 77).

The omission of the *sola fide* formula in the article is not a rejection of the truth that that formula attempts to convey. The article clearly affirms that justification is *through faith*, which is always accompanied with works. That works are part of faith for Bucer has already been established on the paradigm that to know the good is to necessarily perform it. Bucer's view is consistent with this article.

The Truce of Frankfurt and Preparing for a National Colloquy (1539–1540)

Though the Leipzig articles were initially widely circulated, they did not have any lasting effect on the duchy of Saxony. This was partially because they became superfluous upon the duke's death in April 1539, which resulted in his brother's takeover. In addition, the emperor's Frankfurt truce,[53] which promised a forthcoming national negotiation between Roman churches and evangelical churches, overshadowed this preliminary agreement.

Three circumstances led to the emperor's issuing the Frankfurt truce of 1539. The first was that in 1539 Germany was on the brink of civil war over the Minden crisis. In fact, so strong was the tension between the evangelical protesting princes and loyalist princes that even Bucer encouraged the Schmalkaldic League to strike the first blow.[54] Second, the eastern flank of the empire was again being threatened by Suleyman's armies, which were preparing for another large-scale attack. To defend his brother, the emperor needed a united Germany. Finally, the emperor grew impatient with the pope, no longer expecting him to convene an ecumenical council. These events forced the emperor to try to unite Germany.

For this the emperor requested negotiations during the Schmalkaldic League's conference in Frankfurt in February 1539. There he sent Johann von Weeze, the archbishop of Lund, to negotiate the truce with two of his councilors. The result was a negotiated peace for the next fifteen months, which promised a peaceful meeting with reasonable men from both parties to discuss the religious problems in Germany; in addition, this agreement suspended all suits over ecclesiastical property (for fifteen months). These concessions were allowed by the emperor with the stipulations that the protesting estates would

53. On the Truce of Frankfurt, see Paul Fuchtel, "Der Frankfurter Anstand vom Jahre 1539," *Archiv für Reformationsgeschichte* 28 (1931): 145–206.

54. Bucer to the landgrave (May 28, 1539), *Lenz* 1, no. 24, 75; "Wir haben erfaren, wa man das reich Christi zu furdren allein recht furnimet, da geht es furt. Man bedencke doch allein, was zufals E. f. g. (Euer Fürstliche Gnaden) von Gott und den menschen gehebt habe mit Wirtenperg!"

lend support in the war against the Turks and that these estates would also cease to add members to the Schmalkaldic League. Bucer was not pleased with this truce because the membership restriction placed on the Schmalkaldic League was, for him, seen as a suppression of the reign of Christ. In this sense Bucer thought that the prince and elector lacked a vision for expanding Christ's reign in Germany. However, Bucer was encouraged by the emperor's call for a national council, so much so that as soon as it was promised, Bucer began a full-scale assault, writing treatises encouraging the commencemenn of the promised colloquy.[55]

In general these treatises affirmed the priority of justification. Thus the *Concilium Bucerj* on the topic of justification states:

> Furthermore the others must preach justification purely and truly, so that the people especially and clearly are taught to seek, expect and hope for all piety and blessedness from the mercy of God alone and through the merit of Christ, the one and only consolation of all merit for all creatures. Nevertheless, one ought to truly exhort the people toward all types of good works with every promise and urging which scripture has.[56]

Later on he states, "What can or might in some way coexist with the article on justification, the protesting estates must leave uncensored or unreproached in these churches, as long as justification and the proper Christian usage of every

---

55. The first treatise he wrote sometime in the winter of 1539, now titled as the *Concilium Bucerj* in BDS 9/1, 73–78. After first proposing a return to Holy Scripture, the church fathers, and the early church councils as a way forward in negotiations, the *Concilium* proceeds to outline the key topics of the Christian religion, beginning with justification, then baptism, the Eucharist, confession, ceremonies, clerical marriage, and church discipline. Second, was *Etliche gesprech aus götlichem und geschribnen Rechten vom Nürnbergischen fridestand* ... (1539), (*Bibliographie* 91), in BDS 7, 402–502, under the pen name of Konrad Treue von Friedesleben. Then he wrote *Von Kirchengütern* ... (1540), (*Bibliographie* 94), again under the pen name of Konrad Treue von Friedesleben. Part of Bucer's program for reconciliation included a solution to the problem of church property. In *Nürnbergischen fridestand* and *Von Kirchengütern*, he espoused that the church did have a legitimate claim to owning property and wealth, but only insofar as it aided the church's mission of preaching the Word and shepherding souls. Bucer was calling for a much poorer church that used property only to maintain a salary for the church's minister. (There is more work that can be done here in regard to the role and importance of church property in ecumenical dialogues during the sixteenth century). In May 1540, almost immediately after hearing that the colloquy would take place in Hagenau, Bucer wrote a fictional correspondence from two Catholics (an unnamed Decanus and Canonicus) praising the benefits of a national conference. He titled it *An statui et dignitate ecclesiasticorum magis conducat* ... under the pen name of Wahrmund Leuthold (*Bibliographie* 96), in BDS 9/1, 100–145.

56. BDS 9/1, 73, ll. 18–23; "Zum andern musten die andern die justificacion rein und getrewlich predigen, das man das folck eigentlich und clar lehret, alle frömkeit und selickeit allein aus der erbermde gots und durch den verdinst Christj suchen, erwarten und hoffe ane eÿnige vortrosten uf alle vordinst aller Creaturenn. Doch das man daneben zu allen gutten wercken durch alle die vorheischung und bedrawung, ßo die schrift hat, getrewlich vermanet."

ceremony is always taught lucidly, clearly and completely faithfully."[57] As we have repeatedly noticed, justification is central and allows for ἐπιέικια in regard to church ceremonies, albeit they be properly used.

Likewise, in another of these treatises pushing for the promised conference Bucer demonstrated his hope, stating: "I believe that we can come to an agreement on those things which are truly fundamental to the Christian faith, and leave the rest unresolved in Christian freedom, if we only focus on God with all our hearts, not allow Rome to stop us, and come to some kind of agreement on ecclesiastical property."[58] Here, with stronger zeal, Bucer held the belief that unity was founded on an agreement on the chief articles of doctrine and primarily the doctrine of justification.[59] For him it was "the chief article on which the entire reformation depends."[60] In light of what was achieved in Leipzig, Bucer's hope that agreement on justification could be reached was greater than ever. Soon after Leipzig, he wrote: "I am very much hopeful that when God grants that we arrive at consensus on the issues and provided god-fearing, peace-loving, and not quarrelsome people are there, we might then expect to come close in discussion and word and also in agreement."[61]

Repeatedly we observe that Bucer affirmed that it is on the chief article of justification upon which the Reformation hangs and upon which unity is based. The various treatises he wrote during this time, including the *Consilium* and

---

57. Martin Bucer, *Concilium Buceri*, written in the winter of 1539/40, in *BDS* 9/1, 75, ll. 27–31; "Was auch in einigen weg kont ader mocht mit und beÿ dem artickel der justification bestehen, dasselbige musten die protestirenden diesen kirchen vnuorworffen vnd vngetadelt lassenn, So fern das die justification vnd recht Christlicher gebrauch aller Ceremonien jmer hell, klar vnd gantz getrewlich gelert wurden." Earlier on in this short work he affirms again the centrality of justification in negotiations as the "heubtartigkels" (*BDS* 9/1, 75, ll. 10–13). This short work is an advice on how to proceed with a negotiation for unity. As in the other writings of this time period, church property is a central concern of the work. What little it has to say on justification is based on the Leipzig articles. See Ortmann, *Reformation und Einheit*, 75–77.

58. Bucer, *Nürnbergischer fridestand*, in *BDS* 7. 439, l. 33 through 440, l. 2; "Wolan, ich gibe zü, das man in rechten haupstucken christlicher gemeynschafft sich ja wol könde vergleichen und durch Christliche freihey das andere in Christlicher eynigkeyt gleich onverglichen lassen, Wa man alleyn von hertzen uff Gott sehen wolte, sich von Rom nichts hinderen liesse und könde sich der Kirchengütter halben vertragen." On this text, see Ortmann, *Reformation und Einheit*, 90–99.

59. *BDS* 7, 433, ll. 29 through 434, l. 5.

60. *BDS* 7, 434, ll. 4–5; "der hauptarticul, an dem eynmal alle reformation der kirche hanget." He qualifies here what he means by justification, stating that it is not through works but founded upon the grace of God (*sondern allein dadurch vor Gott bestohen*). Works similarly have their place as they always do in Bucer's understanding of faith and the rewards given by God for them. See *BDS* 7, 434, ll. 8–16. Similar expressions are found in his *Von Kirchengütern . . .* (1540), (*Bibliographie* 94), where he again states that unity can be founded on the *huaptstuck* of the doctrine of justification alone from the grace of God and the merit of Christ. See *Von Kirchengütern . . .* (Hiv).

61. *BDS* 7, 435, ll. 25–28; "Wolan, ich bin der hoffnung auch: wann Gott gebe, das wir an der sachen selb zü gleichem verstand kemen und dann gotsförchtige, fridliebende und nit zenckische leüt da sein würden, wir wolten uns alsdann der reden und worten auch etwan vergleichen."

the Nuremberger treatise, fought to ensure the opportunity to discuss the reli-gious issues in Germany through a public colloquy.

The Hagenau Colloquy (1540) and Preliminary
Discussions to Worms

Before entering into negotiations at the Hagenau Colloquy,[62] the elector of Sax-ony asked his theologians to write an opinion clearly stating what areas they were willing to concede on and which points were nonnegotiable.[63] The Wit-tenberg theologians answered their elector, stating that all issues of doctrine were closed to discussion, and thus the *Confessio Augustana* and its *Apology* were not to be compromised at the negotiations.[64] Eleven days later the Wittenbergers put together a document called *Consultation, ob die Evangelischen Fürsten einen weltlichen Friede mit den Bischöffen annehmen* . . . , which stated in a more precise manner how these negotiations were to be approached. In this document they firmly asserted that the teaching of faith was not to be neglected, and that the *sola fide* formula was not to be omitted during negotiations.[65] Because Bucer later signed this document, it will be addressed here.

The *Consultation* is divided into three sections. The first has to do with is-sues of doctrine, the second with the sacraments and ceremonies, and the third with adiaphora. The first section on doctrine begins with a discussion on justification. Here the Wittenberg theologians foresaw three areas that the Roman Church theologians would emphasize, which would compromise the *sola fide* formula.[66]

The first qualification, which the Wittenberg theologians believed the Catholics would make, was in regard to how one becomes righteous: that is, the Catholics would want to affirm that believers are righteous through faith *and* works or that they are righteous through grace, but by grace they would mean love.[67] The Wittenbergers wanted to firmly hold to the *particula*

---

62. On Hagenau, see Eugène Honée, "Über das Vorhaben und Scheitern eines Religionsgesprächs, Ein Ver-fahrensstreit auf dem Konvent von Hagenau (1540)," *Archiv für Reformationsgeschichte* 76 (1985): 195–216; Karl-Heinz zur Mühlen, "Martin Bucer und das Religionsgespräch von Hagenau und Worms 1540/41," in Krieger and Lienhard, *Martin Bucer and the Sixteenth Century Europe,* 2:659–669; and Ortmann, *Reformation und Einheit,* 112–147.

63. This request was made on 19 December 1539; see *CR* 3, 868–871.

64. *CR* 3, 920–921.

65. *CR* 3, 926–945. For an extended analysis of this document, see Lexutt, *Rechtfertigung im Gespräch,* 81–94.

66. *CR* 3, 930; "Sie lassen die hohe und heilsame Lehr vom Glauben nicht unverblendt, werden das *sola fide* nicht leiden wollen, darum werden sie aber etwas daran flikken wollen."

67. *CR* 3, 930; "1) wir sind gerecht durch Glauben und Werke, oder, wir sind gerecht durch die Gnade; und verstehen Gnade die Liebe durch die Gnade; und sennd der Glößlein mancherlei."

exclusiva as a corrective to any "faith *and* . . ." statements because, for them, using the formula *iustificatio sola fide* meant that believers were justified *exclusively* by faith and thus not by works of any kind.[68] They knew that such a stance would inevitably lead to the charge of moral laxity; however, the Wittenbergers were willing to fight that particular battle, since asserting the *sola* safeguarded justification from the view that one could be saved on account of works. Likewise, they knew that the *sola* was not at the exclusion of good works, but rather that it was by faith that one comes to be saved, and that works were an outworking of this same faith.

Their concern over the *sola* highlights the fact that the Wittenbergers perceived that the loyalists would emphasize that one was justified by grace and love as well as faith, using the Thomistic formula that believers are justified by *fides caritate formata*. That is, where there is an infusion of love, a good tree is established and good works follow. The Wittenberg theologians believed that such a stance focused on the justification of the just and not on the justification of the sinner. For them emphasizing the *sola* destroyed any possible reading that would allow works of love to be the works of men, rather than God, as well as maintaining the idea that justification is the justification of the sinner, and love is an aspect or outgrowth of this justification.

The second qualification they foresaw the Roman Church theologians making was in regard to works and merit.[69] Here the Wittenbergers believed that their opponents would want to say that works after an infusion of grace would automatically be seen as warranting merit of condignity, a position that all reformers opposed because the saint is never free from sin. Hence the third area on which they foresaw difficulties arising was in regard to sin. They believed that the Roman Church collocutors would reject the notion that sin remains in the saints.[70] The remaining points in the *Consultation* were in regard to differences over ecclesiology, the invocation of the saints, monastic vows, and the doctrine of purgatory.[71] The *Consultation* presented a rigid stance toward negotiations and in addition advocated a written dialogue rather than a face-to-face dialogue.

It is not surprising that when the landgrave received the document he immediately recognized the hardened stance and was concerned that this

---

68. See Lexutt, *Rechtfertigung im Gespräch*, 86.

69. *CR* 3, 930; "Item vom Merito werden sie zanken, werdens auch glossiren, es sey nicht Verdienst aus eigner Würdigkeit, sondern dieweil es dazu angenommen und verordnet; es sey aber gleichwohl Verdienst, denn ewiges Leben könne nicht ohne Verdienst erlangt werden. Denn der text spricht: 'Euer Lohn wird groß seyn im Himmel.'"

70. *CR* 3, 930; "Item es sey nicht wahr, daß in den Heiligen Sünde bleibe."

71. *CR* 3, 930–932.

statement would hinder any attempt for conciliation.[72] On that account he wrote to Bucer, sending him the Wittenberg opinion and asking him to attend the Schmalkaldic conference in March. On 7 February, Bucer replied to the landgrave with his opinion, stating that he accepted the Wittenberg *Consultation* but that he preferred the manner in which the Leipzig articles spoke of justification, since even Luther was pleased with it.[73] Likewise, he was concerned over the document's preference for a written debate rather than a face-to-face discussion. For Bucer this was not acceptable because written documents are subjected to differing interpretations.[74] In addition, he saw this forthcoming dialogue as an opportunity to explain and advocate the evangelical position, which would then hopefully advance the kingdom of Christ in Germany, especially if the pope did not influence or hinder the proceedings. With these reservations, Bucer signed the Wittenberg opinion at the Schmalkaldic conference in March.[75]

Initially Charles sent invitations for a colloquy to be held in Speyer on 6 June. However, due to an outbreak of the plague, the colloquy was moved to Hagenau and set to commence on 11 June.[76] King Ferdinand facilitated the conference and postponed the colloquy until the fourteenth, in order to allow for preliminary discussions between the Roman Church participants. Prior to the fourteenth, Bucer, Jacob Sturm, and Johannes Brenz met together in Darmstadt.[77]

The Truce of Frankfurt was ambiguous about how these negotiations would be conducted, and therefore the Hagenau conference began with a discussion over mode of procedure. From June to July the main issue revolved around whether or not the *Confessio Augustana* would be used as a starting point for discussion and whether the emperor, though absent from these proceedings, indeed had the authority to convoke such a religious dialogue.[78] Because negotiations seemed to be going nowhere, Ferdinand postponed the discussions to October in Worms. For this forthcoming meeting the two parties were to elect eleven members each and were commissioned to draft a

---

72. Earlier that year, after receiving the Wittenberg document, the landgrave also had his theologians, Adam Fulda, Antonius Corvinus, and Johannes Pistorius, prepare a similar opinion on how to proceed in negotiations. It was written in a more moderate tone, similar to that of the Leipzig articles. However, in preparation for a national council, the Protestant estates chose to take up a more rigid stance on doctrine, following the lead of Wittenberg, advocating the *Consultation* over against the Hessian document, which was more conciliatory in tone. For the *Ein Bedenken hessischer Theologen*, see Gotthold Neudecker, ed., *Merkwürdige Aktenstücke aus dem Zeitalter der Reformation* (Nuremberg, 1838), 177–192. On this report, see Lexutt, *Rechtfertigung im Gespräch*, 90–94.

73. *Lenz* I, no. 47, 135–137.

74. *Lenz* I, no. 47, 135.

75. *CR* 3, 926–945.

76. Leuthold, *An statui et dignitate ecclesiasticorum magis conducat . . .* (*Bibliographie* 96), in *BDS* 9/1, 100–145.

77. See Ortmann, *Reformation und Einheit*, 116–126.

78. See Honée, "Über das Vorhaben," 195–216.

document that would serve as the basis of negotiations. As I have noted, it was here at Hagenau that Bucer first met Johannes Gropper.

The delegates' failure to agree on a mode of procedure was a disappointment. Nevertheless, it led Bucer again to write a treatise championing the need for a national conference.[79] It was written in September and was titled *Who Were Responsible for Preventing a Colloquy Beginning at Hagenau . . . (Per quos steterit, quo minus Haganoae . . . initum colloquium sit).*[80] This work was instigated by Konrad Braun, who challenged the emperor's right to call a council. In this work Bucer argued that there was historical precedent that allowed for an emperor to convene such a meeting. It is noticeable that the failure of Hagenau resulted in Bucer's tone becoming less moderate. He reported that only the loyalist estates of the Nuremberg League desired war and that it was the protesting estates that desired peace. Regardless of the Roman Church intransigence, Bucer continued to push for the commencement of a national conference, since such a meeting would be a great opportunity to implement a reformation throughout Germany and the empire. Those loyal to the pope understood this and thus tried to hamper it. In regard to coming to an agreement over the doctrine of justification he wrote:

> We require that the chief doctrine of Christianity be taught clearly and continually, that the remission of sins and eternal salvation is based on the sole mercy of God and merit of Christ, and not upon any of our merit, and that we secure eternal life by faith not good works, although God generously rewards good works to us by the same boundless and gratuitous love and merit of his son with good things both in the present and the future, however these are the works of Christ in us.[81]

Bucer was convinced that if clearly presented the Roman Church, believers would gradually understand the evangelical doctrine, and thus a true reformation of the Church would ensue.[82] This was the attitude he would take into Worms and Regensburg.

---

79. On this document and Melanchthon's *Confessio Augustana Variata*, see Cornelis Augustijn, "The Quest for *Reformatio*: The Diet of Regensburg 1541 as a Turning-Point," in *The Reformation in Germany and Europe*, ed. Hans Rudolf Guggisberg and Gottfried G. Krodel (Gütersloh: Gütersloher Verlagshaus Gerd Mohn, 1993), 64–80.

80. Martin Bucer, *Per quos steterit, quo minus Haganoae . . . initum colloquium sit* (1540), (*Bibliographie* 105). At the same time, a German edition was published under the title *Vom tag zu Hagenaw*. Both are in BDS 9/1, 162–321.

81. BDS 9/1, 221, l. 23 through 223, l. 3; "Requirimus, ut caput illud doctrinae christianae clare et constanter doceatur, remissionem peccatorem et salutem aeternum ex sola Dei misericordia et Christi merito, nec ullis nostris meritis nobis constare, eoque nos fide, non bonis operibus vitam sempiternam percipere, etiam si Deus bona opera, sed quae Christus in nobis operatur, ex eadem infinita et gratuita sua erga nos charitate meritoque Filii sui liberalissime remuneret bonis tum praesentibus tum futuris."

82. See Bucer's letters to the landgrave from July to August 1539, *Lenz* 1, nos. 27 and 28.

Preparations for the Worms Colloquy

Bucer and Jacob Sturm were invited to Worms by the landgrave in a letter from 23 September.[83] In a reply to the landgrave's invitation on 26 September (which is no longer extant), Bucer outlined his instructions for the way in which they were to enter into negotiations. These instructions were subsequently given to the landgrave's envoys, emphasizing that they were to hold to the opinion of Bucer and Sturm.[84] On 18 October, prior to arriving in Worms, Bucer again wrote to the landgrave describing the task ahead. Here he outlined his threefold desired outcomes for the discussion: first, that there would be a careful explanation of the chief points of evangelical doctrine, which for him included justification; second, that a reformation of the empire would be encouraged; and third, that the basis for negotiations and reform would be the Holy Scriptures and church fathers.[85] With these outcomes in mind Bucer left for Worms.

There was better attendance at Worms than there had been at Hagenau. Bucer arrived in Worms on 1 November. From 9 to 18 November, the Protestant delegates met together and discussed various issues, including justification. Fortunately, these preliminary discussions were recorded by Wolfgang Musculus.[86]

For the first two days the delegates discussed the topic of justification in light of article 4 of the *Confessio Augustana*. Here the delegates examined the article in its negative and positive formulations, that is, the "impossibility of men being justified before God on account of their own virtues, merits, or works,"[87] and the assertion "that men are justified freely on account of Christ through faith."[88] In regard to the first statement the delegates affirmed that it was found in scripture and therefore that the Catholics would not be able to deny it.[89] Some have viewed the article's use of *proprius* as allowing the possibility that certain types of works were allowed;[90] however, they downplay the *negare* in the sentence, excluding this very possibility. The positive description affirmed that justification was *gratis* and *per fidem*. In discussions they agreed

---

83. *Lenz* 1, no. 83, 214.

84. See Friedrich, *Martin Bucer*, 172.

85. *Lenz* 1, no. 85, 217–216.

86. The text from these discussions can be found in Wilhelm H. Neuser, ed., *Die Vorbereitung der Religionsgespräche von Worms und Regensburg 1540/41* (Neukirchen-Vluyn: Neukirchener Verlag, 1974), 116–161. See also Lexutt's note on Neuser's editorial structuring of this text in *Rechtfertigung im Gespräch*, 134n30.

87. Neuser, *Die Vorbereitung*, 119; "negat homines posse iustificari coram Deo propriis viribus, meritis aut operibus . . ." See *CR* 26, 275.

88. Neuser, *Die Vorbereitung*, 119; "asserit eos iustificari gratis propter Christum per fidem." See *CR* 26, 275.

89. Ps. 143:2. See Neuser, *Die Vorbereitung*, 119–121.

90. See Lexutt, *Rechtfertigung im Gespräch*, 135–136.

again that this could not be denied due to the biblical texts that supported this view, especially Romans 3 through 4.

The delegates affirmed the *particula exclusiva* by stating that *sola* and *gratis* are synonymous with *absque operibus* as explained in Romans 11:6 and as testified to by Ambrose, Hilary, and Chrysostom.[91] Therefore, as Lexutt notes, the position of the Wittenberg opinion is weakened, since the word *sola* can be seemingly discarded, replaced by *gratis* and *absque operibus*.[92] However, though the *sola* formula is important to the evangelical position, its replacement with other formulas such as the delegates proposed can and does maintain the integrity of the evangelical position.

After discussing the admission of *gratis* and *absque operibus*, the question of the relationship between Paul and James was posed.[93] The discussion began answering this question with the example of an old man and his gray hair, showing that an old man's gray hair was not the cause of his old age but rather that it revealed him *esse senem*.[94] "Thus good works are from faith, not faith from works."[95] The discussion continued on the nature of faith. In this regard Wenzel Link stated that the grace of Christ is received by faith in the promise.[96] This was followed by a comment from John Calvin, who desired to define faith with the use of *fiducia*.[97]

The discussion on faith and its relation to works then led to a discussion on whether works from faith were *meritum de condigno*. Andreas Osiander began the discussion by offering the following statement: "Righteousness itself is from faith, by which we have been accepted before God," which was "not to say that righteousness is only imputed to us but that it is also infused."[98] This perspective of an infused righteousness concerned Melanchthon and led him to insist that *iustitia* only be spoken about in regard to faith and not through an acquired movement of the heart.[99]

---

91. Neuser, *Die Vorbereitung*, 123.

92. Lexutt, *Rechtfertigung im Gespräch*, 136–137.

93. Neuser, *Die Vorbereitung*, 125–129.

94. Ibid., 125.

95. Ibid.; "Ita opera bona sunt ex fide, non fides ex operibus."

96. Ibid.; "ipse fides in promissione Dei."

97. Ibid., 127; "de fiducia intelligenda sit dictio fidei, qua promissionem divinam de Christo amplectimur, et non de historica illa etc." Calvin also wanted to make sure that justification was understood as *iustum reputare* and not *iustum efficere*; thus, he wished to emphasize a more forensic understanding of justification *propter alienam iustitiam Christi* in contrast to the more ambiguous *pro iustitia* of the *Confessio Augustana*. See Neuser, *Die Vorbereitung*, 127.

98. Ibid., 129; "iustitiam ipsam esse ex fide, qua accepti simus coram Deo. . . . Nec dicendum, quod iustitia nobis tantum imputetur, sed et infundatur." Here Osiander's view that *iustitia* is not only what is imputed but also infused alludes to his forthcoming disputes with Melanchthon and Calvin.

99. Ibid.; "Philippus dicebat hoc esse urgendum, docere nos eam fidei iustitiam, qua propter Christum imputetur, non qua novos motus in corde acquirimus."

On the following day the discussion began by looking at the story of the rich young ruler in Matthew 19. Within the context of this discussion Bucer offered a significant comment, which Musculus prefaced, stating that "Bucer touched the goal which was agreed by the rest."[100] Bucer explained that the manner in which scripture speaks about justification depends on the one to whom the conversation is directed. Therefore, it is difficult to come up with a theological position based on these varying biblical passages. For instance, Jesus' conversation with Nicodemus (John 3) and his speech in Capernaum (John 6:29) state that eternal life is received *sola fide*; however, Jesus' statement to the rich young ruler in Matthew 19:17, Paul's admonition to work out one's salvation in Philippians 2:12, and the story of Abraham offering Isaac in Genesis 22:15–18 seem to suggest that works are integral to salvation.

Based on these texts and others, Bucer stated that "it seems that in scripture the works of a renewed life are in some way [*aliquo modo*] a cause of salvation. We must concede therefore that God uses us as cooperators for the purpose of perfecting this new life and our salvation."[101] Here again we see Bucer's view of works as a secondary cause, as we saw in his *Romans Commentary*.[102]

Lexutt sees this statement and Bucer's approach as clearly and completely against the evangelical reformation teaching which emphasizes *sola fide*.[103] She states that Bucer completely abandons the reformational domain.[104] For her, the reformational doctrine is encapsulated in the *Consultation*, and thus the Wittenberg formulation of the doctrine. As such her perspective of "reformational" seems to be much more rigid than was actually the case for the evangelical reformers, especially since during these discussions *sola* was able to be understood by the biblical terms *gratis* and *absque* by Melanchthon and others.

It must also be granted that Bucer and other evangelical reformers were here attempting to do justice to the entire biblical witness, which affirmed *sola*

---

100. Neuser, *Die Vorbereitung*, 135; "Bucerus . . . scopum tetigit, cui et a reliquis assensum est." It is also surprising that this is the only recorded statement from Bucer at this preliminary discussion. On Bucer's participation at this preliminary meeting, see zur Mühlen, "Martin Bucer und das Religionsgespräch," 662–664. Also both Ortmann and Lexutt give an analysis of Bucer's comments: Ortmann, *Reformation und Einheit*, 166–169; and Lexutt, *Rechtfertigung im Gespräch*, 146.

101. Neuser, *Die Vorbereitung*, 135; "videtur scriptura opera novae vitae aliquo modo causam facere salutis. Concedendum itaque est, quod Deus utatur nobis ad perficiendam novam istam vitam et salutem nostram cooperariis." Cf. Melanchthon's comment on the necessity of works;Neuser, *Die Vorbereitung*, 133.

102. *BRom* (1536), 129–130; (1562), 119; "Nihilominus tamen, cum Deus velit nos sibi bonis operibus ad nostram salutem cooperari, imo etiam eam perficere, κατεργάζεσθαι, Philipp. 2. ac ita statuerit nobis secundum nostra facta rependere, fit etiam suo modo iustificatio nostri, hoc est, adiudicatur nobis vita aeterna, ex operibus, sed tum, quando iam haec nobis vita Dei, ex gratia Dei, et Christi merito ante conditum mundum adiudicata est per electionem nostri, et propositum Dei ante saecula factum. Ephe. 1. et 3."

103. Lexutt, *Rechtfertigung im Gespräch*, 146.

104. Ibid.; ". . . so verläßt Bucer vollends den reformatorischen Bereich . . ."

fide as well as seeming to give some weight to works in regard to salvation. The evangelical position and articulation of the *sola fide* formula was still in flux and being negotiated, evidenced by, as mentioned earlier, Musculus's note that Bucer's comment was agreed to by the rest.[105] The day's discussion ended with the Protestant delegates leaning toward an understanding of justification that allowed "in some manner" a place for works. Thus the more rigid position of the Wittenberg opinion, affirmed by the Protestant estates in March at Schmalkaden, was put aside, leaving open the real possibility of negotiations with Catholics on this issue.

The Worms Colloquy (1540–1541)

Chancellor Granvella opened the Worms Colloquy on 25 November,[106] urging the participants to seek reconciliation in order that the "torn coat of Christ would be sewn back together again."[107] After Granvella's speech Gropper responded for the Catholics and Melanchthon for the Protestants.

Almost immediately difficulties arose over the mode of procedure, as they had previously in Hagenau. The proposed arrangement at Hagenau of selecting two parties of eleven members failed, primarily because the Catholics were split on the reforming issues. Both Brandenburg and the Palatinate were

---

105. The *Confessio Augustana Variata* does speak of works as necessary and as meriting rewards. See *CR* 26, 369–370, esp. 369; "Quanquam igitur haec nova obedentia, procul abest a perfectione legis, tamen est iustitia, et meretur premia, ideo quia personae reconciliatae sunt. Atque ita de operibus iudicandum est, quae quidem amplissimis laudibus ornanda sunt, quod sint necessaria, quod sint cultus Dei et sacrificia spiritualia et mereantur premia." In addition, Calvin's comment, following Bucer's, seems to continue along this trajectory when he states that the promise of eternal life is contained in the law and not just in the gospel. However, because of their sinfulness, humans are unable to fulfill the law and thus depend on the promise of salvation in the gospel. Neuser, *Die Vorbereitung*, 135.

106. A detailed study on the colloquy can be found in Ortmann, *Reformation und Einheit*, 149–229; see also Augustijn, *De Godsdienstgesprekken*, 46–72; Augustijn, "L'espirit d'Erasme," 381–395; Augustijn, "Die Religionsgespräche der vierziger Jahre," in *Die Religionsgespräche der Reformationszeit*, ed. Gerhard Müller (Gütersloh: Gütersloher Verlagshaus Gerd Mohn, 1980), 43–53; Augustijn, "Bucer und die Religionsgespräch der 1540/41," in Krieger and Lienhard, *Martin Bucer and Sixteenth Century Europe*, 2:671–680; and Augustijn, "Das Wormser Buch: Der letzte ökumenische Konsensversuch Dezember 1549," *Blatter für Pfalzische Kirchengeschichte* 62 (1995): 7–46. See also the following works: Lexutt, *Rechtfertigung im Gespräch*, 112–235; Friedrich, *Martin Bucer*, 172–177; zur Mühlen, "Martin Bucer und das Religionsgespräch," 659–669; Basil Hall, *Humanists and Protestants 1500–1900* (Edinburgh: T&T Clark, 1990), 142–170; Stupperich, *Der Humanismus*, 64–65; Stupperich, "Der Ursprung," 88–116; Eells, "The Origin of the Regensburg Book," 355–372. For an abridged English translation of the proceedings between Eck and Melanchthon on original sin at the conference, see Heinz Mackensen, "The Debate between Eck and Melanchthon on Original Sin at the Colloquy of Worms," *Lutheran Quarterly* 22 (1959): 42–56.

107. See the *Oratio Granvellae*, in *CR* 3, no. 2060, 1163–1168, on 1167; "ut Christi Iesu incinsutilem tunicam, tam misere laniatam, laceratam, discissam resarciatis et instauretis."

heavily leaning toward evangelical reform. Likewise, other difficulties arose when the Protestant party proposed using Melanchthon's *Confessio Augustana Variata*, which he drafted in September. A standstill ensued, leading Granvella to force the parties to pick one representative from each side that would enter into negotiations. The Catholic party chose Eck and the Protestants, Melanchthon. From Christmas Eve to 17 January the two theologians discussed the second article of *Confessio Augustana Variata* on original sin, resulting in a joint statement.[108]

The Secret Colloquy at Worms

Before discussion began on Christmas Eve, the monthlong haggling about how the conference would proceed influenced Chancellor Granvella to try a secret means of negotiation. Bucer reported in his *On the One Right Way for the Reconciliation of the German Nation in the Christian Religion* (*Von den einigen rechten Wegen . . .*) (1545) that the secret meeting between reasonable men was the brainchild of Gropper and the imperial secretary Gerhard Veltwyck, who then approached the chancellor with the idea.[109] Granvella invited Bucer to join these secret discussions on 14 December.

Bucer was hesitant to participate in a secret colloquy without the knowledge of his colleagues. Thus he immediately sought the opinion of both Jacob Sturm and the Hessian chancellor Johannes Feige; both responded favorably. In addition, just in case the secret ever got out, Bucer requested from the landgrave a backdated letter granting permission for him to enter into these secret negotiations.[110] In the same letter, after stating that he sought the approval of both Sturm and Feige, he indicated his own confidence for entering into such negotiations, on account that: "the public discussion would not progress, and Your Princely Grace desired that I should speak with Lord Granvella on such things, and likewise you took into consideration that it is the duty of every Christian to lead his neighbor, the authorities, and his superiors to Christ."[111] Bucer asked Granvella for a fourth member, Wolfgang Capito, to be included.

Bucer thus entered into this secret negotiation because the open colloquy was going nowhere, because the landgrave had previously, in a letter from 3

---

108. See Mackensen, "The Debate between Eck and Melanchthon," 42–56. The agreed-upon formula can be found in *CR* 4, no. 2131, 32–33.

109. Bucer, *Von den einigen rechten Wegen . . .* (Strasbourg, 1545), (*Bibliographie* 145), in *BDS* 11/2, 304, ll. 2–11.

110. On Bucer's reticence and his request for a backdated letter, see *Lenz* 1, no. 101, 276–279.

111. *Lenz* 1, no. 101, 274; "das das gemein gesprech nit hat wöllen furgohn, und E.f.g. begeret, das ich mit dem herren von Granzella solte von solichen sachen red haben, dann auch bedacht, das jedem christen zustaht, wie er seine nechsten, schweige seine obren und heupter zu Christo furdre."

December, asked him to speak privately with Granvella,[112] and because he believed that it was his Christian obligation to lead his neighbor to Christ.[113]

In his letter to the landgrave, Bucer noted that prior to the secret conference he and Granvella had a short, one-hour discussion in which Granvella reminded him of the impending danger of war and how that danger could be overcome with a religious compromise.[114] In this conversation Bucer made clear to Granvella that the Protestants would not negotiate over the chief articles of faith, but that they would explain their position in line with the Bible and the fathers in hopes that this could bring about agreement.[115]

The secret meeting, beginning on 15 December, lasted two weeks and took place in the home of Granvella. Here a free discussion over the chief issues of religion took place, resulting in what scholars now call the Worms Book.[116] Whether or not the delegates used a preexisting work to create the Worms Book is debated.[117] What is uncontested, however, is that the theological content was shaped by its principle negotiators: Johannes Gropper[118] and Martin Bucer.[119] I will be showing how the first five articles are compatible with Bucer's view of justification.

Though there are no surviving records from these secret negotiations, we do know from Bucer's letter to the landgrave on 20 December that the group

112. For the landgrave's request that Bucer see Granvella, see the landgrave's letter to Bucer (3 December 1540), *Lenz* I, no. 92, 256; see also *Lenz* I, no. 88, 232–233. The landgrave needed a religious compromise with the emperor on account of his bigamous marriage. Bucer was worried about the landgrave's willingness to compromise with the emperor, who Bucer saw as an enemy. See Bucer's letter to the landgrave (22 November 1540), *Lenz* I, no.89, 235–240. On Bucer's relationship with the landgrave, see Heidi Wulczyn, "The Relationship between Martin Bucer and Philip of Hesse: A Reforming Politician and a Political Reformer, 1534–1539," in Krieger and Lienhard, *Martin Bucer and Sixteenth Century Europe*, 1:451–459; see also Gerhard Müller's article "Landgraf Philipp von Hessen und das Regensburger Buch," in *Bucer und seine Zeit*, ed. Marijn de Kroon and Friedhelm Krüger (Wiesbaden: Franz Steiner, 1976), 101–116.

113. Bucer understood that the failure of negotiations would inevitably lead to a civil war between the Schmalkaldic league and the emperor. He also desired to advance the kingdom of Christ by guiding his German neighbors back to Christ through a reasonable reformation. See Ortmann, *Reformation und Einheit*, 183.

114. On this conversation, see Bucer's letter to the landgrave from Worms (20 December 1540), *Lenz* I, no. 101, 275; and Ortmann, *Reformation und Einheit*, 184–185.

115. *Lenz* I, no. 101, 274–276. Bucer also noted various obstacles that impeded agreement and reformation, especially the pope.

116. Scholars sometimes differentiate between the Worms Book, when pertaining to the original draft of the book, and the Regensburg Book, when pertaining to the amended text at Regensburg.

117. As Ortmann has shown, the attempt to find a model or preliminary outline for the Worms discussion runs into dead ends, primarily because there is a lack of evidence that the *Enchiridion* was used as the basis of negotiations (against Lipgens, *Kardinal Johannes Gropper*, 124) and because the material from 1545 is set in the polemical context of the attempted reform of Cologne, making claims for the articles of the *Wahrhafftigen Antwort* difficult (against Braunisch, "Die 'Artikell' der 'Warhafftigen Antwort,'" 519–545; cf. Ortmann, *Reformation und Einheit*, 187–190).

118. For a comparison of the *Enchiridion* in relation to article 5, see Stupperich, "Der Ursprung" 88–116.

119. Ibid., 101. Stupperich attests that Bucer's *Romans Commentary* played a role in drafting article 5 on justification, an assertion that I agree with and will demonstrate. Likewise, Cardauns traces out how the Leipzig formula influenced articles 2, 5, 11, and 13 of the Worms Book; see Cardauns, *Zur Geschichte*, 16–24.

was able to quickly reach agreement on original sin and justification.[120] They finished working on the Worms Book on New Year's Eve.

On 5 January Bucer left Worms to meet the landgrave in Rosbach to gain his support for the drafted articles. After reading them, Philip recommended that Luther's judgment be sought on them, but to maintain the secrecy of the authorship of the articles he suggested that they be sent to Luther through Joachim II. Bucer returned to Worms on 9 January and the next day sent the book to Joachim II, requesting that, after he reviewed the work, it be sent to Luther for his judgment.[121]

On 17 January the emperor en route to Germany sent a mandate to end the colloquy. Thus concluding with their agreement on original sin, the negotiations between Melanchthon and Eck were postponed to be resumed at the Imperial Diet at Regensburg in March.

The Diet of Regensburg (1541)

During February and March, Regensburg was flooded with visitors, theologians, princes, prince electors, city delegates, and other sundry persons who were arriving for the Imperial Diet.[122] Bucer arrived on 10 March with

---

120. *Lenz* I, no. 101, 276.

121. See Bucer's Letter to Joachim II (10 January 1541), *Lenz* I, no. 15 of appendix 4, 529–538; for Joachim's letter to Luther (4 February 1541), which accompanied the Worms Book, see *WA.Br.*, no. 3573, 322–327.

122. Bucer wrote a report on the colloquy soon after its conclusion; *Acta colloqui in comitiis imperii Ratisponae habiti . . .* (Strasbourg, 1541), (*Bibliographie* 112); and, in German, *Alle Handlungen und Schriften, zu vergleichung der Religion, durch die Key. Mai., Churfürsten, Fürsten, und Ständen, aller theylen, Auch den Päpst. . . .* (Strasbourg, 1541), (*Bibliographie* 114). Both of these texts are now available in *BDS* 9/2; my citations, however, refer to Bucer's original publications. For a partial English translation of *Alle Handlung*, see Donald J. Ziegler, ed. and trans., *Great Debates of the Reformation* (New York: Random House, 1969), 143–177. For secondary resources on Regensburg, see Augustijn, *De Godsdienstgesprekken*, 73–97; Augustijn, "Bucer's Ecclesiology in the Colloquies with the Catholics," 107–121; Peter Matheson, *Cardinal Contarini at the Colloquy of Ratisbon of 1541* (Oxford: Clarendon Press, 1972); Peter Vogelsanger, "Ökumenismus im 16. Jahrhundert: Zur geschichte des Religionsgespräches von Regensburg 1541," in *Unterwegs zur Einheit: Festschrift für Heinrich Stirnimann*, ed. Johannes Brantschen and Pietro Selvatico (Freiburg: Universitätsverlag, 1980), 631–648; Hans-Martin Barth et al., *Das Regensburger Religionsgespräch im Jahr 1541: Rückblick und aktuelle ökumenische Perspektiven* (Regensburg: Friedrich Pustet, 1992); Fuchs, *Konfession und Gespräch*, 429–456; Friedrich, *Martin Bucer*, 178–194; and Ortmann, *Reformation und Einheit*, 233–279. For works that deal specifically with article 5, see Stupperich, *Der Humanismus*, 105–124; Stupperich, "Der Ursprung," 88–116; Walther von Loewenich, *Duplex Iustitia: Luthers Stellung zu einer Unionsformel des 16. Jahrhunderts* (Weisbaden: Franz Steiner, 1972), 29–55; Vinzenz Pfnür, "Die Einigung bei den Religionsgesprächen von Worms und Regensburg 1540/41 eine Täuschung?" in *Die Religionsgespräche der Reformationszeit*, ed. Gerhard Müller (Gütersloh: Gütersloher Verlagshaus Gerd Mohn, 1980), 55–88; Karl-Heinz zur Mühlen, "Die Einigung über den Rechtfertigungsartikel auf dem Regensburger Religionsgespräch von 1541—eine verpaßte Chance?" *Zeitschrift für Theologie und Kirche* 76 (1979): 331–359; Lexutt, *Rechfertigung im Gespräch*, 236–270; and Lane, *Justification by Faith in Catholic-Protestant Dialogue*, 46–60. For an account of the city of Regensburg during the diet, see Hermann Nestler, "Vermittlungspolitik und Kirchenspaltung auf dem Regensburger Reichstag von 1541," *Zeitschrift für bayerische Landesgeschichte* 6 (1933): 389–414.

Calvin and Sturm. The papal legate, Gasparo Contarini, arrived a day later.[123]

Contarini's presence added an optimistic air to the negotiations because he had gained a strong reputation for reform in the Roman Curia.[124] In addition, he shared the Protestant conviction of justification by faith due to an early experience similar to Luther's *Turmerlebnis*.[125] Hubert Jedin suggests that the pope's sending of Contarini was evidence that he wished to "meet the Emperor's aspirations for reunion."[126] Whether or not this was actually the case, it seems that Contarini believed it to be. In a letter to Eck, he stated: "Even in a desperate situation the Christian must not completely abandon hope, but hope against hope. . . . I believe that our task is to carry on the fight with benevolence and good deeds so that our adversaries will be ashamed, or at least should be ashamed because they are separating themselves from loving brothers."[127] It was the papal legate's goal to show the Protestant estates that the Catholics were sincere and loving.

At first Bucer viewed Contarini with suspicion, describing him as a dog and an overly proud man.[128] Within a week Bucer had begun to warm to the legate, due to a meeting he had with the representatives of the emperor and the Catholic estates. Bucer's belief in the possible reformation of the empire was strengthened; he wrote to the landgrave on 21 March, "my hope for aid in the cause has never been greater."[129]

The emperor officially opened the diet on 5 April; however, it was only after Holy Week and celebrating Easter (in separate camps) that on 21 April the

---

123. Contarini's role has been the focus of much of the English scholarship on Regensburg. See Heinz Mackensen, "The Diplomatic Role of Gasparo Cardinal Contarini at the Colloquy of Ratisbon of 1541," *Church History* 27 (1958): 312–337; Mackensen, "Contarini's Theological Role at Ratisbon in 1541," *Archiv für Reformationsgeschichte* 51, no. 1 (1960): 36–57; Marvin W. Anderson, "Biblical Humanism and Roman Catholic Reform (1501–1542): Contarini, Pole, and Giberti," *Concordia Theological Monthly* 39 (1968): 686–707; Peter Matheson, *Cardinal Contarini*; William P. Anderson, "Gasparo Contarini: Sixteenth Century Ecumenist," *Ecumenical Trends* 13, no. 9 (1984): 140–142; Elisabeth G. Gleason, *Gasparo Contarini: Venice, Rome, and Reform* (Berkeley: University of California Press, 1993); and most recently Anthony N. S. Lane, "Cardinal Contarini and Article 5 of the Regensburg Colloquy (1541)," in *Grenzgänge der Theologie: Professor Alexandre Ganoczy zum 75. Geburtstag*, ed. Otmar Meuffels and Jürgen Bründl (Münster: Lit Verlag, 2004), 163–190.

124. Gleason, *Gasparo Contarini*, 194.

125. Mackensen, "The Diplomatic Role of Contarini," 312.

126. Jedin, *History of the Council of Trent*, 1:378. Cf. Matheson, who states that the "dispatch of Contarini was really nothing more than a gesture, a tactical maneuver, dictated by the need to retain the goodwill of the Emperor" (*Cardinal Contarini*, 54); see also Gleason, *Gasparo Contarini*, 199.

127. Contarini to Eck from Rome (6 January 1541), in *Regesten und Briefe de Cordinals Gasparo Contarini*, trans. Franz Dittrich (Braunsberg: Verlag von Huye's Buchhandlung [Emil Bender], 1881), 314–315; quoted and translated in Gleason, *Gasparo Contarini*, 202.

128. On first seeing Contarini, Bucer wrote the following about him on 15 March: "Est canus et satis procerus, vultu vero qui acrem, pertinacem et superbum hominem prodeat." See *Lenz* 2, no. 119, 211n4.

129. *Lenz* 2, no. 121, 23; "daß meer hoffnung der sachen zu helffen, nie gewesen."

theological discussions were initiated by the emperor. At that time he appointed the Catholic and Protestant representatives. For the Catholics he chose Eck, Gropper, and Julius Pflug; for the Protestants, Melanchthon, Bucer, and Johannes Pistorius of Hesse.

The theological discussions began on 27 April. The delegates were presented with the Worms Book, which claimed (to preserve the secret of its origin) to be a formula of concord authored by two deceased scholars from the Low Countries. Prior to its presentation it had been given to Contarini, who with Giovanni Morone and Gropper made around twenty slight revisions.[130]

The Worms Book

The Worms Book is composed of twenty-three articles and is divided into three major sections.[131] The first section is on doctrine, the second section is on the sacraments and ecclesiology, and the third section deals with ceremonies and church discipline.[132] Like the Leipzig articles, the Worms Book begins its discussion with soteriology.[133] By doing so, the sacramental tone that was seen in Gropper's *Enchiridion* on the subject of justification is tempered. The sacramental-incorporational paradigm that was the basis of his understanding of the doctrine is scarcely seen in these first articles.

To demonstrate the compatibility of Bucer's doctrine of justification in the *Romans Commentary* with these articles, I will primarily be referring back to sections in the previous chapters. In addition, I have made use of two works published by Bucer shortly after the colloquy, which shed further light on the agreements reached.

The first is Bucer's *Acts of the Colloquy* (*Acta Colloquii*), which included Melanchthon's "The reply of the princes and estates in agreement with the *Confessio Augustana* concerning the book furnished to the Imperial Majesty Charles, 12 July."[134] In this report Melanchthon includes a section in which he discusses the agreed-upon articles, offering suggestions for further emendation in regard to the ambiguities that remained.

---

130. Matheson, *Cardinal Contarini*, 101.

131. The Worms Book is printed in *BDS* 9/1, which contains both the Latin version and Bucer's German translation of the text.

132. For a breakdown of the articles, see Ortmann's third appendix, *Reformation und Einheit*, 299–301.

133. I will focus only on the first five articles, especially article 5 on justification. For analysis of the first four articles, see Lexutt, *Rechtfertigung im Gespräch*, 193–214. See also Jill Rait, who gives a short summary of the first four articles in "From Augsburg to Trent," in *Justification by Faith: Lutherans and Catholics in Dialogue VII*, ed. H. George Anderson et al. (Minneapolis, MN: Augsburg, 1985), 200–217, see 209–211.

134. In *Acta colloqui*, 41–48; and *CR* 4, 479–491; "Responsio Principium et Statuum coniunctorum Augustanae Confessionis de libro exhibito Imperatori Carolo Aug. 12 Iulii"; partial English translation in Ziegler, *Great Debates*, 152–166.

The second work is Bucer's *On the True Reconciliation and Agreement of the Churches* (*De Vera Ecclesiarum . . . Reconciliatione et Compositatione*), which was a response to the criticisms he received from both Albert Pighius and Eck in regard to the *Acta Colloquii*, in which Bucer placed the blame for the colloquy's failure on the Catholics.[135] In this work he provides commentary on the first five articles.

Both of these latter works confirm that what was agreed upon at Regensburg was consistent with what Bucer had to say on the topic in 1536. Though there are places in these articles where certain topics remain ambiguous, they in no way contradict the evangelical position articulated by Bucer. The representation that article 5 consisted of two views glued together in one document, what some have described as a *Vermittlungstheologie*, does not take into account an independent third or fourth view.[136] As demonstrated in the previous two chapters, the doctrine of justification during this period could be understood in numerous ways. What is presented at Regensburg is one such way compatible with that of the evangelical reformer Martin Bucer.

On the first day of discussions at Regensburg the delegates were able to come to an agreement on the first four articles, with relatively minor revisions to the original. The following analysis of these initial articles looks both at the original form from Worms and at the revisions made at the colloquy of Regensburg.

ARTICLE 1: "CONCERNING THE CONDITION OF MEN AND THE INTEGRITY OF NATURE BEFORE THE FALL."   The first article[137] begins by stating that humanity was created in the image of God,[138] which is correlated to the mental capacity of humanity. Being created in the image of God meant that humanity was endowed with the powers of intellect and will.[139] These powers of intellect and will are

---

135. Bucer, *De Vera Reconciliatione* The first part of this work was published by Walter Friedensburg as "Martin Bucer," 145–191. This was written in response to Albert Pighius's *Ratio componendorum dissidiorum et sarciendae in religione concordiae* (Cologne: M. Novesiani, 1542); and Johannes Eck's *Apologia . . . adversus mucores et calumnias Buceri, super actis Comiciorum Ratisponae* (Cologne, 1542) (my citations come from the 1543 Paris edition); Pighius then replied to Bucer's *De Vera Reconciliatione* with *Apologia Albert Pighii Campensis adversus Martini Buceri calumnias* (Mainz, 1543).

136. Some of those who see this article as a *Vermittlungstheologie* are Stupperich, *Der Humanismus*, 118–124; zur Mühlen, "Die Einigung," 342; Dermot Fenlon, *Heresy and Obedience: Cardinal Pole and the Counter Reformation* (Cambridge: Cambridge University Press, 1972), 55; McGrath, *Iustitia Dei*, 314–315; Gleason, *Gasparo Contarini*, 227–228; and most famously Luther, who said the article of justification was *zusammenleimt* in his letter to John Frederick, *WA.Br.* 9, no. 3616, 406.

137. *BDS* 9/1, 339, ll. 1–12; "De conditione hominis et ante lapsum naturae Integritate." On the first four articles, see Lexutt, *Rechtfertigung im Gespräch*, 193–204; and Rait, "From Augsburg to Trent," 208–212.

138. *BDS* 9/1, 339, ll. 2–3; "Deus hominem ad Imaginem et similitudinem suam, hoc est ad filium qui est Imago patris Invisibilis in spiritu sancto condidit (Gen. 1[27]; Col. 1[15–16]; Heb. 1[3])."

139. *BDS* 9/1, 339, ll. 4–8; "Non in corpore . . . sed in mente, quam intellectus et voluntatis viribus praeditam secundum seipsum virtute vestiuit." For similar statements on Adam before the Fall, see Gropper, *Enchiridion*, 88v–89r; and *BRom* (1536), 401; (1562), 462; *CP* 148.

further described as the freedom of choice, the light of wisdom, and the excellence of innocence.[140]

The article states, "In this complete image and likeness, in which man was created, he possessed in the intellect a true and living knowledge (*viva notitia*) of his God and a right judgment concerning all things, and in the will a burning love and obedience to God."[141] The intellectualist perspective of this article, with its reference to a living knowledge, suggests the influence of Bucer's priority of the intellect.[142]

Though the article is compatible with his basic understanding on the topic of humanity before the Fall, Bucer was more reserved in the *Romans Commentary*, only stating that "the first man was created in the best possible state; he lost it both for himself and for us by sinning, but Christ has restored a better state for believers. That is all we need to believe on the matter. Scripture does not explain what degree of infallibility of judgment and what capacity for uprightness of will Adam enjoyed, and therefore we too must bridle our curiosity."[143] For Bucer the article contained nothing controversial; it acted as an appropriate starting point for a discussion on the renewal of men.[144]

ARTICLE 2: "CONCERNING FREE CHOICE."   This article[145] was organized around four stages of salvation history: before the Fall, after the Fall but before regeneration, after regeneration but before glorification, and glorification.[146] It began by reiterating that before, and only before, the Fall, humanity possessed free choice so that if Adam had so desired, he would have been able to keep the

140. *BDS* 9/1, 339, ll. 4–8; "id est arbitrii libertate, sapientiae luce et innocentiae pulchritudine, ac ita quadam sui participatione mirifice decoravit, ut esset in laudem gloriae ipsius."

141. *BDS* 9/1, 339, ll. 9–12; "In hac Imaginis et similitudinis Integritate constitutus homo in intellectu veram ac vivam dei sui Archetipi notitiam et rectum de rebus Iuditium, In voluntate vero ardentem erga deum amorem et obedientiam possidebat (Eccle. 17[1–9]; Gen. 2; Ps. 8[6–9])."

142. In Bucer's German translation he states, "Hatte er im verstandt ein ware und *lebendige erkanntnuß* seines gottes, demnach er gebildet war, und ein *rechten verstandt* und *urteil* von allen dingen;" adding further emphasis on knowledge and understanding. *BDS* 9/1, 338, ll. 11–14; emphasis added).

Reflecting on the article, Eck offered lengthy comment, which noted the peculiarity of the reference to a *viva notitia*, which neither scripture nor the fathers spoke of. Eck, *Apologia*, 30(v); "Hic nova profert author, prius inaudita, hominem in paradiso vivam habuisse Dei noticiam." Eck did, however, believe that *viva* could be understood for *beatifica*. Bucer responded to Eck's comments on this article by stating that they were superfluous. Bucer, *De Vera Reconciliatione*, 33(r); "Quare Eccius suam merito calumniam, de superfluitate huius articuli, inter suos compotores continuisset, nec Principibus, ad impediendam Ecclesiarum conciliationem, obtrusisset, praesertim, cum post fidem Imperatoriae Maiestati datam, se candide et sincere in hoc negocio versaturum, hunc articulum in colloquio non taxarit, ut nec causam taxandi habuit."

143. *BRom* (1536), 401; (1562), 462; *CP* 148.

144. Bucer, *De Vera Reconciliatione*, 33(r); "De hoc quidem articulo nihil controversum fuit, tamen quia doctrina de reparatione hominis constitui hoc loco debuit, non ineptum initium factum est, a conditione eius ante lapsum."

145. *BDS* 9/1, 339, l. 13 through 343, l. 18; "De libero arbitrio."

146. *BDS* 9/1, 339, ll. 19–21.

command and the image of God intact, albeit with the assistance of grace and the power of the Holy Spirit.[147] Quoting Ecclesiasticus 15:18, the article affirms that man in this state had set before him "life and death, good and evil, that which he will choose will be given to him."[148]

However, because Adam chose his own counsel instead of the counsel of grace and the Holy Spirit, he defiled the image of God that he was given.[149] On account of the Fall, humanity was no longer free to do good and keep from evil. What remained was only a freedom from compulsion.[150] The freedom that remains "is ineffective to begin and perform true righteousness and good works before God."[151] Hence the natural man can no longer perceive the things of the Spirit (1 Cor. 2:14); however, the vestige of freedom that remains is able to choose to do good or evil in relation to outward acts and the goods of this present life.[152]

In De Vera Reconciliatione, Bucer defended the distinction in the article between freedom from necessity and compulsion,[153] in response to Eck's criticism of the statement that "the freedom created to do the good and to keep from evil on account of the Fall of man is lost, and only the freedom from compulsion remains,"[154] as a shameful error contrary to all scripture.[155] Bucer emphasized that God by his certain and infallible judgment effects all in all, so that all that happens is by necessity. In a similar manner, as he had done in his Romans Commentary, he stated that God himself is not free from necessity, since he by necessity wills what is best and right.[156]

When the free will is repaired (reparatio), regenerated humanity (cf. John 8:36, 15:5 and Romans 8:2, 8:26, and 6:18) is described as set free from the law of sin.[157] This freedom is also described positively as being enabled "to keep

147. BDS 9/1, 339, ll. 15–16; "si vellet, posset per acceptam et assistentem gratiam et vim spiritus sancti mandatum servare et Imaginem."

148. BDS 9/1, 339, ll. 22–23.

149. BDS 9/1, 339, l. 25 through 341, l. 3.

150. BDS 9/1, 339, ll. 25–29.

151. BDS 9/1, 339, ll. 28–29; "Inefficax quidem ad inchoandam et efficiendam iustitiam veram et opera coram deo bona."

152. BDS 9/1, 339 l. 30 through 341, l. 1; "valens tantum ad efficienda opera externa et vitae praesentis tam bona quam mala."

153. Bucer, De Vera Reconciliatione, 33(v)–35(r).

154. Eck, Apologia, 32(v); "Author libri. Concreata libertas facienda boni, et continendi se a malo, per hominis lapsum est amissa sola libertate a coactionis retenta, etc." See BDS 9/1, 339, ll. 25–26.

155. Eck, Apologia, 32(v)–33(r); "Pudendus est ille error, et toti sacrae scripturae contrarius." For Eck it was not only a freedom from compulsion that remains in the human after the Fall. In his Enchiridion, he states that the claim that all things happen by necessity is the error of Manichaeism. See Johannes Eck, Enchiridion of Commonplaces: Against Luther and Other Enemies of the Church, trans. Ford L. Battles (Grand Rapids, MI: Baker Book House, 1979), 210–219.

156. Bucer, De Vera Reconciliatione, 33(v)–33(r). See BRom (1536), 361; (1562), 413; CP 102–103. The distinction between sinning by necessity or compulsion is one made by Luther in De servo arbitrio; WA 18, 634.

157. BDS 9/1, 341, ll. 4–10.

himself from sin, to obey God, and to keep the commandments, which he should strive zealously to do, with the assistance of the Spirit toward this end."[158] This latter clause is quite important, for it indicates not that the believer can actually achieve these things, but that with the assistance of the Spirit he should strive toward this end (*huc*). This statement was slightly ambiguous, allowing for the possible interpretation that the law could be fulfilled, and thus the Protestant delegates at Regensburg added in the margin the statement: "The Protestants prefer the following to be put: he is now able to resist sin and to provide an initial obedience."[159] Melanchthon, in Bucer's *Acta Colloquii*, stated that "in this life and on account of the corruption of nature even the reborn are not able to satisfy the law of God, yet they are righteous, that is, accepted by God, through faith for the sake of Christ, our mediator with God."[160] In order to prevent misinterpretation of the statement, Bucer affirmed the Protestant marginal comment, since in this life no one is able to satisfy the law.[161] Nevertheless, the original unannotated article, with the use of *huc*, seems to protect the article from a view that the law can actually be achieved by someone now before glorification.

The positive view expressed in the article after regeneration, in combination with its silence in regard to congruous merit, could, with difficulty, allow for a theology of cooperation in earning one's salvation.[162] However, both Melanchthon and Bucer affirmed that this article should be interpreted as rejecting the view of more recent theologians, which held that unbelievers are able to earn salvation by means of congruous merit.[163] Bucer believed that the article clearly rejected such a stance. He saw the article affirming that "we are born children of wrath and in slavery to sin, so that unless we are freed through the son and inspired by the spirit of adoption (as the article confesses in the second paragraph) our will is ineffective to even begin still less to effect true righteousness and good works before God."[164]

The marginal emendation at Regensburg is cautious about the possibility of a believer being able to fulfill the commands of the law; nevertheless, the Protestant delegates recognized that the article did not deny the evangelical

---

158. *BDS* 9/1, 343, ll. 4–5; "possit nunc se continere a peccato, obedire deo et facere eius mandata, et quod huc adiuvante spiritu summo studio contendere debeat."

159. *BDS* 9/1, 343, ll. 4–5; cf. *BDS* 9/1, 343ni; "Mallent protestantes sic poni: possit possit nunc restistere peccato et praestare inchoatam oboedientiam."

160. Bucer, *Acta colloqui*, 43; "quod in hac vita, et hac naturae corruptione, etiam renati non possint legi Dei satisfacere, sed sint iusti, id est, accepti Deo, fide, propter Christum mediatorem."

161. Bucer, *De Vera Reconciliatione*, 37(v)–38(r).

162. See Lexutt, *Rechtfertigung im Gespräch*, 194–197.

163. Bucer, *Acta colloqui*, 44; and Bucer, *De Vera Reconciliatione*, 33(v).

164. Bucer, *De Vera Reconciliatione*, 33(r); "Hac de re pugnatum quidem est, atqui a nostra parte id solum, ut agnosceretur, sic nos nasci filios irae, et servos peccati, ut nisi per filium liberemur, et spiritu filiorum inspiremur, inefficax sit voluntas nostras, ut confitetur huius articuli, parag: secundus, etiam ad inchoandam, nedum ad efficiendam iustitiam veram, et opera coram Deo bona."

perspective that freedom was found solely in Christ and that true freedom came only after glorification.[165] For Bucer, as I have shown, the view that secondary causes allow for a cooperative role in one's justification articulated in the *Romans Commentary* is compatible with the original draft of the Worms Book, especially since the article both describes this freedom by emphasizing the role of the Spirit and describes the believer, who has been set free from the law of sin, as still prone to sin.[166] The view of the free will after regeneration represented in this article is consistent with Bucer's thought first because it is understood only through the agency of the Spirit, and second because the article repeatedly affirms that the regenerated life is hindered by concupiscence, described as a remaining weakness inclined to evil.[167]

It is also important to note that the article's final paragraph references 1 John 1:8, "No one in this life is without sin," in an attempt to associate the weakness of concupiscence with sin, in line with the evangelical view.[168] In *De Vera Reconciliatione*, Bucer believed that this statement was clear, stating that "none of the saints, while in this life, was able to keep himself from all sin or to offer perfect obedience to God, or to fulfill his commands and satisfy his law."[169] Bucer believed that the article contained the evangelical position, and thus saw this article as solid and perfect for those truly seeking peace.[170]

ARTICLE 3: "CONCERNING THE CAUSE OF SIN."   Article 3[171] is very short and is basically a compilation of John 8:44, Wisdom 2:24, Romans 5:19, and Genesis 3.[172] These passages are used to explain that the cause of sin resides in the devil's and humanity's turning away from God. It is not God who is the source of evil but the devil's jealousy and Adam's fall. Commenting on this article in *De Vera Reconciliatione*, Bucer takes it as an opportunity to affirm the judgment of God,

---

165. See Ortmann, *Reformation und Einheit*, 194.

166. See *BDS* 9/1, 343, ll. 5–6, 14–17. References to the work of the Holy Spirit in this and other articles are another Bucerian influence on the articles. See Stupperich, "Der Ursprung," 115.

167. *BDS* 9/1, 343, ll. 11–15; "Et si interim etiam diligenter inculcandum sit, tantum adhuc in nobis ad bonum infirmitatem et ad malum inclinationem remanere, quae illam vim spiritus dei remoratur et pravas cupiditates gignit, ut impellat ad ea facienda quae non volumus, Quo fit ut nemo sit in hac vita sine peccato (1 John 1[8])." See *BRom* (1536), 267; (1562) 295; *CP* 123.

168. *BDS* 9/1, 343, ll. 11–15.

169. Bucer, *De Vera Reconciliatione*, 38(r); "ut nemo sit in hac vita sine peccato: his certe admodum clare hoc ipsum expressum est, neminem sanctorum, dum in hoc saeculo degit, se continere ab omni peccato, aut perfectam Deo praestare obedinetam, mandatave eius perficere, et legi eius satisfacere." See *BDS* 9/1, 343, ll. 11–17.

170. Bucer, *De Vera Reconciliatione*, 38(v); "Est igitur solida et perfecta de hoc Articulo inter omnes Christum vere invocantes, concordia. Id quod cum Imperatore, universi quoque Principes in hisce Comitiis agnoverunt."

171. *BDS* 9/1, 343, ll. 19–26; "De caussa peccatj."

172. *BDS* 9/1, 343, ll. 20–26.

that is, predestination. According to him, the message that nobody is able to have an impulse of the good unless they are given that impulse from God is in line with the scriptures and the orthodox fathers.[173] God wills to save those whom he wills, and others he wills to hand over to their own base senses. This latter judgment Bucer sees as just because everyone has sin indwelling in them and because everyone has been born from parents tainted by transgressions.[174] To the carnal mind, this is seen as unjust, but because God is the righteous judge, his judgments are just. To criticize these righteous judgments of God is irreligious. They are not open to questioning, as Paul confessed: "Oh the immensity of the wisdom and knowledge of God, how unsearchable are his judgments" (Rom. 11:33).[175]

The article continues, describing Adam as "losing faith and love for God, and in its place conceiving a trust and love of himself."[176] At Regensburg *vivam* was added to *fidem* to distinguish between living faith and what is later described in the book as temporary faith.[177] Adam lost only living faith. The statement that this loss of faith results in a trust and love in oneself echoes Bucer's understanding of sin, as I have shown.[178]

Bucer concludes his commentary on the article by reaffirming it, believing that it piously and in an orthodox manner expresses the truth of this doctrine.[179]

ARTICLE 4: "ON ORIGINAL SIN."   The fourth article[180] is on original sin, which is first defined as a lack of original righteousness (here original righteousness is described as being in the grace of God and possessing the image of God).[181] Original sin is associated with concupiscence, which the article defines as "a corruption and disordered disposition of powers of humanity or a wicked inclination toward evil, which is also on that account the law of members [*lex membrorum*], also called the law of sin and also sin (Rom 7[7–8, 23])."[182] This

---

173. Bucer, *De Vera Reconciliatione*, 38(v).

174. Bucer, *De Vera Reconciliatione*, 38(v).

175. Bucer, *De Vera Reconciliatione*, 38(v)–38(r); see *BRom* (1536), 268; (1562), 297; *CP* 126–127.

176. *BDS* 9/1, 343, ll. 25–26; "cum Adam astu Diaboli circumventus fidem et amorem dei perdit, et horum loco sui fiduciam et amorem imbibit (Genes. 3)."

177. *BDS* 9/1, 343, ll. 25–26; "cum Adam astu Diaboli circumventus fidem <vivam> et amorem dei perdit." In Eck's report on the colloquy, he disagrees with this statement, since nowhere in scripture does it speak of Adam having faith in paradise, let alone a living faith. See Eck, *Apologia*, 33(v).

178. See section 3.4.2.1.3.

179. Bucer, *De Vera Reconciliatione*, 39(v).

180. *BDS* 9/1, 345, l. 1 through 353, l. 21; "De originalj peccato."

181. *BDS* 9/1, 345, ll. 2–5.

182. *BDS* 9/1, 345, ll. 7–10; "concupiscentiam vero intelligimus esse corruptionem et inordinatam dispositionem virium humanarum seu vitiosam inclinationem in malum, quae et ob id lex membrorum, lex peccati et peccatum quoque appellatur."

reference to Romans 7 makes room for the evangelical emphasis that regards concupiscence as sin.[183]

The article proceeds to define these two aspects of original sin using the Thomistic distinction that describes the lack of original righteousness as the formal aspect of original sin, in which guilt exists,[184] and concupiscence as the vicious habit through which actual sins are committed, that is, the material aspect of original sin. Bucer noted in the margin of his German translation that it is this formal aspect of sin associated with guilt that the scholastics (schullerer) called formale peccati.[185]

In his Romans Commentary, Bucer agreed with the scholastics who said that original sin is a loss of original righteousness. However, Bucer saw this loss as completely corrupting humanity and thus qualified the assertion that original sin is only the privation of original righteousness. He stated:

> The Schoolmen make the loss of original righteousness, the state in which all our parts were rightly ordered within us, the chief aspect of this evil of original sin. But surely it is a necessary consequence of this loss that everything in us is now disordered and distorted and the habit of corrupt desire has possession of man. As a result, subjection to eternal death is the lot of all whom the Savior's grace does not restore. This grace, imparted in baptism, annuls the imputation of this evil to us, but nevertheless the "law of our members," our corruption which is ever hateful to God, persists until this perishable nature has put on the imperishable. So long as the Schoolmen accept these corollaries, I do not see any divergence from the orthodox opinion of the Church.[186]

The article clearly affirmed that the law of sin that remains in our members remained after baptism; Bucer's position is compatible with this article.

The distinction between a formal and material aspect of original sin also arose during the discussions at Worms between Eck and Melanchthon. Eck rightly understood that the Protestants wanted to say that concupiscence was not only materially sinful but also formally sinful in that it was both a punishment and worthy of guilt. Over the course of the discussion, Melanchthon emphasized that the distinction made light of one's sinfulness and that to say that the concupiscence in the regenerate is still worthy of guilt does not mean that the regenerate are not forgiven. He stated that "we call that evil which

---

183. See section 3.4.2.1.2.
184. BDS 9/1, 345, ll. 13–16.
185. BDS 9/1, 344, ll. 18–19. See ST 1a 2ae q.82 a.3.
186. BRom (1536), 267; (1562) 295; CP 123.

remains after Baptism not merely a penalty nor a thing indifferent but something which is by its very nature worthy of eternal death unless it were forgiven."[187] Eck pressed him on this issue, wanting him to make the distinction that concupiscence before baptism is both guilt and penalty, but after baptism only a penalty.[188] To this Melanchthon could agree that in baptism guilt was removed through the forgiveness of sins. However, he stated:

> We shall never approve the softening of this to the point of confessing
> that the evil that is left over is only a penalty. . . . Certainly when I
> ponder my own doubts, when I realize how far I am from the fear and
> love of God which God demands, I cannot judge these to be merely
> punishments. I confess and know them to be sins, and therefore the
> whole church prays, "Forgive us our trespasses." For this reason I
> cannot agree with the proposed softening of the doctrine. I rather pray
> that Christians may agree with the Scriptures and with their consciences,
> for they recognize by themselves in their daily life that these evils are not
> merely punishments but are by their very nature sins, but that these sins
> are forgiven the saints who through faith seek forgiveness.[189]

Melanchthon believed that, "If he [Eck] wishes the term 'guilt' to be understood only as an accusation, there is nothing in the way. But if he means that the remnants of the depravity are only a penalty, and that they are not defects opposed to God's law, I shall never assent."[190] Hence Melanchthon did not have a problem with saying that concupiscence did not condemn on account of the forgiveness of sins through Christ; the problem was saying that concupiscence was *only a penalty* and not also *sin*, albeit forgiven. This distinction was accepted by Eck, and agreement was reached at Worms prior to the convening of the Regensburg Colloquy. Thus when the matter was discussed again at Regensburg, *formalis* was, unsurprisingly, stricken out of the Worms Book article.

The next section of the article, which Bucer titled "On the Hereditary Aspect of Original Sin,"[191] affirms that through Adam all of posterity passes away and that death now reigns. On account of the oppressiveness of sin, "God does not see his image or the knowledge and love of him in humanity."[192] All are sons of wrath (Eph. 2:3).[193]

---

187. Mackensen, "The Debate between Eck and Melanchthon" 46; *CR* 4, 41.
188. Mackensen, "The Debate between Eck and Melanchthon," 47; *CR* 4, 44.
189. Mackensen, "The Debate between Eck and Melanchthon," 50; *CR* 4, 54.
190. Mackensen, "TheDebate between Eck and Melanchthon," 53; *CR* 4, 66.
191. *BDS* 9/1, 346, l. 1; "Von der angeburt der erbsünden."
192. *BDS* 9/1, 347, ll. 7–9; "deus in homine hoc peccato oppresso non videt Imaginem suam aut sui notitiam seu amorem."
193. *BDS* 9/1, 347, l. 9.

The article is clear that humanity is oppressed by sin so that it is seen as corrupt, while maintaining that a trace (*vestigium*) of the image of God remains within" "Even if, however, the trace in us from birth is a kind of residue of the image of God, which we call the light of nature, from which we grow in some sort of knowledge of God, nevertheless, because this trace is exceedingly thin on account of its grave contamination, God does not acknowledge that very thing, which is altogether ineffective for producing spirituality and true righteousness."[194] This understanding of some sort (*qualiscunque*) of knowledge of God that remains after the Fall and has the ability to grow is characteristic of Bucer's view of the *notio Dei*.[195] For Bucer this *notio*, akin to the *lumen naturae*, is a gift of God, but devoid of any salvific capacity, because of the potency of original sin and the weakness of the *vestigium*.

Bucer subtitles the next section "On the Dissolution and the Removal of Original Sin."[196] Here the authors show that for the born-again "original sin is destroyed through the washing of regeneration and renovation in the word of life through the merit of Christ's passion (Eph. 5[26])."[197] Bucer's German translation places an emphasis on renewal by the agency of the Spirit, stating that it is the "renovation of the Holy Spirit."[198] Citing Romans 6:4, the authors assert that "we have been buried in him through baptism in death, in order that, just as Christ was raised for the glory of the Father, so also we might walk in newness of life."[199] In baptism grace is returned and guilt is destroyed.[200]

After baptism, concupiscence is repressed (*reprimitur*) by the Spirit moving the regenerated toward holiness; "Hence even if after baptism the material of sin, that is, concupiscence, a serious illness and the root of all bitterness, remains in those born again, nevertheless this is not joined with guilt. For this reason through baptism we have been set free and clothed by Christ and also have been

194. BDS 9/1, 347, ll. 10–15; "Tametsi enim in nobis nascentibus adhuc vestigium quoddam imaginis dei reliquum sit, quod lumen naturae appellamus, quo etiam in qualemcunque dei cognitionem assurgimus, quia tamen hoc vestigium admodum exile est ob contaminationis gravitatem, fit ut deus idipsum non agnoscat, quod ad faciendam spiritualem et veram iustitiam omnino sit inefficax."

195. See section 2.4.1. on Bucer's epistemology. For Gropper this initial knowledge is represented as *credere Deum*; see section 4.3.4.1.

196. BDS 9/1, 346, l. 23; "Vom hinnemen und abthun der erbsünden."

197. BDS 9/1, 347, ll. 16–17; "Dissoluitur autem hoc originale peccatum per lavacrum regenerationis et renovationis in verbo vitae per meritum passionis Christi (Ephes. 5[26])."

198. BDS 9/1, 246, l. 25; "ernewerung des heiligen geists."

199. BDS 9/1, 347, ll. 24–25; "consepulti sumus *ipsi* per *baptisma* in mortem ut, quemadmodum christus est excitatus a mortuis per gloriam patris, *sic* et nos in novitate vitae ambulemus." Ortmann has pinpointed Bucer's direct influence here, showing that the paraphrase of Rom. 6:4 used in the article (a combination of the Vulgate and Erasmus translations) is similar to the paraphrase found in Bucer's *metaphrasis*; see Ortman, *Reformation und Einheit*, 197. B*Rom* (1536), 276; (1562), 305; "Per *baptisma* igitur sumus *ipsi* consepulti, quo participes mortis eius simus; ut quemadmodum Christus gloriosa virtute patris a mortuis excitatus est, *sic* et nos novam vitam nostra conversatione exhibeamus." For the Vulgate and Erasmus versions, see BDS 9/1, 347n14.

200. BDS 9/1, 347, ll. 17–18.

reformed toward the image of the Son of God."[201] Therefore, since the regenerated are without guilt, that which remains, that is, concupiscence, is not imputed as sin (*non imputatur in peccatum*).[202] In this sense concupiscence in the regenerate does not condemn them; it condemns only when it leads to actual sins. The article states that "this law of sin and this remaining concupiscence in the saints, if it produces no evil fruit from itself, is not sin which has some guilt attached to it. For all of its guilt has been taken away through Christ."[203]

As noted earlier, if by guilt is meant accusation, there is no problem for Bucer and the reformers here. At Regensburg, Melanchthon reaffirmed that concupiscence be understood as "a fault which resists the law of God, as was agreed to at Worms."[204] He wanted to make sure that this article took concupiscence seriously; thus he concludes his thoughts on the article on original sin by stating that "the book thereupon acknowledges that this disease brings forth evil fruit in those reborn, and that they ought to seek forgiveness by faith, and that they ought to seek to fight against this disease within them by the Spirit."[205]

Bucer echoed these sentiments in regard to the article in *De Vera Reconciliatione*.[206] He stated: "However, the saints, in their own way, also desire things contrary to God, are turned away from God, oppose God's good will, and the evil that with a renewed mind and the spirit of Christ they hated and fled, in the flesh and old man (which still indwells them) they do; and thus remain in them the senses of the flesh, which is hostile toward God. They are also themselves to this extent enemies of God."[207] Then after quoting Romans 8:1, that there is still no condemnation for those in Christ Jesus, he states that this still remains true for the saint, even though sin still indwells his flesh.[208] Though this evil

---

201. *BDS* 9/1, 349, ll. 1–4; "Proinde etsi post baptismum in renatis remaneat materiale peccati, hoc est concupiscentia, gravis certe infirmitas et radix omnis amaritudinis, tamen haec non habet adiunctum reatum. Nam eo per Baptismum solute et christo induti sumus atque ad Imaginem filii dei saltem inchoatam reformati." See Ortmann, *Reformation und Einheit*, 196–197, esp. 197n246.

202. *BDS* 9/1, 349, ll. 6–8. See *BRom* (1536), 213; (1562), 225.

203. *BDS* 9/1, 351, ll. 3–6; "Itaque docendum est cum Augustino diligenter legem illam peccati et relictam in sanctis concupiscentiam, si ex se nullum fructum malum edit, non esse peccatum quod adhuc eos reatu aliquot teneat. Omnis enim reatus eius per christum sublatus est."

204. *Acta colloqui*, 44; "hoc est concupiscentia, gravis morbus, infirmitas, etc., addantur haec verba, et vitium repugnans legi Dei, ut et Wormatiae convenit." See *BDS* 9/1, 349, ll. 1–3.

205. *Acta colloqui*, 44; "Et liber fatetur subinde, hunc morbum parere malos fructos, adversus quos renati, et fide condonationem petere debent, et eis spiritu repugnare."

206. Bucer, *De Vera Reconciliatione*, 39(v)–45(r). From 45(r) to 117(v), Bucer enters a long discussion against Albert Pighius's view of original sin.

207. Bucer, *De Vera Reconciliatione*, 40(v); "Tamen sancti, suo modo etiam ipsi contra Deum concupiscunt, adversantur Deo, repugnant bonae voluntati Dei, malumque quod mente renovata et spiritu Christi oderunt et fugiunt, carne ac veteri homine, qui adhuc adhaeret, faciunt, habentesque in se sensum carnis, qui est inimicitia cum Deo, sunt et ipsi hactenus inimici deo."

208. Bucer, *De Vera Reconciliatione*, 41(r); "Nihil itaque condemnationis est iis, qui sunt in Christo Iesu: etiamsi in carne illorum inhabitet adhuc peccatum."

and sin still merit condemnation, Christ by his death has removed the deserved condemnation from those who remain in him.[209]

Bucer believed that the severity of the evangelical position was in accord with the quotation from Augustine in paragraph 9,[210] which stated that "this remaining evil in the saints is sin, and not only the penalty or the cause of sin, because disobedience dwells in it against the rule of reason."[211] From Bucer's perspective, the article described concupiscence as sin.

Lexutt, however, believes that the article leaves ambiguous whether or not concupiscence is seen as sin, and on this account this ambiguity is the foundational weakness in both article 4 and article 5.[212] She believes that this weakness highlights an overly positive anthropology, which does not exclude the possibility of a person playing a cooperative role in the *iustificatio impii*. This, however, is not the case. The article is clear that before baptism concupiscence and original sin are materially corrupt,[213] and that the *lumen naturae* does not have any salvific ability in itself.[214] Likewise, if one takes into account Melanchthon's discussion with Eck at Worms, one understands that for the Catholics it was acceptable to understand guilt as accusation, and that concupiscence in those born again was more than just a penalty. Calvin in a letter to Farel on 11 May wrote that agreement was reached without any difficulty in regard to this article.[215] Even Luther stated that this article was in an acceptable form.[216] On this account, Bucer saw in the article nothing that prevented consensus.[217] It represented his position.

Bucer's and Gropper's efforts in secret paid off. In just one day the representative delegates at Regensburg were able to come to agreement on the state

209. Bucer, *De Vera Reconciliatione*, 41(r); "Non ideo est, quod non hac malum et peccatum, condemnationem mereat, sed quia Christus Dominus meritam condemnationem, sua morte ab iis, qui in se manet, submovit."

210. *BDS* 9/1, 351, ll. 3–17.

211. Bucer, *De Vera Reconciliatione*, 44(v); "nam quod in responso nostro de actis Colloquii Impera Maiesta, datum, tantum ob maiorem lucem, et ad avertendum contensiosorum cavillos, adiici optavimus, esse hoc malum vitium repugnans legi Dei id in eo omnino comprehensum imo etiam satis expressum est, quod liber ex Augusti. Adducit parag. 9. Esse malum hoc in sanctis relictum, peccatum: nec tantum penam, aut causam peccati, quia illi insit inobedientia contra dominatum mentis." Cf. *BDS* 9/1, 351, ll. 9–13; "Concupiscentia carnis, adversus quam bonus concupiscit spiritus, peccatum est, quia illi inest obedientia contra dominatum mentis; et poena peccati est, quia reddita est meritis inobedientis; Et caussa peccati est defectione consentientis vel contagione nascentis." See *PL* 44, 787.

212. Lexutt, *Rechtfertigung im Gespräch*, 202–215, esp. 209.

213. *BDS* 9/1, 351, l. 22–353, l.1.

214. *BDS* 9/1, 347, ll. 10–15.

215. Calvin's letter to Farel (11 May 1541), *CO* 11, no. 308, 215; "Delecti nostri de peccato originali non difficulter transgerunt."

216. Luther's letter to John Federick (29 June 1541), *WA.Br.* 9, no. 3637, 463, ll. 127–130; "Der vierde Artickel, von der Erbsunde, ist recht gestalt."

217. Bucer, *De Vera Reconciliatione*, 44(v)–45(r).

of man before the Fall, free will, the cause of sin, and original sin, an impressive achievement.

The First Version of Article 5: "Concerning the Restitution, Regeneration and Justification of Men, Grace and Merit, Faith and Works"

Bucer saw his participation in the secret colloquy as fulfilling the duty that every Christian had to lead his neighbor, the authorities, and his superiors to Christ.[218] In this manner his participation can be seen as consistent with his missiological intent, as indicated in chapter 2.[219] If from the Worms Book concord could be reached, then the reign of Christ would advance; for Bucer this demanded agreement on the evangelical doctrine of justification.[220]

The length of article 5[221] testifies to the centrality of this doctrine during the secret discussions at Worms. During these negotiations Bucer and Capito ensured that the evangelical position was not excluded in the article. It is important to note that Bucer saw the Worms Book not as a confession but as a starting point for more serious discussions yet to come, which was in line with his pedagogical approach, as displayed in his catechism.[222]

The article on justification is ambiguous in parts. Bucer knew this. In the letter written to Joachim II on 10 January accompanying a copy of the Worms

---

218. *Lenz* I, no. 101, 274.

219. See section 2.3.

220. See section 2.3.1.

221. *BDS* 9/1, 353, ll. 22–23; "De restitutione, regeneratio et iustificatio, gratia et merito, fides et operibus." There were at least five versions, outlines, or portions of article 5 before the final version agreed on at Regensburg. Of these drafts, the original and Gropper's second draft, along with the final version, can be found in *ARC* 6, 21–88; the first and final drafts as well as Bucer's German translation of the original article can be found in *BDS* 9/1, 323–483. Eck drew up a manuscript draft that was retained by Pflug and has been posted online by Vinzenz Pfnür at http://ivv7srv15.uni-muenster.de/mnkg/pfnuer/ (accessed 18 July 2007). Melanchthon also offered a contribution, whose contents can be surmised from Caspar Cruciger's dictated report; here Cruciger reveals the manner in which Melanchthon defended *sola fide* and rejected the idea that works before justification were a basis for justification; thus he advocated a strong forensic understanding. See *CR* 4, no. 2209[b], 242–246. Contarini submitted a draft of a portion of the article, which is no longer extant.

Ortmann, Braunisch, and Stupperich provide good commentaries on the origins of certain aspects of the articles. Ortmann focuses on Bucer's contributions (Ortmann, *Reformation und Einheit*, 191–226), and Braunisch and Stupperich explain Gropper's influence; Stupperich focuses on article 5 (Braunisch, "Die 'Artikell'"; Stupperich, "Der Ursprung"). See also Lexutt, *Rechtfertigung im Gespräch*, 204–215.

222. *Lenz* I, no. 15 of appendix IV, 534–535. Here Bucer shows that he saw the Worms Book only as a good starting point for discussions: "Damit aber nun furderlich ein guter anfang in diser sachen gemacht und etlich furneme heubter teutscher nation uff angezeigte weiß in ware und fruchtbare handlung der vergleichung zu kommen erinneret werden, so hat obgemelte personen und kei. oratoren fur gut angesehen, das gedachte schrifft in vertrawen wir E.chf.G. (Euer fürstliche Gnaden) zuschickten, das sie sich in derselben ersehen und demnach, wie E.chf.G. wissen an D. Luther's urteil gegen der unseren hoch gelegen sein wille, und derselbige aber, wa er sicht, das man die lere der iustification zulesset, in allen anderen stucken glinder ist dann unser fil, so sehe uns fur gut und notwendig zu biser sachen an, das E.c.g. dise schrifft bald doctor Luther zusandten, mit solicher anzeig, geding und begere, wie volget." See Ortmann, *Reformation und Einheit*, 226.

Book,[223] Bucer expressed some reservations about the articles. Both he and Capito realized that the articles could have been further corrected;[224] however, it is the nature of compromise that certain areas be left ambiguous.[225] The articles in the Worms Book were carefully pieced together to avoid unnecessary offense.[226] Nevertheless, as I will show, Bucer's understanding of the doctrine of justification is compatible with this first version, albeit as a preliminary step toward further clarification. Like his catechism, by gradual steps one would come to a more clear understanding of the truth. This article was a good first step.

The title of this article highlights the dual approach that the article takes. It is about *iustificatio et* . . . ; hence the term *iustificatio* is not central, and other words, like *regeneratio* and *restitutio*, are used to help describe the justification event. For Lexutt the use of the copula in the title acts as proof that the article must be understood in a Catholic manner; in fact, she cannot see how Bucer, let alone any evangelical, could in good conscience affirm this antireformational formula.[227] However, as she admits, this manner of speaking was in line with what many of the evangelicals had discussed in the preliminary discussions leading up to Worms, where the *sola fide* formula was explained in a less rigid manner.[228] The dual formula in the title and the article was not then and is not here a rejection of the truth of *sola fide* but an elaboration that encompasses the life of faith into the discussion—what Bucer at times called the second and third justifications.[229]

The article is divided into two major sections. The first deals with the causes of justification,[230] faith,[231] grace,[232] the law,[233] and the gospel.[234] The

223. *Lenz* I, no. 15 of appendix IV, 529–538.

224. *Lenz* I, no. 15 of appendix IV, 532; "Doch haben wir [Bucer and Capito] diejenig, so dieselbig schrifft gestellt, nit zu gantzer correction vermöcht." Within the context of the polemics of the attempted reform of Cologne, Bucer also stated that Gropper was responsible for the portions of the article on justification in the Worms Book that "raised higher the ability of man to do good and his righteous deeds than the faith of Christ and the righteousness of God would allow." In *Von den Einigen Rechten Wegen; BDS* 11/2, 299, ll. 23–25; "Doch wie er sich im artikel der Justification immer dahin noch bearbeite, wie er durch schein der h. Schrifft und vaettersprüchen deß menschen vermoegen zum guten unnd sein rechtthun etwz hoeher erhuebe, dann es der glaub Christi und die Gottes gerechtigkeit dulden mage."

225. During the Regensburg colloquy, Luther stated in a letter to Melanchthon (12 May 1541) that all the passages of the Worms Book were "ambigua et dubia." See *WA.Br.* 9, no. 3617, 411, l. 13.

226. *Lenz* I, no. 15 of appendix IV, 534; "Ist vilberurter schrifft in worten dermaßen temperiret und gemeßiget worden, das den guthertzigen auf jenem teil im artikel der justification, an dem alles gelegen, und andern haubtartikeln desto weniger anstoß entgegen geworden würde."

227. Lexutt, *Rechtfertigung im Gespräch*, 209.

228. See section 5.3.1; see Lexutt, *Rechtfertigung im Gespräch*, 209.

229. See *BRom* (1536), 130; (1562), 119.

230. *BDS* 9/1, 357, l. 26 through 359, l. 16.

231. *BDS* 9/1, 359, l. 17 through 361, l. 3.

232. *BDS* 9/1, 361, l. 4 through 363, l. 26.

233. *BDS* 9/1, 365, l. 1 through 367, l. 16.

234. *BDS* 9/1, 367, l. 17 through 387, l. 3.

second section is on works and is titled "On Justification Which Comes from Works of Faith of Which S. James Wrote in Chapter 2."[235]

The article begins by stating:

> Since by nature we are all born sons of wrath (Eph. 2[3]), it is necessary that our sins are forgiven, that we are reconciled with God, and reborn or regenerated, since without this no one is able to see or enter the kingdom of God (John 3[3.5]). Therefore the gratuitous justification and regeneration of men, which occurs through Christ, is the remission of sins and reconciliation with God, bearing the spirit of sanctification. Thus there occurs a spiritual and wonderful metamorphosis or transformation in the human animal, by which, having been snatched by God from the power of darkness, he is transferred into the wondrous light and is led from the innate slavery of his corruption into spiritual freedom.[236]

Here the twofold aspect of the title is affirmed. There is a justification related to forgiveness and one to metamorphosis.

The warrant for this dual manner of speaking of justification is found in scripture, whose authors are apt to speak of justification in two ways, that is, Paul and James.[237] The first manner is described by Christ as *regeneratio* (John 3[5–7]) and by Paul as the *iustificatio impii*, by which we are accepted freely through faith and not by any preceding work or merit; this justification is associated with the remission of sins and the gift of the Holy Spirit.[238] In evangelical terms this is the imputative aspect of righteousness understood as the non-imputation of sins. The second manner in which scripture presents justification is *iustificatio operum*, represented primarily by James, who states that humanity is not justified by faith alone but also by works

---

235. BDS 9/1, 387, l. 4through 397, l. 12; "Restat de Iustificatione operum fidei, de qua apud divum Jacobum cap. 2."

236. BDS 9/1, 353, l. 24 through 355, l. 5; "Cum omnes nascamur natura filii Ire (Ephes. 2[3]), remissione peccatorum et reconciliatione cum deo et renascentia seu regeneratione nobis opus est, sine qua potest videre seu Introire in regnum dei (Ioan. 3[3.5]). Est itaque iustificatio et hominis regeneratio gratuita per christum peccatorum remissio et cum deo reconciliatio, adferens spiritum sanctificationis, quo fit spiritualis et mirifica methamorphosis seu transformatio hominis animalis, qua divinitus e potestate tenebrarum ereptus in admirabile lumen transfertur et a nativa servitute corruptionis in libertatem spiritualem adducitur."

237. BDS 9/1, 355, ll. 10–11; "Iustificationem duplicem in scriptura proponi consideramus." Both Gropper and Bucer had discussed this distinction between Paul and James in their earlier works. See *Enchiridion*, 142 (r)–147(v) [i.e., 149(v)]; and *BRom* (1536), 213; (1562), 224.

238. BDS 9/1, 355, ll. 11–15; "Unam, quam Christus regenerationem appellat (Ioan. 3[5–7]), Apostolus vero paulus iustificationem impii vocat, quae nullis nostris praecedentibus operibus aut meritis debetur, sed gratis per fidem accipitur, qua indepta remissionem peccatorum et spiritum regenerationis seu adoptionis ex impiis et inimicis filii dei efficiuntur qui credunt in eum (Ioan. 1[12])."

(James 2[24]).[239] The authors affirm that this second way of speaking of justification is often described as *sanctificatio*.[240]

These two justifications are described as encompassing two areas: in the
first a human *gratis per fidem accipitur*,[241] and in the second *ex operibus iustificatur homo et non ex fide tantum*.[242] This second justification is clearly shown to be
dependent on the first justification and is seen as a sign of it.[243] This is not a
"double justification" theory *strictu senso*, since the second justification is
dependent on and subordinate to the first justification, which is through faith.
What the article presents is a discussion of what later Protestants would clarify
as justification and sanctification.[244] This terminological distinction between
justification and sanctification for Bucer and Gropper is usually enveloped
within justification's semiotic range, that is, it includes both aspects of justification and sanctification or holiness.[245] For both, the holiness of a believer is
not the basis or formal cause of the forgiveness of sins.[246] The twofold manner
of speaking here is consistent with Bucer's and Gropper's views. However, the
dependence of the justification of works on the first justification of forgiveness
and renewal seems to be a shift in Gropper's position, which tied imputation
more closely to works. When Gropper speaks of a twofold justification, he states
that "justification properly consists in two parts, namely the remission of sins,
and the renewal and purification of the interior mind."[247] For Bucer, when he

239. *BDS* 9/1, 355, ll. 20–21; "idem Apostolus dixit: Vides quoniam ex operibus iustificatur homo et non
ex fide tantum."

240. *BDS* 9/1, 355, ll. 22–23.

241. *BDS* 9/1, 355, l. 13, in reference to the *Confessio Augustana* article 4. See *CR* 26, 275.

242. *BDS* 9/1, 355, ll. 20–21, in reference to James 2:24.

243. *BDS* 9/1, 355, l. 19; "ut indissolubili vinculo priori coheret et tota innititur."

244. Thus what we have here can be taken as a terminological concession as Lane suggests in his analysis
of the final version of the article. "The Reformers all but universally agreed that conversion brings both justification and sanctification. The only concession that Regensburg demanded of them was terminological—to use the
term 'inherent righteousness' of sanctification. This was not much of a concession, since many of them (such
as Bucer and Calvin) were already accustomed to use the word 'righteousness' at least sometimes when referring
to sanctification." See Lane, "A Tale of Two Imperial Cities: Justification at Regensburg (1541) and Trent (1546–1547),"
in *Justification in Perspective: Historical Developments and Contemporary Challenges*, ed. Bruce L. McCormack (Grand
Rapids, MI: Baker Academic, 2006), 119–145, quotation on 129. 245. Thus to express this duality, as we have shown,
they sometimes spoke of a twofold or threefold justification. In Gropper's *Enchiridion* he begins his definition of
justification by stating that "iustificatio duo proprie complectitur, nempe remissionem peccatorum et interioris
mentis renovationem seu repurgationem" (*Enchiridion*, 132(r)). Bucer makes the distinction between a first and
second justification when refering to Rom. 4:1–8; *BRom* (1536), 212, 216, 218; (1562), 224, 229, 232; "Sed illo in
Exodo [Exod. 23:7] non prima iustificatione dictum est. . .. De secundaria, quae iuxta opera sit, iustificatione istuc
dominus dixit"; as well as a threefold scheme in regard to Rom. 2:11–16; see *BRom* (1536), 130; (1562), 119.

246. As I have shown earlier, this did not result in a double justification formula that was based on two
separate formal causes, since for both, as well as for this article, there is one formal cause; *BDS* 9/1, 357, ll. 2–5;
see sections 3.3. and 4.3.4.4.

247. *Enchiridion*, 132(r); "Iustificatio duo proprie complectitur, nempe remissionem peccatorum, et interioris mentis renovationem seu repurgationem."

distinguishes a twofold justification, he typically speaks of a *prima iustificatio*, that is, "absolution from all impiety," and a *secundaria iustificatio*,[248] "which is a result of works."[249] Here Bucer's influence seems to be at play.

Like the *Enchiridion*, the article includes a section that deals with the causal structure of justification.[250] The efficient cause is God; the *subefficiens* is Jesus Christ; the material cause is the *mens hominis*; the formal cause is grace, mercy, and the righteousness of God; the *disponens* (regulating) cause is faith; and the final cause is our glorification.[251] That the material cause is not humanity but the *mens hominis* highlights the intellectualist emphasis in which justification is understood here. Later on the article provides an elaboration on the material cause, now described as the will. There it states:

> When therefore it is sought, how we are justified by the first
> justification, one needs to reply that we are justified freely, not by
> any preceding merits and also without works of the law, that is,
> without the aid of the law; however not simply without the law nor
> without works of the spirit or prevenient grace, . . . to be freely
> justified, is not through one's own will, that is: by the powers of the
> will, yet not without our will; which must grasp healing grace
> through faith, so that having been healed it fulfills the law, not
> placed under the law nor needing the law . . . also as Augustine said
> "He who created you without you, will not justify you without you."
> Thus in this way the will is the material cause of justification.[252]

For Bucer such a causal scheme was not presumably a major issue, since he could at times speak about justification using causal terms, that is, a first cause and second causes. At one point in the *Romans Commentary* he offered a three-fold scheme where the prime cause is God's good will, the second cause is Jesus Christ, and the third cause is attributed to family, friends, and the saints

---

248. Bucer's use of *secundaria* hints not to a following (*secunda*) but to an inferior or second-rate justification that highlights the superiority of the first. In the *Expositio* that precedes this discussion, he correlates this secondary justification to James, stating: "Illud Iacobi dictum est de secundaria iustificatione, quae consequitur opera, non de primaria et substantiali, de qua hic Paulus." *BRom* (1536), 213; (1562), 224.

249. *BRom* (1536), 218; (1562), 232; "secundaria, quae iusta opera fit."

250. See section 4.3.4.4.

251. *BDS* 9/1, 357, l. 28 through 359, l. 18.

252. *BDS* 9/1, 379, ll. 11–20: "Cum ergo quaeritur, quomodo iustificemur iustificatione illa prima, respondendum est, nos iustificari gratis nullis praecedentibus meritis et sine operibus legis, id est sine adiutorio legis; non tamen simpliciter sine lege nec sine operibus spiritus seu gratiae praevenientis, sed non ex illorum merito quod iustificatione sit dignum; Item iustificari gratis, non per propriam voluntatem, hoc est: voluntatis viribus, sed tamen non sine nostra voluntate; quam oportet accipere per fidem gratiam sanantem, Ut sanata 'impleat legem, non constituta sub lege nec Indigens lege,' Ut testatur Augustinus, lib. de spiritu et littera ca. 9; Ut verum sit quod idem ait: 'Qui creavit te sine te, non iustificabit te sine te.' Siquidem voluntas est caussa iustificationis materialis." This Augustinian passage is quoted by Gropper in his *Enchiridion*, 143(v).

who have been used by God in a believer's salvation.[253] Because he had his own causal scheme and because these schemes affirmed, along with this article, that the prime cause was God, in line with Bucer's view of the *Allwirksamkeit* of God, Bucer's doctrine of justification was not threatened here.[254]

The next subsection is on faith. Faith is affirmed as a gift of God and not a human ability.[255] The authors distinguish between a saving faith and a historical faith. The latter faith is given to the *impii* and only has knowledge that God exists and about other things of God;[256] it is related to the *lumen naturae*. Citing Romans 1 and 2, the article states that this historical "faith seems to be added to us either as something new or as a special kindness of God by which God, his will, and other things are known."[257] And it is given as a basis for contemplating the created world and from a literal understanding of the law.[258] This is as we have shown Bucer's understanding of a first level of knowledge.[259] The question of true faith is left for the discussion on the gospel.

The article then moves on to its most characteristically Catholic portion: its discussion of grace. In this subsection the article delineates between the *gratia qua creati sumus* and the *gratia qua predestinati vocamur, iustificamur, sanctificamur et glorificamur*.[260] In regard to the grace by which we are created, it indicates that this grace is a gift of God and that it does not allow for meritorious works to follow.[261] The concept of good works preceding justification is excluded from saving grace. The grace by which we are saved *ex fide Christi* is what the article agrees is especially called grace (*gratia utique proprie dicta*).[262] Here Gropper's hand is evident because saving grace is defined following Lombard's four stages (*gradus*).[263] The first is prevenient grace, which is here related to election and vocation.[264] The second stage of saving grace is justifying grace. Justifying faith is the faith by which God both purifies the heart and imparts the Holy Spirit who grants people the ability to assent to his word.[265] Closely associated with this grace is subsequent

253. *BRom* (1536), 126–127; (1562), 114–115.

254. See Ortmann, *Reformation und Einheit*, 200.

255. *BDS* 9/1, 359, ll. 17–20; "quae est donum dei et non ex nobis (Ephes. 2[8])."

256. *BDS* 9/1, 359, ll. 18–20.

257. *BDS* 9/1, 359, ll. 23–25; "Quae certe fides per lumen naturae sive aliquo novo seu spetiali dei beneficio nobis conciliari videtur, qua deus, deique voluntas utrumque cognoscuntur (Rom. 1 et 2)."

258. *BDS* 9/1 359, l. 25 through 361, l. 3.

259. See sections 3.5.2.1. and 3.4.1.

260. *BDS* 9/1 361, l. 16–17. See section 4.3.4.2.

261. *BDS* 9/1, 361, ll. 12–15.

262. *BDS* 9/1, 363, ll. 1–20.

263. See section 4.3.4.2. See Lombard, *Sentences*, bk. 4, dist. 25–26; *PL* 192, 709–714.

264. *BDS* 9/1, 363, ll. 1–2; "gratia praeveniens, qua praedestinati vocamur et anticipamur, quae et gratia praedestinationis, electionis et vocationis appellatur."

265. *BDS* 9/1, 363, ll.8–9; "Et deinde gratia iustificans, qua quos elegit et vocavit in dilectio etiam filio suos gratos sibi facit, praebens fidem, qua corda purificans spiritum suum Verbo suo assentibus impartitur et immittit."

or cooperating grace. This grace is that by which God works within believers to desire and to accomplish those things that are according to his good will (Phil. 2:13).[266] The article affirms that nothing good can be done except with the aid of God; therefore, to do good God accompanies believers and makes them cooperators with him.[267] Citing Philippians 2:12, "Work out your salvation with fear and trembling," the article states that in this way it is not absurd to call this cooperating grace.[268] Finally, there is perfecting or consummating grace, which is the gift of eternal life. All these grades of grace are understood as being obtained through Christ by faith, by which believers believe in God.[269]

For Lexutt this is the primary weakness of the article, because the idea that man cooperates to complete justification enters in with the inclusion of the concept of cooperating grace. Lexutt believes that the distinction between a first and second justification can no longer exist because both cooperating and perfecting grace fall within the realm of the first justification, thus allowing for a man to cooperate in that first justification.[270] But this neglects what the article states previously about the dependency of the second justification of works depending on the first justification by faith.[271] Likewise, as Volkmar Ortmann states, in comparison with the *Enchiridion*, cooperating grace is here more clearly subordinate to justifying grace, and on that account Ortmann believes one can see the influence of Bucer and Capito.[272] In addition, though Bucer did not speak of stages of grace in his *Romans Commentary*, the article's description of justifying grace as associated with the Spirit and cooperating grace as accomplished with the help of God (*suo auxilio*) does not present an obstacle for agreement.

The article goes on to elaborate the twofold structure of justification, using what was earlier described as the two goals of justification: mortification and vivification, that is, killing the old man and regenerating or resuscitating the new man.[273] Mortification is discussed in the subsection dealing with the law, and vivification in the subsection on the gospel.

---

266. *BDS* 9/1, 363, ll. 11–13; "Ad haec est gratia quae subsequens dicitur, qua deus in nobis operatur velle et perficere pro sua bona voluntate (philip. 2[13])."

267. *BDS* 9/1, 363, l. 14; "nos prosequitur et sibi cooperantes facit."

268. *BDS* 9/1, 363, l. 15; "Quare et cooperans gratia non absurde dicitur."

269. *BDS* 9/1, 363, ll. 19–20; "Hos vero omnes gradus non aliter quam fide, qua deo credimus, per Christum indipiscimur."

270. Lexutt, *Rechtfertigung im Gespräch*, 211.

271. *BDS* 9/1, 355, l. 19.

272. Ortmann, *Reformation und Einheit*, 202.

273. *BDS* 9/1, 359, ll. 8–11; "Iam ut omnis transmutatio duobus terminis et medio conficitur, Ita Iustificatio et regeneratio hosce duos terminus habet, mortificationem et Vivificationem, Mortificationem veteris hominis et regenerationem seu suscitationem novi." For Bucer's and Gropper's uses of mortification and vivification, see *BRom* (1536), 283–285; (1562), 316–318; and *Enchiridion*, 37(r). Cf. Melanchthon's *Romans Commentary*, commenting on Rom. 6:3–4, in *MW* 5, 200–203.

The article states that God makes use of the law at the beginning of justifying grace.[274] It does so at the beginning of justification by inspiring contrition in the person on account of a faith that grasps the *concupiscentia in membris nostris, naturae corruptio*, and *multiplex legis praevaricatio*.[275] At this stage the person becomes knowledgeable of the eternal hellfire he or she deserves, and this is what the article calls *mortificatio* or *contritio*: the first goal of our justification.[276] At this point the document notes that the *Lex est paedagogus in Christum* (Gal. 3:4), which is consistent with Bucer's and the evangelicals' second use of the law.[277]

Ortmann believes that here the association of the law and mortification with the first goal of the first justification leaves interpretational room for works to wiggle in before justifying faith, which is later described in relation to the gospel.[278] This ambiguity exists; however, if these statements are interpreted in line with Bucer's view of *Allwirksamkeit*, this initial stage is seen as a product of the Spirit disclosing sin to the world.[279] Likewise, the manner in which this article describes this beginning of faith is the way in which Bucer describes the beginning of faith in the *Romans Commentary*.[280]

What was earlier described as historical faith is seen here as the basis for mortification, since the article states that "in this manner God implants a kind of faith and thirst for a savior in the man terrified by the law and awakes the mind oppressed by sin to a certain appetite for true salvation."[281] This is the beginning of justifying faith, which is later completed in vivification.[282]

The distinction of an initial faith preceding true faith is compatible with the progression in faith that Gropper described in his *Enchiridion*,[283] and with Bucer's understanding of an initial faith.[284] For both, this stage of faith is a preparation for the gospel and necessary for justifying faith. Thus the section on the law ends by anticipating the section on the gospel, stating:

274. *BDS* 9/1, 365, l. 1; "Porro initium gratiae iustificantis deus a lege facit."

275. *BDS* 9/1, 365, ll. 11–12.

276. *BDS* 9/1, 365, ll. 15–16; "Atque haec est mortificatio seu contritio, primus terminus iustificationis primae et restitutionis nostrae."

277. *BDS* 9/1, 365, l. 6. See chapter 3.

278. Ortmann, *Reformation und Einheit*, 203.

279. *BDS* 9/1, 365, ll. 6–7.

280. See section 3.5.2.1. It is also in line with the way Bucer understands *vocatio* related to *poenitentia*. See *BRom* (1536), 446; (1562), 519.

281. *BDS* 9/1, 367, ll. 1–3; "Deus itaque in hunc modum territo per legem fidem quandam et sitim querendi salvatoris ingenerat et mentem peccato oppressam ad qualemcunque appetentiam verae salutis exuscitat." Cf. *BDS* 9/1, 359, l. 22 through 361, l. 3.

282. *BDS* 9/1, 373, ll. 30–33.

283. See *Enchiridion*, 202(r); and section 4.3.4.1.

284. See *BRom* (1536), 323–324; (1562), 365–366; and section 3.5.2.

> The closer the Holy Spirit leads us to the savior and places him
> before our eyes, so, ever the more, we make progress in obtaining
> justifying grace, so that we are like those walking in the midst of
> deep shadows from whom the fog lifts for the first time, and then a
> light reveals things still uncertain, until at last we see clearly with
> open and uncovered eyes in the clear light of day. In the gospel this is
> represented by the blind man who at first sees nothing, but then he
> sees men just like walking trees, and then he clearly sees all things
> (Mark 8[8–26]).[285]

The subsection on the gospel is where true faith is described.[286] The Holy Spirit reveals to humanity, through the ministry of the Word, that Jesus Christ is both God and man, and thus "we believe him to be God who with divine power has destroyed sin, death and the devil, begins and bestows the new life and the kingdom, abolishes the old man, creates the new, frees us from the spirit of slavery and is able and wills to initiate in us the spirit of adoption of sons of God."[287] This is the gospel, and when "we intensely contemplate this good we understand that God is both able and willing to save."[288]

This contemplation is the gift of faith, which in the gospel appears in two ways (*duplex fides in Deum*). The first way is a faith that begins with the sweetness of the word and persuasion of the truth. This is at times called temporary faith, of which Judas is the prime example.[289] This passage comes directly from Bucer's *Romans Commentary*.[290] This first understanding of faith accepts the truth, but it lacks the fullness of grace that is supplemented in Christ Jesus.[291]

---

285. *BDS* 9/1, 367, ll. 10–16; "Quo propius autem spiritus sanctus nos ad salvatorem adducit eundemque ob oculos ponit, eo magis magisque ad indipiscendam gratiam iustificantem proficimus, ut simus veluti quibus in densissimis tenebris versantibus primum rarescit caligo, deinde dubia quaedam lux ostenditur, donec apertis tandem et reseratis oculis in plena luce perspicue videamus; quod in Evangelio illo caeco adumbratum est, qui primum nihil videt, deinde videt homines veluti arbores deambulantes, mox clare cernit omnia (Mark 8)."

286. *BDS* 9/1, 367, l. 17 through 387, l. 3.

287. *BDS* 9/1, 367, ll. 23–26; "Ut et ipsum esse credamus deum, qui peccatum, mortem et Diabolom divina virtute destruere, vitam novam et regnum auspicari et elargiri, veterem hominem abolere, novum creare, spiritum servitutis eximere et spiritum adoptionis filiorum dei in nos imbuere possit et velit."

288. *BDS* 9/1, 369, ll. 4–6; "cum summe bonum contemplamur, intelligimus eum ut potest ita velle salvare."

289. *BDS* 9/1, 369, l. 20 through 371, l. 17.

290. Here Bucer states that there "is a kind of partial illumination by the divine truth, which stimulates men's hearts to have faith in God's words but only for a time—so long, that is, as they fail to realise that his words conflict with their own desires. . . . This temporary faith is related to the knowledge of God which was granted to the gentiles but yet did not arouse them to the true worship of God." *BRom* (1536), 14; (1562), 14; *CP* 173. See Stupperich, "Der Ursprung," 101–102.

291. *BDS* 9/1, 369, ll. 16–19.

The second understanding of faith is the augmenting of temporary faith by the imparting (*exhibitione*) and reception (*acceptione*) of the truth.[292] This augmented faith is justifying faith, temporary faith strengthened by the Spirit.[293] The article states further on that this faith, "which has a perfect foundation and perfect righteousness in Christ, upon which everything rests, simultaneously grasps and stores away the impartation of this righteousness in the mind according to its measure."[294] The allusion to Christ's perfect righteousness being imparted to the mind echoes the manner in which Bucer understands twofold righteousness in the *Romans Commentary*, where the *iustitia Dei* is imparted to the mind, resulting in a derivative *iustitia*.[295]

The article then proceeds to explain the manner in which the church fathers understood the formula *sola fide* in association with the scholastic concept of a formal cause, described as the *iustitia Christi*.[296] The righteousness of Christ is received by faith. Thus the *sola fide* formula was used by the fathers to show how "only by that living faith and nothing else is the gift of *iustitia* received; that is, it is this faith by which God forgives us from sins, receives us as adopted sons, makes us just from unjust, and now pronounces us accepted."[297] The faith of *sola fide* is described using the Galatians formula of *fides per dilectionem operans*.[298] Stupperich suggests that the formula is clearly due to Gropper's influence.[299] However, Bucer too was able to acknowledge this formula as a valid way of describing justification.[300] Likewise, because the article states also that it is faith that is the *radix operum*, the evangelical view is at least not excluded, and any view that one is justified by love is clearly excluded.[301] However, as a safeguard against antinomianism the article states that when the

---

292. *BDS* 9/1, 369, ll. 16–19; "Est, quae exhibitione quoque et acceptatione veritatis fulcitur et quod adhuc accepto muneri deesse sentit, de plenitudine gratiae, quae est in Christo Jesu, per fidei plenitudinem mutuat ac supplet."

293. *BDS* 9/1, 371, ll. 18–21; "Caeterum iactis his fidei initiis tandem spiritus sanctus fidem suggererit, per quam iustificantur credentes, quae et veritati promissionis et iustitiae, quae est in Christo Jesu, complete et perfecte et indubitato innitutur et exhibitione promissionis, hoc est remissionis peccatorum et promissi spritus fulcitur (Rom. 5 et 8 et Galat. 3)."

294. *BDS* 9/1, 373, ll. 21–23; "Haec ergo fides, quae fundamentum habet perfectam illam et absolutam in Christo Jesu iustitiam, cui tota innititur, et simul huius iustitiae communicationem pro sua mensura et in mente recondit."

295. See section 3.3.

296. Ortmann, *Reformation und Einheit*, 204. See *BDS* 9/1, 381, ll. 10–13.

297. *BDS* 9/1, 381, ll. 15–17; "sola illa fide viva et nulla alia re donum Iustitiae accipitur; Haec est: est ea res, per quam deus nos a peccatis absoluit, in filios adoptionis adsciscit, ex iniustis iustos facit et sibi iam acceptos esse pronunciat."

298. *BDS* 9/1, 377, l. 16.

299. See *Enchiridion*, 143(r)–143(v) [i.e., 145(r)–145(v)]; see Stupperich, "Der Ursprung," 106–109.

300. *BRom* (1536), 22; (1562), 22; *CP* 195–196.

301. *BDS* 9/1, 381, ll. 18–25; "Debet autem hic radix diserte a fructibus discerni: fides per dilectionem operans radix est; opera fidei et charitatis, quae iustificatum sequunter, fructus sunt." See *BRom* (1536), 13–14; (1562), 13–14; *CP* 166.

sola fide formula is preached, in order to avoid moral laxity, people must also be encouraged to have the fear of God and flee from sinful living.[302]

At this point the article notes that love and regeneration are integral to faith and salvation as signs of forgiveness. Citing Bernard, on the story of the paralytic in Matthew 9:2–6, the article states that the forgiven believer ought to walk upright before people, avoiding sin as a testimony of righteousness.[303] As I have indicated, the visibility of justification is similarly described by Bucer in the *Romans Commentary*.[304]

The certainty of one's forgiveness is then taken up. The article affirms that the contemplation of one's imperfect righteousness ought not hinder one's certainty of forgiveness that is confirmed alone through the testimony of the Spirit.[305] It continues, stating that "this great faith in the righteousness which is perfect in Christ, ought to be considered to supply through faith in the present circumstance what is lacking in us."[306] Zur Mühlen suggests that this phrase indicates a Gropperian emphasis that places the imputation of Christ's righteousness as dependent on the works of effective righteousness.[307] However, this is not as clear as zur Mühlen suggests. According to Stupperich, these phrases point back to Bucer's strong emphasis on a certainty of faith empowered by the Spirit,[308] so that what is being spoken of here is a certainty of forgiveness that is given by the Spirit through faith in Christ's perfect righteousness. The phrase does not commit itself to zur Mühlen's suggestion that one's works righteousness is supplemented with Christ's, because it does not define what the believer has that may be supplemented. Likewise, the statement affirms that faith in Christ's righteousness offers the believer a certainty in forgiveness. And as I have noted, the article is explicit that the second justification *ex operibus* is dependent on the first justification *gratis per fidem accipitur*.[309] Works are an outgrowth of forgiveness, the nonimputation of sin. The justification of works is dependent on the justification by faith. On that account Gropper's understanding of imputation as a top-up scheme to one's works is denied, on account of the priority that the article gives to forgiveness as the first justification. What the article here is clear about is that one's own righteousness cannot be depended on, a point Bucer repeatedly expresses.

---

302. *BDS* 9/1, 383, ll. 1–11.

303. *BDS* 9/1, 383, ll. 12–30.

304. See *BRom* (1536), 10; (1562), 10; and section 3.5.4.

305. *BDS* 9/1, 385, ll. 1–4; "Nec hanc certidunem remissionis, modo sit confirmata spiritus testimonio, remorari debet contemplatio Imperfectionis iustitiae nostrae. Sed hoc magis fide in iustitiam, quae in christo absoluta est, intueri oportet, et hic per fidem supplere quod nobis deest."

306. *BDS* 9/1, 385, ll. 2–4; "Sed hoc magis fide in iustitiam, quae in christo absoluta est, intueri oportet, et hic per fidem supplere quod nobis deest."

307. Zur Mühlen, "Die Einigung," 338–339.

308. Stupperich, "Der Ursprung," 110.

309. *BDS* 9/1, 355, l. 19; "ut indissolubili vinculo priori coheret et tota innititur."

The article then briefly touches on the relation of the first justification and infant baptism.[310] It ensures the instrumentality of the church in justification through the sacraments, stating that by the secret breathing of the Spirit, justification is effected in baptized infants:[311] "For by the working of the Spirit of Christ in them through the washing of regeneration and renovation not only is the stain of original sin destroyed and the tinder of concupiscence quenched, but also new spiritual movements are aroused, even if they are unknown to us, which also work so that, when they will mature, they are more suited to understanding the gospel."[312] This ought to be diligently taught to the people so that they understand what a great gift is received in baptism.[313] Stupperich judges that by this statement the authors intend to stir the people to a higher appreciation of the sacraments, in an attempt to remind the people that the church is the mediator of salvation,[314] thus highlighting Gropper's influence. However, the magisterial reformers all affirmed that justification was mediated through baptism by the word of God's promise. In addition, the need to instruct the people on the sacrament is thoroughly Bucerian.[315] At this point the first major section ends.

The second shorter section deals exclusively with the justification of works. It begins with five statements describing the condition of humanity after the Fall, before as well as after justification: first the article affirms that concupiscence remains after baptism, which is ever inclined toward sin; second, that the baptized can never in this life be completely righteous; third, that though believers are commanded after baptism to love God and keep his commands, they will never be able to fulfill these commands perfectly in this life; fourth, that believers must always remember that they are not able to say that they are without sin (1 John 2); and fifth, that this partial righteousness (*iustitia ex parte*) that believers have in this life after baptism will be made complete in the future life.[316] Though this partial *iustitia* is compatible with Gropper, the allusion to 1 Corinthians 13:10 and the "ex parte" at this point in the article can be traced back to Bucer in his *John Commentary*.[317] This aspect of the article also remains

---

310. *BDS* 9/1, 385, ll. 18–23.

311. *BDS* 9/1, 385, ll. 18–20.

312. *BDS* 9/1, 385, ll. 19–23; "operante enim in illis per lavacrum regenerationis et renovationis spiritu christi non tantum labes originalis peccati tollitur et concupiscentiae fomes restinguitur, sed et novi motus spirituales, et si nobis incogniti, gignuntur, qui quoque faciunt ut, cum adoleuerint, ad intelligendum Evangelium sint aptiores."

313. *BDS* 9/1, 385, ll. 24–25.

314. Stupperich, "Der Ursprung," 111. See *BDS* 9/1, 385, ll. 24 through 387, l. 3.

315. See *BRom* (1536), 267; (1562) 295; *CP* 123. In *Einfältiges Bedenken. Entwurf einer Reformationsordnung . . .* (1543), (*Bibliographie* 126), in *BDS* 11/1, 298–315; Bucer offers a model for the way in which baptism ought to be taught. Here he provides a short catechesis for the baptism ceremony.

316. *BDS* 9/1, 387, l. 4 through 388, l. 2.

317. See *BOL* 2, 88–89, 387–388; Ortmann, *Reformation und Einheit*, 206n299.

consistent with Bucer's *duplex homo* view, seen as a partially regenerate judgment and will and a partially unregenerate judgment and will.[318]

At this point the article turns to the concept of *vivificatio*.[319] Vivification is living in Christ and performing works of the Spirit. Thus a believer's works can be called meritorious because they are not their own but the Spirit's work in them on account of their being in Christ.[320] In addition, it is repeated here that these works are the evidence of the first justification.[321]

The article then qualifies how works can be called meritorious. It states that

> even if by God's condescension these works are such, . . . nevertheless the remission of sins is owed to the merit of Christ, who always stands as an advocate for us and works these works in us, so that as we preserve his gifts from the beginning of his substance [Heb. 3:14], through these living works, which he imputes to us as merit, we are justified more and more, just as Rev. 22[11] states: "let the righteous still do right, and the holy still be holy," until at last we prevail on the last day having been stripped of our mortal corruption and clothed and glorified with immortality.[322]

These works are worthy of merit only insofar as they are Christ's works within believers. Here the concept of imputation arises in regard to works, in a similar manner to Gropper's use.[323] However, the claim that works are imputed as merit is compatible with the way works are seen as congruous merits in Bucer's view.[324] On account of God's *pactum*, God has decreed to reward eternal life to the works of faith in the believer, but these works stem from faith in the imputation of Christ's merit, and a believer's works are only secondary dependent causes of salvation for Bucer. The article states that lest these works ever be regarded as an anchor of salvation, one must remember that they are imperfect, and that salvation must be anchored in the living God, who gives and supplies salvation through Christ.[325] A believer's imparted righteousness is clearly affirmed insufficient.

---

318. See section 3.4.2.

319. *BDS* 9/1, 389, ll. 7ff.

320. *BDS* 9/1, 391, ll. 17–25.

321. *BDS* 9/1, 393, ll. 10–19.

322. *BDS* 9/1, 395, ll. 1–7; "et si haec opera dignation[e] dei talia sint, quod nihilominus remissio peccatorum debetur merito christi, qui semper adstat advocatus pro nobis et operatur haec opera in nobis, ut, retinentes initium substantiae eius, per haec opera viva, sua dona, quae tamen nobis in meritum imputat, magis ac magis iustificemur, iuxta illud (Apocalypsis 22[11]): *Iustus iustificetur adhuc et sanctus sanctificetur adhuc*, donec tandem proficientes de die in diem, hac corruptione mortalitatis exutos immortalitate induat et glorificet."

323. See section 4.3.4.3. See also Braunisch, *Die Theologie der Rechtfertigung*, 430–431.

324. See section 3.5.4.

325. *BDS* 9/1, 395, ll. 8–10.

The article teaches that preachers ought to exhort the people diligently to bring about their sanctification by doing good works, "not because they are of themselves the cause of the forgiveness of sins in those born again, but because God purges those sins daily as though with contrary medicines and subdues the power of concupiscence and indeed declares that through those works we have been justified."[326] God declares the just righteous because he crowns his own works. In a manner similar to Augustine, Bucer also states that if a believer "does any good it results from the fact that he is a creation of God, created for good works, works which God himself prepares, makes and performs, so that he rewards in us gifts which are already his."[327] Bucer believes that God requires good works for salvation, but they act as secondary causes stemming from the root of an intellectualized faith within a structure of thought founded on the paradigm that "to know the good is to do the good."[328] Thus, this is compatible with Bucer's thought.

The article ends with the following:

> Therefore it is not absurd to say that those born again are sanctified
> and justified through such works of faith and charity, but only when
> they result from faith, which is received in the first justification. This
> faith returns them to God as the author of every good thing and
> supplies to their imperfection the fullness of righteousness which is
> in Christ Jesus, giving all the glory to God not themselves. By faith
> the just shall live as testified by Habakkuk and confirmed by Paul. [329]

In this manner works are seen as an outgrowth of true faith, and therefore the evangelical formula of *sola fide* is accommodated. The article ends on this note.

Though this article maintained some of the more Gropperian language, for example, grades of grace and causes, here Bucer was able to integrate his understanding of the evangelical position on justification. The *sola fide* formula is presented in the article, and works are included in this scheme only insofar as they stem from faith as their *radix*. Faith is a stimulus; it is the root.

---

326. BDS 9/1, 395, ll. 14–18; "Proindeque exhortationes ad perficiendam sanctificationem nostram bonis operibus diligenter faciendae sunt. Non quod ipsa sint caussa remissionis peccatorum in renatis ex sese, sed quod deus illis peccata illa quotidiana veluti antidotis contrariis expurget et concupiscentiae vim mortificet atque adeo per illa nos iustificatos esse declarat."

327. BRom (1536), 120; (1562), 105. "Si quid benefacit, id inde est, quod figmentum Dei est, ad bona opera conditus, et ea, quae Deus ipse praeparat, facit, et perficit, ut sua iam in nobis dona remuneret."

328. See section 3.5.4.

329. BDS 9/1, 397, 1–5; "Et propterea non est absurdum, dicere quod renati per huiusmodi opera fidei et charitatis sanctificentur et iustificentur, modo fiant in fide, quae in justificatione prima accepta ea ad deum tanquam omnis bonis authorem refert et eorum imperfectionem de plenitudine iustitiae, quae est [in] christo Iesu, supplet, supplet, dans totam gloriam deo, non sibi; qua fide, ut Abacuc [Hab. 2:4] testatur et Paulus [Rom. 1:17] confirmat, *justus vivit.*"

As I have shown, Bucer's view of *sola fide*, understood within his structure of thought, allowed him to speak of the necessity of works for salvation in a secondary manner. Likewise, I have shown how this article and especially the article on original sin affirmed the evangelical emphasis of concupiscence, even though Lexutt sees it as not radical enough and therefore incompatible with her criterion for Reformation teaching during this period.[330] Her criteria are too exacting. There may be ambiguous language, but nothing contradictory to the evangelical position at this stage in the doctrine's development.

Regardless of its merits, when this version of article 5 was read on 28 April, Melanchthon and Eck were immediately displeased with it,[331] on account of its wording, the length, and the absence of any subsections, which resulted in what they saw as an unorganized hodgepodge.[332] Both Melanchthon and Eck demanded that a free and open dialogue over this doctrine be allowed without the hindrance of the Worms Book draft, and Granvella allowed it.

This resulted in the production drafts and counterdrafts. Accounts on the order in which the various drafts were presented differ.[333] However, following Matheson, it is probable that the discussions began with Melanchthon presenting an outline of the Protestant position.[334] According to the preliminary notes, which Melanchthon dictated to Cruciger, we can be fairly certain that this summary defended justification *sola fide* against *propter proprias virtutes*.[335] Likewise, based on this report, he excluded works from justification and advocated a much more forensic view, emphasizing *imputatio*.[336]

His summary was rejected, and a shorter draft of the original article was presented by the Catholic party on 29 April, which Pflug indicated was written by Gropper.[337] It is to this article that I now turn.

---

330. Lexutt, *Rechtfertigung im Gespräch*, 215.

331. See the Saxon delegates' report to Elector John Frederick from 5 May 1541, in *CR* 4, no. 2212, 254; see also Lexutt, *Rechtfertigung im Gespräch*, 236.

332. See Melanchthon's *Historia Conventus Ratisponensis* that he sent to Duke Albert of Prussia on 24 May 1541, in *CR* 4, no. 2246, 332. Melanchthon stated, "Secutus est locus de reconciliatione hominis seu Iustificatione, de quo farrago illa neutri parti satisfaciebat, et quia novas quasdam sententias continebat, et quod pleraque erant obscura, impropria et flexiloqua ut alias videretur recte dicere, fide propter donatas virtutes iusti sumus, ut Thomas seu ut Plato loquitur. Seposito igitur libro summa rei libere disputum est, et tandem ad formulam decursum, in qua recepta et explicata est sententia, Fide propter Christum gratis iustificamur, non propter virtutes nostras."

333. Whether or not Gropper's draft was submitted prior to Melanchthon's is debatable; however, according to Melanchthon's short report to Luther of 30 April 1541 (*CR* 4, no. 2208, 239), his draft was first. Cf. the Saxon delegates' report to Elector John Frederick from 5 May 1541, in *CR* 4, no. 2212, 254.

334. Matheson, *Cardinal Contarini*, 106.

335. See Cruciger's *Annotata a Doctore Casparo Crucigero Ratisbonae ad refutandas praestigias Sophismatum Eccianorum in praecipuis doctrinae Christianae capitibus*, written in early May; *CR* 4, no. 2209[b], 242–250.

336. See zur Mühlen, "Die Einigung," 340n32.

337. The copy of the article in the Zeitz Archive was given the title "Gropperi haec sunt" by Pflug. See Lipgens, *Kardinal Johannes Gropper*, 127n10.

The Second Version of Article 5: "How We Are Freely Justified"

Here I will briefly highlight some of the changes in this article.[338] In general this version represents a reshuffling of the original article in response to the criticism that it was long-winded and unsystematic. Gropper divided this article into nine sections.

Of the nine sections, four have *fides* or *fiducia* in the title, indicating that the Catholics were extending their hand to the Protestants. The first section includes *gratis* in the title, seeming to indicate likewise.[339] Nevertheless, a stronger Catholic influence immediately becomes apparent when the article affirms that the ungodly are justified freely without any preceding merit and without the works of the law, omitting the *per fidem* of the original article.[340] Throughout the article the role of faith is downplayed. Hence, in the last section titled "On the Certainty of Justification and the Remission of Sins,"[341] it states that

> the fear of God, penance, humility and other virtues ought to always grow in the regenerate, since their renovation is incomplete and a major infirmity clings to them. However it ought to be taught that those who truly repent may always consider with a most certain faith that they please God on account of Christ the mediator, because Christ is the propitiator, high priest, and advocate for us, whom the Father gave to us and with him all good things.[342]

338. *ARC* 6, 44, l. 20; "Quomodo iustificamur gratis." For the text of the article, see *ARC* 6, 44–52; for a discussion on this text, see Lexutt, *Rechtfertigung im Gespräch*, 236–243.

339. In the preliminary discussions at Worms, as I have noted, the Protestant delegates affirmed the *particula exclusiva* by stating that *sola* and *gratis* are synonymous with *absque operibus*, as explained in Rom. 11:6 and as testified to by Ambrose, Hilary, and Chrysostom. See Neuser, *Die Vorbereitung*, 123. See Lexutt, *Rechtfertigung im Gespräch*, 237.

340. *ARC* 6, 44, ll. 21–28; "impium iustificari gratis nullis praecedentibus meritis et sine operibus legis, id est adiutorio legis, non tamen simpliciter sine lege nec sine operibus spiritus seu gratiae praevenientis, sed non ex illorum merito, quod iustificatione sit dignum. Item iustificari gratis non per propriam voluntatem, hoc est voluntatis viribus, sed tamen non sine nostra voluntate, ut verum sit, quod idem ait: Qui creavit te sine te, non iustificabit te sine te. Siquidem voluntas est causa iustificationis materialis." Cf. *BDS* 9/1, 379, ll. 12–20; "nos iustificari gratis nullis praecedentibus meritis et sine operibus legis, id est adiutorio legis, non tamen simpliciter sine lege nec sine operibus spiritus seu gratiae praevenientis, sed non ex illorum merito, quod iustificatione sit dignum; Item iustificari gratis non per propriam voluntatem, hoc est: voluntatis viribus, sed tamen non sine nostra voluntate; *quam oportet accipere per fidem gratiam sanatem, ut sanata »impleat legem, non constituta sub lege nec indigens lege«, ut testatur Augustinus, lib. De spiritu et litera ca. 9*; ut verum sit quod idem ait: »Qui creavit te sine te, non iustificabit te sine te«. Siquidem voluntas est causa iustificationis materialis." See Lexutt, *Rechtfertigung im Gespräch*, 237–238.

341. *ARC* 6, 51, l. 1 through 52, l. 32. *BDS* 9/1, 383, ll. 12–25; 385, ll. 1–17; 395, l. 15 through 397, l. 12.

342. *ARC* 6, 51, ll. 17–22; "in renatis semper crescere debent timor dei, poenitentia et humilitas et aliae virtutes, cum renovatio sit imperfecta et haereat in eis ingens infirmitas, tamen docendum est, ut qui vere poenitent semper fide certissima statuant, se propter mediatorem Christum deo placere, quia Christus est propitiator, pontifex et interpellator pro nobis, quem pater donavit nobis et omnia bona cum illo."

Then a bit later on in the same section it admonishes that "the people ought to be taught to pay attention to this increase, and exhortations ought to be diligently made with commands and commendations for the purpose of perfecting our sanctification with both internal and external good works toward God."[343]

The emphasis on works is really of no surprise, since this version of the article incorporates the whole of the second section on works of the original article (less two lines), which constitutes nearly half of the article. This alone reveals the works emphasis that is placed in this article.

Many of the accommodations to the evangelical view in the original draft were diluted. By choosing to present the second part of the original article as a shortened version, and in addition to eliminating any reference to a twofold justification, what is emphasized here is the second justification of works over the first justification of the ungodly. Hence, rather than presenting what might have been a more conciliatory version, we have here a stronger Catholic position that would be rejected and worked over again in the final draft.

The Final Version of Article 5: "On the Justification of Man"

After Gropper's draft was rejected, it seems that Eck and Contarini both provided their own drafts.[344] In Eck's draft he asserts that men were able to provide an initial preparation for justification and that it was a *viva et efficax fides* that justified sinners, "which Paul affirms to work through love, and in the scholastic way of speaking is called *fides formata*."[345] Contarini's draft only provided what seems to have been an amended portion of Gropper's second article[346] in an attempt to keep negotiations going. According to Melanchthon, not only was this draft abominable (*widerwärtig*), but even the Catholic delegates were ashamed of it.[347]

Discussions were at a standstill, and Melanchthon began advocating an end to the negotiations;[348] Bucer, on account of his zealous pursuit to Chris-

---

343. ARC 6, 52, ll. 7–11; "Praeterea docendus est populus, ut det operam huic augmento, et exhortationes ad perficiendam sanctificationem nostram bonis operibus tam internis quam externis a deo mandatis et commendatis diligenter faciendae sunt."

344. *Eccianum de iustificatione*. Eck's ms. draft was retained by Pflug and has been posted online by Vinzenz Pfnür at http://ivv7srv15.uni-muenster.de/mnkg/pfnuer/ (accessed 18 July 2007). Matheson, *Cardinal Contarini*, 106.

345. *Eccianum de iustificatione*; "Itaque fides illa viva et efficax recte dicitur iustificare peccatorem, quam Paulus affirmat per dilectionem operari, et in scolis compendio loquendi dicta est fides formata."

346. Matheson, *Cardinal Contarini*, 106.

347. See Melanchthon's report on Regensburg sent to the Saxon elector John Frederick from around 23 July 23; CR 4, no. 2334, 582.

348. See Melanchthon's *Sententia Melanchthonis de libro collocutoribus oblato [oblatis] anno 1541* written around 24 June 1541, in CR 4, no. 2278, 414, 420.

tianize Europe, pushed Melanchthon to continue.[349] At this point the Catholic party allowed the Protestant party to amend the Catholic draft as they desired.[350] In the Saxon councilors' report to John Frederick, they remark that this new revised version was in no way contradictory to the *Confessio Augustana* and was sufficiently clear,[351] although they declared that due to its brevity, it required further explanation, which could be found in the *Confessio Augustana* and its *Apology*.[352] Although Eck was reluctant, this revision was accepted by both parties on 2 May 1541; hence, Contarini's famous exclamation, "Dio Laudato!"[353]

This version was titled "De iustificatione Hominis"[354] and is composed of roughly ten paragraphs.[355] This article is expressive of Bucer's theology of justification from 1536.

The article begins by reaffirming the doctrine of original sin in that all are born children of wrath and enemies of God.[356] It then goes on in the next paragraph to state that "every Christian must affirm that no one is able to be reconciled to God or freed from the slavery of sin except through Christ the one mediator between God and men."[357] The use of *unus* emphasizes the exclusivity of salvation through Christ. Through his grace Christians are freed from the slavery of sin and reconciled, but also "made sharers in the divine nature and sons of God."[358] The *sed etiam* used to introduce this latter benefit of Christ's mediatorship introduces

---

349. *CR* 4, no. 2334, 581–582. See Ortmann, *Reformation und Einheit*, 237.

350. *CR* 4, no. 2212, 254.

351. *CR* 4, no. 2212, 254; "von den Theologen dieses Theils in der Substanz mit nichten der Confession und Apologia zuwider oder gemäß geachtet wirdet, auch an Worten klar genug, daß er zu Mißverstand mag gedeutet werden."

352. *CR* 4, no. 2212, 254; "Und obwohl solcher Artikel etwas kurz und weiter Erklärung bedürftig, so ist doch derselbige in der Confession und Apologia ganz wohl erklärt, welchen man dieses Theils in alleweg vorzubehalten und darinnen nichts zu vergeben bedacht und entschlossen."

353. Matheson, *Cardinal Contarini*, 111; quoting Contarini's letter to Cardinal Alessandro Farnese (3 May 1541).

354. See *BDS* 9/1, 397, l. 13 through 401, l. 18; "De iustificatione Hominis." On this article, see von Loewenich, *Duplex Iustitia*, 34–38; zur Mühlen, "Die Einigung," 331–359; Lexutt, *Rechtfertigung im Gespräch*, 243–260; Ortmann, *Reformation und Einheit*, 208–209; Pfnür, "Die Einigung," 55–88; R. B. Ives, "An Early Effort toward Protestant-Catholic Conciliation: The Doctrine of Double Justification in the Sixteenth Century," *Gordon Review* 2 (1968–1970): 99–110; and a series of articles by Anthony Lane: "Cardinal Contarini and Article 5," 163–190; "Twofold Righteousness: A Key to the Doctrine of Justification? Reflections on Article V of the Regensburg Colloquy (1541)," in *Justification: What's at Stake in the Current Debates*, ed. Mark Husbands and Daniel J. Treier (Downers Grove, IL: InterVarsity Press, 2004), 205–224; "Calvin and Article 5"; and "A Tale of Two Imperial Cities." Lane plans to expand on these articles in a book on the Regensburg article on justification with the working title *Compromising Patchwork or Ecumenical Breakthrough? The Regensburg Article on Justification (1541): Introduction, Text and Commentary.*

355. Anthony N. S. Lane's translation of this final version of article 5 can be found in appendix D.

356. *BDS* 9/1, 397, ll. 14–15.

357. *BDS* 9/1, 397, ll. 16–17; "nulli christiano ambigendum est nullum hominem posse deo reconciliari itemque liberari a servitute peccati nisi per Christum unum mediatorem dei et hominum."

358. *BDS* 9/1, 397, l. 19; "sed etiam efficimur consortes divinae naturae et filii Dei."

the dual manner in which justification was understood in the original article and is understood by Bucer himself.

In the *Romans Commentary* in reference to the manner in which Paul sometimes speaks of Christ the Lord or the Holy Spirit dwelling in believers, Bucer asks, "What are we to understand by this dwelling and inhabitation other than a more concrete and rather effective sharing of divinity?"[359] Hence it was not foreign for Bucer to speak of becoming "sharers in the divine nature" as a present reality in relation to justification.[360]

The third paragraph speaks of a prevenient movement of the Spirit (rather than prevenient grace) that moves the mind and will to hate sin; the new life begins with repentance. This repentance leads to the Spirit granting a certain faith, which enables a person's mind to believe everything God has transmitted and to assent to the promises God has made.[361]

Here two stages are described. The first is the prevenient movement of the Spirit that leads men to hate sin and seek repentance. This was described in the original article in reference to mortification and the second use of the law.[362] As in the original article, Bucer's doctrine of *Allwirksamkeit* and his understanding of an initial knowledge as a preparation for the gospel are compatible with this understanding of repentance, that is, an initial faith.[363]

In *De Vera Reconciliatione*, Bucer rejects the charge that repentance was inferred to be a preparatory work before faith—what Lexutt describes as justification *sola poenitentia et fide*.[364] Bucer argues that the article excludes such a reading.[365] Bucer asserts that the beginning of the article is written in such a way that nobody ought to doubt that they are children of wrath or that they are unable to reconcile themselves to God except through Christ; for Bucer

---

359. *BRom* (1536), 322–323; (1562), 364. "et Paulus nunc Christum dominum, nunc spiritum sanctum habitare in nobis praedicat, quid hac mansione et inhabitatione aliud quam solidiorem et magis efficacem divinitatis communionem intelligamus?"

360. See also Bucer's *Axiomata Apologetica* (1535); in reference to the Eucharist, he said that "simus . . . consortes naturae eius"; in *BDS* 6/1, 86, l. 27. Contra Lexutt, *Rechtfertigung im Gespräch*, 251–252. On Calvin on this point, see Lane, "Calvin and Article 5," 243.

361. *BDS* 9/1, 397, l. 25 through 399, l. 2; "Deinde a spiritu sancto movetur hominis mens in deum per Christum, et hic motus est per fidem, per quam hominis mens, certo credens omnibus quae tradita sint a Deo, certissime et sine dubio adsentitur promissionibus nobis exhibitis a Deo." Cf. Bucer's *John Commentary*, where he states, "Motus siquidem Spiritus Dei oratio, unde mente Dei in ea homo praesentiscere facile potest." *BOL* 2, 111.

362. *BDS* 9/1, 359, l. 17 through 341, l. 3; and 365, ll. 1–22.

363. See sections 3.5.2.1. and 3.4.2.3. As noted earlier, this beginning of faith is also associated with *vocatio* for Bucer.

364. Lexutt, *Rechtfertigung im Gespräch*, 252; see also Friedrich, *Martin Bucer*, 184; Stupperich, *Der Humanismus*, 121; and Neuser, "Calvins Urteil," 186. Cf. Lane, "Calvin and Article 5," 246.

365. Bucer, *De Vera Reconciliatione*, 164(v)–170(v).

these two initial paragraphs in the article destroyed the ungodly opinion that someone tainted with original sin would be able to offer some degree of good work as a preparation for justification.[366] Here he aligns the article's stance with the church fathers and the *graviores Scholastici*, who taught both that it is necessary that the grace of God come before and prepare the will, and that no one solely in a state of original sin is able to merit according to congruity, and still less according to condignity.[367] The Church anathematizes those who teach that one is able "to love God above all else without the Holy Spirit, and merit the forgiveness of sins by doing what is in himself."[368] The *facere in se quod* of later medieval theology is explicitly rejected.

Bucer states that "concerning the necessity of repentance in paragraph three, it is rightly put that no one is able to receive those benefits of Christ, reconciliation with God, freedom from the servitude of sin, and become a sharer of the divine nature without repentance, which is the detestation of sins."[369] For him repentance was akin to the beginning of faith in relation to the law, as already shown earlier. It is part of faith, albeit an initial part.[370]

Bucer also demonstrates that the view which holds that repentance is by the power of free will is refuted in the article when it states that "adults do not gain these benefits of Christ except by the prevenient movement of the Holy Spirit, by which their mind and will are moved to hate sin."[371] It is the Spirit who renews the mind of believers, moving them to repentance.[372]

366. Bucer, *De Vera Reconciliatione*, 164(v)–165(r); "Primum ergo quoniam plerique visi sunt naturae, peccato originis vitiatae, et depravatae, aliquid bonorum operum, et ad gratiam Dei, ac iustificationem praeparationis tribuere, ut haec falsa ac impia opinio, apud quos esset, tolletur; apud quos non esset, submoveretur eius suspito, positum est statim initio articuli conciliati, nulli Christiano dubitandum esse, non nasci filios irae, inimicos Dei, eoque in mortem et servitutem peccati; et initio secundi para. nullum hominem posse Deo reconciliari, et liberari a servitute peccati, nisi per Christum, unum mediatorem Dei et hominum." See *BDS* 9/1, 397, ll. 14–19.

367. Bucer, *De Vera Reconciliatione*, 165(r); "Sed cum non solum S. patres, sed graviores quoque Scholastici fateantur, et doceant, necese esse, ut nos gratia Dei praeveniat, et voluntatem ipsa nostram sibi praeparet: nos enim, etiam dum solo originis peccato detinemur, nedum iis, quae ipsi admisimus, peccatis, gratiam nobis, qua excidimus, ne de congruo quidem, ne dum de condigno, ut illi loquuntur, mereri posse." See *BRom* (1536), 403; (1562), 464; *CP* 151–152.

368. Bucer, *De Vera Reconciliatione*, 165(r); "hominem posse Deum sine spiritu sancto supra omnia diligere; posse, faciendo quod inse est, remissionem peccatorum mereri."

369. Bucer, *De Vera Reconciliatione*, 166(r); "de necessitate poenitentiae in 3 para. recte positum est, sine poenitentia, et quae sit peccatorum detestatio, benefacia illa Christi, reconciliationem cum Deo, liberationem a peccati servitute, et consortium divinae naturae percipi, a nemine posse."

370. See *BRom* (1536), 87; (1562), 61; "Est ergo cognitio Dei, et veritatis, quae communis est omnibus, satis quidem, ut peccati ipsi nos convincamus, at ut illud vitemus, et quod bonum est, constanter amplectamur, id non nisi novo adflatu dei, et eo multo, quam ille qui contingit promiscue omnibus, potentiore efficitur."

371. Bucer, *De Vera Reconciliatione*, 166(r)–166(v); "adultos haec Christi beneficia, non consequi, nisi praeveniente motu spiritus sancti; quo eorum mens et voluntas moveatur, ad detestationem peccati." *BDS* 9/1 397, ll. 20–21.

372. Bucer, *De Vera Reconciliatione*, 165(v).

Likewise, for him there is a necessary connection between true repentance and faith:

> For both repentance to God and the remission of sins through Christ are announced by *one* gospel and by the name of Christ; the *one* work of the Spirit of Christ opens the heart of the elect and the preordained to live, so that hearing the gospel we acknowledge by that *one* same faith and judge it to be certain that we have not only been shamelessly ungrateful to God, but also insolently ungodly, and that we are thereby deserving of his eternal wrath and rejection.[373]

It is by this faith that the mind acknowledges its deformity, and it is this same faith that upon hearing the gospel causes the mind to assent to it.[374] Thus, for Bucer the article rightly affirms that from this point a believer acquires *fiducia* on account of God's promise of forgiveness and adoption.[375] Those who believe are raised to God and given the Holy Spirit, forgiven their sins, the imputation of righteousness, and other innumerable gifts.[376] The intellectualistic view that faith affects the mind of men, leading to certain and undoubting trust in God,[377] as well as the manner in which faith is said to culminate in *fiducia*, corresponds to Bucer's view that *persuasio* leads to *fiducia*.[378]

Paragraph four describes faith as a *viva et efficax fides*. This no doubt was on account of Eck's influence. Julius Pflug noted that Eck offered the following phrases "fides viva et efficax iustificat" and "ante charitatem non est viva et efficax fides" (citing 1 Cor. 13) during the discussions on justification.[379] Melanchthon's later reference to a certain few taking this article to mean they

---

373. Bucer, *De Vera Reconciliatione*, 167(v); "Uno enim Evangelio, et eodem Christi nomine, et poenitentia in Deum, et remissio peccatorum per Christum, adnunciantur; uno opere spiritus Christi cor aperitur electis, et ad vitam praeordinatis, ut auscultantes Evangelio, una eademque fide agnoscamus, certumque iudicemus, nos, et in Deum, non modo turpiter ingratos, sed etiam contumeliose fuisse impios, aeternamque eo iram eius, et abiectionem meritos esse."

374. Bucer, *De Vera Reconciliatione*, 167(v); "Ex qua fide, quia mens videt, agnoscitque foedissimam suam turpitudinem, et horrendam in illam flagrantem iram Dei, verus de peccatis dolor, certaque impietatis nostrae detestatio, et solidus divini iudicii terror, in animis Evangelio auscultantium existit; et rursus, quia eadem fide, animus firmiter credit, certoque assentitur Evangelio."

375. *BDS* 9/1, 399, ll. 3–4; "et ex eo fiduciam capit propter promissionem Dei, qua pollicitus est se remissurum peccata gratis et adoptaturum in filios credentes in Christum."

376. *BDS* 9/1, 399, ll. 5–7; "et hac fide erigitur in Deum a spiritu sancto ideoque accipit spiritum sanctum, remissionem peccatorum, imputationem iustitiae et innumera alia dona."

377. See *BRom CP* 196n1; 172; (1536), 6, 14; (1562), 6, 14.

378. See section 3.5.2.

379. Julius Pflug, *Notionculae de Dialogis inter Catholicos et Lutheranos Collocutores Ratisponae anno 1541*, ed. Venicio Marcolino. This document contains Pflug's notes (in some places illegible) from the Regensburg negotiations. Vinzenz Pfnur has posted these notes online at http://ivv7srv15.uni-muenster.de/mnkg/pfnuer/PROto. html#art5 (accessed 18 July 2007). See also Eck's draft on justification paragraph 5, where he states in a similar

are saved by love can be seen as directed at Eck and Pighius.[380] In the report printed in Bucer's *Acta Colloquii* Melanchthon stated:

> Where it speaks about an efficacious faith, we understand that certain people have distorted this so that they interpret an efficacious faith to be a working faith; that is, men are justified by faith with works. For it is a shared conviction by some of the other party that when Paul said we are justified by faith, it ought to be taken as if he desired to say we are prepared for righteousness, that is, for love on account of which afterward we are accepted: not by faith on account of Christ. . . . However when our delegates spoke of living or efficacious faith, they intended not to speak about a mere historical knowledge, which is the kind found even in the ungodly, but about *fiducia*, which apprehends the merciful promise on account of Christ, and that lifts terrified minds.[381]

Efficacious faith is a "faith which is by itself a burning movement, consoling, resting in Christ, and living."[382] If it was understood as a preparatory work for love which justifies, then Melanchthon thought that it should be removed from the article.

Catholics repeatedly accused the Protestants of teaching a doctrine of justification that neglected works, something that Jacobo Sadoleto had done in his three-volume *Romans Commentary*.[383] In the *Romans Commentary*, arguing against Sadoleto's calumny that the Protestants taught a dead faith, he explained the nature of true evangelical faith, stating that

---

fashion that "fides illa viva et efficax recte dicitur iustificare peccatorem, quam Paulus affirmat per dilectionem operari, et in scolis compendio loquendi dicta est fides formata." See also *Eccianum de iustificationem*, para. 5; as well as Gropper's draft, ARC 6, 45, ll. 5–9; and the *Enchiridion*, 144(r).

380. See Eck, *Apologia*, 127(r), where he emphasiszes the need for love, citing 1 John 3:14, "Qui non diligit manet in morte." Bucer claimed that Pighius asserted that love is the instrumental cause of justification in *De Vera Reconciliatione*, 177(r).

381. *Acta colloqui*, 44; "In articulo de iustificatione, ubi dicitur, per fidem efficacem, intelleximus id a quibusdam ita depravari, ut interpretentur, efficaci fide, id est operante fide. Hoc est, fide cum operibus iustificari hominem. Est enim quorumdam alterius partis vulgaris persuasio, Paulum sic accipiendum esse, cum ait, fide iustificamur, quasi velit, fide praeparamur ad iustitiam, id est ad dilectione propter quam postea accepti sumus: non fide propter Christum. . . .. Nostri enim cum dixerunt, viva seu efficaci fide, significarunt se loqui, non de sola notitia historiae, qualis est etiam in impiis, sed de fiducia apprehendente misericordiam propter Christum promissam, et erigente perterrefactas mentes."

382. *Acta colloqui*, 44; "In hanc sententiam loquuti sunt nostri de efficacia, qua ipsa fides per se est motus ardens, consolans, innitens Christo, et vivificans."

383. *Iacobi Sadoleti . . . in Pauli epistolam ad Romanos commentarorum Libri tres* (1535). For a brief introduction on this work, see Parker, *Commentaries on Romans*, 25–34.

no man is able to be justified before God except through faith in
Christ, and that between faith and righteousness, which is greater
than any human strength, there is such a bond and link that righteousness never fails to follow true faith. . . . Therefore those who are
held captive by true faith, a certain persuasion of the Holy Spirit
concerning the gospel, cannot but worship, burn for, and live for God
with all their heart and then continually fight against sin which
remains in them and wholeheartedly persevere toward being shaped
into all that which is pleasing to God. . . . This is the character of the
faith which we preach and we commend it to men in this manner in
all our sermons and writings: and whoever makes clear by their
depravity of life that they are lacking in this faith we pronounce that
they are not Christ's.[384]

Bucer assured Gropper of the same at Worms. Looking back at his discussions
with Gropper, he stated: "The faith through which we become righteous and
blessed, for us is nothing that a dead man can imagine. Also for the reborn it is
not only a temporary, partial and powerless inspiration of God, but it is an abid-
ing, full and powerful inspiration of the Holy Spirit, through which men are born
anew, live in Christ, and have Christ dwelling in them in their hearts."[385]

Thus in *De Vera Reconciliatione*, Bucer states that the article in the fourth
and fifth paragraphs clearly taught that believers are pleasing and acceptable to
God on account of Christ through a living and efficacious faith in order to make
sure that dead faith was excluded as true faith.[386] Thus he countered the
popular Catholic accusation.

Bucer understood the underlying connection between faith and love
through what I have argued was an intellectual psychology based on the Socratic dictum. The intellectual nature of faith resulted necessarily in works of love.
Faith and love are connected.[387] The fact that the article states that justification

---

384. *BRom* (1536), 370–371; (1562), 425–426; "Neminem hominum apud Deum, nisi per fidem Christi
posse iustificari, fideique et iustitiae, quae maior omni humana virtute, eam esse societatem et coniunctionem,
ut veram fidem iustitia nunquam non consequatur. . . . Ergo quibus ista contigit vera fides, certa Spiritus sancti
de Evangelio persuasio, hi non possunt Deum non toto pectore colere, ardere, vivere, indeque non perpetuo
contra peccati in se reliquias dimicare, et ut placitis Dei conformentur toti insistere. . . . Hoc ingenium est fidei,
quam nos praedicamus, eam que ad hunc modum nullis non orationibus et scriptis, hominibus commendamus:
et quicunque vitae pravitate declaraverint se huius fidei inopes esse, eos nec Christi esse pronunciamus."

385. *BDS* 11/2, 298, ll.10–16; "das der glaub, durch den wir gerecht und selig werden, bey uns nit ein todt
menschen gedicht, auch nit allein ein zeitliche, stucklechte und zur widergeburt onkrefftige erleuchtung Gottes
seye, sonder ein beharrende, gantze und gewaltige erleuchtung deß h. geistes, durch den der mensch new gebo-
ren, Christo eingeleybet werde und Christum bey sich im hertzen wohnen habe."

386. *BDS* 9/1, 399, ll. 8–9; Bucer, *De Vera Reconciliatione*, 170(r)–170(v).

387. In the *Psalms Commentary*, Bucer even can speak of a *fides formata*. See *BPsalms* (1554), 30.

does not occur without an infusion of charity healing the will, in order that it may begin to fulfill the law, is not problematic for Bucer.[388] In the *Romans Commentary*, he stated:

> Let no one be offended at his [Augustine's] describing love of one's neighbor as the definition of faith, a definition in terms of the effect. He meant to reveal faith by reference to that mark through which its integrity is more easily recognizable. Not for a moment did he hold the opinion that our salvation is based upon the merit of this love or any other kind of merit except Christ's alone, as every page of his works bears lucid testimony. But since true faith in Christ never fails to produce this its proper fruit, he considered that what is not so obvious, the essence and character of true faith, should be exhibited, following the apostle's practice, from the more visible reality of love.[389]

For Bucer it was a characteristic of this faith to excite trust in the mercy of God in the mind, from which this faith burns with a love for God, and induces all manner of virtues.[390]

In addition, Bucer supported Melanchthon's rejection of any interpretation that said men are saved by love. In *De Vera Reconciliatione*, he affirmed that faith, not love, was the dispositive cause, that is, the instrumental cause. Using a similar distinction between three justifications, which he had raised in the *Romans Commentary*,[391] he states that the first justification is the *princeps iustificatio*, which receives the forgiveness of sins, the grace of God, and fellowship with the Father and the Son. It is this justification that is received by faith alone.[392]

For him this understanding of justification is not a *Vermittlungsposition*, as zur Mühlen tries to show.[393] For him it is the accurate description of saving faith

---

388. *BDS* 9/1, 399, ll. 13–14. In the *Acta colloqui*, Bucer states that this phrase could be further clarified by adding that the reborn do not yet satisfy the law because of the sins that remain in them. See *Acta colloqui*, 44.

389. *BRom* (1536), 23; (1562), 22; *CP* 195–196. In addition, as noted earlier in the preliminary discussions to Worms, Bucer could maintain the integrity of *sola fide* without the exact formula of *sola fide*. Thus as he said in the *Psalms Commentary*, "It is surely not the part of Christians to be offended by words, when there is agreement on the sense" (*BPsalms* [1554], 31).

390. Bucer, *De Vera Reconciliatione*, 170(v)–171(r); "Denique quia fidei καθ' αὐτὸ proprium est, excitare in animo, in quo obtinuerit, fiduciam misericordiae Dei; et ex ea accendere quoque charitate in Deum, atque per hanc totum reliquum virtutum chorum adducere . . ."

391. Bucer, *De Vera Reconciliatione*, 172(v)–173(r); "tria genera sunt iustificationem." *BRom* (1536), 130; (1562), 119; "Triplex itaque est nostri iustificatio, hoc est, trifariam nobis Deus vitam aeternam adiudicat."

392. Bucer, *De Vera Reconciliatione*, 172(v)–173(v).

393. See zur Mühlen, "Die Einigung," 342–343.

in Christ that always includes the love of neighbor. Bucer held that the article was clear in stating that it is by faith and not by love or any inhering righteousness that believers are justified, when it stated: "By this faith we are justified, that is, we are accepted, reconciled to God inasmuch as it apprehends the mercy and righteousness, which is imputed to us on account of Christ and his merit, not on account of the dignity or completion of righteousness imparted to us in Christ."[394] Here the imputation of righteousness is associated with living faith and thus is associated with the beginning of justification, not with works.

The fifth paragraph then discusses the nature of inherent righteousness, affirming that the righteousness, which believers receive and have through Christ, indwells them.[395] But this indwelling aspect of righteousness is not the righteousness upon which the justified person can lean. One can only depend "on the righteousness of Christ given to us as a gift"[396] that is, imputed righteousness. The article continues to state that "by faith in Christ we are justified or reputed as righteous: that is, we are accepted through his merits, not on account of our own worthiness or works."[397] The insufficiency of a believer's righteousness is both Bucerian and Gropperian, as previously shown.[398]

The paragraph ends by citing 1 John 3:7, giving a positive definition of this righteousness, stating that "on account of inherent righteousness, we are said to be just, because the works we do are just, as John stated, 'he who does justice is just.'"[399] For Lexutt this statement reveals that it is on account of a weak inherent righteousness that we will be called just, and therefore it is a rejection of the previous assertions in regards to an imputed righteousness.[400] She takes this as evidence of a justification by works. Nevertheless, in light of the previous statements that forgiveness cannot depend on this righteousness, her conclusion is an exaggeration. For Bucer this inherent weak righteousness was described in *De Vera*

---

394. *BDS* 9/1, 399, l. 12; "quod hac fide eatenus iustificamur, id est acceptamur et reconciliamur Deo quatenus aprehendit misericordiam et iustitiam, quem nobis imputatur propter Christum et eius meritum, non propter dignitatem seu perfectionem iustitiae nobis in Christo communicatae." See also Bucer, *De Vera Reconciliatione*, 170(r).

395. *BDS* 9/1, 399, l. 21; "Etiam autem is qui iustificatur, iustitiam adcipit et habet per Christum etiam inhaerentem."

396. *BDS* 9/1, 399, l. 24; "soli iustitiae Christi nobis donatae."

397. *BDS* 9/1, 399, ll. 25–26; "fide in Christum iustificamur seu reputamur iusti, id est: accepti per ipsius merita, non propter nostram dignitatem aut opera." Cf. section 3.3.

398. See sections 3.3. and 4.3.4.3. Bucer affirms that one's own righteousness is weak and insufficient to merit salvation in *De Vera Reconciliatione*, 177(v)–190(v).

399. *BDS* 9/1, 399 ll. 26–27; "et propter inhaerentem iustitiam eo iusti dicimur, quia quae iusta sunt operamur."

400. Lexutt, *Rechtfertigung im Gespräch*, 256; "Hier zeigt sich deutlich der Umschwung von der *iustitia aliena* zu einer Gerechtigkeit des Menschen. Die fremde Gerechtigkeit Christi bewirkt Werke der Gerechtigkeit— und diese sind die Ursache dafür, daß der Mensch gerecht genannt wird; also wird ihm letztendlich doch nicht

Reconciliatione as part of a second-order justification.[401] The article confirms that one is justified only by the merit of the righteousness of Christ given to us.[402]

As Anthony Lane has clearly shown, a "double justification" theory, alleged by various authors, is not taught here.[403] The article is clear that the formal cause of justification is the imputation of righteousness, as Bucer asserted.[404] What is taught is Bucer's twofold view of righteousness as seen in the *Romans Commentary*.[405] For Bucer the imputation of righteousness provided an intellectual image of Christ's perfect righteousness, which the believer then pursued with the aid of the Spirit, resulting in a derivative righteousness. By faith the imputation of this righteousness, understood by Bucer primarily as the non-imputation of sins, is grasped and seen as the prime cause of justification upon which salvation depends.[406] Yet because Bucer believes that God has ordered this world in such a way that what one knows one necessarily does, one's derivative righteousness manifested in works acts as secondary causes of salvation. These secondary causes are not in themselves worthy; they are only worthy in a congruous manner based on the prime cause.[407] Within Bucer's thought the distinction between the primary and secondary causes in justification preserves the truth of the formula *sola fide*.

The next paragraph is taken from Gropper's second version,[408] which affirms that though a believer grows in virtues, the great weakness that remains is cause for them to repent. Likewise, those who truly repent have a certain faith that they are forgiven on account of Christ the mediator.[409] The only alteration that has been made from Gropper's version is that penance was replaced with patience as a virtue in which the believer grows, eliminating a Gropperian sacramental slant.[410]

---

die Gerechtigkeit Christi zum Heil angerechnet, sondern das, was diese *iustitia* in ihm bewirkt." See also Neuser, "Calvins Urteil," 188.

401. Bucer, *De Vera Reconciliatione*, 172(v)–173(r), 177(v)–178(v).

402. Bucer, *De Vera Reconciliatione*, 179(v).

403. See Lane, "Cardinal Contarini and Article 5," 163–190; Lane, "Twofold Righteousness," 205–224; Lane, "Calvin and Article 5," 233–263; and Lane, "A Tale of Two Imperial Cities," 119–145. For instances of the article being described as teaching a double justification theory, see Derek A. Scales, "Illustrations of Compromise in Church History," *Churchman* 102, no. 3 (1988): 215–239, see 221; Henry Chadwick, "Justification by Faith: A Perspective," *One in Christ: A Catholic Ecumenical Review* 20 (1984): 202; and Ives, "An Early Effort toward Protestant-Catholic Conciliation," 99.

404. Bucer, *De Vera Reconciliatione*, 177(v)–179(v).

405. See section 3.3.

406. In *De Vera Reconciliatione*, the notion that it is a positive imputation of Christ's righteousness is further developed than in the *Romans Commentary*. See esp. *De Vera Reconciliatione*, 122(r) and 209(v)–(r).

407. See section 3.5.4.

408. *BDS* 9/1, 399; ll. 28–32; *ARC* 6, 51, ll. 17–22.

409. See Bucer, *De Vera Reconciliatione*, 190(r)–197(r).

410. *BDS* 9/1, 399, l. 28; "in renatis semper crescere debent timor Dei, patientia et humilitas et aliae virtutes." Cf. *ARC* 6, 51, ll. 17–18; "in renatis semper crescere debent timor dei, poenitentia et humilitas et aliae virtutes."

Paragraph seven highlights the experiential doubt that believers have in regard to their salvation on account of the weakness that remains in them. The article here affirms that these doubts ought to be assuaged by focusing on the promises of Christ and praying for an increase of faith.[411]

The next paragraph deals with good works. It states that the born-again Christian should not be idle but should progress in his or her justification by steps.[412] This for Lexutt is unmistakable proof that the infusion of righteousness and its imputation are only the first steps in a longer process that is accomplished through works: justification is understood as being made just.[413] Yes and no. For Bucer it is not one without the other; nevertheless, Bucer and the article repeatedly affirm the priority of the imputation of righteousness upon which the inherent righteousness depends. Likewise, here, in contrast to a Gropperian model, which views impartation as the first step that is supplemented by an imputed righteousness, what is emphasized is the declarative aspect of justification. The first cause includes secondary causes. Without a clear understanding of Bucer's theology, Lexutt's judgment fails to grasp the evangelical manner in which both Bucer and the article accord works a subordinate role to the role of faith in justification. That there is a progression in righteousness is not in dispute, for Bucer understands a progression in faith and righteousness,[414] but this progression is never held as a primary cause of salvation.[415]

The article then goes on to affirm that God has decided to reward these good works:

Thus, although the inheritance of eternal life is due to the regenerate on account of the promise, even when they are first reborn in Christ, nevertheless God also renders a reward to good works, not on account of the substance of the works nor because they come from us, but in so far as they are done in faith and are from the Holy Spirit dwelling in us, with the concurrence of the free will as a partial agent.[416]

411. *BDS* 9/1, 399, l. 33 through 401, l. 2; see Bucer, *De Vera Reconciliatione*, 191(r)–192(v).

412. *BDS* 9/1, 401, ll. 3–5. Cf. Gropper's second version, *ARC* 6, 46, ll. 6–8.

413. Lexutt, *Rechtfertigung im Gespräch*, 257.

414. See section 3.4.2; see also *BRom* (1536), 304, (1562), 341, where, in relation to speaking of mortification in Romans 6, he speaks of the removal of sin as beginning the prosses of sanctification: "ἀποθέωσιν absolvit, reddens nos continuo diviniores."

415. See See Bucer, *De Vera Reconciliatione*, 210(r)–213(r).

416. *BDS* 9/1, 401, ll. 8–12; "Ideoque, quamvis haereditas vitae aeternae propter promissionem debeatur renatis etiam cum primum in Christo renati sunt, nihilominus reddit deus etiam bonis operibus mercedem, non secundum substantiam operam neque secundum quod sunt a nobis, sed quatenus in fide fiunt et sunt a spiritu sancto, qui habitat in nobis concurrente libero arbitrio tanquam partiali agente."

That works are given rewards is consistent with Bucer's view, as I have shown.[417]

The concluding phrase in regard to free will is an addition that corresponds to a more Gropperian position: that is, that the will is a material cause of justification.[418] Lexutt sees this addition as highlighting the fact that this article does not advocate the position that one is justified *sola fide, solo Christo*, or *sola gratia*, but rather that humanity is saved by a collaboration of grace, free will, and works.[419] However, the article is clear that any collaboration is subordinate to grace, and thus Lexutt neglects the explicit hierarchy of causation.[420] Contrary to Lexutt, the article sustains the position of *sola gratia, per Christum unum mediatorem dei*, and *sola fide sed non ex fide tantum* and is clear about it.

The ninth paragraph speaks to the relationship between the quality of the works and the quality of their reward: "And the felicity of those who have done more and greater works will be greater and more complete, on account of the increase of faith and love, in which they have grown through exercises of that kind."[421] This statement ought to be taken as a reaffirmation of the previous paragraph's encouragement, which stated that the justified ought not to remain idle, but that they should perform good works. Nowhere does it state that the justified will be saved by this growth in works; rather, it only seems to affirm that with an increase of faith one ought to see a correlating increase in works. This statement need not be taken as advocating a temporary situated justification of the just.[422]

The last paragraph focuses on the formula of *sola fide*. Here, as in the previous two versions, the one who preaches justification *sola fide* must accompany this teaching with exhortations for good works; that is, "the doctrine of repentance, of the fear of God, of the judgment of God, and of good

---

417. See section 3.5.4.

418. See *Enchiridion*, 143(v); Gropper's second version, ARC 6, 44, ll. 25–28; and the original version of the article BDS 9/1, 379, ll. 11–20.

419. Lexutt, *Rechtfertigung im Gespräch*, 257; "Somit wird nun klar: Es ist nicht der Glaube allein, nicht Christus allein, nicht die Gnade allein, die den Menschen rechtfertigt, ihm das Heil bringt, sondern es ist das Zusammenwirken von Gnade, freiem Willen und Werken, die dies zustande bringen."

420. One must understand that in the scheme of causation the material cause is a passive cause, i.e., it is the wood that the carpenter uses to build a chair. Hence the builder works on the material like God works on the will; both the wood and the will are passive. That the will is a material cause is not necessarily significant if understood in this way.

421. BDS 9/1, 401, ll. 13–14; "Et amplior et maior foelicitas erit eorum, qui maiora et plura opera fecerunt, propter augmentum fidei et charitatis, in qua creverunt huiusmodi exercitiis."

422. Cf. Lexutt, *Rechtfertigung im Gespräch*, 258.

works"[423] ought to be taught as well.[424] The article upholds the evangelical position, clarifying that the doctrine of *sola fide* in no way advocates slothfulness.

Lexutt, however, sees this concession to the Protestant position as a harmful deception in light of the previous statements about faith, for she believes
that in affirming that faith was living and efficacious the article weakened the
ability to teach the radical doctrine of justification *sola fide* without works.[425] But
that here faith is seen as living rather than dead is in no way contradictory to
sola fide. Rather, it is an explanation of that faith which is alone saving. It is
neither fair nor accurate to state that the agreement proved to be a harmful
deception when parties from both sides could sincerely affirm the article
as containing a true representation of the doctrine of justification, albeit a
nuanced one. For Bucer, it was not a deception; it was for him and others an
expression of the evangelical doctrine.

For Bucer works are secondary causes rooted in faith, which is given to a
believer on the basis of the mysterious kindness of God, the prime cause. Justification is *sola fide*. Righteousness is imputed to the believer, and this is the
basis of justification. For Gropper in the *Enchiridion* this is understood from a
sacramental-incorporational perspective related to the supplementation of
works. For Bucer this is understood from an intellectualistic perspective associated with the paradigm that "to know the good is to do the good" and focused
on the beginning of the Christian life.

As a propositional statement of belief both sides were able to agree on this
formulation. From what perspective they read this formulation, however,
affected what was understood. It is evident that the difference between the two
parties was not necessarily over justification but over the place accorded to the
doctrine of justification within their respective theologies.[426] For the Protestants this article described effectively the *foundation* of the Christian life; for
the Catholics this article could be seen as describing the Christian life. For
Gropper justification was a sacramental affair; therefore, the context within
which the issue is discussed matters. When the doctrine is discussed outside
of a context of the sacraments, the incorporational nature of justification as
well as one's progression in grace is diluted. However, Gropper could agree to
this article's formulation because for him it was not the central issue, that is, it
was not understood as the central doctrine. It is and remains subsequent to the

---

423. *BDS* 9/1, 401, ll. 16–17; "simul tradere debent doctrinam de poenitentia, de timore Dei, de iudicio
Dei, de bonis operibus."

424. See Bucer, *De Vera Reconciliatione*, 213(r)–213(v).

425. Lexutt, *Rechtfertigung im Gespräch*, 259.

426. See Pfnür, "Die Einigung," 55.

question of ecclesiology, whereas for the Protestants, and especially Bucer, it was this doctrine of justification that was foundational.

Article 5 after the Colloquy

The agreement on justification was met with high praise. Calvin wrote to Farel, stating:

> I know you will be amazed when you read the article on justification that our adversaries have conceded so much. . . . For the Protestant delegates have retained the essentials of our true doctrine, so that nothing there is held to that does not exist also in our writings. I know that you will desire a more explicit exposition and in that respect I agree with you. But if you consider with what sort of men we have to deal, you will acknowledge that much has been achieved.[427]

On the Catholic side, Contarini wrote in a letter to Cardinal Farnese that the article was both "cattolica et santa."[428] Upon reading the first five articles, Cardinal Pole stated: "When I observed this union of opinion I felt a delight such as no harmony of sounds could have inspired me with; not only because I see the approach of peace and concord, but because these articles [i.e., 1 to 5] are the foundation of the whole Christian faith."[429] After news of the agreement reached the elector of Brandenburg, he immediately sent his musicians to serenade Contarini.[430]

The agreement on justification was seen as a good omen and offered high hopes for the rest of the colloquy. Shortly thereafter, however, the diet began to falter. As Lane states, "The enthusiasm that greeted article V was enthusiasm for the prospect of agreement across the board, not enthusiasm

---

427. To Farel (11 May 1541), *CO* 11, no. 308, 215; "Miraberis, scio, adversarios tantum concessisse, quum legeris exemplar, ita ut postrema manu correctum fuit, quod literis inclusum reperies. Retinuerunt enim nostri doctrinae verae summam: ut nihil illic comprehensum sit, quod non exstet in scriptis nostris: scio, desiderabis clariorem explicationem, et in ea re me tibi assentientem habecis. Verum, si reputes quibuscum hominibus negotium nobis sit, agnosces multum esse effectum."

428. Matheson, *Cardinal Contarini*, 111, quoting from Contarini in *Historisches Jahrbuch der Gorres-Gesellschaft*, 1:371–372.

429. From Quirini, *Epistolae Reginaldi Poli*, t. III, 25; quoted in Leopold von Ranke, *Sammtlicke Werke 37: Die römischen Päpste in den letzten vier Jahrhunderten*, vol. 1 (Leipzig: Duncker und Humblot, 1874), 107; Hall, *Humanists and Protestants*, 166.

430. Lane, "Cardinal Contarini and Article 5," 167.

for the idea of agreeing in one point only."[431] When agreement became impossible on the other articles, the agreement that was met on article 5 was tainted.

The agreement once praised by both sides came into disrepute. Luther described the article as "a verbose bit of patchwork" and considered the article ambiguous on the relationship between the imputation and impartation of righteousness, stating, "So they are right, and so are we."[432] In a similar manner, after the colloquy ended, Bucer and his conciliatory attitude were criticized by various Protestant reformers. Both Melanchthon and Calvin mildly complained of Bucer's willingness to compromise on so many issues.[433] Luther reproached him, stating: "Bucer, the rascal, has absolutely lost all my confidence. I shall never trust him. He has betrayed me too often. Now he has conducted himself evilly at the Diet of Regensburg, for he wanted to be a mediator between me and the pope, and said, "'Surely, it is a sorry thing that so much should be missed for the sake of one or two articles.'"[434] This passage reveals the impossibility of the task—two popes. For Luther anything short of explicitly rejecting the Catholic errors would be seen as a compromise, as Lexutt tries to show.

However, article 5 is not a patchwork of compromise; it is a legitimate evangelical understanding of the doctrine at this stage of the Reformation. As Matheson states:

> It is a finely balanced piece of conciliation, but it exhibits an integrity
> all its own. It falls outside the confessional categories certainly; its
> language, however, is that of conviction, not caution. It is no mere
> mediatorial formula, offering a crumb of theological comfort to every
> grouping. It takes up a clear line, and it is because of this
> uncomfortable clarity, not because of an alleged ambiguity, that it was
> later rejected by Catholic and Protestant confessionalists.[435]

He is right. It is not *Vermittlungstheologie*; it is good Bucerian theology.

---

431. Lane, "A Tale of Two Imperial Cities," 124.

432. Luther's letter to John Frederick (10/11 May 1541), WA.Br. 9. no. 3616, 407, ll. 15–16; "Darin sie recht und wir auch recht haben." For a critique of Luther's criticisms, see von Loewenich, *Duplex Iustitia*, 48–55.

433. See Melanchthon to Joachim Camerario (10 May 1541), CR 9, no. 2225, 281, where Melanchthon criticizes Bucer's willingness to allow the adoration of the host; Calvin to Farel (12 May 1541), CO 11, no. 309, 217.

434. WA.Tr. 5, no. 5461, 166; "Buccerus. Da leckerlein hat den glauben gar bei mir vorlorn. Ich trau im niemer. Er hat mich zu offt betrogen. Er hatt sich auff dem tag ißt zu Regenspurg ubel gehalten; er hat wollen mediator sein zwischen mir und dem babst, hat gesagt: Ei, es ist ein arm ding, das soviel sehlen sollen umbkomen umb eines odr zwen artickel willen!" Translation from Eells, *Martin Bucer*, 296.

435. Matheson, *Cardinal Contarini*, 107–108.

6

Conclusion

Martin Bucer has been predominantly portrayed as a diplomat, who attempted to reconcile divergent theological views, sometimes at any cost, or as a pragmatic pastor, who was more concerned with ethics than theology. These representations have influenced the view that Bucer was a theological lightweight, a *Vermittlungstheologe*, rightly placed in the shadow of Luther and Calvin. This work has argued differently. Bucer was an ecclesial diplomat and a pragmatic pastor, yet his ecclesial and practical approaches to reforming the Church were guided by coherent theological convictions. Central to his theology was his understanding of the doctrine of justification, an understanding that I have argued has an integrity of its own and has been imprecisely represented as *Vermittlungstheologie*. It was this solid doctrine that guided his irenicism and acted as a foundation for entering into discussions with Catholics between 1539 and 1541. He was consistent in his approach and did not sacrifice his theological convictions for ecclesial expediency.

To demonstrate the role of Bucer's doctrine of justification in negotiations with Catholics, I began by highlighting the repeated manner in which Bucer affirmed that agreement was necessary on this doctrine. For him: "The chief point [of our debate] concerns justification, that is, the manner in which a man can reach the point at which he is sure about the divine judgment, certain of the goodwill and mercy of God, persuaded that God regards him as one of the just, and the participants in the blessed life, having been forgiven all things by which he offended him."[1] The doctrine of justification holds prime place in his theology.

Here I also demonstrated how this doctrine provided the theological basis for his strategy of ἐπιείκεια (fairness, equity) within theological negotiations. Justification defined what it meant to be a Christian and therefore was the principal doctrine upon which the extension of Christ's reign throughout the empire depended.

Having established this doctrine's key place in his theology, I focused on clarifying how he understood this doctrine. I demonstrated the internal coherence of his doctrine, which necessarily combined faith and works of love, and argued that to understand his theology correctly, one needs to understand the role of moral philosophy in his thought, that is, the manner in which the Socratic dictum underlies the relationship between faith and works. Chapter 3 thus examined Bucer's epistemology and psychology, highlighting the important role of knowledge in his thought. With the assistance of the dictum that "to know the good is to do the good," I clarified the manner in which Bucer's intellectualistic understanding of true faith results in works of love.

Gropper's understanding of justification in the *Enchiridion*, which incorporated the aspects of imputation and the need to trust in the mercy of God, attracted Bucer's admiration. Bucer saw in Gropper a partner for concord. Gropper's doctrine of justification has been described in a similar manner as Bucer's (i.e., double justification), and therefore it was imperative that we understood Gropper's position to demonstrate the extent to which Bucer's views were consistent and not just similar or compatible with Gropperian doctrine. I demonstrated how in the *Enchiridion* Gropper's doctrine of ecclesiology and the sacraments were foundational for his understanding of justification. Likewise, I demonstrated how his paradigm of incorporation acted as the foundation for his understanding of the imputation of righteousness. For Gropper the impartation of righteousness, understood as being incorporated, plays the leading role. The *iustitia Christi* functions only as a supplement on top of one's own righteousness in the *Enchiridion*. Thus, it is the infusion of grace that is important in justification because through the sacraments one grows in righteousness, and though it is acknowledged as weak and though Gropper emphasizes that the justified should trust in the promise that in the end God will impute them as righteous (on the basis of their incorporation), impartation is always prior. This marks a major distinction between Bucer and Gropper.

---

1. *BOL* 5, 21; "Caput omnium est de iustificatione, hoc est, de ea ratione qua homini possit contingere, ut securus sit iudicii divini, certus benevolentiae et misericordiae Dei, persuasus se haberi Deo inter iustos, et participes vitae beatae, condonatis omnibus quibus ipsum offendit."

Bucer and the reformers reverse this order. For Bucer, every good work stems from the non-imputation of sins, revealed in faith.

Looking at the Colloquy of Leipzig and the preparatory discussions before the Worms Colloquy, we saw the manner in which the doctrine of justification was central to these negotiations, as well as how Bucer remained consistent to his theological convictions. For Bucer, the national colloquies prompted by the emperor were missiological opportunities to advance the Reformation, and he entered these negotiations because he saw it as his Christian duty to lead men to Christ.[2] To do this, there was need of dialogue between reasonable men. Through these dialogues, Bucer articulated the evangelical doctrine of justification by faith alone in a manner that he believed would be understood by the Catholic party. This entailed his explaining the evangelical doctrine of *sola fide* in a manner that combated the calumny that the Protestants taught a dead faith. At the preliminary discussion to Worms we saw the importance of being able to explain the doctrine of *sola fide* with *gratis* and *absque*, since this was the manner in which scripture spoke of justification, and therefore in this manner the *sola fide* doctrine could not be denied. He knew that the truth of the phrase "sola fide" was not restricted to the phrase itself.

At the risk of losing evangelical allies, Bucer demonstrated his commitment to dialogue through his activity at Worms. In the secret discussions with Gropper and others he was able to negotiate on the doctrine of justification in a manner that ensured that the Protestant position was not excluded from the article's formulation. For Bucer the phrasing of the formula remained imperfect and could be improved upon; however, for him it served as a basis for further negotiations. Regardless of the imperfections that remained, Bucer ensured that his foundational principles were left intact. Thus in principle the original article was true by Bucer's standards.

The final version of article 5 removed the ambiguous language of grace and causality that was in the original and in a more concise form provided a clearer representation of the evangelical doctrine. Article 5 affirms that through faith one is imputed righteous at the beginning of the Christian life, and that works of love are a result of this faith. The emphases of supplementation and incorporation that we encountered in the *Enchiridion* are subdued.

Most important, I demonstrated the consistency between these articles and Bucer's thought, both in terms of his *Romans Commentary* and in terms of his later explication of what he took to be article 5's proper evangelical sense.

---

2. *Lenz* 1, no. 101, 274; "das das gemein gesprech nit hat wöllen furgohn, und E.f.g. begeret, das ich mit dem herren von Granzella solte von solichen sachen red haben, dann auch bedacht, das jedem christen zustaht, wie er seine nechsten, schweige seine obren und heupter zu Christo furdre."

This coherence between Bucer's thought and article 5 also helped to demonstrate the evangelical credentials of the article, against those who view it as having discarded Protestant principles based on a rigid understanding of evangelical doctrine at this early sixteenth-century stage. Bucer did not accommodate the evangelical doctrine of justification; he evangelized.

The doctrine of justification articulated at Worms and Regensburg was a product of Bucerian theology, a theology I have shown to have an internal integrity of its own. The claims that the article was a piece of *Vermittlungstheologie* are valid only when Bucer's theological voice is silenced. This work, I hope, has given him back his voice.

Appendix A

English translation of the harmonization from chapter 2,
section 3, dealing with Romans 2:5–10
[BRom (1536), 115–121; (1562), 99–106]

*Harmonization of the statements: "God repays each according to his
works" and "No one will be justified by works."*

"He who will repay each according to his works" [Rom. 2:6] This
statement is repeated frequently in all of scripture and is expressed
everywhere with great importance. The poet in Ps. 62[11–12] says:
"Once God has spoken, twice I have heard this, that power belongs to
God, and kindness, O Lord, belongs to you, because you repay each
according, מעשהו, to his works." And the Lord himself testifies about
himself, in Matt. 16[27]:"He will on the last day repay each κατὰ
τὴνπρᾶξιν αὐτοῦ that is, according to his acts. And speaking concerning the reason for our judgment, he affirms that he will inquire
especially concerning duties of love. Now Saint Paul everywhere with
all his strength defends and teaches this, that no one is justified
before God, that is, absolved in the judgment of God and numbered
among the saints, by his deeds, but all are justified by the mercy
alone of God, who forgives sins on account of himself alone, and by
the grace of Christ before God, on account of whom God forgives
sins. This is affirmed with these words also: "We are justified by
faith," "We are saved by grace," "He who believes in Christ

has eternal life." Likewise, he who believes in me will not come to judgment; however, he who does not believe already is judged. These statements truly seem to be contradictory, and it cannot be said that it was a chance remark that, concerning the reason for divine judgment, it happens according to the deeds of man; for nowhere are they not stressed, and this not only in the law but also in the gospel itself, both by the Lord Jesus and by Paul the supreme herald of faith. Certainly D. Origen gathers from this that the fact that they believe is not alone sufficient for men. And D. Chrysostom says that one must not rely on faith alone, for the judgment in question also inquires concerning deeds. He who would rightly understand the sense of this text and all of these in which our works are proposed as causes of God's benefits, in which the goodness of God is proclaimed as the one sole and entire cause of what we receive from God, must observe four points.

First, that God speaks to us in all of scripture to us according as we can understand, and thereby to the measure of our intelligence. Hence scripture is everywhere replete with human feelings (anthropopathiis). Scripture assigns God to a place, encloses him in time, bestows upon him all kinds of feelings, and everywhere it speaks as if about a man. Second, since God created us with the capacity to learn, and in accordance with the knowledge of good and evil we are attracted to some things and repelled by others, he decided also to lead us to eternal life using teachings and exhortations. Third, we are born such that we are incited toward some things by expediency and deterred from other things by inexpediency. Thence Aristotle, the great investigator of the human mind (ingenii), made the purpose of deliberative discourse συμφέρον and βλαβερόν, the advantageous and the harmful. Fourth, God determined to rule us and to control our affairs, in such a way that he always repays upright deeds with good things and deceitful deeds with evil things, and he desired that we cooperate with him, either for our salvation, steadfastly pursuing a godly way of life, or for our perdition, giving ourselves over to perverse desires. Having weighed these matters, I think that it can be clear what is the true sense of this text that we are discussing.

Moreover, in order that all things may be more clearly known, let us divide the entire discussion into the issues, which are raised in this matter. They are three: first, whether our good works are the causes of the good that God does for us and bestows upon us, and what is the nature of these causes; second, why scripture repeatedly commends good works, so as to speak of them alone as the cause of our salvation; third, whether this sentiment is in agreement with the fact that scripture makes the undeserved kindness of God and merit of Christ the whole and only cause of our salvation and all good things that God does for us both in body and in spirit.

To the first issue: it cannot be doubted that good works are the causes of the benefits of God, since God testifies to it everywhere in scripture. If a person gives a mere cup of cold water to anyone in the name of Christ, the Lord declares that he will receive his reward. If anyone forsakes something for the sake of the name of Christ, he will receive in this life a hundredfold, and eternal life besides. We store up treasures in heaven with our alms [Luke 17:10]. If we make friends for ourselves of the evil of mammon, they will receive us in everlasting habitations (*tabernacula*). In Paul, the man who is generous out of love to his needy brothers sows a seed, out of which he will receive both earthly rewards and heavenly rewards like a harvest. What? Scripture everywhere promises rewards for good works. How often this occurs in the law: "Hear the voice of the Lord and his commands, so as to carry them out in order that it may be well with you, and that you may delight in good things in the land, which the Lord will give to you. [Deut. 4:1]. Isaiah in chapter 1 said: "If it pleases you to listen, you will enjoy in the good things of the earth, if it does not please you, so that you continue to be rebels, you will be devoured by the sword" [Isa. 1:19–20]. Paul states, work out you salvation with fear and trembling [Phil. 2:12], or rather complete it, for he used the term κατεργάζευθε. And elsewhere, in a similar passage, he states that those who act according to the law are justified in the sight of God [Rom. 2:13]. Therefore, it is entirely true that upright deeds are causes of God's doing good to us, but they are not primary causes nor through themselves primary causes, but they are secondary causes, and that only from the undeserved goodwill of God. For however much we may live in a godly and holy manner and do all things rightly, still we are useless servants; neither can any merit of ours be such that we can bind God by any contract or even by any law of extreme generosity, to even the least of all the benefits, which he bestows upon us. For whatever things we do rightly are due to all his works, entirely and totally, as the one who works in us and wills and causes what is fitting, he who fashioned us from nothing. Whatever is not evil in us, is his gift. In the meantime, however, since all things are and are rightly so called, that which God, who created all things by his word from nothing, determined them to be and declares them to be, therefore things that men do honestly are causes of the benefits of God and ought to be so called: for that they are so, God himself testifies everywhere in scripture and commends them by that name.

Therefore, it was taken for granted among the saints that things which men do in a godly and right manner are reasons God bestows his benefits on them, and that they are rightly called merits, just as what God repays to them is called wages. But one accepts this on the basis that we should acknowledge and confess that to the extent that they are certainly causes of the benefits of God they are merits and so called, not by their own merit but by the pure and free goodwill of God towards us. It is just like when parents ask their children to do a task, promising some reward, which is finally given only when the children complete the task. The mother says to her little son, "When you memorize the Lord's prayer, I will give you a nice little bonnet." The boy memorizes the prayer, and the mother gives the bonnet as agreed. In this case who would deny that the reason the boy was given a bonnet was that he memorized the prayer? For the mother would not have otherwise given the bonnet. However, no one will say that this work, that the boy memorized the prayer, was worth this in itself, but it was because the mother, loving the boy so, wanted it thus.

The next question is, why God in scripture so commends his good works, simply making them the causes of our salvation and of all things which he himself generously does for us? This question arises from the former question. For since our good works are not the causes of the benefits of God per se, but they are only so from the pure and free goodwill of God, by which he thus deigned to use us as cooperators in our salvation, it does not seem appropriate that our works should be so immediately commended as if they were alone and in every respect the causes. For this seems to be the case when our works are simply proclaimed as causes of salvation. The Lord himself without doubt said: "If you want to enter life obey the commandments" [Matt. 19:17]. And Moses: "Behold, I have put before you life and death, and goodness, and evil" [Deut. 30:15, 19], and so forth. Truly in this case he calls the commands of God themselves life, and the transgression of them death. And Paul tells us to teach the rich to lay down for themselves a good foundation for the future, in order that they may receive eternal life by good works, that is, generously sharing their wealth [1 Tim. 6:17–15]. Because in these references good works are simply mentioned as the cause of salvation, it could seem that they alone are the cause of salvation and contain in themselves all the good that God bestows on us.

The matter of what truth is in this question will be understood with care if one weighs these things that we put forward, namely, that God teaches us and leads us to salvation according to the measure of our intelligence, and to that end he uses exhortations to us, in which he declares those things that tend to our salvation, those things that tend contrariwise, those things that tend to our advantage, and those things that tend to our disadvantage. And so God in his goodness saw fit that not only other good things but particularly the inheritance of eternal life should gain our zeal for his pleasure, and that by good works, for which he himself created us, and which he himself prepares and perfects, we should cooperate for our own salvation [Eph. 2:10]. Therefore, it is not illogical that when God encourages us to be zealous for good works, that he should especially and particularly mention those which, entirely by that zeal, we gain for ourselves, and prepare also according to our lot, especially when they are such

that they kindle wondrously that much zeal in us and certainly promote blessings of life both in the present and in the future, with God himself so willing it,
and granting it by his undeserved goodness.

Furthermore, in this connection one must notice also that the life of the
saints consists of two aspects, trust in the goodness of God and a zeal for right
living. Therefore, when scripture teaches that trust, when it commends it,
scripture has rightly assigned all things solely to the divine goodwill; it makes
this the sole and unique cause of all things that we must hope for from God,
just as is the case. For since all our affairs are uncertain, or rather they are of
themselves nothing, no account of them must be taken, when one is inquiring
to what end must we trust, to what end must we strive. Without doubt the mind
having regard to them could never be made certain of its own felicity, could
never conceive an opinion worthy of God. For our works, even when regarded
as excellent, are yet always less than what is owed, nor are they in any way ade-
quate to be causes of our salvation, unless God wills it so, and that only out of
his goodness. Therefore, it is necessary that the mind, which ought to cling to
God with certain faith and to place its hope in him with its whole heart, be
raised up and fixed on this sole goodness of God. But since scripture has begun
to excite zeal for works in us and the will to live rightly, nothing is more appropriate than that it should explain abundantly and amply what value we shall set
on the effort to pursue these works and what is going to engender in us that
amount of zeal. We ought indeed to serve God with all our heart, soul, and
strength, to conform ourselves to the things that please him, and to be devoted
to him for the salvation of men. As it is we are born and God has created us in
such a way that with all skill and care, in every action and choice, we should
seek some good. Therefore, scripture especially explains what good and what
advantage there is in holy actions, at the point when it invites us to perform
them. And since God fashioned us of such a kind that we cannot but seek life,
even this present life, good health and all those amenities, with which life is led
comfortably, scripture inflames us toward the duties of holiness by promises
also of these good things. For even if first of all one has prayed to enjoy God's
favor and to be sure of eternal life, nevertheless since it contributes to the glory
of God that we should live here in our own time, even temporary goods have
their own influence for the purpose of encouragement with the saints.

It is indeed an error to think that there is any sin in this appetite for life and
the things this life demands. Certainly, if our Lord Jesus had not earnestly
sought this life, he would not have said to the Father: "If it is possible Father
remove this cup from me" [Luke 22:42]. But as he sought this life, so he also
sought the things which life requires. All the saints have always done and continue to do the same, but as I have said, in the right place. For just as those

things are not good, except when they serve us for our salvation in accordance with God's goodwill toward us, so the saints never have a holy desire for these good things, except insofar as they perform them for the sanctification of God's name and for the extension of his kingdom. However, since good things are to be desired, to have shown that they are the result of good works undoubtedly kindles one toward that zeal for good works. Therefore, it is appropriate that scripture inserts promises of these things with holy exhortations. And since to receive these things from a benevolent God is only for the children of God, who is now our father, as that scripture promises, there is moreover contained in all these promises the promise of eternal life, destined for the children of God, for whom those temporal benefits are proof that God calls them to eternal benefits also. For what father, who in his paternal charity supplies those perishable goods with such goodwill, could bear not also to bestow upon his children what belongs to them, that is, everlasting good things? [Luke 11:11–13]. And this promise of eternal life has the particular power to stimulate us toward all godliness, whence it is more expressly set forth in gospel exhortations, which are appropriately more clear and forceful.

Furthermore, there are those who judge it ungodly to do anything out of desire for eternal life: for one ought, they say, to perform all things for the sake of God, just as one ought to love him above all things, that is, the supreme good. From these people there are those who try to persuade themselves and others also that one should choose hell and endure it with enjoyment, if it is established that such is God's will, and they direct their thoughts concerning this matter to the point that they dare to claim to be of that mind, when in fact they feel nothing less, but are only pretending that they feel so. These people have not yet reached the point where they can with their whole heart seek and undergo those things that are truly good for them, since God wills it so, and they imagine that they are seeking and that they are prepared to undergo that which is the highest evil, which cannot be sought by him who loves God. For hell is nothing other than a declared hatred of God. What? Christ, who was the most perfect of all creatures and was without any sin, prayed to escape not only hell but also immediate death, and yet he did not sin. These people contradict not only their own feeling but that of all the saints and the whole of scripture, and since they have not yet learned to live as men of God, they pretend to themselves that they themselves live as God himself, not according to that lot which is assigned to the elect from the human race, but which God has kept for himself alone. Indeed, it is necessary to love God above all things, to embark on and to do nothing except by grace alone: but not outside ourselves, not to the exclusion of ourselves or of these good things, in which he determined to reveal himself to us as God. For if we love God above all things because he is the highest good, it is necessary that we acknowledge him also as our highest good, that is, we also acknowledge that all that is good for us is in him. Let us seek in him both present life and whatever this life requires and eternal life and whatever leads toward eternal life: then since we live and move and exist in God (and in fact we were created for him as nothing other than the work of God for his glory), by all means no one will seek the glory of God who does not at the same time seek to live in his own time and enjoy these things that this life requires, until freed from this body of death, he lives eternally, already fully united with God. For God decreed these things to be so; therefore, that they should be so is excellent, and on that account they must be chosen by the saints. But what need is there of this philosophy? The word of the Lord teaches us on this point sufficiently and praises in the saints, even as it proposes it to be imitated by us, the fact that they have earnestly prayed to the Lord not only for eternal life but also for present life and whatever is conducive to its being lived pleasantly, and for this reason they have spurred themselves on toward all that is pleasing to God. The incidents when Moses, with love for the salvation of the people of God, prayed to be annihilated from the book of life, and when Paul prayed to be made an anathema for his brothers, are in no way contradictory to these above sentiments. For each prayer was spoken with a clear and sincere mind, although in an ecstasy of love for the people of God. Undoubtedly each mentally added to his prayer, even if it is not expressed in words: "however not my will, but your will be done," just as our Savior added it when he had prayed for the cup of suffering to be removed from him. And as they did not doubt that the will of God required that each should live happily both now and in the future, such they also wished for themselves, and they maintained that it was their reason for living in accordance with the judgment of God, not however for their own sake, but not to their exclusion for the glory of God.

For their happiness was in a sense their share in divine glory, which they realized from his promises, and God instructed them to seek this with singular zeal: they were unable not to seek it, except in accordance with those promises of God. And in this matter they sought not so much their own concerns but the things of God. For since these aspirations depended on the word of God, and from it alone were conceived, they were absolutely unable to be numbered among those who had not denied themselves and in the first place sought the sanctification of the name of God. Therefore, one must seek the things that God has undertaken to give us, and as one must seek these things, so undoubtedly they have some importance and certain power to incite us to good works, which God himself commends to us on this account that they gain for us whatever he promised and we can by any means seek not in fact a special power but his own. For zeal and obedience to God, which is a result of that faith, by which we believe that God wills to behave as a father to us, draws one primarily and with a special power to the things that please God.

Moreover, there is in the fact that scripture proposes a reward for good works, both of this present age and of the future, this advantage, that when any desire for good things comes upon us, either present or future, there immediately comes to one's aid the thought "your God alone bestows these things, and has promised them, to those who tread the path of his commandments." This thought, contemplated with faith, immediately sets the mind on fire for the commands of God, not so much to the extent that we gain these desires as that we make ourselves acceptable to God who is so benevolent to us as besides his other infinite benefits, he invites us with the promise of rewards from every nation, to our salvation, which of course is implicit in a life ordered in a holy manner.

Finally, there are also grades of progress in the knowledge of and zeal for God. The one approaching God must believe that God is also the one who rewards those seeking after him. Hence a great portion of salvation is to know that even external good things are distributed by the one God, and hence one strives after them for oneself from God and from no creature. For we were created such that we cannot but strive after the things that we perceive to be good for us. Therefore, when it has been given to men, not to doubt that the one God bestows these things according to his free decision, an overwhelming necessity is now laid upon him to take pains to make himself pleasing to God and devote himself completely to his commands. And soon from the same fact that he now acknowledges God as the fount of all good things he will by himself excellently advance to awed contemplation of God, and he will progress to the point that now he seeks nothing but God's own glory. It is for this reason, as scripture everywhere proclaims, that God alone dispenses all the good things and bad things of this life, and that he bestows and protects life, prosperous health, wealth, peace, and all things desired on those who keep his commands: something that can be seen not only in the books of Moses but also in the Prophets and Psalms, and finally in the New Testament. For nothing is less true than what certain people wickedly propound as dogma, that the happiness that God promised to his ancient people living in accordance with his precepts has reached its end with these external goods. God still wanted these blessings to be better known in order that the more ignorant might be brought to the knowledge of him. For whoever progresses to the point that he does not doubt that life and whatever its preservation requires are given to him by the one God, and as nothing is beyond these things, which we seek by nature, so God is now for this man the supreme good, from whom he seeks all things for himself, including therefore eternal life, for desire for this too is inborn. Thus man is gradually brought to the point that he wants nothing other than God, he admires nothing other than God, and he is conformed completely to the things that please God. By what other way would he reach this state, when it is impossible that anyone acknowledge the God of himself and of everyone who also has not previously acknowledged that God is the supreme good both for himself and for everyone? For no one is able to acknowledge this for the first time on the basis of eternal good things, since "eye has not seen, ear has not heard, nor have they entered into the heart of man" [1 Cor. 2:9]: therefore that fact must be learned in the beginning from present good things that are seen and that we daily enjoy.

As a result of this, I suppose, it can now be very clear to anyone and completely appropriate that scripture, when it spurs us on to good works, also mentions and promises generally that God will give a reward for good works, and that by a zeal for the divine will, we shall enjoy all kinds of good things both present and future. That our mind is thus kindled directly corresponds with our ability, that is, the condition in which it pleased God to fashion us. For when one attributes to good works the idea that they are causes of our happiness, one is not however attributing to them the idea that they are sole causes or even the main causes. In fact, these exhortations are addressed to those who already believe in God, and thereby depend in all things on his free generosity alone, attributing nothing entirely to their own strength. For whom would the good things, which God has promised to them who live rightly, spur on to live rightly, unless he already has faith in the promises? Now where the promise is, there is the undeserved goodwill, on which he who embraces the promise by faith must depend. For everybody easily realizes that his own deeds in no way correspond to these good things that God has promised to give as a reward for them. It seems that these things answer the second question comprehensively: but this matter exercises and wearies the world so much that it cannot be made clear in a few words.

The third question asks how these exhortations in which good works are put forward as a cause of our salvation and the statements that God rewards each in accordance with his deeds, match those places in which scripture witnesses that we are justified before God by his grace alone and the merit of Christ, that is, that in the judgment of God we are absolved from the guilt of sins and judged worthy to be admitted into the inheritance of eternal life. This eternal life, we embrace and receive as the grace of God and the merit of Christ, while we believe in Christ. Whence the sentiment that Paul is in the habit of expressing, "we are justified by faith," which as has already been repeatedly stated, is nothing other than that we acknowledge that God judges us as absolved from sins and deserving to be numbered as heirs of salvation, and so we receive salvation by faith: for God deals with each according to his faith.

These two sets of sentiments seem to be incompatible. The former statements, namely, that we are judged according to our deeds, that we are repaid in accordance with what we have done: the reward of good works is salvation, seem to imply that God judges us by considering our works. The latter statement, that we are justified by grace or by faith, says, equivalently, that God judges us with no consideration of our works, but only by the contemplation of his own goodness, free mercy, and merit of Christ. Now that God in judging us takes account of our works and yet does not take account of our works seems completely contradictory, and they would contradict each other even if "habere rationem" (to take account) were understood in the same sense in each set of propositions.

And yet this phrase "habere rationem" is understood in one way when one says that God justifies us taking no account of our works, but he justifies us on account of himself alone, that is, he awards eternal life to us: and in another way when one says that God takes account of our works with the result that it is in accordance with our works that he imparts his benefits to us, and judges that we deserve to inherit his kingdom. For in the former statement one denies that in our works themselves there is any inherent cause why God should favor us, and number us among his own, and do good to us. In the latter statement, however, one affirms nothing beyond the fact that God takes account of our works to the extent that he rewards them, and that in accordance with the quality of our deeds. Hence scripture states in general that God repays us according to our works and that we receive from him, πρὸς ἇ, on account of that which each has done [2 Cor. 5:10]. There is in fact also elsewhere, "quia," or "propterea," and "ut" and other markers of causality: for as I said, good works are causes of the things with which God rewards us for them, but not the prime cause and not per se: for even good works themselves are gifts of the divine goodwill.

Then the fact that he rewards them is not because these works deserve it, as we have said, but because God of his own free goodness deems them worthy of that honor. Whatever good God does to us depends once and for all in every respect on his own goodness and undeserved generosity. Just as if a king were to designate for himself some nobles for which he were to appoint certain tournaments with most generous prizes: in that situation none receives the prize except the one who contends legitimately, and each is repaid in accordance with how he behaved in the tournament, and on these terms the legitimate effort expended in the contest is in its own way the reason for the prize. But that effort alone does not deserve a prize of itself nor of its own merit: for many others undergo much more effort and indeed danger in fighting on the prince's behalf; as is also the case when one is fighting earnestly in battle where no prize is awarded, still less such a prestigious and generous prize as is awarded to the participants in the tournament. The fact therefore is that in this situation for the nature of the contest there is awarded a generous prize by the prince who established that order of nobility by his own decision and appointed to it those whom he pleased and who has then announced such prizes as he willed for the contestants. And yet God's generosity to us while he awards prizes for good works that he established is greater by the measure that even the good works are his works in us and are free gifts no less than the actual prizes. For nobody can perform good works unless God has breathed his Spirit into them, hence God himself has not brought it about that they desire and perform these works, and to that extent it is all God's doing and nothing is our doing. He first elects those whom he wills into the order of the sons of God before they exist, still even less before they have done anything good, then he breathes into each the Spirit of right doing, just as he pleases. And so although God repays good works, which he also prescribed in accordance with his goodwill, with undeserved prizes, and in one way or another pays these rewards in accordance and on account of these works and so in some way takes account of these works, namely, so as to return good for good and evil for evil, to that extent these prizes are nothing other than gifts and free benefits of God, so that scripture rightly declares that God provides these for his own, taking account only of his own goodness and the merit of Christ and of absolutely no merit at all in any work of man. Therefore, the fact persists and always remains true that we are justified by the grace and mercy of God alone, that is, we are reckoned among the righteous, we are preserved and we receive whatever benefits God bestows upon us. And nevertheless this equally is true that "God rewards each in accordance with his works"; therefore we are justified by works, that is, judged as sharing the lot of the righteous and as heirs of life. But in the use of the terms "secundum" (according to) and "ex" (as a result of), nothing more is signified than the order that God established, that he should reward our good deeds with his benefits and the condescension by which God deems us worthy of this honor, so that we should cooperate with him for our salvation in accordance with what Paul says: "Work out your own salvation with fear and trembling" [Phil. 2:12–13]. But the idea that we should make any independent contribution to our works, however good, which God might regard and so bestow upon us even the smallest benefit, is found neither in these statements nor in any place in scripture, any more than the idea that when God repays us according to our good works he equates the reward with the works. For what contribution of ours could be equal to the divine benefits? For if one were to have as much holiness and righteousness as all the saints who have been in the world, one's deeds would still not be the equal of even the slightest benefit of God. Indeed, we are useless servants, even when we have carried out all that we have been commanded to do. On the other hand, no one has ever lived such an accursed life but that when he was saved he was repaid according to his works. For suppose that somebody lived in the most ungodly manner throughout his entire life. The Lord, however, converts him at the end of his life just as he did with the thief who was crucified with our Savior. Now as soon as he has embraced the goodness of God by faith, his mind truly burns for the glory of God. If he can do nothing else, he confesses his sins to the glory of God and urges others to repent. Even if he cannot do it by prayer, he does it by groans and sighs. In this he now has good works according to which he may be justified, that is, for which he may be judged to deserve admission to the inheritance of eternal life. In fact they are for this man the works of a penitent, they are the works of a mind seeking the glory of God, they are works of the sort that God determined to reward with eternal life, forgetting all that was previously done wickedly in accordance with the sentiment: "When man turns away from his ungodliness." But how so? Are these works worth so much in themselves? Far from it. It is because such is the extent of God's mercy and goodwill. Now if as a result of these works, even of whatever quality, God justifies him and the justification is in some way a result of works, is it then untrue that justification is a result of faith, so that absolutely no regard be had of works? Far from it once again. For even if those works be in their own way the cause of justification, that is, so that man would be numbered among the heirs of life, all this yet comes entirely from the goodness of God alone, so that on the one hand salvation and justification are absolutely not the result of any regard for works: but on the other hand these works indeed have in themselves some power which of itself may grant to this man that God may look with favor on him and bestow upon him his good things. For man himself is from nothing, therefore, all his works are of themselves of no value. If he does any good, it results from the fact that he is a creation of God, created for good works, works that God himself prepares, makes and performs, so that he rewards in us gifts that are already his.

Because all the former statements are consistent with the latter: God pays to each according to his works; those who have performed good works will enter life; those who have performed wicked works will enter hell; and whatever of the sort is read in scripture, it is abundantly evident, therefore, that there is nothing in these texts that does not accord with the things we are saying. We are saved only by the grace of God not by works; we are justified by faith without works; those who believe have eternal life; and whatever sentiments of this sort are contained in Holy Scripture.

Concerning only infants, who are called hence before they are able to do good works, it is a different matter. However, all those statements in Holy Scripture, which mention that the judgment of God will be according to our works, are exhortations that were written for adults, whom God wills by this means to arouse toward a zeal for right living: in their case the ordinance holds good that upright deeds are rewarded, for they are people of the sort that the Lord has determined shall cooperate with him for their salvation. Therefore, since this does not apply to babies who are carried off in infancy, it is not appropriate that on the basis of statements that are designed to apply expressly to adults, we should make a judgement concerning infants.

We consider that these statements are a sufficient answer to the third question, and from them, and from our answers to the first two questions, we think that there is an excellent harmony between the passages of scripture in which the judgment of God is declared to be exercised upon us on the basis of works, and those which affirm that our salvation and all the benefits of God depend on no consideration for our works but only on the goodness of God and on the merit of Christ.

With regard to what the fathers gather from the statement "God will repay each according to his works," namely, that faith alone and belief alone are not sufficient for salvation, they have no wish to contradict what is the certain conclusion from Saint Paul: that we are justified and saved by faith, which the fathers also maintain in these very words, as we argued above in the prefaces. For the fathers speak sometimes by imitation concerning faith and belief, that is, utilizing these terms in a sense in which evil lives bandy the words "faith" and "belief," although they have no true faith and only give assent to God's words; just as all those who live however wickedly acknowledge in general terms that it is good to live virtuously, although in the meantime they judge and act in an entirely different manner when action is required now, and a decision is needed on an occasion about what must be done. This is not the true faith and firm belief, which the Spirit of Christ brings about only in the elect. True faith, which is the work and gift of the Holy Spirit by which the sons of God are sealed, results in one being able to judge for certain that what God approves is the best thing to do and is also able to accomplish it with the greatest zeal. Whence the apostle declares that faith ἐνεργεῖν, that is, works through love, by which the whole law is fulfilled. That faith certainly cannot exist without good works, and if it lacks good works, that is, depends on no works, it must embrace the salvation offered by the sole mercy of God. If you say concerning this faith, "Faith without works does not suffice for life," it is just as if you were saying, "Fire does not suffice for warmth without heat." Such useless talk, I imagine, was not allowed by the fathers. Hence it seems probable to me that when they wrote that faith alone is not sufficient for salvation, they understood concerning faith, what men are commonly accustomed to bandy about, when in the meantime they are in bondage to sin and are lacking in true faith. For even as by this faith the righteous live, and live the life of God so he is unable to lack zeal for good works. At this point I have finished this particular harmonization.

Appendix B

English translation of the harmonization from chapter 2, section 3, dealing with Romans 2:11–16
[*BRom* (1536), 129–130; (1562), 118–119]

Harmonization II: "That those who act according to the law are justified"; with: "That no one is justified as a result of the works of the law."

The apostle here writes: "ὅι ποιηταὶ, (those who do) the law, will be justified." This seems to contradict that which he everywhere demonstrates: that we are justified by faith and not by any works. "Those who act according to the law are justified": what else does this mean if not: "They are justified as a result of the works of the law"? That these two are in agreement can be sufficiently seen from the harmonization of this text: "God will reward each according to his deeds," which we explained above in section 2. God will certainly judge us according to our deeds, and he will bid us pass into eternal life if those deeds are good; thus far, then, it is correctly said that they are justified, that is, that judgment is given in God's assize in the case of those who have acted according to the law, meaning those who have earnestly applied themselves to the precepts of the law. This of course is something that those who truly believe in God cannot fail to do.

What we have just said is contradicted by absolutely nothing said earlier, as we abundantly proved above: that God saves us by his mercy alone and by the contemplation of the merit of Christ, which, when we believe in Christ, is bestowed on us and becomes ours. For those very deeds done rightly in accordance with which God justifies us, that is, assigns to us eternal life, are the works of Christ in us, bestowed on us with Christ out of the pure and free goodwill of God. As a result, the goodness of God is in itself the prime and the whole cause of our salvation, as is expressed by the phrases "by grace alone" and "by faith alone." By this faith, of course, we embrace and receive this grace, namely, that we are justified—and not as a result of works. Accordingly in regard to these statements one is inquiring into what is the first cause, and in itself the cause, of our justification, and thereby one rightly denies that this cause can be works, which no one can possess unless he is already justified and in possession of eternal life. Whence Augustine says that the phrase "Works do not justify" signifies "Good works follow justification and do not precede justification" in *Concerning Faith and Works*, chapter 14. Nevertheless, when God wants us to cooperate with him by good works for our salvation, or rather, even to "work it out" ($\kappa\alpha\tau\epsilon\rho\gamma\dot{\alpha}\zeta\epsilon\sigma\theta\epsilon$) [Phil. 2:12], and has thus determined to repay us according to our deeds, there is brought about also in its own way our justification; that is, eternal life is assigned to us as a result of works. But this is the case only when through our election and the purpose of God formed before the ages, there is already assigned to us before the foundation of the world this life of God as a result of the grace of God and the merit of Christ [Ephesians 1 and 3]. This life, moreover, is assigned to us through faith, that is, after we believe in Christ and have in some way become already possessed of him. This of course comes about at that blessed beginning of faith that belongs to the sons of God through the Spirit, who is the pledge of this inheritance. For good works are the fruit of this faith and of the Spirit.

Therefore, our justification is threefold, that is, God assigns eternal life to us in three ways. The first is that by which he destines us to eternal life, and it exists solely by his goodness and regard for the merit of Christ. The scholastics add the consideration of the merits, which God foresees will be in his own. But whence, I ask, does he foresee those things that no one will ever have except by his gift, things that he also determined to grant at the very moment when he determined to grant salvation?

The second way is that by which he already reveals eternal life in some way and grants that one enjoy it, by the gift of the Spirit, in which we cry, "Abba Father." This justification exists in addition to our faith, but that too is something that God out of his free goodness gives, and brings about by his Spirit in us. The third way is when he now reveals actually and fully the eternal life or even blessings that we enjoy, no longer only by faith and hope. Our deeds contribute to this justification, but they too are the gifts and works of the free goodness of God.

The statement that God reveals eternal life to us to be enjoyed to the full according to our works in no way contradicts the statement that we conceive the hope of this eternal life solely through confidence in the goodness of God and merit of Christ by faith in the Gospel (both faith and hope themselves being assigned to us by God's sole goodness and on account of the merit of Christ). These statements are in no way incompatible with the fact that the sole goodness of God and merit of Christ is the prime and in itself entire cause of all those facts; hence there is also no lack of harmony in these texts of scripture, which declare all these things whether separately or together. When scripture is especially concerned to commend good works to us, and so invites us to perform them, it is easily seen how helpful it is that scripture states and expounds only that good works contribute to our felicity. For it is by the will of God that good works have this advantage, that an abundant reward is paid for them, that God judges us in accordance with them and declares us heirs of eternal life; more than that he now fully reveals this eternal life, that is, he justifies us finally and completely. Why, then, would scripture not express, proclaim, and inculcate this, and all the more so when it has begun to arouse and kindle in us the zeal for good works? From where the actual good works befall us, from where it is that they are rewarded by eternal life, how completely they fail to match such a reward, in short, how they are never such that we can trust them, but must yet depend utterly and solely on the mercy of God and satisfaction of Christ, all these things scripture most abundantly proclaims in the various appropriate texts; and these statements concerning good works it proclaims only to those who already honestly hold all those beliefs concerning the undeserved goodness of God, the merit of Christ, the nature of faith, and lastly the defectiveness of our works.

In these three harmonizations of such texts, I opted to discuss these matters so extensively because the principle religious disagreements in the whole world have arisen and been sustained from the fact that very few indeed have yet examined the question of what status should be accorded to our works and how they have the nature of merits and earn the wages of eternal life. For thereupon it is exposed that some invent for humanity a sort of entrance into good works, on their own initiative, while others claim that our whole salvation depends on the fact that we grasp by faith the mercy of God, who decides for his own sake to bless us and provides this through the merit of Christ, by which he wills that full expiation be made for our sins; thus these proclaim and reject works in such a way that they seem openly to others to contradict all those texts in which good works also become causes of our salvation and what these works merit. What good man does not deplore the trouble this one question causes today, that we are justified by faith alone without works? The situation is such that the passages of scripture—some of which proclaim the grace of God, some faith, some works—are clear and beautifully harmonious, such that if only godlessness ceased along with that greatest destroyer of truth φιλονικεία, that is, lust for victory, and it pleased people to speak as scripture speaks, both about faith and about works and all that it everywhere inculcates, we would not make use of these texts as mere chance remarks by either completely avoiding them, or by very rarely permitting ourselves to make use of them; but on the contrary, what scripture contains in one place or another, always suitably, we would not mishandle anyway whatsoever, especially out of the context that we see observed by the sacred writers; I tell you, if we paid attention to these terms [i.e., in the contexts where the writers apply them], we would both see more clearly than in the light of midday how, happily, these texts agree, and we would employ them always to our certain edification, far from all disagreements and strife. May he at last grant us this, who is our peace, Jesus Christ our Lord. Amen.

Appendix C

English translations of harmonizations I and II from
chapter 4, section 1, dealing with Romans 4:1–8
[*BRom* (1536), 217–219; (1562), 230–233]

*Harmonization (I) of the texts "The Law removes the reason for boast-
ing"; and "The believer has reason to boast before God."*

Previously the apostle made the removal of boasting for any reason a
property of faith, which of course the law of works would not remove.
But here when he writes that Abraham did not have any reason to
boast before God on the grounds of works, he indicates that he had
reason to do so as a result of faith; therefore, faith both removes and
supplies reason to boast, which seems a contradiction, but boasting
of one's own righteousness is one thing, boasting of God's righteousness is another thing; boasting of our works is one thing, boasting of
the condescension of God another thing; the one certainly faith
removes, the second certainly faith gives grounds for καύχημα, that
is, boasting, is the proud expression of a confident and joyful mind in
something that presents itself as one's own. Now he who truly
believes God through Christ, acknowledges that he is saved by the
mercy of God alone and that all that is his own, far from escaping
God's curse, necessitated the death of the son of God to accomplish
its expiation. Hence it is impossible to boast of anything other than
the grace and goodness of God toward oneself and the cross of

our Lord Jesus Christ. Hence the apostle wrote in the epistle to the Ephesians concerning our salvation: "It is a gift from God not as a result of works, lest anyone should boast" [Eph. 2:8b–9]. Now as faith is convinced that it has been granted eternal felicity without any merit of its own, so it has reason to boast, but only in the Lord; and in fact in the Lord who is so favorable and benevolent to it. Concerning this boasting Paul writes later in the fifth chapter: "Through him we have access by faith to this grace in which we stand and make our boast in the hope of glory of God" [Rom. 5:2]; and not only that, but we glory even in our afflictions. For the saints are so certain of God's love toward them that they do not doubt that it is as a result of this love that adversities are sent to them and that these undoubtedly work together for their salvation. Hence they glory too in these very adversities as the greatest and most certain goods. But how are they described as "goods"? Because they are ordained by God for good. And therefore this boasting in the Lord's goodwill is also grace. So also Paul writes that those whom he brought to faith in Christ are his boast and that he is their boast, that is, each is the boast of the other. But even this boast was the result of the Lord's kindness who had sent to his elect such a useful and salutary apostle and who had given his apostle such docile hearers, ready to follow Paul to the Lord's kingdom. Moreover, in what he wrote in Galatians 6, he seems to make works themselves grounds for boasting. For he wrote: "If anyone thinks he is something when he is nothing, he is deceiving himself. But let each test his own works, then he will have reason to boast of himself alone, not of another" [Gal. 6:3]. But here Paul rejects the boast which anyone presumes to make by reviling others and making them inferior to himself, whereby he himself may seem to be superior. In this way he is actually boasting not about himself but about others whom he puts down and in comparison with whom he prides himself. But he who lives with a pure conscience and truly pursues good works has within himself a reason to boast; but not because it is his own doing, but a gift of God. This is the boast of a good conscience, which Paul mentions in 2 Corinthians 1. All things are true among the saints, including therefore also the gifts of good works and a purity of mind. Therefore, they can and must boast about these, that is, proclaim them with the apostle confidently but in the proper place and give thanks for them to the Lord. This is rightly called boasting about them in God. Paul swears by the Lord that he must not abandon in the territory of Achaia the boast that he had preached the gospel for nothing. For that was the gift of God and an excellent one. Why, then, would he have not proclaimed it in the proper place to the glory of God, that is, for the strengthening of his apostolate, which was for the salvation of those to whom he had been sent as an apostle and in fact for the increase of the kingdom of Christ?

In all this he ascribed nothing to himself but everything to God; he had all this reason to boast in the sight of God, that is, depending on the testimony of God. Therefore, faith absolutely removes all reasons for men to boast about themselves and their own deeds, for whatever good is present, he acknowledges that he receives it all by the gift of the divine goodwill. But at the same time he knows for certain that he enjoys God's favor, and that what God bestows are true steadfast goods, and that one day it will be revealed that they truly exist and are held by him, so when that can happen by the *ère* of men, he may proclaim these truths also before men, that is, he boasts of them to the glory of God and he has this reason to boast before God, for God confirms of course those goods now in the consciences of believers and will one day confirm them before the whole assembly of the saints in the day of the last judgment. Hence Paul boasts that his glory will be the Corinthians and Thessalonians in the day of the Lord. Therefore, the fact that the apostle here attributes to the faith of Abraham, that he had reason to boast before God, that is, imputed righteousness of which he was able to boast, with God confirming that boasting by his own testimony is in no way contrary to what he wrote above in chapter 3, that all boasting is removed by the law of faith. For at present he attributes to faith boasting which depends on the mercy of God, who justifies his own freely, and hence also bestows a true communion of righteousness and good works. However, above he speaks about boasting which depends on our works and which faith causes to vanish completely.

Harmonization II of the texts "He who believes in him who justifies" and what we read in Exodus 23: "God does not justify the ungodly."

The Lord himself spoke thus: "Thou shalt not kill the innocent and the righteous for I will not justify the wicked, אצדיק, that is, I will not absolve, I will not hold him guiltless. This therefore seems diametrically opposite to what Paul here teaches: the whole of salvation depends on our believing that God justifies the wicked, that is, he absolves him and indeed he accounts him righteous. But the text in Exodus did not refer to the first justification, that is, absolution from all impiety; "For everybody is born wicked." Wherefore, if God does not justify the wicked and ungodly, absolutely nobody will be saved. Concerning the second justification that is made according to works, the Lord said, "I will not justify the wicked"; for in this justification God repays each according to his deeds. But how these two statements may be the case and how they may honestly not contradict each other, that God forgives sins freely and yet takes vengeance and exacts punishment from sinners according to the nature of their offenses, can be more fully ascertained from our previous discussions in the second conciliation in section 3, chapter 2.

First God must certainly go before us with his mercy and forgive all our impiety. It is thus that he justifies the ungodly but while forgiving and remitting impiety, and hence also bestowing his spirit to shun all impiety and zealously pursue godliness, so that he may in this way reward us with his subsequent benefits as the prize and reward of godliness, but a godliness that is given by him. However, he whose impiety God does not at the same time both forgive and take away, just as he persists in his ungodliness that cannot but be hateful to a just God, so also he is hated by God on account of his ungodliness and he must pay in full the penalty of his ungodliness, at the time when God will judge according to his deeds. So God does not justify the ungodly, that is, while he continues to be ungodly, that is, God does not leave him unpunished; for as the apostle wrote above in chapter 2, he sends affliction and distress into the soul of every evildoer. Therefore, the text "I will not justify the ungodly" means nothing other than "I will condone no one's wickedness and ungodliness; no one while I am judge will be absolved while he pursues wickedness and godliness."

Appendix D

English translation of Article 5 by Anthony N. S. Lane

The Justification of Man

(1) No Christian should doubt that after the fall of our first parent all men are, as the apostle says, born children of wrath [Eph. 2:3] and enemies of God [Rom. 5:10] and thereby are in death [Rom 5:21; Eph. 2:1] and slavery to sin [Rom. 6:16–20].

(2) Likewise, no Christian should question that nobody can be reconciled with God, nor set free from slavery to sin, except by Christ the one mediator between God and men [1 Tim. 2:5], by whose grace, as the apostle said to the Romans, we are not only reconciled to God [5:10] and set free from slavery to sin [6:18, 22], but also made sharers in the divine nature [2 Pet. 1:4] and children of God [Rom. 8:14–16].

(3) Likewise, it is quite clear that adults do not obtain these blessings of Christ, except by the prevenient movement of the Holy Spirit, by which their mind and will are moved to hate sin. For, as Saint Augustine says, it is impossible to begin a new life if we do not repent of the former one. Likewise, in the last chapter of Luke, Christ commands that repentance and forgiveness of sin should be preached in his name [24:47]. Also, John the Baptist, sent to prepare the way of the Lord, preached repentance, saying: "Repent [*Poenitentiam agite*], for the kingdom of heaven is drawing near" [Matt. 3:2]. Next, man's mind is moved toward God by the Holy Spirit

through Christ and this movement is through faith. Through this [faith] man's mind believes with certainty all that God has transmitted [*tradita*], and also with full certainty and without doubt assents to the promises made to us by God who, as stated in the Psalm, is faithful in all his words [144/5:13]. From there he acquires confidence [*fiduciam*] on account of God's promise, by which he has pledged that he will remit sins freely and that he will adopt as children those who believe in Christ, those I say who repent of their former life. By this faith, he is lifted up to God by the Holy Spirit and so he receives the Holy Spirit, remission of sins, imputation of righteousness and countless other gifts.

(4) So it is a reliable and sound doctrine that the sinner is justified by living and efficacious faith, for through it we are pleasing and acceptable to God on account of Christ. And living faith is what we call the movement of the Holy Spirit, by which those who truly repent of their old life are lifted up to God and truly appropriate the mercy promised in Christ, so that they now truly recognize that they have received the remission of sins and reconciliation on account of the merits of Christ, through the free [*gratuita*] goodness of God, and cry out to God: "Abba Father" [Rom. 8:15; Gal. 4:6]. But this happens to no one unless also at the same time love is infused [*infundatur*] which heals the will so that the healed will may begin to fulfill the law, just as Saint Augustine said. So living faith is that which both appropriates mercy in Christ, believing that the righteousness which is in Christ is freely imputed to it, and at the same time receives the promise of the Holy Spirit and love. Therefore the faith that truly justifies is that faith which is effectual through love [Gal. 5:6]. Nevertheless it remains true, that it is by this faith that we are justified (i.e., accepted and reconciled to God) inasmuch as it appropriates the mercy and righteousness which is imputed to us on account of Christ and his merit, not on account of the worthiness or perfection of the righteousness imparted [*communicatae*] to us in Christ.

(5) Although the one who is justified receives righteousness and through Christ also has inherent [righteousness], as the apostle says: "you are washed, you are sanctified, you are justified, etc." [1 Cor. 6:11] (which is why the holy fathers made use of [the term] "to be justified" even to mean "to receive inherent righteousness"), nevertheless, the faithful soul depends not on this, but only on the righteousness of Christ given to us as a gift, without which there is and can be no righteousness at all. And thus by faith in Christ we are justified or reckoned to be righteous, that is, we are accepted through his merits and not on account of our own worthiness or works. And on account of the righteousness inherent in us we are said to be righteous, because the works which we perform are righteous, according to the saying of John: "whoever does what is right is righteous" [1 John 3:7].

(6) Although fear of God, patience, humility and other virtues ought always to grow in the regenerate, because this renewal is imperfect and enormous weakness remains in them, it should nevertheless be taught that those who truly repent may always hold with most certain faith that they are pleasing to God on account of Christ the mediator. For it is Christ who is the propitiator, the High Priest, and the one who prays for us, the one the Father gave to us and with him all good things [Rom. 8:32].

(7) Seeing that in our weakness there is no perfect certainty and that there are many weak and fearful consciences, which often struggle against great doubt, nobody should be excluded from the grace of Christ on account of such weakness. Such people should be earnestly encouraged boldly to set the promises of Christ against these doubts and by diligent intercession to pray that their faith may be increased, according to the saying: "Lord increase our faith" [Luke 17:5].

(8) Likewise, every Christian should learn that this grace and this regeneration have not been given to us so that we might remain idle in that stage of our renewal which we at first obtained, but so that we may grow in everything into him who is the head [Eph. 4:15]. Therefore, the people must be taught to devote effort to this growth which indeed happens through good works, both internal and external, which are commanded and commended by God. To these works God has, in many passages from the Gospels, clearly and manifestly promised on account of Christ a reward— good things in this life, as much for the body as for the soul (as much as seems right to divine providence) and after this life in heaven. Therefore, although the inheritance of eternal life is due to the regenerate on account of the promise, as soon as they are reborn in Christ, nevertheless God also renders a reward to good works, not according to the substance of the works, nor because they come from us, but to the extent that they are performed in faith and proceed from the Holy Spirit, who dwells in us, free choice concurring as a partial agent.

(9) The joy of those who have performed more and better works will be greater and more abundant, on account of the increase of faith and love, in which they have grown through exercises of that kind.

(10) Now those who say that we are justified by faith alone should at the same time teach the doctrine of repentance, of the fear of God, of the judgment of God and of good works, so that all the chief points of the preaching may remain firm, as Christ said: "preaching repentance and the remission of sins in my name" [Luke 24:47]. And that is to prevent this way of speaking [i.e., *sola fide*] from being understood other than has been previously mentioned.

Bibliography

PRIMARY SOURCES

Aquinas, Thomas. *Summa Theologiae*. Ed. and trans. Blackfriars. 60 vols. London: Eyre and Spottiswoode, 1962–1980.

Bellarmino, Roberto. *Disputationes Roberti Bellarmini Politiani, . . . de controversiis christianae fidei, adversus huius temporis haereticos opus*. 4 vols. Ingolstat, 1606.

Bucer, Martin. *Enarrationum in Evangelia Matthaei, Marci, & Lucae. . . .* Strasbourg: Johann Herwagen, 1527 (*Bibliographie 22*).

———. *Epistola D. Pauli ad Ephesios. . . .* Strasbourg: Johann Herwagen, 1527 (*Bibliographie 25*).

———. *Metaphrasis et Enarrationes Perpetuae . . . in Epistolam ad Romanos. . . .* Strasbourg: Wendelin Rihel, 1536 (*Bibliographie 76*).

———. *In Sacra Quatuor Evangelia, Enarrationes perpetuae. . . .* Strasbourg: Johann Herwagen, 1536 (*Bibliographie 77*).

———. *Von Kirchengütern. . . .* Strasbourg: Johann Prüss, 1540 (*Bibliographie 94*).

———. *Acta colloqui in comitiis imperii Ratisponae habiti. . . .* Strasbourg: Wendelin Rihel, 1541 (*Bibliographie 112*).

———. *De vera Ecclesiarum . . . Reconciliatione et Compositione. . . .* Strasbourg: Wendelin Rihel, 1542 (*Bibliographie 124*). The first part of this work was published in an article by Walter Friedensburg. "Martin Bucer, Von der Wiedereinigung der Kirchen (1542)." *Archiv für Reformationsgeschichte* 31 (1934): 145–191.

———. *Psalmorum libri quinque ad Hebraicam Veritatem Traducti. . . .* Genf: Robert Stephanus, 1554 (*Bibliographie 201*).

————. *Metaphrasis et Enarrationes Perpetuae . . . in Epistolam ad Romanos. . . .* Basel: Petrus Perna, 1562 (*Bibliographie* 223).

————. *Praelectiones Doctiss. in Epistolam D. P. ad Ephesios. . . .* Basel: Petrus Perna, 1562 (*Bibliographie* 229).

————. "Quomodo S. Literae pro Concionibus Tractandae sint Instructio" (1531). In "Un Traité d'exégèse pratique de Bucer," Latin and French translation, ed. and trans. Pierre Scherding and François Wendel. *Revue d'Histoire et de Philosophie Religieuses* 26 (1946): 32–75.

————. *Instruction in Christian Love (1523).* Trans. Paul T. Fuhrmann. Richmond, VA: John Knox Press, 1952.

————. *Martini Buceri Opera Latina.* Vols. 1–. Paris, 1955; Leiden, 1979–.

————. *Martin Bucer Études sur la Correspondance.* Ed. J. V. Pollet. 2 vols. Paris: Presses Universitaires de France, 1958–1962.

————. *Common Places of Martin Bucer.* Trans. and ed. David F. Wright. Appleford, England: Sutton Courtenay Press, 1972.

————. *Martin Bucers Deutsche Schriften.* Ed. R. Stupperich et al. Vols. 1–. Gütersloh: Gerd Mohn, 1979–.

————. *Correspondance de Martin Bucer.* Ed. J. Rott. Vols. 1–. Leiden: Brill, 1979–.

————. *Concerning the True Care of Souls.* Trans. by Peter Beale. East Peoria, IL: Versa Press, 2009.

Calvin, John. *Iohannis Calvini Opera Quae Supersunt Omnia.* Ed. W. Baum, E. Cunitz, and R. Reuss. 59 vols. Berlin and Brunswick: Schwetschke, 1863–1900.

Concordia. Christliche Widerholete einmütige Bekentnüs . . . Augspurgischer Confession und verselben zuende des Buchs underschriebener Theologen Lere und glaubens. . . . Dresden, 1580.

Council of Trent. *Canons and Decrees of the Council Trent.* Trans. H. J. Schroeder. Rockford, IL: Tan Books and Publishers, 1978.

Eck, Johannes. *Apologia . . . adversus mucores et calumnias Buceri, super actis Comiciorum Ratisponae.* Cologne, 1542.

————. *Enchiridion of Commonplaces: Against Luther and Other Enemies of the Church.* Trans. Ford L. Battles. Grand Rapids, MI: Baker Book House, 1979.

Erasmus. *Opera Omnia Desiderii Erasmi Roterodami Recognita et Adnotatione Critica Instructa Notisque Illustrata.* 9 vols. Amsterdam: North Holland, 1969–2003.

Gropper, Johannes. *Antididagma seu christianae et catholicae religionis. . . .* Louvain: Servatius Zassenus, 1544.

————. *An die Roemsche Keyserliche Maiestat . . . Warhafftige Antwort und gegenberichtung.* Cologne: Iaspar Gennepaeus, 1545.

————. *Canones Concilii Provincialis Coloniensis . . . quibus adiectum est Enchiridion christianae institutiones.* Paris: Nicolaus Boucher, 1545.

————. *Briefwechsel, I: 1529–1547.* Ed. Reinhard Braunisch. Munster: Aschendorff, 1977.

Herminjard, A. L., ed. *Correspondence des réformateurs dans les pays de langue française, ecuellie et publiée.* Vol. 3. 2nd ed. Paris: H. Georg, Libraire-Editeur, 1878.

Lenz, Max. *Briefwechsel Landgraf Philipps des Grossmüthigen von Hessen mit Bucer.* 3 vols. Stuttgart: Verlag von S. Hirzel, 1880–1891.

Luther, Martin. *Luthers Werke. Kritische Gesamtausgabe.* 72 vols. Weimar: H. Böhlau, 1883–1993.

Melanchthon, Phillip. *Philippi Melanchthonis Opera Quae Supersunt Omnia.* Ed. Karl Bretschneider and H. Bindseil. 28 vols. Halle: Schwetschke, 1834–1860.

———. *Melanchthons Werke in Auswahl.* Ed. R. Stupperich et al. 5 vols. Gütersloh: Gerd Mohn, 1961–1965.

———. *Commentary on Romans (1540 ed).* Trans. Fred Kramer. St. Louis, MO: Concordia, 1992.

Pfeilschifter, G, ed. *Acta Reformationis Catholicae ecclesiam Germaniae concernantia saeculi XVI.* 6 vols. Regensburg: Friedrich Pustet, 1959–1974.

Pighius, Albert. *Ratio componendorum dissidiorum et sarciendae in religione concordiae.* Cologne: M. Novesiani, 1542.

———. *Apologia Albert Pighii Campensis adversus Martini Buceri calumnias.* Mainz, 1543.

Rott, Jean, ed. *Quellen zur Geschichte der Täufer. (Täuferakten Elsass I–IV).* 4 vols. Gütersloh: Gerd Mohn, 1959–1988.

Schiess, T, ed. *Briefwechsel der Brüder Ambrosius und Thomas Blaurer 1509–1548.* 3 vols. Freiburg: Fehsenfeld, 1908–1912.

Witzel, Georg. *Typus ecclesiae prioris: Anzeigung, wie die heilige Kyrche Gottes, inwendig siben und mehr hundert jaren, nach unsers Herrn Auffart, gestalt gewesen sey.* Mainz: Behem, 1541.

———. *Warer Bericht von den Acten der Leipsischen und Speirischen Collocution zwischen Mar. Bucern und Georg. Wilcelien.* Cologne: Johann Quentel Erben, 1562.

Zwingli, Huldreich. *Huldreich Zwinglis Sämtliche Werke.* Ed. Emil Egli et al. 15 vols. Leipzig: Heinsius; Zurich: Verlag Berichtshaus, Theologischer Verlag, 1905–1966.

SECONDARY SOURCES

Althaus, Paul. *The Theology of Martin Luther.* Trans. Robert C. Schulz. Philadelphia: Fortress Press, 1966.

Anderson, Marvin W. "Biblical Humanism and Roman Catholic Reform (1501–1542): Contarini, Pole, and Giberti." *Concordia Theologica! Monthly* 39 (1968): 686–707.

Anderson, William P. "Gasparo Contarini: Sixteenth Century Ecumenist." *Ecumenical Trends* 13, no. 9 (1984): 140–142.

Anrich, Gustav. *Martin Bucer.* Strasbourg: Karl J. Trübner, 1914.

Arnold, Matthieu, and Berndt Hamm, eds. *Martin Bucer zwischen Luther und Zwingli.* Tubingen: Mohr Siebeck, 2003.

Atkinson, James. "Martin Bucer (1491–1551): Ecumenical Pioneer." *Churchman* 79 (1965): 19–28.

Augustijn, Cornelis. *De Godsdienstgesprekken tussen Rooms-Katholieken en Protestanten van 1538 tot 1541.* Haarlem: F. Bohn, 1967.

———. "L'espirit d'Erasme pendant le Colloque de Worms (1540)." In *Colloquia Erasmiana Turonensia.* Ed. Jean-Claude Margolin, 381–395. Toronto: University of Toronto Press, 1969.

———. "Strasbourg, Bucer et la politique des Colloques." In *Strasbourg au cœur religieux de XVI⁰ siècle: hommage à Lucien Febvre: actes du Colloque international de Strasbourg (25–29 mai 1975)*. Ed. Georges Livet and Francis Rapp, 197–206. Strasbourg: Librairie Istra, 1977.

———. "Die Religionsgespräche der vierziger Jahre." In *Die Religionsgespräche der Reformationszeit*. Ed. Gerhard Müller, 43–53. Gütersloh: Gütersloher Verlagshaus Gerd Mohn, 1980.

———. "Bucer und die Religionsgespräch der 1540/41." In *Martin Bucer and Sixteenth Century Europe: Actes du Colloque de Strasbourg (28–31 août 1991)*. Ed. Christian Krieger and Marc Lienhard. Vol. 2, 671–680. Leiden: Brill, 1993.

———. "The Quest for *Reformatio*: The Diet of Regensburg 1541 as a Turning-Point." In *The Reformation in Germany and Europe*. Ed. Hans Rudolf Guggisberg and Gottfried G. Krodel, 64–80. Gütersloh: Gütersloher Verlagshaus Gerd Mohn, 1993.

———. "Bucer's Ecclesiology in the Colloquies with the Catholics, 1540–1541." In *Martin Bucer: Reforming Church and Community*. Ed. David F. Wright, 107–121. Cambridge: Cambridge University Press, 1994.

———. *Erasmus: His Life, Works, and Influence*. Trans. J. C. Grayson. Toronto: University of Toronto Press, 1995.

———. "Das Wormser Buch: Der letzte ökumenische Konsenversuch Dezember 1540." *Blätter für Pfälzische Kirchengeschichte* 62 (1995): 7–46.

Backus, Irena. "Martin Bucer and the Patristic Tradition." In *Martin Bucer and Sixteenth Century Europe: Actes du Colloque de Strasbourg (28–31 août 1991)*. Ed. Christian Krieger and Marc Lienhard. Vol. 1, 55–69. Leiden: Brill, 1993.

———. "The Early Church as a Model of Religious Unity in the Sixteenth Century: Georg Cassander and Georg Witzel." In *Conciliation and Confession: The Struggle for Unity in the Age of Reform, 1415–1648*. Ed. Howard P. Louthan and Randall C. Zachman, 106–133. Notre Dame, IN: University of Notre Dame Press, 2004.

Barnikol, Horst-Martin. "Bucers Lehre von der Rechtfertigung: Dargestellt an seinem Römerbriefkommentar." Ph.D. diss., Georg-August-Universität Göttingen, 1961.

Barth, Hans-Martin et al. *Das Regensburger Religionsgespräch im Jahr 1541: Rückblick und aktuelle ökumenische Perspektiven*. Regensburg: Friedrich Pustet, 1992.

Baum, Johann W. *Capito und Butzer: Strassburgs Reformatoren: Nach ihrem handschriftlichen Briefschatze, ihren gedruckten Schriften und anderen gleichzeitigen Quellen*. Elberfeld: Verlag von R. L. Friderichs, 1860.

Bäumer, Remigius, ed. *Von Konstanz Nach Trient: Beiträge zur Geschichte der Kirche von den Reformkonzilien bis Tridentinum: Festgabe für A Franzen*. Munich: Verlag F. Schöningh, 1972.

Bornkamm, Heinrich. *Martin Bucers Bedeutung für die europäische Reformationsgeschichte*. Schriften des Vereins fur Reformationsgeschichte 169, 1–42. Gütersloh: C. Bertelsmann Verlag, 1958.

———. *Das Jahrhundert der Reformation: Gestalten und Kräfte*. Göttingen: Vandenhoeck & Ruprecht, 1961.

Brady, Thomas A. "Martin Bucer and the Politics of Strasbourg." In *Martin Bucer and Sixteenth Century Europe: Actes du Colloque de Strasbourg (28–31 août 1991)*. Ed. Christian Krieger and Marc Lienhard. Vol. 1, 129–143. Leiden: Brill, 1993.

Brandi, Karl. *The Emperor Charles V: The Growth and Destiny of a Man and of a World-Empire.* Trans. C. V. Wedgewood. London: Jonathan Cape, 1939.

Braunisch, Reinhard. "Die 'Artikell' der 'Warhafftigen Antwort' (1545) des Johannes Gropper: Zur Verfasserfrage des Worms-Regensburger Buches (1540/41)." In *Von Konstanz nach Trient: Beiträge zur Geschichte der Kirche von den Reformkonzilien bis zum Tridentum.* Ed. Remigius Bäumer, 519–545. Munich: Verlag Ferdinand Schöningh, 1972.

———. "Johannes Gropper zwischen Humanismus und Reformation: Zur Bestimmung seines geistigen Standorts bis 1543." *Römische Quartalschrift* 69 (1974): 192–209.

———. *Die Theologie der Rechtfertigung im "Enchiridion" (1538) des Johannes Gropper: Sein Kritischer Dialog mit Philipp Melanchthon.* Münster: Aschendorff, 1974.

———. "Johannes Gropper (1503–1559)." In *Katholische Theologen der Reformationszeit.* Ed. Erwin Iserloh. Vol. 1, 117–124. Münster: Aschendorff, 1984.

Bray, Gerald L., ed. *Ancient Christian Commentary on Scripture: New Testament VI, Romans.* Downers Grove, IL: InterVarsity Press, 1998.

Brecht, Martin. "Martin Bucer und die Heidelberger Disputation." In *Calvin: Erbe und Auftrag.* Ed. Wilhelm H. Neuser and Willem van't Spijker, 214–218. Kampen: Kok Pharos, 1991.

Burnett, Amy Nelson. "Martin Bucer and the Anabaptist Context of Evangelical Confirmation." *Mennonite Quarterly Review* 68 (1994): 95–122.

———. *The Yoke of Christ: Martin Bucer and Christian Discipline.* Kirksville, MO: Sixteenth Century Journal Publishers, 1994.

———. "Confirmation and Christian Fellowship: Martin Bucer on Commitment to the Church." *Church History* 64 (1995): 202–217.

Brecht, Martin, and Reinhard Schwarz, eds. *Bekenntnis und Einheit der Kirche: Studien Zum Konkordienbuch.* Stuttgart: Calwer Verlag, 1980.

Camelot, Th. "Credere Deo, Deum, in Deum: Pour l'Histoire d'une Formule Tradition-nelle." *Revue des Sciences Philosophiques et Théologiques* 30 (1941–1942): 149–155.

Cameron, Euan. *Reformation of the Heretics.* Oxford: Clarendon Press, 1984.

Cameron, James K. "Cologne Reformation and the Church of Scotland." *Journal of Ecclesiastical History* 30 (1979): 39–64.

Cardauns, Ludwig. *Zur Geschichte der kirchlichen Unions-und Reformbestrebungen von 1538 bis 1542.* Rome: Loescher, 1910.

Cavallera, Ferdinand. "L'Enchiridion Christianae Institutionis de Jean Gropper (1538)." *Bulletin de Litterature Ecclesiatique* 40 (1939): 25–47.

Chadwick, Henry. "Justification by Faith: A Perspective." *One in Christ: A Catholic Ecumenical Review* 20 (1984): 191–225.

Chrisman, Miriam Usher. *Strasbourg and the Reform: A Study in the Process of Change.* New Haven, CT: Yale University Press, 1967.

Cross, F. L., ed. *The Oxford Dictionary of the Christian Church.* 3rd ed. Ed. E. A. Livingstone. Oxford: Oxford University Press, 1997.

de Kroon, Marijn. *Studien zu Martin Bucers Obrigkeitsverständnis: Evangelisches Ethos und politisches Engagement.* Gütersloh: Gütersloher Verlagshaus Gerd Mohn, 1984.

————. "Martin Bucer and the Problem of Tolerance." *Sixteenth Century Journal* 19 (1988): 157–68.

————. *Martin Bucer und Johannes Calvin: Reformatorische Perspektiven Einleitung und Text.* Trans. Hartmut Rudolph. Göttingen: Vandenhoeck & Ruprecht, 1991.

de Kroon, Marijn, and Friedhelm Krüger, eds. *Bucer und seine Zeit.* Wiesbaden: Franz Steiner, 1976.

de Vogel, C. J. "Erasmus and His Attitude toward Church Dogma." In *Scrinium Erasmianum.* Ed. J. Coppens, 101–132. Leiden: Brill, 1969.

Ditsche, Magnus. "Das 'Richtscheit der Apostolischen Kirche' biem Leipziger Religionsgespräch von 1539." In *Reformata Reformanda.* Ed. Erwin Iserloh and Konrad Repgen. Vol. 1, 466–475. Münster: Aschendorff, 1965.

Eells, Hastings. "Martin Bucer and the Conversion of John Calvin." *Princeton Theological Review* 22 (1924): 402–419.

————. "The Origin of the Regensburg Book." *Princeton Theological Review* 26 (1928): 355–372.

————. *Martin Bucer.* New Haven, CT: Yale University Press, 1931.

Ehresnsperger, Kathy, and R. Ward Holder, eds. *Reformation Readings of Romans.* New York: T&T Clark International, 2008.

Elliott, Mark W. "Romans 7 in the Reformation Century." In *Reformation Readings of Romans.* Ed. Kathy Ehrensperger and R. Ward Holder, 171–188. New York: T&T Clark, 2008.

Erbes, Jean. "Martin Bucers Concordienbestrebungen und die heutige Lage der Ökumene." *Kirchenblatt für die Reformirte Schweiz* 121 (1965): 196–201.

————. "Martin Bucer (1491–1551): Enfant de Sélestat, réformateur de Strasbourg, précurseur de l'Oecumenisme." *Annuaire de la Société des amis de la Bibliothèque de Sélestat* 4 (1954): 131–147.

Erichson, Alfred. *Martin Bucer: Zum 400 jährigen Todestag des elsässischen Reformators.* Strasbourg: Librairie Oberlin, 1951.

Evans, Gillian R, ed. *Christian Authority: Essays in Honour of Henry Chadwick.* Oxford: Clarendon Press, 1988.

Fenlon, Dermot. *Heresy and Obedience: Cardinal Pole and the Counter Reformation.* Cambridge: Cambridge University Press, 1972.

Filser, Hubert. *Ekklesiologie und Sakramentenlehre des Kardinals Johannes Gropper: Eine Glaubenslehre zwischen Irenik und Kontroverstheologie im Zeitalter der Reformation.* Münster: Lit Verlag, 1995.

Fink, David C. "'The Doers of the Law Will Be Justified': The Exegetical Origins of Martin Bucer's *Triplex Iustificatio.*" *Journal of Theological Studies* 58 (2007): 485–524.

Fraenkel, Pierre. *Einigungsbestrebungen in der Reformationszeit: Zwei Wege—Zwei Motive.* Wiesbaden: Franz Steiner, 1965.

————. "Bucer's Memorandum of 1541 and a 'Lettera Nicodemitica' of Capito's." *Bibliothèque d'Humanisme et Renaissance* 36 (1974): 575–587.

————. "Die Augustana im Gespräch Mit Rom, 1540–1541." In *Bekenntnis und Einheit der Kirche.* Ed. Martin Brecht and Reinhard Schwarz, 89–104. Stuttgart: Calwer Verlag, 1980.

Friedensburg, Walter. "Martin Bucer, Von der Wiedereinigung der Kirchen (1542)." *Archiv für Reformationsgeschichte* 31 (1934): 145–191.

Friedrich, Reinhold. "Martin Bucer—Ökumene im 16. Jahrhundert." In *Martin Bucer and Sixteenth Century Europe; Actes du Colloque de Strasbourg (28–31 août 1991)*. Ed. Christian Krieger and Marc Lienhard. Vol. 1, 257–268. Leiden: Brill, 1993.

———. *Martin Bucer—"Fanatiker der Einheit"?: Seine Stellungnahme zu theologischen Fragen seiner Zeit (Abendmahls- und Kirchenverständnis) insbesondere nach seinem Briefwechsel der Jahre 1524–1541*. Bonn: Verlag für Kultur und Wissenschaft, 2002.

Fuchs, Thomas. *Konfession und Gespräch: Typologie und Funktion der religionsgespräche in der Reformationszeit*. Weimar: Böhlau Verlag, 1995.

Fuchtel, Paul. "Der Frankfurter Anstand vom Jahre 1539." *Archiv für Reformationsgeschichte* 28 (1931): 145–206.

Gäumann, Andreas. *Reich Christi und Obrigkeit: Eine Studie zum reformatorischen Denken und Handeln Martin Bucers*. Bern: Peter Lang, 2001.

Gleason, Elisabeth G. *Gasparo Contarini: Venice, Rome, and Reform*. Berkeley: University of California Press, 1993.

Greschat, Martin. "Die Anfänge der reformatorischen Theologie Martin Bucers." In *Reformation und Humanismus*, 124–140. Witten: Luther Verlag, 1969.

———. "Martin Bucers Bücherverzeichnis Von 1518." *Archiv für Kulturgeschichte* 57 (1975): 162–185.

———. "Martin Bucer als Dominikanermönch." In *Bucer und seine Zeit*. Ed. Marijn de Kroon and Friedhelm Krüger, 30–53. Wiesbaden: Franz Steiner, 1976.

———. "Der Ansatz der Theologie Martin Bucers." *Theologische Literaturzeitung* 103 (1978): 81 96.

———. "TheRrelation between Church and Civil Community in Bucer's Reforming Work." In *Martin Bucer: Reforming Church and Community*. Ed. David F. Wright, 17–31. Cambridge: Cambridge University Press, 1994.

———. "Martin Bucers Konzept der Erneuerung der Kirche in Europa." In *Die Christliche Mitgift Europas: Tradition der Zukunft*, 46–62. Stuttgart: Kohlhammer, 2000.

———. "Martin Bucer and Church Renewal in Europe." *Reformation and Renaissance Review* 5, no. 1 (2003): 92–101.

———. *Martin Bucer: A Reformer and His Times*. Trans. Stephen E. Buckwalter. Louisville, KY: Westminster John Knox Press, 2004.

Greschat, Martin, and J. F. G. Goerters, eds. *Reformation und Humanismus: Robert Stupperich Zum 65 Geburtstag*. Witten: Luther Verlag, 1969.

Gundry, Robert. "The Nonimputation of Christ's Righteousness." In *Justification: What's at Stake in the Current Debates*. Ed. Mark Husbands and Daniel J. Treier, 17–45. Downers Grove, IL: InterVarsity Press, 2004.

Hall, Basil. *Humanists and Protestants 1500–1900*. Edinburgh: T&T Clark, 1990.

Hammann, Gottfried. *Martin Bucer: Zwischen Volkskirche und Bekenntnisgemeinschaft*. Trans. Gerhard Ph. Wolf. Speyer: Verlagsgemeinschaft Evangelischer Presseverlag Pfalz, 1989.

———. "The Creation of the 'Christlichen Gemeinschaften.'" In *Martin Bucer: Reforming Church and Community.* Ed. David F. Wright, 129–143. Cambridge: Cambridge University Press, 1994.

Hampson, Daphne. *Christian Contradictions: The Structures of Lutheran and Catholic Thought.* Cambridge: Cambridge University Press, 2001.

Hauerwas, Stanley and Samuel Wells, ed. *The Blackwell Companion to Christian Ethics.* Oxford: Blackwell, 2004.

Hazlett, Ian P. "A Pilot-Study of Martin Bucer's Relations with France 1524–1548." In *Martin Bucer and Sixteenth Century Europe: Actes du Colloque de Strasbourg (28–31 août 1991).* Ed. Christian Krieger and Marc Lienhard. Vol. 2, 513–521. Leiden: Brill, 1993.

———. "Bucer." In *The Cambridge Companion to Reformation Theology.* Ed. David Bagchi and David C. Steinmetz, 100–112. Cambridge: Cambridge University Press, 2004.

Hendrix, Scott H. *Recultivating the Vineyard: The Reformation Agendas of Christianization.* Louisville, KY: Westminster John Knox Press, 2004

Henze, Barbara. *Aus Liebe zur Kirche Reform: Die Bemühungen Georg Witzels (1501–1573) um die Kircheneinheit.* Münster: Aschendorff, 1995.

Higman, Francis. "Bucer et les Nicodémites." In *Martin Bucer and Sixteenth Century Europe: Actes du Colloque de Strasbourg (28–31 août 1991).* Ed. Christian Krieger and Marc Lienhard. Vol. 2, 645–658. Leiden: Brill, 1993.

Hillerbrand, Hans J., ed. *The Oxford Encyclopedia of the Reformation.* 4 vols. Oxford: Oxford University Press, 1996.

Hobbs, R. Gerald. "An Introduction to the *Psalms Commentary* of Martin Bucer: The Commentary in Its Historical and Exegetical Setting." Ph.D. diss., Universite de Strasbourg, Faculte de Theologie Protestante, 1971.

———. "Martin Bucer on Psalm 22: A Study in the Application of Rabbinic Exegesis by a Christian Hebraist." In *Histoire de l'exégèse au XVIe siècle: Textes du Colloque International Tenu a Genève en 1976.* Ed. Olivier Fatio and Pierre Fraenkel, 144–163. Geneva: Droz, 1978.

———. "How Firm a Foundation: Martin Bucer's Historical Exegesis of the Psalms." *Church History* 53 (1984): 477–491.

———. Review of *Martin Bucer: Ein Reformator und seine Zeit,* by Martin Greschat. *Church History* 61 (1992): 243–244.

Honée, Eugène. "Über das Vorhaben und Scheitern eines Religionsgesprächs, Ein Verfahrensstreit auf dem Konvent von Hagenau (1540)." *Archiv für Reformationgeschichte* 76 (1985): 195–216.

Irwin, Terence. *Plato's Ethics.* Oxford: Oxford University Press, 1995.

Ives, Robert B. "An Early Effort toward Protestant-Catholic Conciliation: The Doctrine of Double Justification in the Sixteenth Century." *Gordon Review* 2 (1968): 99–110.

Jedin, Hubert. *A History of the Council of Trent.* Trans. Ernest Graf. Vol. 1. London: Nelson, 1957.

Jones, W. T. *A History of Western Philosophy: The Classical Mind.* 2nd ed. Vol. 1. Fort Worth, TX: Harcourt Brace Jovanovich, 1980.

Kantzenbach, Friedrich W. *Das Ringen um die Einheit der Kirche im Jahrhundert der Reformation: Vertreter, Quellen und Motive des 'ökumenischen' Gedankens von Erasmus von Rotterdam bis Georg Calixt.* Stuttgart: Evangelisches Verlagswerk, 1957.

———. "Martin Butzer: Streiter für Einheit der Kirche in der Reformationszeit." In *Ökumenische Profile: Brückenbauer der einen Kirche.* Ed. Günter Gloede. Vol. 1, 42–50. Stuttgart: Evang. Missionsverlag, 1961.

Kaufmann, Thomas. "Bucers Bericht von der Heidelberger Disputation." *Archiv für Reformationsgeschichte* 82 (1991): 147–170.

———. *Die Abendmahlstheologie der Straßburger Reformatoren bis 1528.* Tübingen: J. C. B. Mohr, 1992.

———. "Streittheologie und Friedensdiplomatie die Rolle Martin Bucer's im Frühen Abendmahlsstreit." In *Martin Bucer and Sixteenth Century Europe: Actes du Colloque de Strasbourg (28–31 août 1991).* Ed. Christian Krieger and Marc Lienhard. Vol. 1, 239–256. Leiden: Brill, 1993.

Kittelson, James M. *Wolfgang Capito: From Humanist to Reformer.* Leiden: Brill, 1975.

———. "Martin Bucer: Forgotten Man in the Late 16th Century?" In *Martin Bucer and Sixteenth Century Europe: Actes du Colloque de Strasbourg (28–31 août 1991).* Ed. Christian Krieger and Marc Lienhard. Vol. 2, 705–714. Leiden: Brill, 1993.

Koch, Karl. *Studium Pietatis: Martin Bucer als Ethiker.* Neukirchener: Neukirchener Verlag, 1962.

Kohls, Ernst-Wilhelm. *Die Schüle bei Martin Bucer in ihrem Verhältnis zu Kirche und Obrigkeit.* Heidelberg: Quelle & Meyer, 1963.

———. "Martin Bucer als Anhänger Luthers." *Theologische Zeitschrift* 33 (1977): 210–218.

———. "Martin Bucer: Erasmien et Martinien tel que la Montre su Conception du Baptême." In *Strasbourg au cœur religieux de XVIe siècle: hommage à Lucien Febvre: actes du Colloque international de Strasbourg.* Ed. Georges Livet and Francis Rapp, 167–183. Strasbourg: Librairie Istra, 1977.

Köhn, Mechtild. *Martin Bucers Entwurf einer Reformation des Erzstiftes Köln: Untersuchung der Enststehungsgeschichte und der Theologie des "Einfaltigen Bedenckens" von 1543.* Wittenberg: Luther Verlag, 1966.

Kok, Joel Edward. "The Influence of Martin Bucer on John Calvin's Interpretation of Romans: A Comparative Case Study." Ph.D. diss., Duke University, 1993.

Kraft, Sigisbert. "Martin Bucers Theologie—Eine Wegweisung Im Ökumenischen Gespräch." *Ökumenische Rundschau* 50 (2001): 524–535.

Kretschmar, Georg. "The Imperial Diet of Regensburg 1541 and the Confessio Variata of 1542." In *Piety, Politics, and Ethics: Reformation Studies in Honor of George Wolfgang Forell.* Ed. Carter Lindberg, 85–102. Kirksville, MO: Sixteenth Century Journal Publishers, 1984.

Krieger, Christian, and Marc Lienhard, eds. *Martin Bucer and Sixteenth Century Europe: Actes du Colloque de Strasbourg (28–31 août 1991).* 2 vols. Leiden: Brill, 1993.

Krüger, Friedhelm. *Bucer und Erasmus: Eine Untersuchung zum Einfluss des Erasmus auf die theologie Martin Bucers (bis zum Evangelien-Kommentar von 1530).* Wiesbaden: Franz Steiner Verlag, 1970.

————. "Bucer and Erasmus." *Mennonite Quarterly Review* 68 (1994): 11–23.

Kuhaupt, Georg. *Veröffentliche Kirchenpolitik: Kirche im publizistischen Streit zur Zeit der Religionsgespräche (1538–1541)*. Göttingen: Vanderhoeck & Ruprecht, 1998.

Lane, Anthony N. S. *Justification by Faith in Catholic-Protestant Dialogue: An Evangelical Assessment*. London: T&T Clark, 2002.

————. "Calvin and Article 5 of the Regensburg Colloquy." In *Calvinus praeceptor Ecclesiae: Papers of the International Congress on Calvin Research*. Ed. Herman J. Selderhuis, 233–263. Geneva: Droz, 2004.

————. "Cardinal Contarini and Article 5 of the Regensburg Colloquy (1541)." In *Grenzgänge der Theologie: Professor Alexandre Ganoczy zum 75. Geburtstag*. Ed. Otmar Meuffels and Jürgen Bründl, 163–190. Münster: Lit. Verlag, 2004.

————. "Twofold Righteousness: A Key to the Doctrine of Justification? Reflections on Article V of the Regensburg Colloquy (1541)." In *Justification: What's at Stake in the Current Debates*. Ed. Mark Husbands and Daniel J. Treier, 205–224. Downers Grove, IL: InterVarsity Press, 2004.

————. "A Tale of Two Imperial Cities: Justification at Regensburg (1541) and Trent (1546–1547)." In *Justification in Perspective: Historical Developments and Contemporary Challenges*. Ed. Bruce L. McCormack, 119–145. Grand Rapids, MI: Baker Academic, 2006.

Lang, August. *Der Evangelienkommentar Butzers und die Grundzüge seiner Theologie*. Leipzig: Neudruck der Ausgabe, 1900. Reprint, Aalen: Scientia Verlag, 1972.

Leijssen, Lambert. "Martin Bucer und Thomas von Aquin." *Ephemerides Theologicae Lovanienses* 55 (1979): 266–296.

Levit, Georges, and Francis Rapp, eds. *Strasbourg au cœur religieux de XVIᵉ siècle: hommage à Lucien Febvre: actes du Colloque international de Strasbourg (25–29 mai 1975)*. Strasbourg: Librairie Istra, 1977.

Lexutt, Athena. *Rechtfertigung im Gespräch: Das Rechtfertigungsverständnis in den Religionsgesprächen von Hagenau, Worms und Regensburg 1540/41*. Göttingen: Vandenhoeck & Ruprecht, 1996.

Lienhard, Marc. "Bucer et la Tetrapolitaine." *Bulletin de la Societe de l'Histoire du Protestantisme Francais* 126 (1980): 269–286.

Lindberg, Carter, ed. *Piety, Politics, and Ethics: Reformation Studies in Honor of George Wolfgang Forell*. Kirksville, MO: Sixteenth Century Journal Publishers, 1984.

Lindsay, Thomas M. "Martin Bucer and the Reformation." *Quarterly Review* 220 (1914): 116–133.

Lipgens, Walter. *Kardinal Johannes Gropper, 1503–1559 und die Anfänge der katholischen Reform in Deutschland*. Münster: Aschendorff, 1951.

Lohse, Bernhard. *Martin Luther's Theology: Its Historical and Systematic Development*. Trans. Roy Harrisville. Minneapolis, MN: Fortess Press, 1999.

Lössl, Josef. "Augustinus im 'Regensburg Buch' (1541)." *Zeitschrift für Kirchengeschichte* 111 (2000): 28–55.

MacCulloch, Diarmaid. *Reformation: Europe's House Divided 1490–1700*. London: Allen Lane, 2003.

Mackensen, Heinz. "The Diplomatic Role of Gasparo Cardinal Contarini at the Colloquy of Ratisbon of 1541." *Church History* 27 (1958): 312–337.

———. "The Debate between Eck and Melanchthon on Original Sin at the Colloquy of Worms." *Lutheran Quarterly* 22 (1959): 42–56.

———. "Contarini's Theological Role at Ratisbon in 1541." *Archiv für Reformationsgeschichte* 51, no. 1 (1960): 36–57.

Matheson, Peter. *Cardinal Contarini at the Colloquy of Ratisbon of 1541*. Oxford: Clarendon Press, 1972.

———. "Martyrdom or Mission? A Protestant Debate." *Archiv für Reformationsgeschichte* 80 (1989): 154–172.

———. "Martin Bucer and the Old Church." In *Martin Bucer: Reforming Church and Community*. Ed. David F. Wright, 5–16. Cambridge: Cambridge University Press, 1994.

———. *The Rhetoric of the Reformation*. Edinburgh: T&T Clark, 1998.

McCormack, Bruce L. "What's at Stake in the Current Debates over Justification?" In *Justification: What's at Stake in the Current Debates*. Ed. Mark Husbands and Daniel J. Treier, 81–117. Downers Grove, IL: InterVarsity Press, 2004.

McCue, James F. "Simul Iustus et Peccator in Augustine, Aquinas, and Luther: Toward Putting the Debate in Context." *Journal of the American Academy of Religion* 48 (1980): 81–96.

———. "Double Justification at Trent." In *Piety, Politics, and Ethics: Reformation Studies in Honor of George Wolfgang Forell*. Ed. Carter Lindberg, 39–56. Kirksville, MO: Sixteenth Century Journal Publishers, 1984.

McGrath, Alister E. "Forerunners of the Reformation? A Critical Evaluation of the Evidence for Precursors of the Reformation Doctrines of Justification." *Harvard Theological Review* 75 (1982): 219–242.

———. "Humanist Elements in the Early Reformed Doctrine of Justification." *Archiv für Reformationsgeschichte* 73 (1982): 5–20.

———. "Justification: The New Ecumenical Debate." *Themelios* 13 (1988): 43–48.

———. *Iustitia Dei: A History of the Christian Doctrine of Justification*. 3rd ed. Cambridge: Cambridge University Press, 2005.

McLaughlin, R. Emmet. "The Politics of Dissent: Martin Bucer, Caspar Schwenckfeld, and the Schwenkfelders of Strasbourg." *Mennonite Quarterly Review* 68 (1994): 59–78.

McNeill, John T. *Unitive Protestantism: The Ecumenical Spirit and Its Persistent Expression*. London: Epworth Press, 1964.

Mehl, Roger. "Strasbourg et Luther: La Tetrapolitaine." *Strasbourg au cœur religieux du XVIe siècle: hommage à Lucien Febvre: actes du Colloque international de Strasbourg (25–29 mai 1975)*. Ed. George Livet and Francis Rapp, 145–152. Strasbourg: Librairie Istra, 1977.

Meier, Johannes. "Das 'Enchiridion christianae institutionis' (1538) von Johannes Gropper Geschichte seiner Entstehung: Verbreitung und Nachwirkung." *Zeitschrift für Kirchengeschichte* 86 (1975): 289–328.

Monteil, Michèle. "Le petit catéchisme (1529) de Luther et la brève explication écrite (1534) de Bucer: Deux modèles d'instruction catéchétique." *Études Germaniques* 50 (1995): 447–466.

Müller, Gerhard. "Landgraf Philipp von Hessen und das Regensburger Buch." In *Bucer und seine Zeit*. Ed. Marijn de Kroon and Friedhelm Krüger, 101–116. Wiesbaden: Franz Steiner, 1976.

———, ed. *Die Religionsgespräche Der Reformationszeit*. Gütersloh: Gütersloher Verlagshaus Gerd Mohn, 1980.

Müller, Gerhard, and Vinzenz Pfnür. "Justification—Faith—Works." In *Confessing One Faith: A Joint Commentary on the Augsburg Confession by Lutheran and Catholic Theologians*. Ed. George Wolfgang Forell and James F. McCue, 117–146. Minneapolis, MN: Augsburg Press, 1982.

Müller, Johannes. *Martin Bucers Hermeneutik*. Gütersloh: Gerd Mohn, 1965.

Murphy, Roland E. *Word Biblical Commentary: Ecclesiastes*. Vol. 23a. Dallas, TX: Word Books, 1992.

Nestler, Hermann. "Vermittlungspolitik und Kirchenspaltung auf dem Regensburger Reichstag von 1541." *Zeitschrift für bayerische Landesgeschichte* 6 (1933): 389–414.

Neudecker, Gotthold, ed. *Merkwürdige Aktenstücke aus dem Zeitalter der Reformation*. Nuremberg, 1838.

Neuser, Wilhelm H. "Calvins Urteil über den Rechtfertigungsartikel des Regensburger Buches." In *Reformation und Humanismus*. Ed. Martin Greschat, 176–194. Witten: Luther Verlag, 1969.

———, ed. *Die Vorbereitung der Religionsgespräche von Worms und Regensburg 1540/41*. Neukirchen-Vluyn: Neukirchener Verlag, 1974.

———. "Bucers Programm einer 'guten' leidlichen reformation" (1539–1541)." In *Horizons Européens de la Réforme en Alsace*. Ed. Marijn de Kroon and Marc Lienhard, 227–239. Strasbourg: Librairie Istra, 1980.

Neuser, Wilhelm H. and Willem van't Spijker, eds. *Calvin: Erbe und Auftrag*. Kampen: Kok Pharos, 1991.

Oberman, Heiko A. "'Iustitia Christi' and 'Iustitia Dei': Luther and the Scholastic Doctrines of Justificiation." *Harvard Theological Review* 59 (1966): 1–26.

———. *Luther: Man between God and the Devil*. Trans. Eileen Walliser-Schwarzbart. New York: Image Books, 1992.

———. *The Reformation: Roots and Ramifications*. Trans. Andrew C. Gow. Edinburgh: T&T Clark, 1994.

———. *Forerunners of the Reformation: The Shape of Late Medieval Thought*. Cambridge: James Clarke, 2002.

———. *The Harvest of Medieval Theology: Gabriel Biel and Late Medieval Nominalism*. 3rd ed. Grand Rapids, MI: Baker Academic, 2002.

Ortmann, Volkmar. *Reformation und Einheit der Kirche: Martin Bucers Einigungsbemühungen bei den Religionsgesprächen in Leipzig, Hagenau, Worms und Regensburg 1539–1541*. Mainz: Verlag Philipp von Zabern, 2001.

———. "Martin Bucers Bemühungen um Reformation und Einheit der Kirche bei den Religionsgesprächen 1540/41." In *Martin Bucer zwischen Luther und Zwingli*. Ed. Matthieu Arnold and Berndt Hamm, 127–146. Tübingen: Mohr Siebeck, 2003.

Parker, T. H. L. *Commentaries on Romans, 1532–1542*. Edinburgh: T&T Clark, 1986.

Pas, P. "La doctrine de la double justice au Concile de Trent." *Ephemerides Theologicae Lovanienses* 30 (1954): 5–53.

Pauck, Wilhelm. "Calvin and Butzer." *Journal of Religion* 9 (1929): 237–256.

Pfnür, Vinzenz. "Die Einigung bei den Religionsgesprächen von Worms und Regensburg 1540/41 eine Täuschung?" In *Religionsgespräche der Reformationszeit*. Ed. Gerhard Müller, 55–88. Gütersloh: Gütersloher Verlagshaus Gerd Mohn, 1980.

Pils, Holger, Stephan Ruderer, and Petra Schaffrodt, comps. *Martin Bucer—Bibliographie*. Gütersloh: Gütersloher Verlagshaus Gerd Mohn, 2005.

Pollet, Jacques V. "Bucer et l'ecole." *Bibliothèque d'Humanisme et Renaissance* 26 (1964): 559–572.

———. "Origine et structure du *De Sarcienda Ecclesiae Concordia* (1533) d'Erasme." In *Scrinium Erasmianum: Mélanges historiques . . . à l'occasion du cinquième centenaire de la naissance d'Erasme*. Ed. Joseph Coppens. Vol. 2, 183–196. Leiden: Brill, 1969.

Rack, Henry D. *The Reasonable Enthusiast: John Wesley and the Rise of Methodism*. 3rd ed. London: Epworth Press, 2002.

Rait, Jill. "From Augsburg to Trent." In *Justification by Faith: Lutherans and Catholics in Dialogue VII*. Ed. H. George Anderson et. al., 200–217. Minneapolis, MN: Augsburg, 1985.

Reventlow, Henning Graf. "Martin Bucer." In *The Authority of the Bible and the Rise of the Modern World*, 73–87. London: SCM Press, 1984.

Richter, Aemilius L. *Die evangelischen Kirchenordnungen des sechzehnten Jahrhunderts: Ukunden und Regesten zur Geschichte des Rechts und der Verfassung der evangelischen Kirche in Deutschland*. Vol. 1. Weimar: Landes-Industriecomptoir, 1846.

Ritschl, Otto. *Dogmengeschichte des Protestantismus. Grundlagen und Grundzüge der theologischen Gedanken- und Lehrbildung in den protestantischen Kirchen*. Vol. 3, *Die reformierte Theologie des 16. und 17. Jahrhunderts in ihrer Entstehung und Entwicklung*. Göttingen: Vandenhoeck & Ruprecht, 1926.

Roussel, Bernard. "Martin Bucer lecteur de l'épître aux romains." 2 vols. Ph.D. diss., Universite de Strasbourg, Faculte de Theologie Protestante, 1970.

———. "Martin Bucer et Jacques Sadolet: La Concorde possible (automne 1535)?" *Bulletin de la Société de l'Histoire du Protestantisme Français* 122 (1976): 507–524.

———. "Martin Bucer Exégète." In *Strasbourg au cœur religieux de XVIᵉ siècle: hommage à Lucien Febvre: actes du Colloque International de Strasbourg (25–29 mai 1975)*. Ed. George Livet and Francis Rapp, 153–166. Strasbourg: Librairie Istra, 1977.

Rupp, Gordon. *Protestant Catholicity: Two Lectures*. London: Epworth Press, 1960.

———. "Martin Bucer: Prophet of a New Reformation." In *Prospect for Theology: Essays in Honour of H. H. Farmer*. Ed. F. G. Healey, 183–199. Digswell Place: James Nisbet, 1966.

Ryrie, Alec. "Reform without Frontiers in the Last Years of Catholic Scotland." *English Historical Review* 119 (2004): 27–56.

Scales, Derek A. "Illustrations of Compromise in Church History." In *Churchman* 102, no. 3 (1988): 215–239.

Scheibe, Max. *Calvins Prädestinationslehre: Ein Beitrag zur Würdigung der Eigenart seiner Theologie und Religiosität*. Halle: M. Niemeyer, 1897.

Schneckenburger, Matthias. *Vergleichende Darstellung des lutherischen und reformirten Lehrbegriffs*. Vol. 1. Stuttgart: Verlag der JBM, 1855.

Seeberg, Reinhold. *Lehrbuch Der Dogmengeschichte*. Vol. 2, *Die Dogmengeschichte des Mittelalters und der Neuzeit*. Erlangen: A. Deichert'sche Verlagsbuchhandlung Nachf (George Böhme), 1898.

Séguenny, André. "Why Bucer Detested the Spiritualists: Some Reflections on Reading Bucer's Dialogues of 1535." *Mennonite Quarterly Review* 68 (1994): 51–58.

Selderhuis, Herman J. "*Vera Theologia Scientia Est*: Bucer and the Training of Ministers." *Reformation and Renaissance Review* 3, no. 1 (2001): 125–139.

Simoncelli, Paolo. "Vom Humanismus zur Gegenreformation. Das Schicksal des Regensburger Buches in Italien. Versuch Einer Rekonstruktion." In *Pflugiana: Studien Uber Julius Pflug (1499–1564): Ein Internationales Symposium*. Ed. Elmar Neuss and Jacques V. Pollet, 93–114. Münster: Aschendorff, 1990.

Spijker, Willem van't. "Bucer und Calvin." In *Martin Bucer and Sixteenth Century Europe: Actes du Colloque de Strasbourg (28–31 août 1991)*. Ed. Christian Krieger and Marc Lienhard. Vol. 1, 461–470. Leiden: Brill, 1993.

———. "Bucer's Influence on Calvin: Church and Community." In *Martin Bucer: Reforming Church and Community*. Ed. David F. Wright, 32–44. Cambridge: Cambridge University Press, 1994.

———. "Calvin's Friendship with Bucer: Did it Make Calvin a Calvinist?" In *Calvin Studies Society Papers (1995, 1997): Calvin and Spirituality (1995) & Calvin and His Contemporaries: Colleagues, Friends and Conflicts (1997)*. Ed. David Foxgrover, 169–186. Grand Rapids: MI: CRC Product Services, 1998.

Stählin, Rudolf. "Martin Butzer und die Einheit der Kirche." *Evangelisch-lutherische Kirchenzeitung* 6 (1952): 55–59.

Steinmetz, David C. "The Superiority of Pre-critical Exegesis." *Theology Today* 37 (1980): 27–38.

———. *Reformers in the Wings: From Geiler von Kaysersberg to Theodore Beza*. 2nd ed. Oxford: Oxford University Press, 2001.

Stephens, W. Peter. *The Holy Spirit in the Theology of Martin Bucer*. Cambridge: Cambridge University Press, 1970.

———. "The Church in Bucer's Commentaries on the Epistle to the Ephesians." In *Martin Bucer: Reforming Church and Community*. Ed. David F. Wright, 45–60. Cambridge: Cambridge University Press, 1994.

Strohl, Henri. "Deux etudes sur Bucer." *Revue d'Histoire et Philosophie Religieuses* 10 (1930): 571–578.

———. "Théologie et humanisme à Strasbourg au moment de la création de la Haute-Ecole." *Revue d'Histoire et de Philosophie Religieuses* 17 (1937): 435–456.

———. "Bucer, interprète de Luther." *Revue d'Histoire et Philosophie Religieuses* 18 (1939): 223–261.

———. "Un aspect de l'humanisme chrétien de Bucer." *Revue d'Histoire et Philosophie Religieuses* 18 (1939): 432–447.

Stump, Eleonore. "Aquinas's Account of Freedom: Intellect and Will." In *Aquinas's Summa Theologiae: Critical Essays*. Ed. Brian Davies, 203–222. Lanham, MD: Rowman and Littlefield, 2006.

Stupperich, Robert. *Der Humanismus und die Wiedervereinigung*. Leipzig: M. Heinsius Nachfolger, 1936.

———. "Der Ursprung des 'Regensburger Buches' von 1541 und seine Rechtfertigungslehre." *Archiv für Reformationsgeschichte* 36 (1939): 88–116.

———. *Martin Bucer: Der Reformator des Elsasses und Einiger des deutschen Protestantismus*. Berlin: Heliand, 1941.

———. "Martin Bucer als Theologe und Kirchenmann." *Die Zeichen der Zeit* 5 (1951): 253–258.

———. "Schriftverständnis und Kirchenlehre bei Butzer und Gropper." *Jahrbuch des Vereins für Westfälische Kirchengeschichte* 44 (1951): 109–128.

———. "Stande und Aufgabe der Butzer-Forschung." *Archiv für Reformationsgeschichte* 42 (1951): 244–259.

Tait, Edwin W. "A Method for the Christian Life: Martin Bucer and the Sermon on the Mount." Ph.D. diss., Duke University, 2005.

———. "The Law and Its Works in Martin Bucer's 1536 Romans Commentary." In *Reformation Readings of Romans*. Ed. Kathy Ehrensperger and R. Ward Holder, 57–69. New York: T&T Clark, 2008.

Temmel, Leopold. "Glaube und Gewissheit in der Theologie Martin Bucers, vornehmlich nach seinem Römerbriefkommentar." Ph.D. diss., Erlangung, 1950.

Thompson, Bard. "Bucer Study since 1918." *Church History* 25 (1956): 63–82.

Thompson, Nick. *Eucharistic Sacrifice and Patristic Tradition in the Theology of Martin Bucer 1534–1546*. Leiden: Brill, 2005.

Torrance, Thomas F. *Calvin's Doctrine of Man*. London: Lutterworth Press, 1949.

———. *Kingdom and Church: A Study in the Theology of the Reformation*. 1956. Reprint, Eugene, OR: Wipf and Stock, 1996.

Venema, Cornelis P. *Accepted and Renewed in Christ: The "Twofold Grace of God" and the Interpretation of Calvin's Theology*. Göttingen: Vandenhoeck & Ruprecht, 2007.

Vogel, C. J. de. "Erasmus and His Attitude toward Church Dogma." In *Scrinium Erasmianum*. Ed. J. Coppens. Vol. 2, 101–132. Leiden: Brill, 1969.

Vogelsanger, Peter. "Ökumenismus im 16. Jahrhundert: Zur geschichte des Religionsgespräches von Regensburg 1541." In *Unterwegs zur Einheit: Festschrift für Heinrich Stirnimann*. Ed. Johannes Brantschen and Pietro Selvatico, 631–648. Freiburg: Universitätsverlag, 1980.

von Loewenich, Walther. *Duplex Iustitia: Luthers Stellung zu einer Unionsformel des 16. Jahrhunderts*. Wiesbaden: Franz Steiner, 1972.

von Ranke, Leopold. *Sammtlicke Werke 37: Die römischen Päpste in den letzten vier Jahrhunderten*. vol. 1. Leipzig: Duncker und Humblot, 1874.

Wartenberg, Günther. "Der Leipziger Religionsgespräche von 1534 und 1539: Ihre Bedeutung für die sächsisch-albertinische Innenpolitik und für das Wirken Georgs von Karlowitz." In *Religionsgespräche der Reformationszeit*. Ed. Gerhard Müller, 35–41. Gütersloh: Gerd Mohn, 1980.

Weber, Hans Emil. *Reformation, Orthodoxie und Rationalismus*. Vol. 1. Gütersloh: Gütersloher Verlagshaus Gerd Mohn, 1937.

Wendel, François. *Martin Bucer: Esquisse de sa vie et sa pensée publiée à l'occasion du 4e centenaire de sa mort, 28 février 1551*. Strasbourg: Société Pastorale, 1951.

Wright, David F. "Martin Bucer and England—and Scotland." In *Martin Bucer and Sixteenth Century Europe: Actes du Colloque de Strasbourg (28–31 août 1991)*. Ed. Christian Krieger and Marc Lienhard. Vol. 2, 523–532. Leiden: Brill, 1993.

———, ed. *Martin Bucer: Reforming Church and Community*. Cambridge: Cambridge University Press, 1994.

———. "Martin Bucer." In *Historical Handbook of Major Biblical Interpreters*. Ed. Donald K. McKim, 157–164. Downers Grove, IL: InterVarsity Press, 1998.

Wulczyn, Heidi. "The Relationship between Martin Bucer and Philip of Hesse: A Reforming Politician and a Political Reformer, 1534–1539." In *Martin Bucer and Sixteenth Century Europe: Actes du Colloque de Strasbourg (28–31 août 1991)*. Ed. Christian Krieger and Marc Lienhard. Vol. 1, 451–459. Leiden: Brill, 1993.

Yarnold, Edward. "*Duplex Iustitia*: The Sixteenth Century and the Twentieth." In *Christian Authority: Essays in Honour of Henry Chadwick*. Ed. G. R. Evans, 204–223. Oxford: Clarendon Press, 1988.

Ziegler, Donald J., ed. and trans. *Great Debates of the Reformation*. New York: Random House, 1969.

zur Mühlen, Karl-Heinz. "Die Einigung über den Rechtfertigungsartikel auf dem Regensburger Religionsgespräch von 1541—eine verpaßte Chance?" *Zeitschrift für Theologie und Kirche* 76 (1979): 331–359.

———. "Martin Bucer und das Religionsgespräch von Hagenau und Worms 1540/41." In *Martin Bucer and the Sixteenth Century: Actes du Colloque de Strasbourg (28–31 août 1991)*. Ed. Christian Krieger and Marc Lienhard. Vol. 2, 659–669. Leiden: Brill, 1993.

Index